What experts say abo

Great asset. This guide is really good. It covers all the topics and guides you step-by, prepare you to take the SAT. I found it useful to have the exercises with an example of how to answer them; great way to help students with the approach.

– **Maria D'hyver, High School Teacher**

Digital SAT Supreme Guide by Vibrant Publishers is an educational non-fiction book designed to help students master the Digital SAT. It offers a comprehensive breakdown of Reading, Writing, and Math concepts, with step-by-step strategies to solve questions more efficiently. The guide includes realistic practice drills, a performance review sheet, and access to online tests that simulate the actual exam environment. It also provides updated information on the Digital SAT format, scoring system, and a 6-week targeted study plan, making it an essential resource for anyone preparing for this critical test.

Vibrant Publishers have outdone themselves with this easy-to-use guidebook that will prepare students for the world of Digital SATs no matter what their starting level is. Complex SAT concepts are presented in a clear and accessible manner, making it easier for students to grasp challenging material with good visual cues to enhance clarity and comprehension. The guide's well-structured layout and strategic approach allow for efficient study sessions, helping students maximize their preparation time and making it easy to split the book into 'lessons' they can do in their own time. I was also really impressed with the inclusion of realistic practice drills and detailed explanations for both correct and incorrect answers, as it's so essential to understand not only what you got wrong, but precisely why it was wrong, and what could be improved on. Vibrant Publishers' ability to stay current with the evolving SAT format also ensures that students are well-prepared for the specific challenges of the Digital SAT compared to in-person learning, making this a truly invaluable guide. Overall, I'd certainly recommend Digital SAT Supreme Guide as a book that delivers everything it promises.

– **K.C. Finn, Readers' Favorite**

The book looks good as it provides a detailed approach for each question type on the Digital SAT. The strategies suggested can definitely help you improve your scores from any level that you start. The practice questions make you think just the way the real SAT questions do. This book can provide good practice and the online tests are an additional benefit. I recommend this book to everyone who is looking to prep for the SAT.

– **Praveen Sharma, Director, Wizius Careers**

The structure and content of this book are praiseworthy. The number of practice questions (450+) and the variety of the topics is excellent. I do like that the online practice test will be adaptive just like the Digital SAT.

As with most other such books, the content is divided topic-wise, with each topic containing tips, strategies, and practice questions with detailed explanatory answers. As I used to teach the Verbal section to entrance exam aspirants, I admit I focussed more on the RW section than the Math one. I found the quality of the questions and tips to be of a high standard.

I especially appreciate the below points:
- The six-week study plan.
- The dual level strategies – per subject level as well as test-taking tips.
- The inclusion of common SAT vocabulary.

With the SAT turning digital just lately, this updated and comprehensive version ought to be helpful to every SAT aspirant. As the SAT is usually the first major entrance of a child's life, keeping the book user-friendly and structured is a great idea.
Definitely recommended.

– Roshni D'Souza, SAT Trainer

The "Digital SAT Supreme Guide" is a stellar piece of work put together to shine the spotlight on the topic-wise nuances vital for the test takers. The easy-to-understand, structured, and logical explanations underscore the relevance and efficacy of its content, especially for tutors and zealous students. The practice tests mimicking the layout and problem types in College Board-administered SAT act as a cherry on the cake to groom students to ace the Reading/Writing and Math sections.

– Jyotika Bhalla, Senior SAT Faculty

VIBRANT
PUBLISHERS

Digital SAT®

SUPREME GUIDE

Master the Digital SAT® with this guide!

450+ practice questions

---

1 FREE diagnostic test

---

2 full-length practice tests
(1 in-book; 1 online)

Expert strategies for solving
questions

Digital SAT® Supreme Guide

Paperback ISBN–10: 1-63651-236-4
Paperback ISBN–13: 978-1-63651-236-5

This publication is designed to provide accurate and authoritative information in regard to the subject matter covered. The Author has made every effort in the preparation of this book to ensure the accuracy of the information. However, information in this book is sold without warranty either expressed or implied. The Author or the Publisher will not be liable for any damages caused or alleged to be caused either directly or indirectly by this book.

Vibrant Publishers books are available at special quantity discount for sales promotions, or for use in corporate training programs. For more information please write to **bulkorders@vibrantpublishers.com**

Please email feedback / corrections (technical, grammatical or spelling) to **spellerrors@vibrantpublishers.com**

For general inquires please write to **reachus@vibrantpublishers.com**

To access the complete catalogue of Vibrant Publishers, visit **www.vibrantpublishers.com**

Want to **maximize** your **Digital SAT**® score?

Check out our other offerings!

Digital SAT
MATH PRACTICE QUESTIONS

360+ MATH QUESTIONS

PRACTICE TESTS FOR THE Digital SAT

5 PRACTICE TESTS

Digital SAT
READING AND WRITING PRACTICE QUESTIONS

360+ RW QUESTIONS

SCAN TO ORDER

bit.ly/dsatcollections

USE COUPON CODE

SAT15

to avail flat 15% off

Table of Contents

How to use this book

Introducing the Digital SAT Supreme Guide

Welcome to the first step on the journey to preparing for the Digital SAT! This Supreme Guide will be your mentor and best friend the entire way, equipping you with the knowledge and practice required to become an expert on the Digital SAT.

Before diving in, take a moment to set your goals. Are you aiming for a specific score? Is there a college you're eager to attend that has a score requirement? Write these down and keep them in mind as you study. Remember, every question you answer correctly brings you one step closer to your goal!

What's In This Book

This book is designed to guide you through each type of question in the Reading and Writing and Math sections. Dive into the details about the Digital SAT in the first chapter and acquaint yourself with aspects like scoring, number of questions asked, types of questions, timing, etc.

The format of this book is as follows:

- 1 FREE diagnostic mini-test (online)
- Comprehensive guidance and tips for each skill covered in the **Reading** and **Writing** sections
- Drill questions to practice each **Reading** and **Writing** skill
- Comprehensive guidance and tips for each skill covered in the **Math** section
- Drill questions to practice each **Math** skill
- 1 Full-length test (in-book)
    - Module 1: Medium level (easy, medium, and hard questions)
    - Module 2: Easy level (easy, medium, and hard questions)
    - Module 2: Hard level (easy, medium, and hard questions)
- 1 Full-length adaptive test (online)

The First Steps

Start by taking the free diagnostic mini-test included with this book. The purpose of this diagnostic test is to identify your areas of strength and weakness, enabling you to create a targeted, focused study plan to improve your deficient skills and maintain your strongest skills. For all practice tests, set aside a block of time and take the test in a comfortable, quiet environment without any distractions. Analyze your score results from the diagnostic test, taking note of the questions or skills where you scored the lowest.

Access the free tests in 3 steps:

1. *Scan this QR code*

2. *Login to your account or sign in if you haven't created one*

3. *Take your free diagnostic test and full-length test!*

Create a study plan (or follow the one given in this book) that covers how often you will study, for how long, which skills will be covered, and in which chronological order. We recommend setting aside a couple of hours a few times a week and working chronologically through this book, dedicating more time to the skills where you are lacking. Record a study journal where you track the following each week:

- The number of hours studied

- Scores on practice tests

- Areas of strength and areas needing improvement

- Next week's goals and skills to target

Learning and Practicing

The first section dives deep into the Reading and Writing portion, breaking down each question type and providing clear, actionable strategies. You'll learn how to spot and approach different question formats, with detailed explanations followed by step-by-step examples that demonstrate how to apply the techniques.

To reinforce your understanding, each explanation is paired with a set of ***drill questions.*** These exercises come in varying levels of difficulty, ensuring you're well prepared for the range of questions you may face in the real test.

The second section of the book is dedicated to Math, following a structure similar to the Reading and Writing section. This part is packed with essential formulas, mathematical rules, and strategic tips. This is accompanied by clear explanations and examples to ensure you understand not just how to use them, but why they work.

Practice Tests

When you are ready for the practice tests after going through all the topics and drill questions, take the 3-module practice test to know if you are prepared for the test or need further practice.

1. Start with the first module, which has a mix of questions with varying levels of difficulty, and note down your raw score (the number of questions that you get right).

2. If you get less than 15 questions correct, take Module 2 (Easy).

3. If you get more than 15 questions correct, take Module 2 (Hard).

4. At the end, make sure to finish all the questions in the three modules as they will give you extra practice. Again, note down the areas where you are scoring the lowest and revisit the skill explanations, tips, and drill questions as necessary.

Additionally, this book includes access to an online adaptive test, which simulates the real exam experience with dynamic adaptive technology. It mirrors the SAT's adaptive testing format and adjusts the difficulty of questions based on your performance as you progress through the exam.

Our resources closely reflect the content on the test day, so thoroughly comb through this book and practice diligently to prepare yourself. Good luck!

Icons in this Book and Their Meanings:

   –   Key points to remember

   –   Important cautions and warnings

   –   Solved examples

   –   Expert tips to help you excel

Chapter 1
About the Digital SAT

Now that you have made the important decision to head to college/university, there is one last thing you need to do to achieve your goal — take the SAT. Most universities or colleges, including Ivy League schools, expect you to have a good SAT score to secure admission in any course of your choice.

The College Board has transitioned the famous pencil-and-paper test into a fully digital one in 2023. The College Board's decision to go digital was based on giving a fair testing experience to students. The digital test is easier to take, easier to administer, is more secure, and more relevant.

For giving the Digital SAT, you need to be aware of the format of the test, the time that you will be given to answer each question, the possible complexity of the questions, and the scoring method employed to assess your performance in the test. In this chapter, you will discover important information including the SAT policy of inclusive accessibility, the newly introduced Multistage Adaptive Testing feature, the modular format of the test, and much more.

The College Board has also streamlined the method of delivery of the Digital SAT. With the latest test delivery platform for the Digital SAT Suite of Assessments, students can have access to all their tests and their content, as well as enjoy the chance to practice with the full-length, adaptive practice tests offered for free on the platform.

If you are attempting the Digital SAT for the first time, it could be scary not knowing exactly what to expect in the test. This is why this book is specifically designed to expose you to everything you need to know about successfully taking the Digital SAT.

Customized test delivery platform

The College Board has set up a customized test delivery platform for the Digital SAT Suite of Assessments. This platform called **Bluebook** is designed according to the principles of UDA (Universal Design for Assessment) and the main goal of it is to make the testing experience accessible to a maximum number of students. The most useful features of this platform are that: (i) all test takers can have complete access to the tests and their content; (ii) students will be able to take full-length, adaptive practice tests for free on the platform so that they can assess their knowledge levels or have an understanding of similar test materials before attempting the real tests.

Multistage Adaptive Testing

The College Board changed from a linear testing mode, which had been the primary mode of SAT administration, to an adaptive mode.

The main difference between the linear and adaptive testing modes is that for the linear testing mode, students are given a test form that contains some questions that have already been set before the test day and do not change during testing, irrespective of the student's performance.

On the other hand, the adaptive testing model makes it possible for the test delivery platform to adjust the questions' difficulty level based on the performance of the individual test takers. Therefore, each student will be given test questions that match their level of understanding.

This adaptive test mode is known as **Multistage Adaptive Testing (MST)**. The MST is administered in two stages, and each stage comprises a module or set of questions. The first module consists of test questions with different ranges of difficulty levels (easy, medium, and hard). The performance of the test takers in the first module is appropriately assessed, and the results are used to determine the level of difficulty of questions to be administered to them in the second module.

The set of an administered first-stage module and its second-stage module are referred to as a ***panel.***

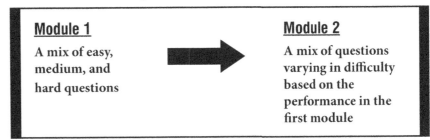

Embedded pretesting

The Digital SAT also included embedded pretesting in its design. What this means is that a small number of pretest (unscored) questions are incorporated among the operational (scored) questions. Even though they are not administered for a score, you may not be able to distinguish these pretest questions from the operational ones on which your scores are based. The number of pretest questions is few so you will not be asked to focus mainly on questions that won't be used to estimate your final Digital SAT score. The pretest questions are mainly used to gather your performance information so that it can be utilized to assess if these questions are appropriate for operational use in the future.

Discrete questions

One interesting aspect of the Digital SAT is that all questions are in a **discrete format** i.e. they are **standalone.** You can answer each question on its own, which doesn't necessarily require any reference to a common stimulus such as an extended passage. This is one of the striking differences between the paper-and-pencil SAT and the Digital SAT in the sense that the former uses both discrete questions and question sets. In practice, the question sets expect you to refer to a common stimulus.

Scoring

You will obtain a section score based on your final performance in the Reading and Writing and Math section. For the Digital SAT, you can get a score between 400-1600. Hence, for each of the sections of the Digital SAT, there will be three scores reported: (1) A Reading and Writing section score; (2) A Math section score; (3) A total score, which is the sum of the two section scores. It is important to note that the scales for these scores have the same ranges as for the paper-based SAT. This indicates that the Digital SAT total score is on the familiar 400–1600 scale.

Score scale of the Digital SAT Suite of Assessments

Test	Total score scale	Section score scale
PSAT 8/9	240-1440	120-720
PSAT/NMSQT & PSAT 10	320–1520	160–760
SAT	400–1600	200–800

The precise scoring process remains undisclosed, but your score is influenced by several factors, including your raw score (number of correct answers), performance in the initial modules, and ability to solve questions with higher weightage. For an approximate estimation of potential scores, please refer to the below table. It's important to note that these scores are not indicative of your actual test scores and are provided solely to assess your preparedness for the exam.

Raw Score Conversion Table

When you take the full-length test at the end of the book, note down your raw scores for each section and compare them with the scaled scores given beside them in the below table. Note that these scores are not indicative of your actual SAT scores.

RAW SCORE	SCALED SCORES		RAW SCORE	SCALED SCORES	
	Reading and Writing	Math		Reading and Writing	Math
1	200	200	28	550	620
2	220	210	29	550	630
3	240	230	30	560	640
4	260	250	31	570	650
5	280	270	32	580	660
6	300	290	33	590	670
7	320	300	34	600	680
8	340	320	35	620	690
9	360	340	36	630	700
10	380	360	37	640	720
11	400	370	38	650	740
12	420	380	39	670	750
13	430	390	40	680	760
14	450	410	41	690	770
15	460	420	42	700	780
16	470	440	43	710	790
17	480	450	44	710	800
18	490	460	45	720	
19	490	480	46	720	
20	500	500	47	730	
21	500	510	48	740	
22	510	520	49	750	
23	510	540	50	760	
24	520	560	51	770	
25	530	580	52	780	
26	540	590	53	790	
27	540	610	54	800	

Overall test specifications

As you know, the Digital SAT is made up of two sections: A *Reading and Writing* (RW) section and a *Math* section. In the linear model, the test had separate sections for Reading and Writing. However, in the Digital SAT, both the Reading and Writing sections are combined in one section. The questions in these two sections concentrate primarily on the skills and knowledge that students need to use in college and/or to get ready for their careers. Although all the testing programs within the Digital SAT Suite, whether it is the SAT, PSAT/NMSQT, PSAT 10, or PSAT 8/9 have similar designs, these tests allow for differences in test takers' ages and levels of understanding.

Digital SAT Suite: Overall Test Specifications

Characteristic	Reading and Writing section	Math section
Administration	Two-stage adaptive design; this section contains two separately timed modules	Two-stage adaptive design; this section contains two separately timed modules
Number of questions	54 questions; 25 questions in each module with 2 pretest questions	44 questions; 20 questions in each module with 2 pretest questions
Time	64 minutes	70 minutes
Time per question	1.19 minutes	1.59 minutes
Time per module	32 minutes	35 minutes
Content domains	Information and Ideas, Craft and Structure, Expression of Ideas, and Standard English Conventions	Algebra, Advanced Math, Problem–Solving and Data Analysis, and Geometry and Trigonometry

Test length

There are a total of 54 questions in the Reading and Writing section and 44 questions in the Math section. These 54 questions are divided into two equal-length modules; that is, one for each of the section's two stages. Out of the 27 questions for each module, 25 questions are operational—which means that test takers' performance on them is used to calculate their section score, and 2 questions are pretests. For the Math section, the first module has 20 operational questions and 2 pretest questions.

Time per module

You will have **32 minutes** to complete each module of the Reading and Writing section and **35 minutes** to complete each module of the Math section. Once the time for the first module has expired, you will be automatically advanced to the second module. The second module may contain questions that are of higher or lower difficulty, depending on your performance in the first module. You will not have the opportunity to return to the first-module questions.

Total time allotted

You will have **64 minutes** to complete the Reading and Writing section and **70 minutes** to complete the Math section.

Average time per question

You will, on average, have **1.19 minutes** to answer each Reading and Writing question and **1.59 minutes** to answer each Math question.

Question format(s) used

The Reading and Writing section mostly utilizes four-option multiple-choice questions, and each question has a single best answer (which is referred to as the **keyed response** or **key**). Roughly 75% of questions in the Math section also adopt the same four-option multiple-choice format, while the remaining part of the section utilizes the student-produced response (SPR) format. This means that students will be required to answer the latter type of questions by inputting their responses in a box next to the questions. These questions measure your ability to solve math problems by yourself. The SPR questions can have more than one correct response; however, you are required to provide only one answer.

Text complexity

It is assumed that the complexity test takers can read is directly related to how ready they are for college and their careers. Therefore, the idea of text complexity is strictly considered when designing and developing the Digital SAT questions. The texts in the Reading and Writing section are given three complexity bands (grades 6–8, grades 9–11, and grades 12–14).

Texts for grades 12-14 have the highest complexity, followed by the texts for grades 9-11, while grades 6-8 have texts with the lowest complexity. While it is possible to use the same texts for grades 12-14 and grades 9-11, those difficult texts cannot be used for grades 6-8 because they don't appropriately assess the literacy knowledge and skills of students in eighth and ninth grades.

On the other hand, text complexity is not an issue in the Math section because it is not formally measured. It is estimated that about 70% of Math questions don't necessarily have a context. You are only required to use the information/data provided to solve some questions that may be related to science, social studies, history, etc.

What has changed

The College Board continues to maintain fairness and high quality in its administration of the Digital SAT Suite, but some aspects of its operations have changed. These changes include:

- The Digital SAT Suite tests are particularly shorter than their paper-and-pencil predecessors—they can be taken in **2 hours 14 minutes** instead of 3 hours.

- You now have more time on your hands to answer each question.

- It is now possible for you to receive scores in days instead of weeks, faster than the predecessor paper-and-pencil SAT.

- The Digital SAT Suite now connects students to opportunities based on their scores. They can be connected to information and resources concerning local 2-year colleges, career options, and workforce training programs.

- States, schools, and districts are given more flexibility concerning when they could give the Digital SAT Suite.

- The Digital SAT will now have a single Reading and Writing section instead of separate Reading and Writing and Language sections. More importantly, the Reading and Writing section's passages are significantly shorter and more diverse.

- A single (discrete) question is associated with each passage (or passage pair) instead of having several questions associated with a small number of longer passages, as it was for the paper-and-pencil SAT.

- You can now use calculators throughout the Math section.

What has stayed the same

Despite the changes mentioned above, some aspects of the SAT Suite tests have remained the same, such as:

- The Digital SAT still measures skills and knowledge that you are learning in school that can be used in college and/or your future career.

- The test is scored on the same scales as the paper-and-pencil test.

- The test is administered in schools and test centers with a proctor.

- You will still be connected to scholarships and the College Board National Recognition Programs.

- Support will be given to all students who need accommodations and/or support to access the tests and their content.

- The Reading/Writing passages cover a wide range of academic disciplines and text complexities.

- The test still has both multiple-choice and student-produced response question formats.

More questions answered about the Digital SAT

1. **How will I take the Digital SAT?**

   You can take the Digital SAT on a laptop or tablet using a custom-built digital exam application called **Bluebook** that can be downloaded in advance of the test day.

2. **How is the Digital SAT more secure?**

   For the linear test, if one test form is compromised, it can mean that the scores for all the students in that group or at the same test centers will be canceled. However, going digital will make it possible to give every student a unique test form so that it won't be technically possible to share answers.

3. **How will the College Board address test day issues and technical support challenges?**

   The College Board has dedicated customer service resources ready to troubleshoot issues on test day for students and test centers. There is a technology coordinator for each test center to provide additional support and technical help when needed.

4. **What kinds of tools will be available in Bluebook for students taking the Digital SAT?**

   You can use the following tools while using the software:

   - Flag questions to come back to them later
   - A countdown clock to know when you are running out of time. You can decide to show or hide it at the top of the testing screen
   - A built-in graphing calculator that you can use on the entire Math section (or you can bring your own calculators)
   - A reference sheet of basic math formulas

The Reading and Writing section at a glance

The table below summarizes the specifications of the types of questions and their distribution in the Reading and Writing section.

Content Domain	Skill/Knowledge	Question distribution
Information and Ideas	• Central Ideas and Details • Command of Evidence (Textual and Quantitative) • Inferences	12–14 questions (26%)
Craft and Structure	• Words in Context • Text Structure and Purpose • Cross–Text Connections	13–15 questions (28%)
Expression of Ideas	• Rhetorical Synthesis • Transitions	8–12 questions (20%)
Standard English Conventions	• Boundaries • Form, Structure, and Sense	11–15 questions (26%)

The Math section at a glance

The table below summarizes the specifications of the types of questions and their distribution in the Math section.

Content Domain	Skill/Knowledge	Question Distribution
Algebra	• Linear Equations in One Variable • Linear Equations in Two Variables • Linear Functions • Systems of Two Linear Equations in Two Variables • Linear Inequalities in One or Two Variables	13–15 questions (35%)

Content Domain	Skill/Knowledge	Question Distribution
Advanced Math	• Equivalent Expressions • Nonlinear Equations in One Variable and Systems of Equations in Two Variables • Nonlinear Functions	13–15 questions (35%)
Problem–Solving and Data Analysis	• Ratios, Rates, Proportional Relationships, and Units • Percentages • One–variable Data: Distributions and Measures of Center and Spread • Two–variable Data: Models and Scatterplots • Probability and Conditional Probability • Inference from Sample Statistics and Margin of Error • Evaluating Statistical Claims: Observational Studies and Experiments	5–7 questions (15%)
Geometry and Trigonometry	• Area and Volume • Lines, Angles, and Triangles • Right Triangles and Trigonometry • Circles	5–7 questions (15%)

The Bluebook App

As you now know, you'll be taking your Digital SAT on the College Board **Bluebook app**, most probably on your own personal device. When you open and log in to the app with a student account, you'll have the opportunity to take full-length practice tests on the app to become familiar with the user interface. This is very important! Don't wait until test day to get to know the app; otherwise, you'll be wasting precious testing time.

Once you start your test on the app, your device will be locked, preventing access to other programs or apps while you are taking the test. A timer will be running to indicate how much time remains for each section or module.

You have the option to hide the timer if you want. There are many keyboard shortcuts for zooming, navigating, and other actions that you might find helpful if you prefer using the keyboard over the mouse. Just get used to them before the test. You can access the list of shortcuts by clicking on the three dots labeled "More", and then clicking on "Shortcuts".

At the start of each test section, directions will appear and remain accessible throughout the section. Please get familiar with these directions long before the test day, so that on the test day, you can close these directions and save some time to spend on the questions.

You may navigate back and forth in each section during the allotted time for that section only. To do this, just click on the "Next" and "Back" buttons. There is also another very useful option to navigate between questions. At the middle bottom of each question screen, if you click on the question number, a small pop-up menu will appear showing you the numbers of all the questions, and you can go to any question by simply clicking on its number. This pop-up menu also shows which questions you've answered, which you haven't, and which you've marked for review.

To mark a question for review, click on the ribbon-like icon found beside the question number of each question on the screen with a "Mark for Review" note beside it. Once you click on this icon, it will be filled with a maroon color, and the note "Mark for Review" will be bolded. If you like a larger view of the review menu, you can click on "Go to Review Page" also accessible from the pop-up menu which appears when you click on the bottom middle of the screen.

For each multiple-choice question, there are four choices titled A, B, C, and D. Only one of these choices is correct. There is also another option for multiple choice questions, which is marked by the icon "ABC" with a forward slash crossing the "ABC". This icon is found beside the question number to the right of the "Mark for Review" note. Once clicked, it will turn blue, and a new icon will appear beside each choice. If you click this icon beside the choice, it crosses it out, allowing you to focus on the other choices, and an "Undo" clickable word appears beside the choice if you want to undo crossing out the choice.

For a student-produced response question, there will be a blank that you need to fill in. Once you enter your answer into the blank, an answer preview will appear to show you how the app interprets your answer. For example, if you enter '3/5', the answer preview will show $\dfrac{3}{5}$.

While there is no "Annotate" tool in the Math section, there are two other buttons specific to the Math section. One of them is the 'Reference' button on the top right of the screen. If you click "Reference", a reference sheet of formulas will appear. It includes formulas for calculating the areas and volumes of common shapes, in addition to some properties of right triangles, and other information about the sum of degree and radian measures of central angles in a circle, and the sum of angle degree measures in a triangle. The other button is the "Calculator" which will be explored in the "Introduction to the Math Section" chapter.

Study Plan

This 6-week study plan provides a comprehensive roadmap to prepare for the Digital SAT. While following this plan is optional, having a well-structured guide can greatly enhance the effectiveness of your preparation and help you achieve your best results.

Week 1: Foundation Review

Day 1-3: Review fundamental concepts in math, grammar, and reading comprehension (1-2 hours per day).

Day 4: Take a diagnostic test (free along with this book) to identify baseline performance.

Day 5-7: Analyze diagnostic test results and set specific goals for improvement.

Week 2: Content Review

Day 1-3: Focus on math concepts and problem-solving strategies (1-2 hours per day).

Day 4: Review grammar rules and writing conventions.

Day 5-7: Practice reading comprehension strategies and techniques.

Week 3: Practice Questions and Timed Tests

Day 1-3: Practice SAT-style questions for math, grammar, and reading comprehension (1-2 hours per day).

Day 4: Take a timed practice test for one section (e.g., Math).

Day 5-7: Review and analyze practice test results; identify areas for improvement.

Week 4: Strategy Development

Day 1-3: Learn and practice test-taking strategies for each section (1-2 hours per day).

Day 4: Experiment with different strategies and approaches; find what works best for you.

Day 5-7: Continue practicing with timed tests, focusing on implementing strategies effectively.

Week 5: Simulated Exams

Day 1-3: Schedule full-length practice tests for Reading and Writing and Math (3-4 hours per day).

Day 4: Analyze performance, and identify patterns of strengths and weaknesses.

Day 5-7: Review and reinforce weak areas; focus on improving time management and accuracy.

Week 6: Final Review and Relaxation

Day 1-3: Prioritize a final review of key concepts and strategies (1-2 hours per day).

Day 4: Ensure you get adequate rest and relaxation to maintain focus.

Day 5-7: Stay calm and confident; mentally prepare for the exam.

Adjust the study plan according to your individual needs and schedule, ensuring a balance between content review, practice, and relaxation. Stay committed, stay focused, and trust in your preparation as you approach the Digital SAT

This page is intentionally left blank

Chapter 2

Introduction to the Reading and Writing Section

As mentioned before, the Reading and Writing section comprises **54 questions** that are divided into **two equal-length modules**. Each module is for each of the test's two stages, and it has **27 questions**, of which 25 are operational and 2 are pretest. However, only answers to the operational questions are used in estimating the section's final score.

You are given a total of **64 minutes** to complete your Reading and Writing section. Since this time is equally divided between the two modules, you can spend 32 minutes answering the questions in each module. After the time for the first module has been used up, you have to immediately proceed to the second module and answer questions with lower or higher difficulty levels as per their initial performance in the first module. After moving on to the second module, you will not be able to go back to the questions in the first module.

All Reading and Writing questions are in a multiple-choice format with four answer options that you can choose from. There will be a single best answer referred to as the keyed response or the key. The questions are discrete in the sense that they all have their own specific passages (or passage pairs).

The passages used in the Reading and Writing section are obtained from the following subject areas:

> *Literature, history/social studies, humanities, and science*

However, you are not expected to have prior knowledge of each subject.

The passage (or passage pair) for each Reading and Writing question is between **25 and 150 words.** A word in a passage is made up of six characters (these could be numbers, spaces, letters, symbols, and, of course, punctuation). As a standard, the total number of characters in a passage is divided by six; therefore, when a test question has two short passages as its stimuli, the final word count for the two passages must be between 25 and 150 words.

You will find some **informational graphics** in certain passages in the Reading and Writing section. They are basically provided to assess your ability to identify and interpret data. Some examples of informational graphics include **bar graphs, tables, and line graphs,** which are the most common methods of displaying information/data in the subjects the questions are prepared from. However, *you are not required to perform any mathematical calculations on the provided data in the informational graphics.* You need to use your quantitative and literary skills to discover the relevant information in the graphics, interpret it, and then use that information to make a reasonable conclusion about the appropriate answer for each question.

Domain structure

The questions in the Reading and Writing section depict one of four content domains, which are as follows:

- **Information and Ideas:** Questions in this domain require you to utilize your knowledge, comprehension, and analytical skills to understand what is stated and implied in texts. You must use the associated informational graphics to identify, interpret, evaluate, and process the information and ideas.

- **Craft and Structure:** In this case, you are expected to use your synthesis, comprehension, vocabulary, analysis, and reasoning skills and knowledge to discover the meaning of high-utility academic words and phrases in context, evaluate texts rhetorically, and make supportable connections between multiple topically related texts.

- **Expression of Ideas:** For this domain, you must use your revision skills and knowledge to make the written expression effective based on the expected rhetorical goals.

- **Standard English Conventions:** You will be expected to utilize your editing skills and knowledge which should be in accordance with the core conventions of Standard English sentence usage, structure, and punctuation.

General test-taking tips

To achieve a high score on the Reading and Writing section, pay attention to these general tips:

1. **Learn to identify the context and the main theme in a passage: Almost all questions on the Digital SAT are based on context.** Even questions that require you to choose the correct punctuation require context. Therefore, practice recognizing the context and the main theme in all texts that you read. The main theme is usually the subject that is being discussed and you can easily identify it. Look for the subject that is being described, criticized, or expanded upon. For example, read this text picked from Jane Austen's novel, *Sense and Sensibility* (this passage is taken from a sample test provided by the College Board).

> *Elinor, this eldest daughter, whose advice was so effectual, possessed a strength of understanding, and coolness of judgment, which qualified her, though only nineteen, to be the counsellor of her mother, and enabled her frequently to counteract, to the advantage of them all, that eagerness of mind in Mrs. Dashwood which must generally have led to imprudence. She had an excellent heart;—her disposition was affectionate, and her feelings were strong; but she knew how to govern them: it was a knowledge which her mother had yet to learn; and which one of her sisters had resolved never to be taught.*

Here, the passage describes Elinor's qualities like her coolness of judgment, her understanding, and her affectionate nature at a young age which led her to advise her mother on matters. Therefore, the main theme of the passage is Elinor's mature disposition at a young age.

2. **Eliminate three wrong options:** Each question in the Reading and Writing section has four answer choices; you need to train yourself to eliminate three of the four options to find the correct answer. Watch out for options that are:

   (i) not related to the question;

   (ii) not specifically addressing the point raised in the question (not supporting the point in the question);

   (iii) not grammatically correct; and

   (iv) expressing an opposing view to the point in the question.

   You will learn to identify the correct answer and eliminate the wrong options in the forthcoming chapters

3. **Recognize the question stems to answer questions quickly**: Digital SAT questions have a pattern of question stems that they follow. For example, for Central Ideas and Details questions, the question stem is usually "What is the main idea of the text?" or "Which choice best states the main idea of the text?" **Studying and learning to recognize question stems can help you avoid confusion.** Questions for Text Structure and Purpose questions ask questions like "Which choice best states the main purpose of the text?" which can be confusing at times as you may think it is asking the central idea of the passage.

4. **Improve your reading skills:** You can improve your level of reading comprehension by practicing with some passages included in this guide. To do this, you should **pay attention to these elements of a passage: its big picture, words, and phrases in context, perspective, word choice, textual evidence, inference, and its details.** If you analyze each passage, you will discover that they all have the elements mentioned above, and familiarizing yourself with them will help you analyze the passage appropriately.

5. **Work on your vocabulary:** Though the Digital SAT tests your analytical and reasoning abilities, it also requires you to have a working knowledge of the English language. You can improve your vocabulary by reading books, articles, journals, blogs, etc. Mind you that though reading fictional novels is a good way to enhance your vocabulary, reading nonfiction pieces will also greatly help you crack the SAT. How and why you ask? Because the Digital SAT does not only focus on literature; it includes passages from a variety of domains like science, history, and social studies. So, cultivating **a habit of reading informative blogs, statistical reports, historical pieces, newspapers, etc, will exercise your reasoning and analytical abilities and expose you to a variety of words in different contexts. You can also use tools like flashcards, play word games, and watch videos in English.**

6. **Use your extra time to double-check your answers:** If you can finish with extra time on your hands, use that time to double-check. You may be able to discover some mistakes you have committed in the course of answering the test questions.

Chapter 3
Information and Ideas

Topics covered in this chapter:

- Central Ideas and Details
- Command of Evidence
    - Textual
    - Quantitative
- Inferences

Central Ideas and Details

Central Ideas and Details questions are designed to evaluate your reading comprehension by assessing your ability to discern the main idea of a passage or hone in on a specific detail in the passage.

Central Ideas

To tackle Central Ideas questions effectively, you must first identify them within the test. These types of questions typically take the form of questions like:

> *"Which choice best describes the main idea of the text?"*

The question may refer to either a non-fiction passage or an excerpt from a literary work.

Let's define a *main idea* now.

The main idea is the central point or primary message of a passage that unifies all the content in the passage. It is the most important concept or theme that the author is trying to convey in the text. Take note that the main idea isn't always explicitly stated and often requires inference and interpretation.

Now, let's discuss the elements that can typically be present in a passage and how they help you identify the main idea.

Topic sentence	Some passages will start with topic sentences that introduce the main idea or focus that the paragraph will discuss. If the passage has a clear topic sentence, the main idea can usually be found in that sentence.
Supporting examples or details	These are specific pieces of information, evidence, or examples that support and elaborate on the main idea. They help to illustrate and clarify the main idea. If there are no clear topic or concluding sentences, the supporting details and examples will hint at the main idea. The main idea should be supported by all the details, explanations, and examples in the passage. If any sentence does not contribute to the main idea, you most likely have the wrong main idea identified.
Transitions	Transition words and phrases, such as "however," "for example," "on the other hand," "in addition," etc., are used to connect ideas within a paragraph and guide the reader from one point to the next. Transitions will clarify the progression of the main idea. Pay close attention to transition words in a passage. When there are seemingly multiple arguments in a passage, transition words will guide you in identifying the correct main idea. For instance, a passage may start with one main point, include the transition word "however," and end with another main point. Thus, the correct choice should focus on this contrasting, opposing relationship between the main points.

Concluding sentence	Some passages will end with concluding sentences that summarize the main idea or focus of the paragraph. If the passage has a clear concluding sentence, the main idea can usually be found in that sentence.

In summary, Central Ideas questions require a deep understanding of the main idea within a passage. The main idea, which is often implicit, **unites all the elements and details within the passage.** By recognizing and analyzing elements like topic sentences, supporting details, transitions, and concluding sentences, you can effectively discern and articulate the main idea in the context of the passage.

Details

The question stem for Details questions usually starts with:

> **"*According to the text/Based on the text*" and then goes on to focus on a specific detail**

The question may refer to either a non-fiction passage or an excerpt from a literary work.

Since each passage discusses a different subject, there is no defined scope for the types of details these questions may ask. Nonetheless, you will be well-equipped to answer correctly if you pay attention to the words used in the question and try to find the same words in the passage — this will be your starting point for finding the specific answer.

 What you need to keep in mind

For Central Ideas questions:

Look for topic or concluding sentences: By examining both the introductory and concluding sentences of the passage, you may be able to find the main point right away.

Avoid choices that are too specific: The SAT will include answer choices that are highly specific to distract you. While the answer choice does address information directly from the passage, **information that is too specific cannot be a main idea** that adequately summarizes all the details in the passage. Be careful because there is usually at least one answer choice that directly matches a specific part of the passage but doesn't apply to the entire reading.

For Details questions:

Locate the answer by searching for words from the question: SAT questions will not be able to ask you for a specific detail in the passage without referring to the context around the detail or the detail itself. This is great news for you – simply locate the same words that are used in the question in the passage. The answer should be found in the lines that you identify.

How to solve Central Ideas and Details questions?

Step 1

Summarize the passage: If there is no clear topic or concluding sentence, start by summarizing the passage in your own words in a succinct sentence before you read the answer choices. This exercise can help you distill the main idea solely from the details of the passage without being distracted or swayed by the answer choices. Then, find the answer choice that most closely matches your own summary. Make sure your summary is one concise sentence. Otherwise, you may end up rephrasing the whole passage, which will not help you identify the main idea.

Summarizing the passage will also be helpful for Details questions because having a firm grasp of the passage's argument will provide the context and understanding required to identify specific details.

Step 2

Avoid choices that bring in outside information: The SAT will also include answer choices that seem relevant at first, but these choices will actually include information that is not discussed in the passage. The correct choice will only refer to information from the passage without requiring any outside knowledge.

Step 3

Avoid making assumptions: Focus on what the text explicitly states. Avoid the temptation to make unwarranted inferences or assumptions regarding the main idea that lack substantiation within the paragraph's context. The SAT will include answer choices that seem correct at first. However, on a second glance, the answer choice actually makes assumptions beyond what is stated in the passage.

Step 4

Be open to choices with rephrased words or different vocabulary: The correct choice will not always use the exact same phrasing or words in the passage. Do not immediately eliminate these choices. The correct choice will accurately state the main idea, sometimes using different words or phrases from the passage.

Pro Tips -

Pay attention to absolute or extreme words: These words include but are not limited to "all," "always," "many," "most," "least," and "only." Some answer choices will strategically use these words that are too extreme to misguide you. For example, a passage may refer to several times an event or phenomenon occurs. A misleading answer choice could state the correct idea while using an extreme word like "always." This answer would be incorrect because the passage does not explicitly confirm that the event always happens all the time. The passage merely mentioned several instances of the event.

Focus on the verbs of the choices: The SAT will include some answer choices that are 90% correct to confuse you. However, you will notice that these answer choices actually use inaccurate verbs. If even one word in the answer choice is wrong, the whole answer choice is wrong. For instance, if a passage is talking about a hypothesis using verbs like "believe" or "speculate", then avoid answer choices that use words like "confirm" or "determine."

Questions to ask yourself if you are stuck between two choices:

Does any choice leave out any critical information or essential details stated in the passage? If yes, eliminate that choice.

Does any choice include information not directly supported in the passage? If yes, eliminate that choice.

Does any choice include absolute or extreme words? If yes, reevaluate if the passage directly supports the extreme nature of the answer choice.

Have you eliminated choices simply because of new words or phrasing? If yes, reevaluate those eliminated choices because the correct choice does not always use the same vocabulary as the passage.

? Let's solve a Central Ideas question now:

The following text is from Franz Kafka's 1915 novella *The Metamorphosis*.

When Gregor Samsa woke up one morning from unsettling dreams, he found himself changed in his bed into a monstrous vermin. He was lying on his back as hard as armor plate, and when he lifted his head a little, he saw his vaulted brown belly, sectioned by arch-shaped ribs, to whose dome the cover, about to slide off completely, could barely cling. His many legs, pitifully thin compared with the size of the rest of him, were waving helplessly before his eyes.

Which choice best states the main idea of the text?

A) Gregor feels like an insect due to his physical insecurities.

B) Gregor has undergone a physical transformation and feels powerless in this new state.

C) Gregor is having a vivid and strange dream about a monster.

D) Gregor is struggling to get out of bed in the morning.

Solution:

Let's start by using some tips we have learned.

Look for topic or concluding sentences: The first sentence describes an event that occurs at the very start of the passage, with Gregor waking up as a type of vermin. The last sentence describes an event that happens at the chronological end of the narrative. Therefore, there is no clear topic or concluding sentence in this case, since the sentences chronologically describe the events that are occurring.

Summarize the passage: Remember, the summary should only be one sentence long. In this passage, Gregor has taken on the form of an insect, which leads to shock, confusion, and clumsiness.

Now, let's take a look at each answer choice.

A) Gregor feels like an insect due to his physical insecurities.

Choice A is somewhat similar to our own summary. However, remember to **focus on the verbs**. In the passage, does Gregor "feel" like an insect, or has he literally transformed into an insect? Observe that there are no words in the text indicating that Gregor is merely "feeling" like an insect. With one wrong word, this choice can be eliminated.

B) **Gregor has undergone a physical transformation and feels powerless in this new state.**

Choice B is similar to our own summary as well. Gregor indeed has physically transformed into an insect. The supporting details in the passage state that Gregor has "pitifully thin" legs that wave "helplessly." These details all contribute to the main idea that Gregor feels powerless in his new body. So far, this answer choice seems the most suitable.

C) **Gregor is having a vivid and strange dream about a monster.**

Choice C is quite different from our summary. There is nothing stated in the passage to suggest that this event is merely a dream. We should not assume this frightening transformation is a nightmare, since this is not directly supported in the passage. This choice can be eliminated.

D) **Gregor is struggling to get out of bed in the morning.**

Choice D is partially correct. The passage does suggest that Gregor is struggling to get out of bed in his new body. However, we need to **avoid choices that are too specific.** This choice does not mention anything about Gregor's new insect body, which is the entire premise behind why he is struggling to leave his bed. This choice can be eliminated.

Using the tips and strategies, we can conclude that the best answer is **Choice B**.

(?) Let's solve a Details question now:

The following text is from Franz Kafka's 1915 novella *The Metamorphosis*.

When Gregor Samsa woke up one morning from unsettling dreams, he found himself changed in his bed into a monstrous vermin. He was lying on his back as hard as armor plate, and when he lifted his head a little, he saw his vaulted brown belly, sectioned by arch-shaped ribs, to whose dome the cover, about to slide off completely, could barely cling. His many legs, pitifully thin compared with the size of the rest of him, were waving helplessly before his eyes.

According to the text, why is Gregor "waving [his arms] helplessly"?

A) He is often clumsy in his surroundings.

B) He just woke up from a nightmare.

C) He doesn't want to get started with his day.

D) He is unfamiliar with his new body.

Solution:

Start by **locating the answer by searching for words from the question.** The phrase "waving helplessly" can be found in the last sentence of the passage. This sentence describes the physical attributes of Gregor's new body, including multiple stick-thin legs. Remember to use this sentence as a starting point as we go onto evaluate the answer choices.

A) **He is often clumsy in his surroundings.**

For **Choice A, pay attention to absolute or extreme words.** In this case, the word is "often," which suggests that Gregor is frequently clumsy. However, there is not enough information or evidence in the passage to prove that he is known to be a clumsy person or to showcase various instances of his clumsy nature. This passage is only about one instance of Gregor's clumsiness, so this choice can be eliminated.

B) **He just woke up from a nightmare.**

Choice B is indeed mentioned in the beginning of the passage: "Gregor…woke up…from unsettling dreams." However, there is no direct link between the dream and the helpless waving of Gregor's legs. The passage clearly states that, in reality, Gregor has transformed into an insect and cannot control his new body, so this choice can be eliminated.

C) **He doesn't want to get started with his day.**

Choice C could be true if we make an assumption that Gregor is waving his arms because he is feeling lazy or apprehensive about starting his day. We must make this assumption because Gregor's motivation or lack thereof is not explicitly stated in the passage. Now, remember that correct answer choices will **not require assumptions to be made beyond what is mentioned in the passage.** This choice should be eliminated.

D) **He is unfamiliar with his new body.**

Choice D draws accurate, specific information from the passage. Gregor's body has undergone a sudden transformation, whereby Gregor now has many, thin legs that are waving beyond his control. The supporting details in the passage further suggest that he is not used to any part of his new body, including his hard back and domed belly. Thus, choice is correct.

INFORMATION AND IDEAS

The following text is from Alfred Lord Tennyson's poem, "Crossing the Bar"

> Sunset and evening star,
> > And one clear call for me!
> And may there be no moaning of the bar,
> > When I put out to sea,
>
> But such a tide as moving seems asleep,
> > Too full for sound and foam,
> When that which drew from out the boundless deep
> > Turns again home.

Which choice best states the main idea of the text?

A) The poet talks about death and his fear of being forgotten by the world.

B) The poet likens death to crossing a sandbar, asking for a passing so peaceful that no one cries at his death.

C) The poet hears the call of death, hoping that he is asleep when he passes.

D) The poet wants a quiet and full tide to carry him out beyond the bar of death.

The notion that individuals can be categorized as either right-brained or left-brained is a misconception. While we undoubtedly possess diverse talents, attributing these distinctions to one brain hemisphere's dominance lacks scientific validity. Recent research by Nielsen and team, employing advanced brain imaging technologies, has failed to uncover any evidence supporting the notion of right or left brain dominance. This myth suffers from a fundamental flaw: it hinges on vague concepts attempting to account for various abilities. For instance, mathematics, often associated with logical thinking and left-brain activity, is, in reality, a blend of logical and creative thinking. Similarly, artistic creativity extends beyond emotion, with many masterpieces arising from precise thought processes.

Which choice best states the main idea of the text?

A) Before the study by Nielsen and the team, individuals were categorized as right-brained or left-brained based on their talents and abilities.

B) The myth of being right-brained or left-brained rests upon incorrect ambiguous definitions, where mathematics is associated with logic and art is creative.

C) The oversimplification of human abilities has led to the idea of individuals being right-brained or left-brained.

D) The categorization of humans into right-brained and left-brained lacks scientific validity and does not accurately represent brain function.

3 ⎙ Mark for Review

Microscopes are a special type of scientific tool – mostly used in biology and medicine – that use magnification to enable close viewing of certain objects for study. The use of this tool has led to several scientific advancements over the last century, but electronic microscopes are very expensive, and thereby not many institutions can afford such devices. To overcome this risk, researchers have developed an affordable version by attaching affordable photons that travel about 20 times faster than electrons in a chip.

According to the text, what is one advantage of attaching photons when using electronic microscopes?

A) Adding a certain chip enhances the convenience and speed of electron microscopes.

B) Reducing the photon locating time accelerates the microscopic process.

C) Researchers can utilize a superior version at a more affordable price.

D) It significantly speeds up the process without being too expensive.

Answers & Explanations

1. **Level:** Easy | **Skill/Knowledge:** Central Ideas and Details

    Key Explanation: Choice B is the correct answer. The poet states that he wants "no moaning" when he crosses the sandbar, i.e., when he dies. He also wishes for a tide that is "Too full for sound and foam." "Too full for sound and foam" indicates that there is no place for sound and foam in the tide. "Foam" refers to the crashing of waves against the shore. Thus, because there is no foam and sound, the tide is peaceful, much like how the poet wishes to die.

    Distractor Explanations: Choice A is incorrect because the text does not provide any information to support the idea that the poet is afraid of death and being forgotten after he dies. **Choice C** is incorrect because the poet does not hope that he is asleep when he dies. Rather, he wishes for a tide that seems asleep because it is "too full for sound and foam." **Choice D** is incorrect because the bar is not a metaphor for death itself. Rather, it is the boundary between life and death, wherein the poet's crossing of the bar refers to him dying.

2. **Level:** Medium | **Skill/Knowledge:** Central Ideas and Details

    Key Explanation: Choice D is correct. The main idea of the text is that the notion that individuals can be categorized as either right-brained or left-brained is a misconception because this idea lacks scientific validity. The main idea also includes Nielsen's recent research using advanced brain imaging technologies which failed to provide evidence supporting the concept of right or left brain dominance. Choice D comes closest to capturing the main idea of the text and hence, is the correct option.

    Distractor Explanations: Choice A is incorrect because the text mentions that "recent research by Nielsen and team … has failed to uncover any evidence supporting the notion of right or left brain dominance." However, the text does not provide direct evidence that before this study, individuals were categorized as right-brained or left-brained based on their talents and abilities. Since this option also does not capture the main idea of the text, it is not the best choice. **Choice B** is incorrect because it focuses on a specific aspect of the text – the categorization of right-brained or left-brained is based on unclear definitions, such as the association of mathematics with logic and art with creativity. It does not address the broader main idea of the passage. **Choice C** is incorrect because while it is generally correct in addressing the oversimplification of human abilities, it does not explicitly mention the lack of scientific validity or the inaccuracy of representing brain function. It is slightly less precise and comprehensive in conveying the main idea presented in the passage as compared to Choice D.

3. **Level:** Hard | **Skill/Knowledge:** Central Ideas and Details

Key Explanation: Choice D is correct. The text states that electronic microscopes are expensive, making them inaccessible to many institutions. However, researchers have developed an affordable version by attaching affordable photons. Since photons travel about 20 times faster than electrons, attaching photons to the microscope facilitates the speed of the microscopic process. This means that researchers can achieve faster results without the high cost associated with the previous version of electron microscopes. Therefore, Choice D is the correct choice.

Distractor Explanations: Choice A introduces the concept of adding a chip to the electronic microscope, but the text does not mention any specific chip being added. It only mentions attaching affordable photons to the microscope. Therefore, this option is not supported by the given information. **Choice B** suggests that attaching photons decreases the time it takes for the photons to locate objects and speeds up the microscopic process. However, the text does not provide any information about the time it takes

for photons to locate objects. It only states that photons travel faster than electrons. Therefore, this option is not supported by the given information. **Choice C** suggests that attaching photons allows researchers to use a more premium version of the microscope. However, the text does not mention anything about a more premium version. It simply states that researchers have developed an affordable version by attaching affordable photons. Therefore, this option is not supported by the given information.

Command of Evidence – Textual

Command of Evidence (Textual) questions evaluate how well you can identify a piece of textual evidence to either support or undermine a claim.

You will first be presented with a brief paragraph on a specific topic. Following the paragraph, Command of Evidence (Textual) questions look like:

> *"Which quotation most effectively illustrates the claim?"*
>
> **OR**
>
> *"Which finding, if true, would most strongly support/undermine the hypothesis?"*

The **first step** is to identify and understand the argument the question is asking you to find supporting evidence for or against. The argument will either be a **scientific argument** presented in a study or **a claim from a literary work**. Command of Evidence (Textual) questions are like the opposite of Central Ideas questions. *Instead of identifying the main argument based on supporting points, you are given the main argument for which you need to find the best supporting point.* Let's revisit the most common types of supporting points:

Common types of Supporting points

1. **Specific examples:** A supporting point can be a specific data point, anecdote, or example that directly supports or justifies the argument. If the question includes a quote from a book stating that the protagonist is a selfless individual, a description of the protagonist donating her meager savings to the local shelter is a solid supporting example.

2. **Detail that elaborates or expands on the argument:** A supporting point can also add more detail or explanation to the main point. If the question includes a scientific study's conclusion that higher levels of sunlight are associated with taller sunflowers, an explanation of how photosynthesis contributes to both faster and more efficient plant cell generation is a supporting point that elaborates on the conclusion.

As always, eliminate the obvious wrong choices and spend more time evaluating the ones that are remaining. For Command of Evidence (Textual) questions that ask you to <u>support</u> the argument, wrong choices will either directly refute the argument or support an irrelevant argument. For questions that ask you to <u>undermine</u> the argument, the wrong choices will either directly support the argument or support an irrelevant argument. When you notice these, it's time to eliminate them!

How to solve Command of Evidence (Textual) questions?

 ## Step 1

Underline the verb in the question: The first step is to identify whether you should be finding a point that supports or refutes the argument. Underline the verb in the question immediately to avoid getting confused. Supporting keywords include illustrates, supports, and justifies, while counterpoint keywords include undermines and refutes.

Step 2

Use keywords to identify the argument: In some cases, the claim is directly underlined for you. However, in other cases, you have to correctly identify the argument in order to find the relevant supporting evidence. For scientific questions, the argument may be a study's hypothesis or conclusion. Look for words such as "speculate", "claim", "argue", "hypothesize", "found", or "concluded" to locate the argument within the passage.

 Step 3

Underline the argument or restate it in your own words: If the argument is concisely stated in a few words or a sentence, underline it to help you remember and focus on this claim. Otherwise, restate the argument in your own words and jot it down to ensure you understand the argument.

☝ Remember

If one word is wrong, the whole choice is wrong. Be very specific while evaluating the answer choices. If even one word does not support or refute the argument, eliminate the entire answer choice.

Let's take the example of finding a supporting point for a main argument about the relationship between birds and seasons. One of the answer choices is almost perfect, describing how seasonal changes lead to migration patterns. However, rather than discussing birds, the answer choice focuses on butterflies. Because of the wrong subject, the answer choice is no longer relevant and should be eliminated. This example is pretty easy to catch, but there can be more subtle differences – remember that each word counts.

> **Questions to ask yourself if you are stuck between two choices:**
>
> Are you sure you are looking for the correct one based on the question: supporting point or counterpoint?
>
> Does any choice include even one word that slightly mismatches the argument? If yes, eliminate that choice.

 ## Let's solve a Command of Evidence (Textual) question now:

Frida Kahlo was a Mexican painter who is famous for her self-portraits and other works of art, which were heavily influenced by her Mexican culture. In an essay about Kahlo's work, a student claims that Kahlo's paintings can be classified as belonging to the Surrealism movement in art, a movement wherein artists depicted unexpected and typically unrealistic scenes.

Which quotation from a journalist best supports the student's claim?

A) "In a 1930 painted self-portrait in the show, the exotic look is still in formation. She sits alone in a chair in front of a plain pink wall, staring, evaluating."

B) "In one particularly beautiful Kahlo painting – she thought highly of it – called "My Nurse and Me" (1937), we see Kahlo reduced to the size of an infant and suckled by a dark-skinned Madonna with a Teotihuacan mask for a face."

C) "Wearing indigenous Mexican skirts and shawls that minimized the physical evidence of the accident, she became a piece of multicultural theater."

D) "In a family picture of a teenage Kahlo, taken by her father, an immigrant from Germany, she is already tailoring life to her taste: she is wearing a three-piece man's suit."

Solution:

First, let's **underline the verb** in the question:

Which quotation from a journalist best **supports** the student's claim?

Now we know we are looking for a supporting point.

Next, time to identify the argument. Notice the **keyword** in the sentence below that suggests where the argument can be found:

In an essay about Kahlo's work, a student **claims** that Kahlo's paintings can be classified as belonging to the Surrealism movement in art, a movement wherein artists depicted unexpected and typically unrealistic scenes.

Since the argument is slightly long, summarize it in your own words: Kahlo paints unexpected and unrealistic scenes.

Let's move to evaluating the answer choices.

A) **"In a 1930 painted self-portrait in the show, the exotic look is still in formation. She sits alone in a chair in front of a plain pink wall, staring, evaluating."**

Choice A describes a painting of Kahlo sitting in a chair. This point does not directly support the argument since there is nothing unexpected or unrealistic occurring. This choice can be eliminated.

B) **"In one particularly beautiful Kahlo painting – she thought highly of it – called "My Nurse and Me" (1937), we see Kahlo reduced to the size of an infant and suckled by a dark-skinned Madonna with a Teotihuacan mask for a face."**

Choice B describes a painting where Kahlo's face is on a baby's body being held by a masked figure. Since Kahlo is a grown woman, it is unexpected to see her in a small baby's body. So far, this answer choice seems to support the argument.

C) **"Wearing indigenous Mexican skirts and shawls that minimized the physical evidence of the accident, she became a piece of multicultural theater."**

Choice C describes Kahlo wearing cultural garments. Further, this answer choice does not directly allude to a painting. This choice can be eliminated because the argument to support is about the subject and style of Kahlo's paintings.

D) **"In a family picture of a teenage Kahlo, taken by her father, an immigrant from Germany, she is already tailoring life to her taste: she is wearing a three-piece man's suit."**

Choice D describes a picture of young Kahlo. This answer choice also does not directly allude to a painting. This choice can be eliminated because the argument to support is about the subject and style of Kahlo's paintings.

Using the tips and strategies, we can conclude that the best answer is **Choice B**.

INFORMATION AND IDEAS

1 ☐ **Mark for Review**

"Auguries of Innocence" can be viewed as a single poem encapsulating the themes found in William Blake's longer poetic volumes. It employs the same principles seen in "Songs of Innocence" and "Songs of Experience," constructing both an innocent, child-like narrative, and a mature, adult narrative within a single poem. Throughout the poem, there is a recurring shift from the smaller microcosm to the larger macrocosm.

Which quotation from "Auguries of Innocence" most effectively illustrates the underlined claim?

A) "To see a World in a Grain of Sand / And a Heaven in a Wild Flower/ Hold Infinity in the palm of your hand / And Eternity in an hour"

B) "A dog starvd at his Masters Gate / Predicts the ruin of the State / A Horse misusd upon the Road / Calls to Heaven for Human blood"

C) "The Questioner who sits so sly / Shall never know how to Reply / He who replies to words of Doubt / Doth put the Light of Knowledge out"

D) "Some to Misery are Born / Every Morn and every Night / Some are Born to sweet delight / Some are Born to sweet delight / Some are Born to Endless Night"

2 ☐ **Mark for Review**

Renowned Nigerian author Chimamanda Ngozi Adichie has made significant contributions to the world of literature through her novels and essays. In a recent analysis of Adichie's work, a critic posits that she effectively incorporates elements of her personal experiences into her fictional narratives.

Which quotation from a literary critic best supports the critic's claim?

A) "Adichie's compelling storytelling reveals the emotional depth of her characters and the profound connection to her own childhood spent in Nsukka."

B) "One of Adichie's most celebrated essays explores her personal history in a way that differs significantly from her approach to creating fictional characters in her novels."

C) "Adichie's novels resonate with readers due to her vivid portrayal of fictional characters, yet her essays provide a more direct window into her personal experiences and inspirations."

D) "While Adichie's essays often delve into her personal history, her novels demonstrate a distinct sense of detachment from her own life, creating compelling fictional worlds."

3 🔖 **Mark for Review**

During a study conducted on a rare species of orchid only found in a remote rainforest, botanists discovered that these orchids only bloom at night for a single night, and their pollination is supported by specific nocturnal insects that are also active during this phase. By observing the behavior of the orchids over several days and analyzing data collected from camera traps set up around their habitat, the botanists concluded that the plant's reproductive cycle is intricately linked to the rising and setting of the sun.

Which discovery, if confirmed, would most directly weaken the botanists' conclusion?

A) Depending on factors like rainfall and temperature, the orchids display different blooming patterns in different years.

B) The nocturnal insects responsible for pollinating the orchids are not found exclusively in the rainforest where the orchids grow.

C) Other plant species in the same rainforest also show a correlation between their reproductive cycles and the rising and setting of the sun.

D) Observations of the same species of orchid in a different rainforest region indicate that they bloom consistently regardless of the sun.

Answers & Explanations

1. **Level:** Easy | **Skill/Knowledge:** Command of Evidence (Textual)

   Key Explanation: Choice A is the best answer. The underlined claim focuses on the constant shift between the microcosm and macrocosm, i.e., the shift between something that is seen as a small version of a larger structure (microcosm) and the entire large structure itself (macrocosm.) The quote in Choice A speaks about seeing the world in a grain of sand, holding infinity in one's palm, and enjoying Eternity in an hour. Thus, this choice best illustrates the shift from the microcosm to the macrocosm, emphasizing the ability to perceive vast, universal concepts in small, everyday elements. It aligns with the underlined claim.

   Distractor Explanations: Choice B is incorrect because it touches on social and political themes in the poem but does not directly illustrate the shift from the microcosm to the macrocosm, as mentioned in the claim. **Choice C** is incorrect because it addresses the theme of questioning and knowledge but does not specifically illustrate the shift from the microcosm to the macrocosm. **Choice D** is incorrect because it focuses on the themes of human destinies and the contrasting fates of individuals but does not directly illustrate the shift from the microcosm to the macrocosm.

2. **Level:** Medium | **Skill/Knowledge:** Command of Evidence (Textual)

   Key Explanation: Choice A is the best answer. This choice mentions "…the profound connection to her own experiences." It highlights the idea that Adichie's storytelling reveals the emotional depth of her characters and the profound connection to her own experiences. This suggests that her personal experiences are incorporated into her fictional narratives, aligning with the critic's assertion.

   Distractor Explanations: Choice B is incorrect because it discusses one of Adichie's celebrated essays exploring her personal history, which is distinct from her approach to creating fictional characters in her novels. While it addresses her essays and personal history, it does not directly confirm the incorporation of personal experiences into her fictional narratives. **Choice C** is incorrect because it talks about the resonance of her novels with readers and suggests that her essays provide a more direct window into her personal experiences and inspirations. While it hints at the idea that her personal experiences may influence her work, it does not directly address the incorporation of personal experiences into her fictional narratives. **Choice D** is incorrect because it mentions that her essays often delve into personal history but a sense of detachment from her own life is seen in her novels. This option directly contradicts the incorporation of personal experiences into her fictional narratives.

3. **Level:** Hard | **Skill/Knowledge:** Command of Evidence (Textual)

    Key Explanation: Choice D is correct. This discovery directly weakens the botanists' conclusion by indicating that the orchids' blooming behavior is consistent across different regions, regardless of the environmental conditions or the presence of sunlight. This consistency suggests that the orchids' reproductive cycle is not linked to the absence of sunlight, weakening the botanists' findings in the original rainforest.

    Distractor Explanations: Choice A is incorrect because it introduces variability in the orchids' blooming patterns based on external factors but does not directly contradict the botanists' conclusion about the orchids' specific night-blooming behavior. **Choice B** is incorrect because it focuses on the habitat of the pollinating insects rather than the behavior of the orchids themselves, which is the main subject of the botanists' conclusion. **Choice C** is incorrect because it introduces a correlation between other plant species and the rising and setting of the sun, which is not directly relevant to the orchids' behavior as observed by the researchers.

Command of Evidence – Quantitative

Command of Evidence (Quantitative) questions aim to assess your ability to analyze and interpret data, as well as use that knowledge to complete a statement about the data. The data is usually presented in the form of a table, bar graph, or line graph.

Command of Evidence (Quantitative) questions will start with a brief context about the data and end with a question like:

> *"Which choice most effectively uses data from the table to complete the text?"*
>
> *OR*
>
> *"Which choice most effectively uses data from the graph to justify the underlined claim?"*

 A Word of Caution

Not all Command of Evidence (Quantitative) questions will ask for data that supports the statement or argument presented in the question. The questions may also ask you to look for data that undermines the presented argument.

Let's take a look at the type of statements these questions will include, starting with the examples below.

- The survey responses reflect that, compared to other age groups, younger adults have higher levels of _____.

- To emphasize how high the rate in the U.S. is relative to that of other countries: _____.

- Although the number of shows produced by this broadcasting company has varied significantly over the period, the number overall has increased since 2005.

- For some farms, more fruit was harvested in April than in the other months. For example, _____.

Notice that there are two types of keywords in these statements that are crucial hints. The first type of keyword will inform you of the specific subject or topic you should look for within the graph or table. These keywords are marked in bold below.

- The survey responses reflect that, compared to other age groups, **younger adults** have higher levels of _____.

- To emphasize how high the rate in the **U.S.** is relative to that of other countries: _____.

- Although the number of shows produced by this broadcasting company has varied significantly over the period, the number overall has increased since **2005**.

- For some farms, less fruit was harvested in **April** than in the other months. For example, _____.

The second type of keyword calls out the comparison that can be found within the data. They serve as a guiding point to tell you whether you should be looking for the lowest point in the graph, the median number in the table, or the highest bar in the graph. These keywords are underlined below.

- The survey responses reflect that, compared to other age groups, younger adults have <u>higher</u> levels of _____.

- To emphasize how <u>high</u> the rate in the U.S. is relative to that of other countries: _____.

- Although the number of shows produced by this broadcasting company has varied significantly over the period, the number overall has <u>increased</u> since 2005.

- For some farms, <u>less</u> fruit was harvested in April than in the other months. For example, _____.

Once you have identified both types of keywords, you will be equipped to hone in on specific rows, columns, bars, or points in the data and evaluate the correct answer based on the type of comparison.

How to solve Command of Evidence (Quantitative) questions?

 ### Step 1

Underline the verb of the question: Verbs like "support" or "justify" suggest that the selected data needs to align with the statement in the question. On the other hand, verbs like "undermine" or "refute" indicate that you should look for data that contradicts the statement in the question. Start by underlining the verb to ensure you are looking for the data that is relevant to the question.

 ### Step 2

Identify the keyword that identifies the subject in question: Each table or graph can present multiple points of information, but not every point will be necessary to answer the question. In fact, trying to understand all the data presented in the graphic will take up too much time and prevent you from answering the questions quickly and accurately. In order to hone in on the details relevant to the question, start by understanding the specific subject the question wants you to evaluate. For example, if the table presents the population levels of countries in South America and the statement mentions Paraguay, start by looking at the column or row that contains data relevant to Paraguay. You can even cross out or hide the countries that are not required to answer the question to block out the extraneous details.

 ### Step 3

Identify the keyword that is a comparative or superlative word: Comparative words are words that compare two objects in some quality. Some examples include: more, worse, better, and faster. Superlative words are words that indicate the most or least of some quality. Examples of superlatives include best, most, least, and strongest. It is not important to remember the terms "comparative" and "superlative", but you should be able to identify and pay extra attention to these keywords.

Step 4

Read the title of the graph or table: Every graph or table will have a title that describes the data being presented. Do not ignore the title. The title is often a succinct, straightforward description that will quickly give you the context and a higher level of understanding of the data, which is crucial before diving deeper into each of the data points.

Step 5

Immediately eliminate choices that misread the data in the graph or table: Every quantitative command of evidence question will include some answer choices that are factually incorrect based on the data in the graph or table. If you identify these choices, immediately eliminate them. There is no need to further evaluate if they are relevant to the claim in the question or if they support or refute that claim because the SAT will never ask you to pick an answer choice that misinterprets the data presented.

☝ Remember

Choices that are factually correct based on the graphic are not always the correct answer: If all you had to do was eliminate choices that misread the data in the graph or table, quantitative command of evidence questions would be too easy. While that is the first step, the next step is to evaluate whether the remaining choices are relevant to the question or not.

Questions to ask yourself if you are stuck between two choices:

Is the choice factually supported by the data in the graph or table? If the answer is no, eliminate the choice.

Does the choice directly relate to the statement from the question? If the answer is no, eliminate the choice.

 Let's solve a Command of Evidence (Quantitative) question now:

% of U.S. Adults Who Say They Use or Have Used the Following Types of Technology

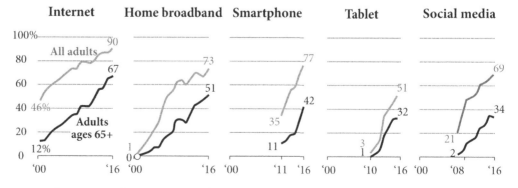

A research center in the U.S. surveyed 3,015 adults across the country in 2016 to understand

adoption rates of smart devices like phones and tablets, as well as use of the internet and social media, over time. The majority of the adults included in the survey reported that they believe technology has an overall positive impact on society and the economy. Based on the survey results, older adults above the age of 65 had adoption rates more than _____.

Which choice most effectively uses data from the graphs to complete the statement?

  A) triple for smartphones from 2008 to 2016.

  B) triple for social media from 2000 to 2016.

  C) multiply by fivefold for the internet from 2000 to 2016.

  D) those of all adults for tablets from 2010 to 2016.

Solution:

First, let's mark the **subject keyword** in bold and underline the comparative or superlative keyword in the question.

> Based on the survey results, **older adults above the age of 65** had adoption rates <u>more</u> than _____.

Now we know we should focus on adults above the age of 65, which is the age group represented by the dark-colored line in the graph. We also know we need to focus on how this age group has higher adoption rates than other groups.

Next, let's take a look at each answer choice.

A) triple for smartphones from 2008 to 2016.

  Choice A cannot be interpreted from the line graphs, simply because data for adoption rates for smartphones was not available from 2000 to 2010. This choice can be eliminated.

B) triple for social media from 2000 to 2016.

  Choice B cannot be interpreted from the line graphs as data for adoption rates for social media was not available from 2000 to 2007. This choice can be eliminated.

C) multiply by fivefold for the internet from 2000 to 2016.

  Choice C is correct. The graph shows that the adoption rate for the internet was 12% for adults aged 65+ in 2000. In 2016, the adoption rate for the same was 67%, which is more than fivefold of 12%. This answer is both factually correct based on the graph and relevant to the question about adoption rates for adults over the age of 65.

D) those of all adults for tablets from 2010 to 2016.

  Choice D is incorrect based on the data in the line graphs. The graph shows that the adoption rates for all adults for tablets is consistently higher than the same for adults aged 65+ from 2010 to 2016. This choice can be eliminated.

1   ☐ Mark for Review

Opinions towards Incentives to Produce More Affordable Housing

Incentive	% of respondents who believe the incentive is helpful to produce more affordable housing
Reduced parking and road width requirements	19
Fee reductions/financing programs	24
Bigger floor area ratio	13
Reduced minimum lot sizes	22
Expedited building permit issuance	22
Reduced setback requirements	18
Expedited rezoning process	20
Additional height allowances	19
Land subsidy (for acquisition)	18

The availability and quality of affordable housing are growing concerns in many countries. The challenges of introducing more affordable housing can be related to zoning regulations, labor laws, costs of materials, and various other factors. In a survey among developers, respondents shared potential incentives governments could introduce to push developers to build more affordable housing units. Assuming the respondents' opinions are reliable, if governments can only prioritize a few top incentive programs, governments should _____

Which choice most effectively uses data from the table to complete the statement?

A) implement bigger floor area ratios, reduced setback requirements, and land subsidies for acquisition.

B) implement reduced parking and road width requirements, fee reductions, and expedited rezoning processes.

C) not implement bigger floor area ratios, reduced setback requirements, and land subsidies for acquisition.

D) not implement fee reductions, reduced minimum lot sizes, and expedited building permit issuances.

% of U.S. adults ages 25 to 34 with a bachelor's degree

In 2021, an annual survey collected data on college graduation rates among U.S. adults. Based on the results, in the mid-1990s, the percentage of women with a bachelor's degree surpassed the percentage of men with a bachelor's degree for the first time in history. This change may be attributed to changes in personal choice, more opportunities for women, and shifts in cultural norms. While the percentage of men with bachelor degrees was 8 percentage points higher than the same percentage for women in 1970, _____

Which choice most effectively uses data from the graph to complete the statement?

A) the percentage of women with bachelor degrees was 10 percentage points higher than the same percentage for men in 2021.

B) the percentage of women with bachelor degrees was 20 percentage points more than the same percentage for men in 2021.

C) the percentage of men with bachelor degrees was 10 percentage points higher than the same percentage for women in 2021.

D) the percentage of men with bachelor degrees was 10% more than the same percentage for women in 2021.

3   ☐ Mark for Review

**% of Adults in Each Group (Oppose/Favor Use of Animals in Research)
who Believe Genetic Engineering of Animals is Appropriate**

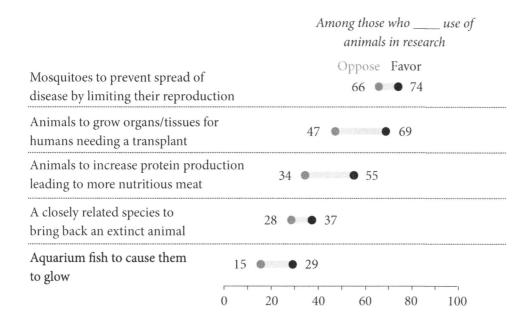

Modifying the DNA sequences of an organism to alter a trait is known as genetic engineering. Genetic engineering can have ethical implications, which often leads to a diversity of opinions. Researchers surveyed 2,537 adults, some who oppose animal research and some who favor animal research, to explore their opinions about genetic engineering for different use cases. The adults included in the survey are nationally representative in terms of gender, religious views, and education levels. The survey found that _____

Which choice most effectively uses data from the graph to complete the statement?

A) those favoring the use of animals in research are less likely to believe genetic engineering of animals is appropriate.

B) those opposing the use of animals in research are less likely to believe genetic engineering of animals is appropriate.

C) the majority of those favoring the use of animals in research also support genetic engineering of animals.

D) the majority of those opposing the use of animals in research also support genetic engineering of animals.

Answers & Explanations

1. **Level:** Easy | **Skill/Knowledge:** Command of Evidence (Quantitative)

   Key Explanation: Choice C is correct. The governments should not implement the incentive programs with the lowest percentages of respondents who believe the incentive is helpful to produce more affordable housing. Therefore, the incentive programs with the lowest percentages are: bigger floor area ratios (13%), reduced setback requirements (18%), and land subsidies for acquisition (18%).

   Distractor Explanations: Choice A is incorrect. The governments should implement the incentive programs with the highest percentages of respondents who believe the incentive is helpful to produce more affordable housing. However, the incentive program with the lowest percentage is bigger floor area ratios (13%). **Choice B is incorrect.** The governments should implement the incentive programs with the highest percentages of respondents who believe the incentive is helpful to produce more affordable housing. However, the incentive program with one of the lowest percentages is reduced parking and road width requirements (19%). **Choice D is incorrect.** The governments should not implement the incentive programs with the lowest percentages of respondents who believe the incentive is helpful to produce more affordable housing. However, the incentive program with the highest percentage is fee reductions (24%).

2. **Level:** Medium | **Skill/Knowledge:** Command of Evidence (Quantitative)

   Key Explanation: Choice A is correct. The percentage of women with bachelor degrees in 2021 was 46%, which is 10 percentage points higher than 36%, the percentage of men with bachelor degrees in 2021.

   Distractor Explanations: Choice B is incorrect because it inaccurately interprets the data in the graph. The percentage of women with bachelor degrees is 10 percentage points more than men in 2021 as shown in Choice A. **Choice C is incorrect.** The percentage of women with bachelor degrees in 2021 was 46%, which is 10 percentage points higher than 36%, the percentage of men with bachelor degrees in 2021. **Choice D is incorrect.** If the percentage of men with bachelor degrees was 10% more than the same percentage for women in 2021, 50.6% of men would have bachelor degrees in 2021. (46% + 4.6% = 50.6%)

3. **Level:** Hard | **Skill/Knowledge:** Command of Evidence (Quantitative)

   Key Explanation: Choice B is correct. The graph shows that the percentages of people who oppose the use of animals in research and believe genetic engineering of animals is appropriate in the defined use cases is consistently lower than the percentages of people who favor the use of animals in research and believe genetic engineering of animals is appropriate in the defined use cases.

   Distractor Explanations: Choice A is incorrect. The graph shows that the percentages of people who oppose the use of animals in research and believe genetic engineering of animals is appropriate in the defined use cases is consistently lower than the percentages of people who favor the use of animals in research and believe genetic engineering of animals is appropriate in the defined use cases. **Choice C is incorrect.** The majority of those favoring the use of animals in research also support genetic engineering of animals in some use cases, but this is not true in all the use cases in the graph. **Choice D is incorrect.** The majority of those opposing the use of animals in research also support genetic engineering of animals in some use cases, but this is not true in all the use cases in the graph.

Inferences

Inference questions on the SAT evaluate how well you can critically understand an argument and logically link pieces of information together to the argument.

These questions start with a non-fiction passage and ask:

> **"Which choice most logically completes the text?"**

First of all, **an inference is defined as a conclusion that is drawn through reasoning, often based on evidence.** The passage you are given provides all the pieces of evidence, and you need to draw the conclusion by choosing the sentence or phrase that most logically ties into these pieces of evidence. The correct answer should logically follow the points in the paragraph and support the overall argument clearly.

> The main reason you will eliminate answer choices for inference questions is when there is **no evidence in the passage** to support the statement.

Inference questions are tricky because finding the answer is not about which point is factually correct; any of the answer choices could technically be true. Let's look at a simplified example to help you understand how you should be conceptually thinking about inferences.

> Cities are more crowded than rural areas because cities are more densely populated. Many people drive to work in the morning in cities. Therefore, _____

Which choice most logically completes the text?

A) people work longer hours in cities.

B) cities are more likely to have traffic jams in the morning.

C) rural areas are more likely to have traffic jams in the morning.

D) cities have higher birth rates than rural areas.

The flow of logic in the passage starts with a statement that cities are more crowded than rural areas. The next point states that people in cities drive their cars to commute to work. While these two statements seem to be discussing separate points, what can you logically conclude when you put them together?

> Crowded + driving to work in the morning = traffic jams in the morning

Choice B is the closest answer to this conclusion. You'll notice that while the other answers could technically be true, none of them are fully supported by the combined pieces of evidence in the passage. For Choice A, longer working hours are not related to driving to work or living in densely populated areas. Choice C is actually refuted by the points in the passage since the passage suggests that cities are more likely to have traffic jams than rural areas. Lastly, for Choice D, birth rates are not related to driving to work or living in densely populated areas.

Note that you will likely not be able to come up with a logical conclusion yourself first; you will need to browse through the answer choices to find the one that matches your own conclusion.

The SAT questions will not be as simple as the example above, so your best bet is to plug in each answer choice one by one and eliminate as you go.

How to solve Inference questions?

Step 1

Understand the flow of logic in the passage: In the simple example above, we quickly jotted down the notes "Crowded + driving to work in the morning" to summarize the pieces of evidence in the passage concisely. Try to also write down or underline a few keywords in the passage to remember these pieces of evidence. If you don't have a firm grasp of the evidence, it will be hard to logically reason through the rest of the question.

Step 2

Pay attention to absolute or extreme words: Words like "all," "always," "many," "most," "least," and "only" could be trying to misguide you. For example, a passage may refer to an event or phenomenon occurring several times. A misleading answer choice could state the correct idea while using an extreme word like "always." This answer would be incorrect because the passage does not explicitly confirm that the event always happens all the time. The passage only mentions several instances of the event.

Step 3

Transition words are key clues: Transition words and phrases, such as "however," "for example," "on the other hand," "in addition," etc., are used to connect ideas within a paragraph and guide you from one point to the next. They basically outline the flow of logic for you! A passage may introduce a general claim and include the transition phrase "for instance." In this case, the correct choice should provide a specific example to logically follow this transition phrase.

Step 4

Focus on keywords in the last sentence to complete: Similar to transition words, the keywords in the final sentence can provide some clues about whether the correct answer will be an example, a conclusion, or another type of point. Passages about scientific studies will often end with a sentence like, "Researchers then concluded that ____." The keyword "concluded" indicates that the correct answer will provide a conclusion based on the results of the study.

⚡ Pro Tip --

Relevance, relevance, relevance: One way to think about inference questions is to focus on the most relevant answer choice. Take the example of a passage describing a study about the relationship between the words in a song and an audience's reaction to the song. The sentence that logically completes the text is supposed to provide a summary of the findings of the study. Which keyword is the most relevant to the passage: pitch, beat, production, or vocabulary? Since the study is about the words in the song, vocabulary should be the most relevant one.

The correct choice could describe how using sophisticated vocabulary leads to more positive reactions to the song. Could it be true that a higher production quality leads to more positive reactions to the song? Certainly, but it is not relevant to the study in the passage, so this is not the answer we are looking for.

Questions to ask yourself if you are stuck between two choices:

Is the choice relevant to the points in the passage? Does the choice have any evidence or reasoning in the passage, whereby it logically flows from the other sentences?

Does any choice include absolute or extreme words? If yes, reevaluate if the passage supports the extreme nature of the answer choice.

Have you noted any transition words and checked how they hint at the flow of logic in the passage?

Have you checked the keywords in the last sentence of the passage? Does the answer choice logically follow what the keyword is suggesting?

(?) Let's solve an Inferences question now:

A group of researchers came across a new carnivorous pitcher plant species called Nepenthes pudica during a trip to Borneo. The pitchers were actually located underground, where the plants wait for ants, mites, beetles, and other insects to fall or stumble into the pitchers. Further, the pitcher plants were only found at elevations of 3,600 to 4,265 feet above sea level, where the presence of other organisms is more scarce. The researchers then posited that _____

Which choice most logically completes the text?

A) the plant had never been unearthed before this discovery.

B) the pitcher plants were underground as a result of a landslide.

C) the pitcher plants adapted to be able to capture prey not commonly found above ground.

D) the pitcher plants were biologically different from other pitcher plants.

Solution:

First, let's try to document the **flow of logic** in the passage.

Insect-eating plants found underground + at high elevations without many living things

Also notice that the last sentence in the passage includes the **keyword** "posited", which suggests that the correct answer will be a conclusion based on the researchers' findings.

A) **the plant had never been unearthed before this discovery.**

Right away, we can be wary of **Choice A** because it includes an **absolute word**, which is "never." There is no evidence in the passage to suggest that the plants have never been unearthed before this particular group of researchers.

B) **the pitcher plants were underground as a result of a landslide.**

Choice B is also incorrect because there is no evidence in the passage about a landslide. Discussion of a landslide is **not relevant**.

C) **the pitcher plants adapted to be able to capture prey not commonly found above ground.**

Choice C seems correct. Remember our notes that "insect-eating plants found underground + at high elevations without many living things." Therefore, it is logical to reason that the pitcher plants grow underground because it was hard to find enough prey above ground, so they adapted to be able to find insects underground. Further, the plants can also live at high elevations without many other visible organisms since they only eat insects underground. We should only confirm this choice is the right answer if we are also able to eliminate all other choices safely.

D) the pitcher plants were biologically different from other pitcher plants.

Choice D is incorrect because the text does not compare different types of pitcher plants, so this topic is **not relevant**.

Using the tips and strategies, we can conclude that the best answer is **Choice C**.

1 ☐ **Mark for Review**

For migratory birds, knowing when to depart their winter habitats is a critical factor that can mean the difference between life and death. During the spring season, approximately one in five bird species depart from their winter habitats on a lengthy journey, ultimately leading to mating, nesting, and the hatching of their offspring. Determining the precise moment to commence this migration is a delicate calculation for these creatures. They must arrive at their breeding grounds with sufficient time to ensure successful reproduction. However, _____

Which choice most logically completes the text?

A) if they arrive too late, their migratory timeline may be over for the season.

B) if they arrive after spring, their endocrine system may not be prepared for reproduction.

C) if they arrive too soon, winter may not be quite over, putting the birds at risk of starving to death.

D) migration is a complicated process that differs from species to species.

2 ☐ **Mark for Review**

In 2001, the Marine Corps introduced the Marine Corps Martial Arts Program (MCMAP), an internally developed martial arts program. The purpose of MCMAP was to equip marines with a wider range of non-lethal techniques to effectively handle situations in domestic urban areas that involve hostile individuals who are unarmed. The implementation of MCMAP was driven by the increasing encounters between marines and unarmed American civilians. Therefore, the expectation behind the introduction of the MCMAP is that _____

Which choice most logically completes the text?

A) an increased number of Marine Corps will need to be deployed over the next decade.

B) more Marine Corps stations will be established.

C) more Marines will be involved in urban peacekeeping missions within America in the coming years.

D) the MCMAP will be successful in lowering urban crime rates across the country.

| 3 | ☐ **Mark for Review** |

Dogs have long been considered to be man's best friend. However, animal behaviorists have long wondered if it is possible that dogs end up taking on the personalities of their owners. Considering the fact that dogs spend a considerable amount of time with humans, human personality could influence dog behavior. In 2012, dog personality was reported by owners and friends. The ratings found that there was _____.

Which choice most logically completes the text?

A) no link between owners and their dogs for neuroticism, extraversion, conscientiousness, and agreeableness.

B) a link between owners and their dogs for neuroticism, extraversion, conscientiousness, and agreeableness.

C) a link between owners and their dogs for many physical traits and overall appearance.

D) no link between owners and their dogs for many physical traits and overall appearance.

Answers & Explanations

1. **Level:** Easy | **Skill/Knowledge:** Inferences

   Key Explanation: Choice C is the correct answer. The text mentions that birds "must arrive at their breeding grounds with sufficient time to ensure successful reproduction", meaning that they need to reach early. The usage of "however" before the blank suggests that the remainder of the sentence will also show a contrasting idea. Therefore, the birds need to reach the breeding sites early but not too early, further emphasizing on the information provided in the first sentence ("a critical factor that can mean the difference between life and death")

   Distractor Explanations: Choice A is incorrect because the usage of "however" indicates that the remaining text will show a contrasting idea. Since this choice neither shows an opposite idea nor touches upon reproduction, it is not the best answer. **Choice B** is incorrect because the choice does not offer a contrasting idea. It touches upon the endocrine system and the text gives no indication that the endocrine system plays a role in reproduction. **Choice D** is incorrect because it is completely unrelated to the previous sentence and hence does not contrast the idea of birds reaching migratory sites in plenty of time.

2. **Level:** Medium | **Skill/Knowledge:** Inferences

   Key Explanation: Choice C is the correct answer. The usage of "therefore" in the last sentence implies that a conclusion has been drawn based on information previously provided in the text. If the Marine Corps are facing "increasing encounters between marines and unarmed civilians" and that they are being taught a "wider range of non-lethal techniques," it can be inferred that they will participate in a task(s) that involve unarmed/hostile civilians. Choice C comes closest to this inference and hence is the best option.

Distractor Explanations: Choice A is incorrect because it does not draw upon previous information to create a logical conclusion to the text. **Choice B** is incorrect because the text provides no information about the number of Marine Corps stations. **Choice D** is incorrect because it does not directly relate to the previous sentence in the text and is not a suitable conclusion that can be drawn based on the information provided.

3. **Level:** Hard | **Skill/Knowledge:** Inferences

   Key Explanation: Choice B is the best answer because it takes into account the topic of the passage: that there is possibly a connection between human behavior and canine pets.

   Distractor Explanations: Choice A is not logical because it says there is no connection. The passage considers the possibility that there is a connection between dog and owner behavior. This choice makes an illogical inference. **Choice C** focuses on physical similarities when the passage discusses personalities. **Choice D** is wrong because not only does it focus on physical traits, but it also makes the illogical conclusion that there is no connection when the entire passage has been leading the reader to the conclusion that there is a link between dogs and their owners.

This page is intentionally left blank

Chapter 4
Craft and Structure

Topics covered in this chapter:

- Words in Context
- Text Structure and Purpose
- Cross–text Connections

Words in Context

Words in context (WIC) questions test your reading comprehension and knowledge of vocabulary. Mastering Words in Context questions demands not only a robust vocabulary but also a keen understanding of how words function within the fabric of a passage.

These questions include a fiction or a non-fiction passage that has a missing word to be filled in or an underlined word and asks:

> *"Which choice completes the text with the most logical and precise word or phrase?"*
>
> **OR**
>
> *"As used in the text, what does the word "example" most nearly mean?"*

Your task is to identify the option that not only aligns accurately with the intended meaning of the word to be inserted but also maintains a consistent tone and connotation with the overall paragraph. As you tackle these questions, keep in mind that the passages *typically introduce a central idea, and the missing underlined word serves as a pivotal piece to complement and enhance that idea.* Hence, you can begin searching for hints within the passage.

In general, regular reading of both fiction and non-fiction texts is the best way to fortify your vocabulary for the Digital SAT. As you read, you not only expand your word bank but also develop an understanding of how words operate in different contexts. This proficiency in contextual comprehension becomes particularly valuable when tackling Words in Context questions, making regular reading a valuable method of test preparation.

How to solve Words in Context questions?

 ### Step 1

Read the whole paragraph: Don't focus solely on the sentence containing the blank/underlined word. The words and phrases in the sentences surrounding the blank/word can offer significant hints about the intended meaning.

 ### Pro Tip

Be attentive to transitions, comparisons, and contrasts in the text.

 ### Step 2

Underline context clues: After reading the paragraph in full, find the part of the paragraph that corresponds with the sentence containing the missing/underlined word. How do you know if there is correspondence or not? Look for a key subject that is repeated or an idea that is restated. Underline any relevant context clues which should only consist of a few words. The correct answers are often the synonyms of these context clues. Take a moment before even looking at the answer choices to predict what kind of word or phrase might fit into the blank or what could the underlined word mean based on the context of the passage.

Step 3

Eliminate antonyms and irrelevant answers: Words can easily be eliminated if they convey the opposite meaning of the intended word. For example, if the passage is describing a vivid, colorful landscape and the intended word is an adjective used to describe that setting, an antonym like "bland" that conveys a dull, boring visual can be eliminated right away. Further, some answer options will simply be irrelevant to the topic of the passage. Those options can also be eliminated.

 Pro Tips -

The following tips should be applied for more difficult questions when you are unable to eliminate choices or you do not recognize the words in the answer options:

1. **Determine the tone:** Try to identify whether the author expresses positivity, negativity, neutrality, or any other nuance in tone in the passage. This awareness is crucial because the tone often guides the meaning of the unfamiliar word. If the sentence exudes positivity, eliminate negative or neutral-sounding answer choices. Similarly, if the tone is negative, disregard options with positive or neutral connotations. Recognizing the tonal context enhances your ability to pinpoint the right word that fits with the overall sentiment of the sentence.

2. **Deconstruct word:** Breaking a word down to its root, prefix, and suffix can demystify its meaning. Roots carry core definitions, prefixes modify these meanings, and suffixes alter the word's grammatical function. For example, "benevolent" breaks down into 'bene' (good) and "vol" (will), suggesting goodwill. Another example is the prefix "in-" which often implies negation, as seen in words like "inactive" or "ineffective." Similarly, the suffix "-tion" indicates a process or action, helping you deduce the meaning of words like "determination" or "information." This **deconstruction** method provides valuable clues to decipher the intended sense of the word in the given sentence.

- -

Questions to ask yourself if you are stuck between two choices:

Are there relevant context clues in the passage to support this answer choice? If not, eliminate this choice.

Does this word match the overall tone and connotation expressed throughout the passage? If not, eliminate this choice.

(?) **Let's solve a Words in Context question now:**

Medical researchers have coined a new term called the "commercial determinants of health." The term refers to the growing _____ of companies in the realm of public health. While these impacts can be either positive or negative, researchers argue that the degree to which companies can control health-related policies should be limited.

Which choice completes the text with the most logical and precise word or phrase?

A) influence

B) deception

C) delight

D) mistrust

Solution:

After reading the passage, we can gather that the passage is about the role that companies play in public health policies. Let's now focus on the sentence with the missing word: the sentence indicates that we need to find a word that describes something about the companies *in relation to* public health.

We can now underline the context clues that correspond with the aforementioned sentence.

> Medical researchers have coined a new term called the "commercial <u>determinants</u> of health." The term refers to the growing _____ of companies in the realm of public health. While these <u>impacts</u> can be either positive or negative, researchers argue that the degree to which companies can <u>control</u> health-related policies should be limited.

This passage offers context clues at various points. The initial context clue, "determinants," is chosen because the term "commercial determinants of health" involves the key elements of this discussion: "commercial," which pertains to companies, and "public health." Consequently, the term "determinants," meaning deciding factors, establishes a crucial connection between companies and public health.

The second context clue "impacts" is relevant because of the word that precedes it: "these." The word "these" indicates that the "impacts" relate to the information that was presented in the previous sentence, which happens to be the sentence that includes the missing word. Therefore, the correct answer choice should also relate to "impacts".

Finally, the last sentence includes the context clue "control" because the last sentence also links the two subjects "companies" and "health" together.

The three clue words all seem to indicate control, influence, and power. The answer choice that most closely aligns with these is Choice A) influence.

To be safe, we should still review the other three choices to ensure they can be eliminated.

Choice B has a more negative connotation since deception refers to an act of lying or deceit. However, the passage has a more neutral tone since companies can have "positive or negative" impacts, so this choice can be eliminated due to its mismatch in connotation.

Choice C is irrelevant. There are no clues in the passage to indicate that companies are delighted, or excited in the public health landscape. We can eliminate this choice.

Choice D is incorrect because there are no context clues to suggest that there is mistrust, or suspicion in relation to companies and public health policies. This choice can also be eliminated.

Using the tips and strategies, we can conclude that the best answer is **Choice A**.

(?) Let's see how the second type of question is solved:

The following text is adapted from Honoré de Balzac's 1835 novel *Le Père Goriot*. The narrator describes a previous tenant of a boarding house.

At that time one of the rooms was tenanted by a law student, a young man from the neighborhood of Angouleme, one of a large family who pinched and starved themselves to spare twelve hundred francs a year for him. Misfortune had <u>accustomed</u> Eugene de Rastignac, for that was his name, to work. He belonged to the number of young men who know as children that their parents' hopes are centered on them, and deliberately prepare themselves for a great career, subordinating their studies from the first to this end, carefully watching the indications of the course of events, calculating the probable turn that affairs will take, that they may be the first to profit by them.

As used in the text, what does the word "accustomed" most nearly mean?

A) Overwhelmed

B) Ritualized

C) Consumed

D) Familiarized

Solution:

We can start by underlining the context clues for the word "accustomed."

> At that time one of the rooms was tenanted by a law student, a young man from the neighborhood of Angouleme, one of a large family who pinched and starved themselves to spare twelve hundred francs a year for him. Misfortune had accustomed Eugene de astignac, for that was his name, to work. He belonged to the number of young men who know as children that their parents' hopes are centered on them, and deliberately <u>prepare</u> themselves for a great <u>career,</u> <u>subordinating</u> their <u>studies</u> from the first to this end, carefully watching the indications of the course of events, calculating the probable turn that affairs will take, that they may be the first to profit by them.

In this case, there do not seem to be many context clues that directly correlate to the word "accustomed." Instead, we can identify related phrases that refer to the statement of Eugene being accustomed to work due to misfortune.

The passage suggests that Eugene does not come from a wealthy family. He makes an effort to create a "great career" and prioritizes his job over his "studies." Therefore, these hints indicate that Eugene is no stranger to work. It makes sense that this reality is caused by "misfortune", which is the word that closely precedes "accustomed," since the lack of wealth creates this need to generate income by working rather than inheritance.

Remember that we should also evaluate the tone of the answer choices. **Choice A** may be too strong of a choice as there is no evidence to support the statement that Eugene is overwhelmed or cannot handle work. The same reasoning goes for **Choice C**.

Choice B is not relevant because there are no context clues to suggest a ritual or custom taking place.

Choice D is the word with the most appropriate definition and neutral tone. Due to his family's misfortune and lack of wealth, Eugene is familiar with having to work to earn a living and support his family.

List of Important Vocabulary Words

This list contains carefully selected words that have appeared in previous SAT tests. These words are important for the SAT and valuable additions to your everyday vocabulary. Mastering these words will not only help you excel in the SAT but also enhance your reading comprehension and writing skills. Each word is accompanied by definitions and sample sentences to help you understand and remember them.

Word	Part of Speech	Meaning	Sentence
absolve	verb	To free someone from guilt, blame, or responsibility for a wrongdoing	The court's decision to **absolve** the defendant of all charges surprised many legal experts.
amass	verb	To gather or collect a large amount of something, typically over a period of time	Over the years, he had managed to **amass** a fortune through wise investments.
brunt	noun	The main impact or force, especially of a blow or attack	The coastal towns bore the **brunt** of the hurricane's destructive force.
coin	verb	To invent or devise a new word or phrase	The author **coined** a term to describe the unique cultural phenomenon she was studying.
conclusive	adjective	Serving to settle an issue; decisively final	The DNA evidence was **conclusive** in proving the suspect's innocence.
curtail	verb	To reduce in extent or quantity; to impose a restriction on	The government decided to **curtail** spending in order to reduce the national debt.
cynical	adjective	Believing that people are motivated purely by self-interest; distrustful of human sincerity or integrity	After years of working in politics, she had become **cynical** about the motives of politicians.
determinate	adjective	Having exact and fixed limits or boundaries	The committee set a **determinate** deadline for the completion of the project.
disjunction	noun	A disparity or disconnection between two things	The **disjunction** between his public persona and private life surprised many of his fans.
dwindle	verb	To become smaller or lose substance	As the days passed, the food supplies in the shelter began to **dwindle**.
earthy	adjective	Of or resembling earth or soil; practical and down-to-earth	Her cooking was praised for its **earthy** flavors and simple, rustic presentation.
embattled	adjective	Engaged in battle or conflict; faced with difficulties	The **embattled** nation refused to surrender despite facing overwhelming odds.
expository	adjective	Intended to explain or describe something	The textbook contained a detailed **expository** section on the causes of the Civil War.
extemporaneous	noun	Spoken or done without preparation	Her **extemporaneous** speech impressed the audience with its eloquence and coherence.
fancied	adjective	Imagined or believed to be true, typically without evidence or proof	She had a **fancied** notion that her neighbors were spying on her.
fatalism	noun	The belief in fate, or that all events are predetermined and inevitable	His **fatalism** prevented him from taking proactive steps to improve his situation.
fitful	adjective	Not steady; irregularly intermittent	The baby's sleep was **fitful**, waking up every few hours throughout the night.

Word	Part of Speech	Meaning	Sentence
furor	noun	An outbreak of anger or excitement	The announcement of the new retirement policy caused a **furor** among the employees.
gloss	verb	To attempt to hide something unfavorable through misrepresenting the truth or making it more attractive	The marketing brochure was designed to **gloss** over the company's recent financial troubles.
hale	adjective	Healthy and strong, especially in old age	Despite his advanced age, the **hale** old man still enjoyed hiking and gardening.
harbor	verb	To give shelter or refuge to; to conceal or hide	The fugitive was **harbored** by sympathetic villagers until he could escape across the border.
homage	noun	A public show of special honor or respect	The film director's latest work was an **homage** to classic Hollywood cinema.
incarnate	adjective	Embodied in human form; personified	She was the very spirit of kindness **incarnate**.
innate	adjective	Natural; existing from birth	His **innate** talent for music was evident from a very young age.
incidence	noun	The occurrence or rate of something, usually something undesirable	The **incidence** of diabetes has been increasing worldwide.
iota	noun	A very small amount	She didn't show an **iota** of fear during the interview.
jargon	noun	Specific, technical words or expressions that are used by a particular group that may be difficult for others to understand	The legal document was full of **jargon** that was difficult for the average person to decipher.
jollity	noun	Lively and cheerful celebration	The festival was filled with music, dance, and general **jollity**.
kismet	noun	Predetermined fate or destiny	They believed it was **kismet** that they met on that fateful day.
laity	noun	Ordinary people who are not identified as professionals or experts	The priest gave a special sermon aimed at the **laity** rather than the clergy.
leaven	verb	To add a substance such as yeast to dough or batter to make it ferment and rise; to modify something to make it better	A small amount of humor can **leaven** a serious speech.
licentious	adjective	Promiscuous; without legal or moral restraints	The novel was criticized for its portrayal of **licentious** behavior among the characters.
luminary	noun	An inspirational and influential person in a particular discipline or group	She was a **luminary** in the field of medicine, known for her groundbreaking research.
malcontent	noun	A person who complains and rebels	The **malcontents** in the group were always stirring up trouble.
marital	adjective	Relating to marriage	They sought counseling to improve their **marital** relationship.
mitigate	verb	To reduce the severity or pain of something	Planting trees can help **mitigate** the effects of climate change.

Word	Part of Speech	Meaning	Sentence
motley	adjective	Having diversity in appearance or other characteristics	The **motley** crew of adventurers set off on their journey.
multiplicity	noun	A large number or variety	The **multiplicity** of opinions made it difficult to reach a consensus.
mutable	adjective	Able to be changed	The weather in spring is famously **mutable**, with sudden changes from sunshine to rain.
nuptial	adjective	Relating to marriage	The couple exchanged vows in a beautiful **nuptial** ceremony attended by friends and family.
nullify	verb	To invalidate or make void, often in a legal context	The contract was **nullified** because it had been signed under duress.
omnipresent	adjective	Commonly found or present; widespread	The influence of technology is **omnipresent** in modern society.
ordination	noun	The act of making someone a priest or minister, or the act of giving holy orders	His **ordination** as a priest was a momentous occasion for the small parish.
ossify	verb	To turn into bone; to become rigid or inflexible in habits, attitudes, or opinions	As people age, their cartilage **ossifies** and becomes less flexible.
panache	noun	Flamboyant confidence of manner or flair	She entered the room with **panache**, drawing all eyes to her.
penance	noun	Actions done to repent or punish oneself for wrongdoing	The monk performed acts of **penance** to atone for his sins.
pestle	noun	A heavy tool with a rounded end, used for crushing and grinding substances into smaller parts, like a powder	She used a **pestle** to crush the herbs for her homemade remedy.
portent	noun	A sign or warning that something bad is likely to happen	The sudden appearance of dark clouds was a **portent** of the coming storm.
preternatural	adjective	Beyond what is normal or expected	The athlete's **preternatural** speed and agility amazed spectators.
privy	adjective	Having knowledge of something exclusive or secret	Only a few were **privy** to the details of the confidential agreement.
quietude	noun	A quiet and calm state	The library was a haven of **quietude**, perfect for studying.
ravel	verb	To tangle something	The threads of the sweater began to **ravel** after being washed.
redress	noun	Repair or compensation of something done wrong	The company offered financial **redress** to customers affected by the faulty product.
replete	adjective	Abundantly filled with something	The buffet was **replete** with a variety of delicious dishes.
resonant	adjective	Deep and echoing, typically used to describe sounds	His voice was **resonant**, carrying across the auditorium without the need for a microphone.
rueful	adjective	Expressing sorrow or regret, often humorously or lightly	She gave a **rueful** smile as she realized her mistake.

Word	Part of Speech	Meaning	Sentence
sleeper	noun	Something that becomes successful after a period of obscurity	The low-budget indie film turned out to be a **sleeper** hit at the box office.
succor	verb	To give support or aid to	The Red Cross **succored** the victims of the natural disaster.
surmise	verb	To suppose that something is true without having evidence	From his nervous demeanor, she **surmised** that he was hiding something.
synchronous	adjective	Occurring at the same time	The dancers moved in **synchronous** harmony, creating a mesmerizing performance.
tarry	verb	To delay or be late	We can't **tarry** any longer if we want to catch the train.
tenet	noun	A core principle or belief	The **tenets** of democracy include freedom of speech and equal rights for all citizens.
turgid	adjective	Hard to understand; swollen, typically with fluids	The **turgid** river threatened to overflow its banks after days of heavy rain.
unerringly	adverb	In a way that is always right or accurate	She could **unerringly** find her way through the maze of streets in the old city.
venerate	verb	To greatly respect or honor	In many cultures, elders are **venerated** for their wisdom and experience.
vie	adjective	To compete eagerly with someone in order to do or achieve something	The two companies **vied** for the lucrative contract.
viscid	adjective	Having a glutinous or sticky consistency	The painter struggled with the **viscous** paint that refused to flow smoothly.
votary	noun	A person who is devoted to a particular religion or deity	The temple was crowded with **votaries** offering prayers and seeking blessings.
winsome	adjective	Attractive in appearance or character	The child's **winsome** smile charmed everyone she met.
wrest	verb	To pull something from a person forcefully	He managed to **wrest** the gun from the robber's hand and escape.
wastrel	noun	A person who wastes their time, money, skills, etc.	The novel's protagonist is a **wastrel** who squanders his inheritance on frivolous pursuits.
yoke	verb	To join together closely	The two countries were **yoked** by a common history and shared values.
zany	adjective	Unusual or surprising in a silly and humorous way	The comedian's **zany** antics kept the audience entertained throughout the show.
zeal	noun	Intense enthusiasm or passion	She tackled her new job with **zeal**, eager to learn and contribute.
zephyr	noun	A gentle breeze	The **zephyr** rustled the leaves of the trees, creating a soothing sound.

CRAFT AND STRUCTURE

1   ◫ Mark for Review

A survey has found that 42% of millennials and Gen-Z respondents _____ a strong inclination toward secondhand shopping, a move that is expected to have positive environmental implications. According to latest estimates, if each consumer were to purchase only one secondhand garment this year instead of a new one, it could reduce over 2 billion pounds of CO_2 emissions, saving approximately 23 billion gallons of water and 4 billion kilowatt-hours of energy.

Which choice completes the text with the most logical and precise word or phrase?

A) expressed

B) evoked

C) substantiated

D) cherished

2   ◫ Mark for Review

The complex nature of numerous urban health issues frequently makes them unsuitable to be studied under conventional research methods. This frustration has introduced the necessity for an alternate paradigm. Combined with the community's plea for authenticity in the research procedure, this multifaceted nature of urban health issues has significantly _____ the requirement of an approach like community-based participatory research (CBPR), a collaborative approach that combines various dynamics to tackle urban health problems.

Which choice completes the text with the most logical and precise word or phrase?

A) featured

B) highlighted

C) exposed

D) announced

3   ◫ Mark for Review

Set in the 1930s, *Closed Casket* is an Agatha Christie novel that finds Christie's iconic detective Hercule Poirot with Edward Catchpool at the home of a famous writer, where several guests have gathered at her request to celebrate a family event. But as is often the case, something goes _____.

Which choice completes the text with the most logical and precise word or phrase?

A) seamlessly

B) awry

C) adrift

D) askew

Answers & Explanations

1. **Level:** Easy | **Skill/Knowledge:** Words in Context

   Key Explanation: Choice A is correct. The passage mentions a global survey conducted in 2021, where millennials and Gen Z respondents were surveyed about their shopping preferences. The passage is discussing the results of this survey and, specifically, the respondents' attitude toward secondhand shopping. Therefore, the missing word should reflect how these respondents conveyed or communicated their inclination toward secondhand shopping. "Expressed" is a precise word choice that directly communicates the idea that respondents conveyed their preferences.

   Distractor Explanations: Choice B is incorrect because "evoked" is a less precise word choice in this context. While it can imply that the survey results triggered a response, it doesn't clearly convey the idea that respondents themselves actively communicated their inclination toward secondhand shopping. **Choice C is** incorrect because "substantiated" means to provide evidence or support for something. Therefore, it does not directly convey the idea of expressing an inclination, making it an unsuitable choice for the context. **Choice D is incorrect** because "cherished" implies a deep affection or appreciation for something or someone. This is not the same as expressing an inclination, therefore making it an incorrect choice.

2. **Level:** Medium | **Skill/Knowledge:** Words in Context

   Key Explanation: Choice B is the correct answer. The passage talks about how the complexity of urban health problems are beyond traditional approaches. It also mentions that "this frustration has introduced the necessity for an alternate paradigm." With these details in mind, we need a word that positively emphasizes the need for an alternative solution to complete the text. Since "highlighted" means to call attention to something, it is the most suitable answer as the need for an alternate paradigm has already been introduced earlier in the text.

   Distractor Explanations: Choice A is incorrect because "featured" does not best emphasize the need for an alternative paradigm. "Featured" usually means to be an important part of something or to be on display. **Choice C is** incorrect because "exposed" as a verb refers to the act of uncovering something, often with a slight negative connotation. In this context, it does not suitably complete the sentence – to "expose the importance of an alternative paradigm" does not sound positive. **Choice D is incorrect** because to announce something is to make a declaration or a statement about a particular event or occurrence. The need for an alternative solution does not need to be announced, since it has already been introduced earlier in the text.

3. **Level:** Hard | **Skill/Knowledge:** Words in Context

   Key Explanation: Choice B is the correct option. The text mentions that Poirot and Catchpool are at the home of the writer to celebrate an event. This is a positive sentiment. However, the sentence to be completed begins with "but", implying that despite the initial positive intention, something unexpected and possibly problematic happens. In this case, the word "awry" fits best because it conveys the sense of something going wrong or not according to plan. It implies that an unexpected event or situation arises, potentially causing confusion or disturbance.

   Distractor Explanations: Choice A is incorrect because it implies that everything progresses smoothly and without any noticeable disruptions. The sentence to be completed begins with "but", which gives us the idea of something going differently from what is expected at a family celebration. Therefore, everything is not going to go seamlessly. **Choice C is incorrect** because "adrift" typically refers to something floating without direction or purpose, which is not the most appropriate word to describe a situation going wrong. **Choice D is incorrect** because "askew" means crooked or not in proper alignment, which does not accurately capture the sense of something going wrong or awry.

Text Structure and Purpose

Text Structure and Purpose questions assess your ability to comprehend and analyze the organization, main ideas, and overarching purpose of a given passage. Mastering these questions involves a keen understanding of a passage's main idea, the role of specific sentences, and the overall purpose of the text.

Text Structure and Purpose questions usually take the form of questions like:

> *"Which choice best describes the overall structure/purpose of the text?"*
> **OR**
> *"Which choice best describes the function of the underlined sentence in the text as a whole?"*

The question may be referring to a non-fiction passage or an excerpt from a literary work.

Structure

The **structure of a text** refers to the organization and arrangement of its content, including *how* ideas, information, and elements are presented and interconnected. Understanding the structure is essential for comprehending the author's intended meaning, identifying key points, and following the flow of the text.

For text structure, you will be offered answer options that include verb(s) and noun(s) that are paired together, such as:

- The speaker explains the reason…

- The speaker evaluates the critique…

- The speaker conveys excitement…

- The speaker concedes to the opposition…

Carefully assess the passage to determine how the author is presenting information. Look for cues, keywords, and the overall tone.

Check whether the verbs accurately describe the action being taken in the passage, and if the nouns appropriately represent the subject or theme under consideration.

Purpose

The **purpose** of a text refers to the author's intention or objective in creating and presenting that particular piece of writing. Why did they write this passage? An author's purpose can include, but is not limited to:

- To inform or explain

- To convince or persuade

- To illustrate or describe

- To compare or contrast

- To offer advice or solutions

- To express an opinion, whether in support of or against something

- To evaluate or analyze

When encountering questions related to the author's purpose, consider the overall tone and content of the passage. For example, if the author uses a neutral tone, the author's purpose is more likely to express or explain a point rather than advocate for or argue against something. In these questions, you need to pay attention to the nuances between the verbs used in each answer choice.

How to solve Text Structure and Purpose questions?

Step 1

Identify whether the question is about structure or purpose: While both text structure and purpose require a keen understanding of the passage, structure focuses more on *how* and purpose focuses more on *why*. The question stem will typically include the word "structure" or "purpose" explicitly, so underline the keyword to narrow down your focus.

Step 2

Summarize the passage: Use your own words and jot down a few notes on the key ideas and information from the passage. Do this before you read the answer choices so you can derive the essence of the passage solely from the text itself rather than getting distracted by the answer choices. When you summarize something in your own words, you are getting a deeper understanding of the flow of information, which will help you determine the text's structure and purpose.

Step 3

Do not make assumptions: Only refer to what the text explicitly states. Refrain from making unwarranted inferences or assumptions about the text that lack substantiation within the paragraph's content. The questions might present choices that seem correct initially, but upon closer inspection, they make assumptions beyond what the passage states.

Step 4

Avoid choices that are too specific: The questions might throw in choices that are very detailed just to throw you off. Make sure the answer you choose is relevant to the passage but also encompasses the overall passage rather than focusing on only a specific portion. The tricky thing to remember is these answer options aren't necessarily wrong; they just aren't as good as the answer option that is both accurate and comprehensive.

 Step 5

If one word is wrong, the whole choice is wrong: You want to be strict with every word in the answer options, including the verbs, nouns, and adjectives. If even one word is not supported by the passage, eliminate the entire answer choice.

Questions to ask yourself if you are stuck between two choices:

Does any choice focus only on a part of the passage rather than encompassing the overall flow of information? If yes, eliminate that choice.

Does any choice include information not directly supported in the passage? If yes, eliminate that choice.

Does any choice include even one word that seems inaccurate? If yes, eliminate that choice.

(?) Let's solve a Text Structure and Purpose question now:

The following text is adapted from Sayaka Murata's 2018 novel *Convenience Store Woman*. The speaker is describing her thoughts about her job as a convenience store worker.

I'd always had a lot of respect for manager #8. He was a hard worker and I'd thought of him as the perfect colleague, but now I was sick to death of him only ever talking about [my boyfriend] whenever we met. Until now, we'd always had meaningful worker-manager discussions: "It's been hot lately, so the sales of chocolate desserts are down," or "There's a new block of flats down the road, so we've been getting more customers in the evening," or "They're really pushing the ad campaign for that new product coming out the week after next, so we should do well with it." Now, however, it felt like he'd downgraded me from store worker to female of the human species.

Which choice best states the main purpose of the text?

A) To express frustration at the change in the manager's concerns and behavior

B) To exemplify the work-related conversations that frequently occur at the convenience store

C) To explain the reason behind the speaker's plan to resign from her job

D) To show sorrow about the way the speaker is being treated at her workplace

Solution:

After reading the question, we notice that this question is explicitly asking about the **purpose of the text,** so we know to focus on the why.

Next, let's **summarize the passage** with a few concise notes. Below are some examples of what these notes could look like. Remember that everyone takes notes differently, so don't worry if yours doesn't match any of the examples below. As long as your notes are not too long and capture similar main ideas as the examples, you are on the right track.

● Respect for manager → now annoyed at the manager

● Manager talking about personal life, contrast with previous discussions

● Work talk → relationship talk

We can now go through each of the answer choices and eliminate the ones that are too specific, not supported by the passage, etc.

A) **To express frustration at the change in the manager's concerns and behavior**

"express frustration" is accurate because the speaker states she is "sick to death" of the manager's behavior. *Change in the manager's behavior* is also accurate because the speaker contrasts the manager's previous "meaningful…discussions" to "only ever talking about [the speaker's] boyfriend." This answer is both supported by the passage and encompasses the overall flow of ideas in the passage well.

B) **To exemplify the work-related conversations that frequently occur at the convenience store**

"exemplify the work-related conversations" is accurate because the speaker includes multiple examples of the discussions between her and her manager. However, this choice is **too specific** and is not fully relevant to the summary notes we had written. The conversation examples are specifically used to illustrate the change in the manager's behavior, which is not covered in this answer choice. Thus, this choice should be eliminated.

C) **To explain the reason behind the speaker's plan to resign from her job**

This choice is not supported by the passage and includes an **unsubstantiated assumption:** that the speaker wants to "resign from her job". While the passage does reflect the speaker's grievances towards her manager, there is no direct evidence to support the statement that the speaker is planning on resigning. Thus, this choice should be eliminated too.

D) **To show sorrow about the way the speaker is being treated at her workplace**

The passage is indeed about the way the speaker is *"being treated at her workplace"*. However, the word *"sorrow"* does not seem entirely accurate to the tone of the passage. The words "sick to death" indicate a tone of annoyance or frustration towards the speaker's manager. Therefore, because **one word** (sorrow) is **not accurate**, this entire choice should be eliminated.

Using the tips and strategies for Text Structure and Purpose questions, we can conclude that the best answer is **Choice A.**

Text Structure and Purpose questions don't only include passages; they also provide excerpts of poems where you have to analyze the structure of the poem or deduce the purpose of an underlined sentence.

(?) Let's look at an example:

The following text is from "A Tree Design", a poem written by Arna Bontemps in 1927.

A Tree is more than a shadow

Blurred against the sky,

More than ink spilled on the fringe

Of white clouds floating by.

A tree is more than an April design

Or a blighted winter bough

Where love and music used to be.

<u>A tree is something in me,</u>

<u>Very still and lonely now.</u>

Which choice best states the function of the underlined sentence in the overall structure of the text?

A) To reveal that the narrator is a tree

B) To contrast with the positive tone of the previous descriptions of the tree

C) To summarize the key purpose of a tree's life

D) To underscore the central theme of the tree as a symbol beyond its physical presence

Solution:

Since this question is asking about the function of the sentence in the overall structure, we should focus on how the specific underlined sentence achieves its meaning and function.

Begin by breaking down the poem. Each line of the poem introduces a physical aspect of a tree and affirms that the tree holds more significance than its physicality. The phrase "more than" is repeated three times to emphasize this point. We can interpret this repetition as showcasing the symbolic depth of a tree, moving beyond its physical form to represent emotional and existential themes. Each line contrasts the tree's physical presence with its deeper meaning, culminating in the final line's introspective reflection on the tree's significance within the speaker's inner world. While the first three lines reflect generally on the tree, the symbolism in the last line becomes personal in relation to the speaker.

D) To underscore the central theme of the tree as a symbol beyond its physical presence

The correct answer that reflects this is **Choice D.** *How* the underlined sentence contributes to the overall poem is by emphasizing the main theme of a tree's symbolism.

A) To reveal that the narrator is a tree

Choice A is not supported by the text, as the narrator states that the tree is something in him or her self rather than claiming that the tree is literally him or her self.

B) To contrast with the positive tone of the previous descriptions of the tree

Choice B is inaccurate because not all the previous descriptions were positive. For example, the tree being described as a "blighted winter bough" portrays an empty, scarce image that is devoid of life.

C) To summarize the key purpose of a tree's life

Choice C is not supported by the text, as the narrator does not discuss the main purpose of a tree's life.

1 ⬚ **Mark for Review**

Although many types of birth control have been used since the 1960s, there is still a great deal unknown about their impact on the body. Recently, a group of women, some on birth control and some not, were tested by having their blood taken. The results showed that those on birth control experience higher levels of the stress hormone even while completing activities that are not associated with stress.

Which choice best states the main purpose of the text?

A) To persuade readers not to use birth control

B) To discuss the potential side effects of taking birth control

C) To provide information about what causes high levels of stress

D) To present a brief history of the birth control pill

2 ⬚ **Mark for Review**

The following text is an adapted excerpt from "Aeneid", an epic poem by Virgil.

I sing of arms and the man, he who, exiled by fate, first came from the coast of Troy to Italy, and to Lavinian shores – hurled about endlessly by land and sea, by the will of the gods, by cruel Juno's remorseless anger, long suffering also in war, until he founded a city and brought his gods to Latium: from that the Latin people came, the lords of Alba Longa, the walls of noble Rome. Muse, tell me the cause: how was Juno offended in her divinity, how was she grieved, the Queen of Heaven, to drive a man, noted for virtue, to endure such dangers, to face so many trials? Can there be such anger in the minds of the gods?

Which choice best describes the function of the underlined sentence in the text as a whole?

A) It suggests that the Gods might be angry with the man mentioned by the poet.

B) It describes the dangerous journey the man had to undertake to establish a city that was the precursor of Rome.

C) It offers a look into the man's background and achievements.

D) It indicates that the man will be the primary character of the epic poem.

3 · Mark for Review

This text is adapted from Alexandre Dumas's 1849 novel, *The Three Musketeers*.

It was, then, into the midst of this tumult and disorder that our young man advanced with a beating heart, ranging his long rapier up his lanky leg, and keeping one hand on the edge of his cap, with that half-smile of the embarrassed provincial who wishes to put on a good face. When he had passed one group he began to breathe more freely; but he could not help observing that they turned round to look at him, and for the first time in his life D'Artagnan, who had till that day entertained a very good opinion of himself, felt ridiculous.

What is the main purpose of the underlined portion in the overall structure of the text?

A) It warns the reader of a coming conflict.

B) It indicates a temporal change in the passage.

C) It describes the appearance of a scene.

D) It stresses the emotional state of a character.

Answers & Explanations

1. **Level:** Easy | **Skill/Knowledge:** Text Structure and Purpose

   Key Explanation: Choice B is the best choice since the passage introduces the topic of birth control and then leads into a study that has shown birth control can lead to elevated levels of stress. This is a discussion of birth control and one of its possible side effects. The main purpose of the text needs to include the main idea which will be reflected in the topic sentence and confirmed in the concluding sentence.

   Distractor Explanations: Choice A is inaccurate as the language of the passage is not strong enough to show that the author is trying to convince readers not to use birth control at all. The author merely wants to inform readers about one possible side effect for consideration. **Choice C** is wrong because it does not consider the main idea, which is focused on birth control. The high level of stress is a possible side effect of birth control, but not the main topic of the passage. **Choice D** is incorrect because this answer choice only focuses on one part of the passage. It does not consider the latter half of the passage and is therefore too narrow of an answer choice.

2. **Level:** Medium | **Skill/Knowledge:** Text Structure and Purpose

   Key Explanation: Choice A is the correct choice. The underlined sentence in the poem mentions "by the will of the gods, by cruel Juno's remorseless anger." Juno has been mentioned as "the Queen of Heaven," and hence an assumption can be made that She is a God too. The poet mentions that the man has been "exiled by fate" and towards the end of the poem, asks the Muse "Can there be such anger in the minds of the gods?" This serves to indicate that the Gods might be angry with the man, which is why he has been subjected to problems such as being "hurled about endlessly by land and sea."

Distractor Explanations: Choice B is incorrect because it focuses more on the man's journey rather than the suggestion of the gods' anger. However, while the underlined sentence alludes to the sufferings of the man, it underscores the anger that the Gods may have towards him. **Choice C** is incorrect because it inaccurately states that the underlined sentence is about the man's background and achievements. The underlined sentence does not delve into the man's background and achievements but instead emphasizes his suffering and the possible anger of the Gods. **Choice D** is incorrect because it focuses on the man being the primary character. However, the underlined sentence does not indicate this and instead focuses on the Gods' anger and the man's suffering.

3. **Level:** Hard | **Skill/Knowledge:** Text Structure and Purpose

   Key Explanation: Choice D is the best answer. The fact that D'Artagnan notices that people turn around to look stresses that he is very nervous about appearing like an "embarrassed provincial." He realized that they saw through his front and "felt ridiculous." By mentioning the fact that he saw them, it is clear to the reader why his "very good opinion of himself" changed.

   Distractor Explanations: Choice A is incorrect because there is no conflict in the text. **Choice B** is incorrect because a "temporal change" is a shift in time, but the time sequence remains consistent. **Choice C** is incorrect because the reader has no idea what the scene really is; one knows D'Artagnan is walking by a group of people, but there is no clue how many or where they are.

Cross-text Connections

Cross-text Connections questions on the SAT assess your ability to establish connections between multiple passages, showcasing your comprehension and analytical skills in identifying relationships, similarities, and differences between texts. Excelling in these questions requires a discerning understanding of the main ideas in each passage, as well as recognizing how they interrelate and contribute to an overall theme or concept.

Questions that ask you to compare two texts will look like:

"Based on the texts, how would…from Text 2 respond to …from Text 1?"

Note that the questions will not be asking how the author from one text would generally perceive the author from the other text; each question will refer to a specific viewpoint or argument.

The first thing to do is identify the specific goal to compare or contrast so that you can read through the two texts while specifically keeping this goal in mind. Here are some examples of Cross-text Connections questions with their goals underlined:

- Based on the texts, what would the author of Text 2 most likely say about the conclusion of the study presented in Text 1?

- Based on the texts, how would the author of Text 2 most likely describe the description of mangroves in Text 1?

- Based on the texts, how would the author of Text 2 most likely react to the software developer job requirements described in Text 1?

- Based on the texts, the authors of Text 1 and Text 2 would most likely agree with which statement?

Now we can break down the structure and content of answer options for Cross-text Connections questions.

For questions that ask you to identify what the author of Text 2 would "describe", "characterize", or "say about" something from Text 1:

- It is inaccurate because… / As inaccurate because…

- It is effective and has been proven in multiple studies. / As effective and proven because…

- It illustrates an example of… / As an example of …

For questions that ask you to identify how the author of Text 2 would "respond to" or "react to" something from Text 1:

- By defending the importance of…

- By speculating that…

- By contending that…

- By conceding to the point that…

As you may begin to see, *you need to have a firm understanding of the perspectives of each author/text to be able to draw a comparison between the viewpoints.* While you will not directly need to state that author 1 believes X and author 2 argues that Y, you need to know if the authors agree or disagree and on which specific point(s).

How to solve Cross-text Connections questions?

Step 1

Identify the goal: Underline the specific comparison the question is asking for between the two texts. **Identify the goal *before* you read the two texts.** To avoid being inundated with digesting all the information across the two texts, always be aware of the goal so you can focus on the relevant points as you read.

Step 2

Summarize the passages: In your own words, jot down a few notes on the key ideas and information from both passages. In addition to these summaries, evaluate whether the passages are agreeing, disagreeing, or having some other nuanced view on the specific goal. This will help you immediately eliminate some answer options. For example, if the passages are clearly agreeing on the benefits of some topic, you can eliminate the choices that suggest that the authors have differing viewpoints on this topic. Once you have a general understanding of whether the authors agree or disagree, go more specific. What do they agree or disagree on? Why? The correct answer should be specific and relevant.

Step 3

If one word is wrong, the whole choice is wrong: By now, this tip should feel like second nature to you. You want to be strict with every word in the answer options, including the verbs, nouns, and adjectives. There is no such thing as a correct answer that kind of or slightly conveys the relationship between the two passages. The correct answer must be entirely supported by the passages with each and every word, without any ambiguity.

Step 4

Be careful of absolute or extreme words: These words include but are not limited to "all," "always," "many," "most," "least," and "only." Verbs conveying extreme emotions like "hate" or "despise" also count as extreme words. Some answer choices will use a more extreme version of the right answer to misguide you. For example, imagine the author of Text 2 has the same opinion as the author of Text 1, albeit with a few differences in their reasoning. An extreme and incorrect answer choice may state that the author of Text 2 "heavily disagrees" or "disputes" the perspective of the author of Text 1.

Step 5

Do not make assumptions: Again, this should feel like second nature to you to *only choose answer choices that are directly supported by the passages.* Differentiate between what the text is explicitly suggesting and what is an assumption-based conclusion that goes further than the content in the text.

A Word of Caution

Keep the order of the texts clear: Make sure you are not confusing the content and perspectives from Text 1 with that of Text 2. It's a simple and silly mistake, but it can happen.

Questions to ask yourself if you are stuck between two choices:

Does any choice include even one word that seems inaccurate? If yes, eliminate that choice.

Does any choice include information not directly supported in the passage? If yes, eliminate that choice.

Does any choice use extreme or absolute language? If yes, take a second look to check if this choice is overly extreme and should be eliminated.

(?) Let's solve a Cross-text Connections question:

Text 1

According to the American Society of Nutrition, most non-dairy alternatives to milk are healthier than cows' milk in terms of fat and calories. Plant-based milk not only reduces the amount of sugar in one's diet but also is widespread in various forms. Plant-based milk can be made from almonds, rice, soybeans, coconuts, cashews, and more. Given the same amount of milk, most plant-based milks have anywhere from 37% to 75% less fat than cows' milk. Just one cup of cow's milk contains 12 grams of carbohydrates from milk sugars; in comparison, one cup of plant-based milk typically has 1 gram of carbohydrates.

Text 2

Although one cup of cow's milk contains 12 grams of sugar, all of the sugar is naturally occurring lactose, which will not spike metabolism or blood sugar like refined sugars will. On the other hand, plant-based milks often contain refined sugars like cane sugar or rice syrup. Plant-based milks also do not contain sufficient levels of key nutrients like protein, potassium, and vitamin D. Cows' milk naturally contains high levels of protein, calcium, potassium, vitamin D, and B vitamins.

Based on the texts, how would the author of Text 2 most likely respond to Text 1's description of the benefits of plant-based milk?

A) By rejecting the superficial assumption that all fat and sugars are bad

B) By praising the analysis of both macronutrients and micronutrient

C) By acknowledging that both plant-based milk and cows' milk have fats and sugars

D) By agreeing that both milks have a number of nutrients available

Solution:

First, **the goal** is to determine how the second author would <u>most likely respond to the first author's description of the benefits of plant-based milk.</u> With this goal in mind, we can now read the two texts and pay special attention to opinions towards plant-based milk.

Here is an example of the **summary notes** of the two texts:

Text 1: plant milk healthier than cows' milk, less fat and carbs

Text 2: cow milk's sugar and nutrients are beneficial

The two authors definitely disagree on the nutritional benefits of plant-based milk versus cows' milk. Based on this generally conflicting relationship between the two texts, we can preliminarily eliminate **Choices B** and **D** since these two choices clearly convey a more positive relationship between the two texts by using words like "praising" and "agreeing."

A) By rejecting the superficial assumption that all fat and sugars are bad

Choice A seems to be supported by both texts. The author of Text 1 argues that plant-based milk is healthier than cows' milk by using the high levels of fat and milk sugars in cows' milk as the key supporting point. The underlying reasoning here is that fat and milk sugars are bad for your health. However, the author of Text 2 discusses the nuances of different types of sugar, arguing that natural milk sugars in cows' milk do not have the same negative effects as refined sugars used in plant-based milk. Therefore, it is reasonable to state that the author of Text 2 would reject author 1's assumption that all fat and sugars are bad.

C) By acknowledging that both plant-based milk and cows' milk have fats and sugars

Choice C is incorrect because the author of Text 2 focuses on the fact that some fats and sugars are healthier than others, so it is not enough to simply look at the presence of fats and sugars. This choice is not relevant to the main ideas from the passages.

To be safe, we can take a closer look at **Choices B** and **D** to ensure that they can be eliminated.

B) By praising the analysis of both macronutrients and micronutrients

Choice B is incorrect because both authors discuss and analyze the nutrients in the milk, so it is unlikely that the second author would praise the first author for his or her analysis. Furthermore, you can see this choice does not match our summary notes at all, so we can eliminate this choice.

D) By agreeing that both milks have a number of nutrients available

Choice D is incorrect because our summary notes show that the number of nutrients, in general, is not a focal point in either text. This choice is too vague.

Using the tips and strategies, we can conclude that **Choice A** is the correct answer. This exercise is a good example to show that understanding general agreement or disagreement between the author's viewpoints is not enough: some Cross-text Connections questions will require you to go deeper to understand the exact points or ideas the authors may agree or disagree on and why.

1 ☐ Mark for Review

Text 1

The term "curry" was coined by European colonists to refer to spiced sauces from India. While the term has roots in the Tamil word "kari", meaning "sauce", curry was used as a catch-all term for a multitude of diverse sauces. Given the distinct heritage of each dish, using one term to define them is oversimplified and dismisses each cuisine's identity.

Text 2

In the eighteenth century, Indian dishes were adapted to suit the taste of British migrants. While each Indian dish was named based on ingredients and preparation, "curry" was used to refer to the altered British-Indian version of food. When the British traveled to Africa and Southeast Asia, each region adapted Indian food, creating a range of regionally modified "curries."

Based on the texts, how would the author of Text 2 most likely respond to the critique described in Text 1?

A) By disagreeing with the premise that the term originated from colonial roots

B) By pointing out that "curry" expanded beyond Asia into Africa as well

C) By acknowledging "curry" is a highly generalized term, while also recognizing its use to refer to fusion dishes

D) By agreeing with the critique and further proposing for the term "curry" to be retired

2 ☐ Mark for Review

Text 1

Researchers have observed how wild female killer whales live for years after the whales are no longer able to reproduce more offspring, but the exact reason has been unclear. Previous research speculated that after giving birth to the last calf, female killer whales focus on providing food for their offspring since they continue to hunt during their non-reproductive years.

Text 2

A new study examined scars that indicated fighting between orcas. The researchers found that whales with non-reproducing mothers had fewer scars than whales whose mothers were no longer alive and whales whose mothers were still reproducing. This finding led researchers to believe that non-reproducing female killer whales spend a significant amount of time protecting their offspring and preventing fights.

Based on the texts, how would the author of Text 2 most likely respond to the theory as described in Text 1?

A) By commending the theory for recognizing that non-reproducing female killer whales provided social support

B) By agreeing with the theory's emphasis on providing resources to peers

C) By cautioning that the theory fails to pinpoint a significant role played by non-reproducing female killer whales

D) By arguing that the theory is based on unreliable and biased evidence

3	🔖 **Mark for Review**

Text 1

Buttons on women's clothing appear on the left side as a remnant of historical fashion customs. In the eighteenth and nineteenth centuries, servants often helped women get dressed since women's fashion typically involved multiple layers. Designers began to put buttons on the left so servants would be able to help women button their clothes from the outside.

Text 2

Men's clothing has buttons that appear on the right side because of adaptations from military uniforms. In the army, men are trained to hold weapons using their right hand, leaving their left hand free to adjust their jacket buttons. Further, the jacket flap on the left overlaps to the right to provide an extra precaution against weapons slipping inside the jacket.

Based on the texts, how would the author of Text 2 most likely respond to the claim described in Text 1?

A) By stating that women without servants would have difficulty buttoning their clothes

B) By arguing that women's military uniforms actually have buttons on the right side

C) By noting it is another example of how fashion is influenced by history

D) By comparing the utility of buttons for men with the utility of buttons for women

Answers & Explanations

1. **Level:** Easy | **Skill/Knowledge:** Cross-text Connections

    Key Explanation: Choice C is correct. Text 1 critiques the use of the term "curry" as oversimplified and dismissive of cultural differences. Text 2 also explains that "curry" was used as a general term referring to many dishes, but it further expounds on the fact that it was used specifically to refer to fusion dishes and "curries" developed into a range of multicultural dishes. Therefore, the author of Text 2 is most likely to acknowledge the generalized nature of "curry", while also recognizing its value in capturing these multicultural, fusion dishes.

    Distractor Explanations: Choice A is incorrect because the author of Text 2 does not dispute the fact that the term began when British colonists lived in India. **Choice B** is incorrect. While this fact is true, the author of Text 2 does not make this fact the main focus on the text. **Choice D** is incorrect because the author of Text 2 sees the value and unique meaning of the term, so the author is not likely to want to retire the term completely.

2. **Level:** Medium | **Skill/Knowledge:** Cross-text Connections

    Key Explanation: Choice C is correct. Text 1 presents a theory that non-reproducing female killer whales are focused on hunting and providing food. However, Text 2 describes a study suggesting that these whales play an important role in preventing fights among their offspring and others. Therefore, the author of Text 2 is most likely to believe that the theory from Text 1 fails to consider the important role of ensuring social harmony that is taken on by non-reproducing female killer whales.

Distractor Explanations: Choice A is incorrect because the theory in Text 1 is related to providing food rather than providing social support. **Choice B** is incorrect because the author of Text 2 would not agree that the whales are focused on providing resources to peers. **Choice D** is incorrect because the author of Text 2 does not discuss the reliability or bias of evidence.

3. **Level:** Hard | **Skill/Knowledge:** Cross-text Connections

Key Explanation: Choice C is correct. Text 1 explains the origin behind women's buttons being on the left side for servants to help women get dressed. Text 2 describes the military origins behind men's buttons being on the right side. Therefore, the author of Text 2 is likely to note that the observation described in Text 1 is another example of how historical practices, like servitude or war, influence clothing.

Distractor Explanations: Choice A is incorrect because the author of Text 2 does not discuss women's clothing. **Choice B** is incorrect because the author of Text 2 does not assert that all military uniforms have buttons on the right side. **Choice D** is incorrect because the author of Text 2 does not make a comparison between the utility of buttons based on the type of clothing.

Chapter 5
Expression of Ideas

Topics covered in this chapter:

- Rhetorical Synthesis
- Transitions

Rhetorical Synthesis

Rhetorical Synthesis questions often require you to utilize information from some given notes effectively to derive a specific insight from the notes. **Rhetorical Synthesis questions evaluate your ability to synthesize information from multiple sources and communicate a clear and accurate response.**

Rhetorical Synthesis questions first present a list of around 5 or less facts on a topic in bullet point format. The question stem will start with a specific goal and follow up with:

> *"Which choice most effectively uses relevant information from the notes to accomplish this goal?"*

The correct answer will be a statement that accurately synthesizes information from the facts presented. Each question will ask you to focus on a different goal that is specific to the topic.

 Remember

Always identify the goal first to ensure you are synthesizing information into a relevant statement. Refer to some examples of goals:

- Introduce a study and its results

- Give a definition and example of something

- Compare and contrast

- Explain an idea or argument

As with all Reading and Writing SAT questions, you do ***not*** need outside information to answer Rhetorical Synthesis questions. This good news means that you should not spend time evaluating •whether the notes are factually accurate, grammatically sound, or punctuated correctly. In the context of the question, all the notes are factually and grammatically accurate. All you need to focus on is using information across the notes to identify the answer option that addresses the goal specifically. Further, since these questions are about synthesizing multiple pieces of information, make sure that your answer uses information from more than one bullet point.

If we were asked to create a statement from scratch to answer the question, we could come up with endless variations and possibilities. Thus, it is not a good use of your time to formulate a suitable statement in your own head first and find the answer option that matches your ideal statement. Instead, go ahead and try out each of the answer options, employing the **process of elimination** to land on the final answer.

How to solve Rhetorical Synthesis questions?

 ## Step 1

Understand the goal: Use the tip "addressing the goal" as the first criterion for elimination. While this seems simple, the correct answer will fulfill all aspects of the goal. For example, if the question asks you to define and exemplify climate change based on the notes, the correct answer needs to explicitly include both a definition and an example. Eliminate any answer choice that only includes one of the above or none at all. Even if an answer choice synthesizes information from multiple notes, it should be eliminated if it is not relevant to the goal at hand.

 ## Step 2

Start by testing each answer choice: It is not critical to fully grasp every detail from the list of notes provided. In fact, oftentimes, the correct answer will include information from 2-3 notes rather than the entire set of notes. Therefore, it is a better use of your limited time to directly test each answer choice out, checking relevance to the goal and matching the information to specific notes. If you start by reading the full list of notes, you might get inundated with an overwhelming amount of information and struggle with evaluating the answer choices.

 ## Step 3

Ensure that your choice includes information from more than one note: For the most part, all answer choices will include information from more than one note. However, you can always double-check to ensure that the answer choice actually synthesizes information by referring to ideas from more than one note. If the answer only includes information from one point, it is not the correct answer.

Questions to ask yourself if you are stuck between two choices:

Does any choice include even one word that seems inaccurate? If yes, eliminate that choice.

Does any choice include information not directly supported in the passage? If yes, eliminate that choice.

Does any choice use extreme or absolute language? If yes, take a second look to check if this choice is overly extreme and should be eliminated.

---

⑦ Let's solve a Rhetorical Synthesis question now:

While researching a topic, a student has taken the following notes:

- The International Union for Conservation of Nature's Red List of Threatened Species records the conservation status and extinction risk of species all around the world.

- In 2022, a group of researchers developed a machine-learning computer model to evaluate the extinction risk of 4,369 reptile species based on existing data.

- Upon gathering the results of the model, the researchers compared the results with the Red List's assessment of extinction risk.

- The researchers found that the number of threatened species identified by the machine learning computer model is much higher than portrayed in the Red List.

- The researchers encourage the use of machine learning tools to increase the accuracy of evaluating extinction risk.

The student wants to present the study and its findings. Which choice most effectively uses relevant information from the notes to accomplish this goal?

A) In 2022, a group of researchers used machine learning to assess the extinction risk of reptiles.

B) The IUCN's Red List was used by a group of researchers as the basis for comparison against a machine learning model in a 2022 study.

C) In 2022, a group of researchers utilized machine learning to determine that more reptile species were at risk for extinction than previously defined in the Red List.

D) A group of researchers encourage other researchers to also use machine learning to improve predictive accuracy.

Solution:

The question stem asks us to "present the study and its findings" – always **keep this goal in mind.** We will use this goal as the first criterion for elimination.

Feel free to take a quick glance at the notes, but for efficiency's sake, we will go straight to the answer choices and start to eliminate the ones that do not fully address the goal of presenting the study and its findings.

Choice A starts to introduce the study, mentioning that the study was conducted in 2022 and focused on using "machine learning to assess the extinction risk of reptiles." However, this choice fails to address the study's findings. Therefore, this choice does not meet the goal and can be eliminated.

Choice B also provides details about the study, including the use of "IUCN's Red List" data and a machine learning model. That being said, this choice also fails to discuss the findings from the study and can be eliminated.

Choice C introduces the 2022 study, incorporating details like the use of machine learning and the reference to the IUCN's Red List. In addition, this choice also includes the finding that "more reptile species were at risk for extinction" than previously thought by the IUCN. This choice successfully and comprehensively addresses the goal of presenting the study and its findings. We can also confirm that this choice synthesizes information from multiple notes.

Choice D mentions an implication of the study: machine learning is a promising research mechanism for predictive accuracy. However, it lacks an introduction to the study itself and the study's results.

Since we were able to find the correct answer, **Choice C**, purely by checking which choice fulfilled the specific goal from the question stem, we did not have to check for specificity in each word or whether assumptions were used in this case. Remember to use these as follow-up criteria if required for more difficult questions.

1 🔖 **Mark for Review**

While researching a topic, a student has taken the following notes:

- While bears typically have an omnivorous diet, there are exceptions such as the carnivorous polar bear and the vegetarian giant panda.

- Despite their large size, bears often consume relatively small items like berries and nuts, which might seem unexpected.

- Grizzlies, a bear species native to North America, are renowned for their remarkable fishing abilities, particularly during the salmon spawning season.

- The Asian sloth bear has a penchant for termites and larvae and is known for ransacking termite nests using its funnel-like lips.

- The giant panda is exclusively herbivorous and sustains itself on a diet consisting solely of bamboo.

The student wants to explain the diet of bears to a new audience. Which choice most effectively uses relevant information from the notes to accomplish this goal?

A) Bears, with the exception of the polar bear and giant panda, usually eat food of both plant and animal origin, including berries, nuts, fish, and insects.

B) Most bears eat berries, nuts, and other food that may seem small for such a large animal.

C) Grizzly bears eat a great deal of fish, especially salmon.

D) Most bears consume foods of animal origin barring the giant panda that only eats bamboo.

2 🔖 **Mark for Review**

While researching a topic, a student has taken the following notes:

- Spanish, Italian, and French are all Romance languages.

- These languages share a common root in Latin.

- However, each has developed its own unique set of grammatical rules and vocabulary.

- Spanish is known for its distinctive sound patterns and pronunciation.

- Italian is renowned for its melodious quality and is often used in opera.

- French, often referred to as "the language of love," has a rich literary tradition.

The student wants to emphasize a similarity between the three European languages. Which choice most effectively uses relevant information from the notes to accomplish this goal?

A) Spanish, Italian, and French, all Romance languages, differ in their grammatical rules and vocabulary.

B) While Spanish is known for its distinctive sound patterns, Italian is often used in opera and French has a rich literary tradition.

C) As Romance languages, Spanish, Italian, and French all have their roots embedded in Latin.

D) Often hailed as "the language of love," French not only boasts a robust literary tradition, but also has its roots planted in Latin as a member of the romance languages.

EXPRESSION OF IDEAS

While researching a topic, a student has taken the following notes:

- Pliosaurs were a type of plesiosaur with short necks and massive skulls.

- In 2023, a team led by Sven Sachs of the Naturkunde-Museum Bielefeld analyzed and finally identified fossils found in 1983 to be a new pliosaur genus: Lorrainosaurus.

- The Lorrainosaurus reached over 6m from snout to tail, had jaws over 1.3m long with large conical teeth, and a bulky torpedo-shaped body propelled by four flipper-like limbs.

- Other than a brief report published in 1994, the fossils of Lorrainosaurus remained obscure until this new study re-evaluated the finds.

- The classification of the Lorrainosaurus indicates that the reign of gigantic mega-predatory pliosaurs must have commenced earlier than previously thought.

The student wants to present the primary aim of the study. Which choice most effectively uses relevant information from the notes to accomplish this goal?

A) The previously unrecognized pliosaur genus: Lorrainosaurus had short necks, large skulls, and grew to more than 6m long.

B) The Naturkunde-Museum Bielefeld team wanted to re-evaluate the mysterious fossils and their significance for the broader field of paleontology.

C) Sven Sachs' team reinvestigated the obscure fossils found over 40 years ago and classified the genus, Lorrainosaurus, and its implications for the history of mega-predatory pliosaurs.

D) The Lorrainosaurus fossils were discovered in 1983 but were largely ignored until the Naturkunde-Museum Bielefeld team reinvestigated them.

Answers & Explanations

1. **Level:** Easy | **Skill/Knowledge:** Rhetorical Synthesis

   Key Explanation: Choice A is the correct answer. This option effectively conveys the general diet of bears, mentioning their omnivorous nature with some exceptions, and listing various types of food they typically consume. It uses the information provided in the notes in a comprehensive manner.

   Distractor Explanations: Choice B is incorrect because while it summarizes the fact that bears often consume relatively small items like berries and nuts, it does not provide a complete overview of their diet. It neglects information like bears being omnivorous. **Choice C** is incorrect because it focuses specifically on grizzly bears and their preference for fish, particularly during the salmon spawning season. While it is aligned with some information from the notes, it does not cover the broader diet of bears as a whole. **Choice D** is incorrect because it only mentions the giant panda eating bamboo and that most bears consume animal origin food. It neglects to mention that bears are omnivorous and other pieces of information relating to their diet.

2. **Level:** Medium | **Skill/Knowledge:** Rhetorical Synthesis

   Key Explanation: Choice C is correct because it informs us that all three languages share the commonality of being Romance languages rooted in Latin. This statement emphasizes both similiarities that the languages share: being Romance languages and sharing Latin roots.

   Distractor Explanations: Choice A is incorrect because while it does mention that these are all Romance languages, it focuses on their unique grammatical rules and vocabulary, thus emphasizing their differences. **Choice B** is incorrect because it provides unique characteristics of each language, accentuating their differences rather than their similarities. **Choice D** is incorrect because it fails to mention the other two languages, Spanish and Italian, and does not show how they are similar to French.

3. **Level:** Hard | **Skill/Knowledge:** Rhetorical Synthesis

    Key Explanation: Choice C is the correct answer. It effectively encapsulates the primary aim of the study, emphasizing the investigation of the newly classified genus and its implications for the history of mega-predatory pliosaurs.

    Distractor Explanations: Choice A is incorrect because it describes the characteristics of the Lorrainosaurus but does not effectively address the primary aim of the study, which is to investigate and classify the new genus and understand its implications. **Choice B** is incorrect because while it mentions the re-evaluation of the fossils, it does not specifically address the classification of the new genus and its implications, which are the primary aims of the study. **Choice D** is incorrect because it mentions the reinvestigation of the fossils but does not directly address the classification of the new genus and its broader implications, which are the primary aims of the study.

Transitions

Transition questions on the SAT assess your ability to navigate the flow of information within a given text. In the context of writing and language, *a transition refers to a word, phrase, or sentence that connects ideas and creates a smooth flow between different parts of a text*. Transition questions aim to evaluate how effectively you can identify the most logical transition to complete a passage, ensuring that the text maintains cohesion and coherence.

These questions take the form of:

> *"Which choice completes the text with the most logical transition?"*

Transition questions are most often paired with a non-fiction text.

While there are numerous transitions, here is a list of common transitions. Notice how you can broadly categorize the transitions into a few types based on how the transition changes the flow of ideas and information in a passage.

A Comprehensive List of Transitions

Category	Transition	Example
Adding additional information or a supplementary point	Moreover	Apples are healthy and delicious. Furthermore, they are cheap and easily accessible.
	In addition	
	Furthermore	
Indicating disagreement or a contrasting or conflicting point	However	I wanted to go to the art museum today. However, the museum was closed for an exclusive private event.
	In contrast	
	Conversely	
	Still	
	Nonetheless	
	On the other hand	
Providing a specific example	For example	Dogs are friendly, social animals. For example, labrador retrievers love to spend time with their owners and other dogs.
	In particular	
	For instance	
Conveying a sequence or order	First	First, whisk the eggs and butter together until well incorporated. Next, pour in the flour and baking soda.
	Next	
	Lastly	
	In turn	

Category	Transition	Example
Suggesting a cause-and-effect-relationship	Therefore	Sarah had a splitting headache this morning. As a result, she decided to stay home from school to rest.
	Consequently	
	As a result	
	Thus	
Leading to a conclusion or summary	In sum	The environment provides crucial ecosystem services for humans, plants, and animals. Natural landscapes can also have calming effects. Overall, the environment has many benefits that should be carefully preserved.
	Overall	
	To conclude	

In order to identify the best transition, you need to read the sentence(s) preceding the transition and the sentence(s) following the transition.

> What is the relationship between two sentences? Is it a relationship of agreement, disagreement, cause and effect, or other more nuanced relationship?

Answering this question will help you select a category of transitions and narrow down the possible options.

How to solve Transitions questions?

 ## Step 1

Understand the flow of logic in the passage: In the Command of Evidence (Textual) section, we practiced jotting down a few notes to summarize the ideas in the passage. This practice can also be useful for Transition questions to help you concisely understand the information in the passage and decipher what type of transition would best connect the separate pieces of information. For instance, consider a paragraph that discusses the optimistic attitude towards a new technology and ends with a failure to deploy the technology. You might jot down "hopeful new tech" + "failed to launch" as the summary notes. There is clearly a big shift happening in the paragraph, from a positive outlook to a negative outcome, which suggests the best transition will be one indicating contrast or conflict.

 ## Step 2

Anticipate the transition: Before looking at the answer choices, first try to anticipate the type of transition needed based on the context. By anticipate, we mean think of a suitable transition in your head first. This proactive approach can help you focus purely on the flow of logic in the passage and guide you in identifying the correct transition more efficiently. You will also avoid being distracted by the answer options when you anticipate the transition yourself.

 ## Step 3

Eliminate similar choices: The SAT will never ask you to choose between two answer choices that are essentially the same (e.g. "moreover" and "furthermore".) Thus, if you see two answer choices that convey the same transition, you can safely eliminate these choices. Note that not all transitions in the same transition category mean the exact same thing. There may be some nuances between the transitions, so spend some time studying lists of transitions if you are not confident in your knowledge of them.

 Remember

The answer is the most suitable option, not the perfect one: While you may have an idea of the perfect transition to complete the sentence, you may not always find that transition in the answer choices. Remember that you need to find the most suitable choice out of the options, so don't spend time stressing over why the perfect transition is not listed in the answer options.

Questions to ask yourself if you are stuck between two choices:

Are there answer options that are very similar transitions? If so, eliminate these choices.

Are you failing to find an answer option that matches the transition you believe is the most suitable? If yes, forget about the ideal transition and find the most suitable one among the answer choices.

(?) Let's solve a Transitions question now:

To keep food fresh for longer periods of time, people in the Philippines devised multiple techniques to preserve food. _____ moist-heat cooking methods such as steaming and boiling were commonly used to preserve the nutrients in the food without leading to spoilage. In order to extend the freshness of their food, they also relied on the abundant use of vinegar and salt since the high levels of acid and sodium created an unfavorable environment for bacteria to grow.

Which choice completes the text with the most logical transition?

A) Moreover,

B) Consequently,

C) In turn,

D) In particular,

Solution:

We'll start by reading the full paragraph and **jotting down some notes** for each sentence.

- To keep food fresh for longer periods of time, people in the Philippines devised multiple techniques to preserve food. → **Philippine methods to preserve food**

- _____ moist-heat cooking methods such as steaming and boiling were commonly used. → **Examples of such methods**

- In order to extend the freshness of their food, they also relied on the abundant use of vinegar and salt since the high levels of acid and sodium created an unfavorable environment for bacteria to grow. → **More examples of such methods**

Don't worry if you aren't able to jot down concise notes during your first read-through of the paragraph. In some cases, you'll need the full context of the paragraph before you understand the main points from the first few sentences to jot down. The more you practice jotting down notes, the more naturally this exercise will come to you.

Before looking at the answer options, let's **anticipate the transition**. From the first sentence to the next sentence, there seems to be a relationship of exemplification linking the two. The first sentence states an idea, and the second sentence presents an example of the same idea. We could use transitions like "for example", "in particular", or "for instance."

Now, let's check if there are any **similar answer choices we can eliminate.**

- Moreover: adding additional information

- Consequently: indicating a cause-and-effect relationship

- In turn: indicating a succession or sequence

- In particular: providing an example

Each answer option offers distinct transitions, so there are no choices we can safely eliminate.

Finally, we can conclude that **Choice D** is the best answer because "in particular" matches the transition we had anticipated which suggests a specific example is being provided.

EXPRESSION OF IDEAS

1 ☐ **Mark for Review**

Wordsworth's "A Letter to the Bishop of Llandaff" stands out because he appears to have started abandoning its principles almost as soon as he had written them. _____ he continued to strongly endorse the French Revolution at that time, the poetic aspect of Wordsworth's character began to assert itself. This led the poet to reevaluate his commitment to Republicanism especially between 1793 and 1796.

Which choice completes the text with the most logical transition?

A) While

B) Notwithstanding,

C) Regardless,

D) Therefore,

2 ☐ **Mark for Review**

Seaweed has recently garnered the status of being a superfood, celebrated for its health related advantages and sustainable nature. _____ as compared to the rest of the world, Europeans seemed to be ahead of the trend, having consumed this nutrient-rich plant for many centuries. Scientists have uncovered conclusive archaeological proof indicating that seaweeds and additional native freshwater plants were part of their diet even before the onset of the Middle Ages.

Which choice completes the text with the most logical transition?

A) Moreover,

B) However,

C) Therefore,

D) Similarly,

3 ☐ **Mark for Review**

A group of students from Imperial College London has found themselves in a state of uncertainty following the loss of the £150,000 rocket they launched into space on September 24, 2023. Volunteers are currently combing the Mojave Desert in California, searching for clues that will determine the outcome of the mission. However, the Mojave Desert is known for its harsh conditions. _____ experts say that it is unlikely they will find any remains.

Which choice completes the text with the most logical transition?

A) Indeed,

B) Notwithstanding,

C) Regardless,

D) Therefore,

Answers & Explanations

1. **Level:** Easy | **Skill/Knowledge:** Transitions

   Key Explanation: Choice A is the correct answer. This choice provides a logical transition indicating that two contrasting actions or situations are happening simultaneously. It connects the poet's abandonment of the principles with his strong endorsement of the French Revolution, highlighting the contrast.

   Distractor Explanations: Choice B is incorrect because it suggests that the second statement does not contradict the first and also does not emphasize the simultaneous nature of the actions. **Choice C** is incorrect because it does not provide a strong logical connection between the two statements. It implies that the poet's abandonment of principles is unrelated to his endorsement of the French Revolution. **Choice D** is incorrect because it implies a cause-and-effect relationship, which is not the intended connection between the two statements. It suggests that the poet abandoned the principles as a result of strongly endorsing the French Revolution, which is not accurate.

2. **Level:** Medium | **Skill/Knowledge:** Transitions

   Key Explanation: Choice B is the correct answer as it effectively introduces a contrast between the recent reputation of seaweed and the historical consumption by European ancestors.

   Distractor Explanations: Choice A is incorrect because "moreover" is used when the upcoming information adds to the previous statement. In this case, it suggests that the recent reputation of seaweed as a superfood is connected to the historical consumption by European ancestors which is not the case. Thus, it does not convey the contrast in the information presented. **Choice**

   C is incorrect because "therefore" suggests a cause-and-effect relationship between the current nutritional information of seaweed and the historical consumption by Europeans but we require a word that indicates the contrast between the two ideas. **Choice D** is incorrect because "similarly" is used to indicate that the upcoming information aligns with the previous statement, showing a similarity or connection. In this case, the intention is to emphasize the contrast between the recent reputation of seaweed as a superfood and the historical consumption by European ancestors.

3. **Level:** Hard | **Skill/Knowledge:** Transitions

   Key Explanation: Choice D is the correct answer. The use of "therefore" is appropriate in cases where there is a cause and effect situation. The cause in this context is "the Mojave Desert is known for its harsh conditions." The effect is "experts say that it is unlikely they will find any remains." In this context, "therefore" is the most appropriate transition word.

   Distractor Explanations: Choice A is incorrect because "indeed" suggests that the harsh conditions in the Mojave Desert are confirming or emphasizing the experts' opinion. It doesn't provide a cause-and-effect relationship. **Choice B** is incorrect because "notwithstanding" is similar in meaning to "in spite of." In this context, using "notwithstanding" would not be a logical transition as the experts would not say that remains of the rocket would not be found in spite of the harsh conditions of the desert. **Choice C** is incorrect because "regardless," similar to Choice B, means "in spite of something." Using this would not be a logical transition as the experts would not say that remains of the rocket would not be found in spite of the harsh conditions of the desert.

This page is intentionally left blank

Chapter 6
Standard English Conventions

Topics covered in this chapter:

- **Boundaries**

    I. Punctuation

    II. Supplements

    III. Coordination and Subordination

- **Form, Structure, and Sense**

    I. Subject-verb Agreement

    II. Pronoun-antecedent Agreement

    III. Verb Forms

    IV. Subject-modifier Placement

    V. Plural and Possessive Nouns

Boundaries I: Punctuation

Punctuation questions are a subset of the Boundaries topic in the SAT. Punctuation questions test your grasp of punctuation rules around commas, semicolons, colons, dashes, and periods and your ability to apply them effectively within a given context.

These questions typically present a sentence or passage with an underlined portion to be filled in, prompting you to choose the choice with the most appropriate punctuation. All Boundaries questions have the same question stem:

> *"Which choice completes the text so that it conforms to the conventions of Standard English?"*

Your task is to select the option that not only adheres to the rules of punctuation but also enhances the clarity and coherence of the sentence. As you approach these questions, consider the role of punctuation marks in signaling pauses, indicating relationships between elements, and conveying the intended meaning.

First, let's understand some key terms.

- **Independent Clause:** a group of words that contains a subject and a predicate (verb) and expresses a complete thought. It can stand alone as a complete sentence.

    Visiting a ski resort during winter is a lovely experience.

    My teacher likes to review answers together right after a quiz.

- **Dependent Clause:** also known as a subordinate clause, they are a group of words that contains a subject and a predicate but does not express a complete thought. It relies on an independent clause to form a complete sentence.

    Because she was late

    If you want to win

- **Conjunction:** a word or a group of words that connects words, phrases, or clauses. There are different types of conjunctions, including coordinating conjunctions and subordinating conjunctions.

    And

    But

    Or

    Because

    Although

    If

- **Participle/Participial Phrase:** a word based on a verb that ends in present tense or past tense and functions as an adjective / a phrase with a participle.

    Anticipating the worst

    Hesitant to step up

A Comprehensive List of Rules and Conventions around Commas, Semicolons, Colons, Dashes, and Periods

Punctuation	Function	Examples
Commas (,)	Separate items in a list.	I bought apples, oranges, and bananas.
	Set off nonessential information, such as additional details or phrases that could be removed without changing the essential meaning of the sentence.	My friend, <u>who lives in Canada</u>, visited last week.
	Use a comma and a coordinating conjunction (and, but, for, nor, or, so, yet) to join two independent clauses.	The sun was setting, and the sky turned orange. The restaurant was closed, but the lights were on.
	If the dependent clause comes before the independent clause, use a comma to separate them.	Because it was raining, we decided to stay indoors.
	Separate a participial phrase from an independent clause.	Excited for school, Jack hopped on the bus.
Semicolons (;)	Separate two closely related independent clauses (complete sentences) without a conjunction.	She loves to read; he prefers watching movies. She enjoys hiking; however, he prefers biking.
	When listing items that contain internal commas, use semicolons to separate each item in the list to maintain clarity.	The team included players from New York, New York; Chicago, Illinois; and Los Angeles, California.
Colons (:)	Introduce a list or series. The colon must be used after an independent clause (complete sentence).	The ingredients for the recipe are: flour, sugar, eggs, and butter.
	Introduce an explanation or example that elaborates on the preceding statement. The colon must be used after an independent clause (complete sentence).	There was only one solution: hard work.
Dashes (—)	Set off nonessential information, such as additional details or phrases that could be removed without changing the essential meaning of the sentence.	My friend — who lives in Canada — visited last week.

Punctuation	Function	Examples
Periods (.)	Separate two independent clauses.	The mountain was filled with rangers today. A crowded mountain often means limited resources.

How to solve Punctuation questions?

 ### Step 1

Identify punctuation questions: Since all Boundaries questions share the same question stem, being able to identify punctuation questions will help you understand the objective and focus right away. Answer options of punctuation questions will use mostly the same words, but they will slightly vary in terms of punctuation used. There may also be a conjunction in one of the answer options.

 ### Step 2

Label independent clauses, dependent clauses, and conjunctions: The punctuation rules outlined above have specific criteria relating to clauses and conjunctions. Quickly labeling these components as you read the passage will clarify the structure of the passage. One way is to label independent clauses with an "I", dependent clauses with a "D", participial phrases with a "P", and underline conjunctions. You can create more labels if you like to break the sentence structure down even further, but this could take more time.

Step 3

Focus on the sentence with the underlined blank: For punctuation questions, you can often ignore additional sentences and concentrate primarily on the sentence featuring the missing blank. All the information necessary to identify the correct answer should be found within that specific sentence.

⑦ Let's solve a Punctuation question now:

Derived from the Greek words "bio" meaning life, and "morphe" meaning form, biomorphism does not directly refer to a life form. Instead, it refers to the inclination of exhibiting the characteristics or visual traits of living _____ the term may sound scientific, its earliest usage was actually in relation to biomorphic art, as observed in the Cubism and Abstract Art exhibition held at MoMA in 1936.

Which choice completes the text so that it conforms to the conventions of Standard English?

A) organisms and while

B) organisms while

C) organisms. While

D) organisms, while

First, we know this is a Punctuation question because the answer options differ both in terms of punctuation used and the presence of a conjunction.

Next, we can **ignore the first sentence** for now since the missing blank is in the second sentence. You can cross it out if you'd like to avoid getting distracted by it.

Now, let's **label the components** of the second sentence with the missing portion to fill in. We will substitute the words from the answer choices, but we won't analyze the punctuation yet.

1. Instead, it refers to the inclination of exhibiting the characteristics or visual traits of living organisms

2. while the term may sound scientific, its earliest usage was actually in relation to biomorphic art, as observed in the Cubism and Abstract Art exhibition held at MoMA in 1936.

The first clause is independent because it has a subject (it) and a verb (refers), expressing a complete thought on its own. The second independent clause also stands as a complete thought on its own.

Reviewing the punctuation rules we learned, remember that only a semicolon (;) or a period (.) can be used to separate two independent clauses. A comma (,) can also be used if there is a coordinating conjunction. With this in mind, time to evaluate each answer choice.

Choice A is incorrect because there needs to be both a comma and a coordinating conjunction to link two independent clauses together. However, Choice A has only a coordinating conjunction and no comma.

Choice B is incorrect because there is no punctuation present to separate the two independent clauses.

Choice C looks like the best choice so far because a period (.) can be used to separate two independent clauses.

Choice D is incorrect because there needs to be both a comma and a coordinating conjunction to link two independent clauses together. However, Choice D has only a comma and no coordinating conjunction.

Choice C is the correct answer.

Exercises

For the following sentences, all punctuation has been removed except the full stop. Your task is to fill in the required punctuation to follow the SAT rules. Use commas, colons, semicolons, and dashes to solve these exercises. You can include one or more types of punctuation. Each sentence requires at least one punctuation mark to be added.

1. The school play featured actors from the drama club the dance team and the music department.

2. His favorite subject history always fascinated him.

3. Excited for the trip the students packed their bags early.

4. The assignment was challenging however the students completed it with dedication.

5. The meeting which lasted for hours was finally adjourned.

6. She couldn't believe her luck she had won the lottery.

For the following sentences, <u>one</u> punctuation mark has been removed. Please fill in the blank with the correct punctuation mark.

7. The teacher's advice was simple _ study hard, ask questions, and never give up.

8. Despite the challenges _ they managed to finish the project on time.

9. We went to the beach _ but it started raining heavily without any warning.

10. Sam, a famous linguist _ presented his thesis in front of the department faculty today.

11. The event was a success _ everyone enjoyed the food, music, and activities.

12. Calgary _ a Canadian city — is the largest city in the province of Alberta.

Answers

1. The school play featured actors from the drama club, the dance team, and the music department.

2. His favorite subject, history, always fascinated him.

3. Excited for the trip, the students packed their bags early.

4. The assignment was challenging; however, the students completed it with dedication.

5. The meeting, which lasted for hours, was finally adjourned.

6. She couldn't believe her luck; she had won the lottery.

7. The teacher's advice was simple: study hard, ask questions, and never give up. OR The teacher's advice was simple — study hard, ask questions, and never give up.

8. Despite the challenges, they managed to finish the project on time.

9. We went to the beach, but it started raining heavily without any warning.

10. Sam, a famous linguist, presented his thesis in front of the department faculty today.

11. The event was a success; everyone enjoyed the food, music, and activities. OR The event was a success: everyone enjoyed the food, music, and activities.

12. Calgary — a Canadian city — is the largest city in the province of Alberta.

Boundaries II: Supplements

Supplements questions are a subset of the Boundaries topic in the SAT. These questions test your ability to understand sentence structure, identify essential and nonessential elements, and apply the correct punctuation.

Supplements consist of the following elements:

1. **Essential elements are integral components of a sentence that are necessary for it to convey a clear and complete thought.** In other words, essential elements are required for the sentence to be an independent clause. These elements do not require punctuation for separation from the rest of the sentence.

2. **Nonessential elements are components that provide additional information but are not essential for the sentence's overall meaning.** These elements must be set off by punctuation, such as commas, to indicate their separation from the main sentence. Even when nonessential elements are removed, the sentence should still be an independent clause.

While you need to be able to differentiate between these two types of supplements, Supplements questions also require a keen understanding of punctuation to be able to set nonessential elements off correctly. Remembering the punctuation rules from the previous section, both commas (,) and dashes (—) can be used to set off nonessential information. Since nonessential elements can appear in different parts of a sentence, let's look at each scenario. The nonessential element in each scenario is italicized.

Scenario	Example	Rule
Start of sentence	*In the room,* a large chandelier lit up the space	Only one comma is required to set off "in the room".
Middle of sentence	The concert, *featuring famous musicians,* was a huge success.	Two commas are required to set off nonessential information "featuring famous musicians".
End of sentence	The team won the championship, *a significant achievement for such a young group of players.*	Only one comma is required to set off "a significant achievement…"

While commas are used in the above examples, dashes function in the same way. Parentheses () can also be used to set off nonessential information but this is rare.

 Remember

You do **not** need to differentiate between when to use commas, dashes, or parentheses when setting off nonessential information: they are interchangeable in the eyes of the SAT. However, **remember to always pair the same type of punctuation** together when setting off nonessential information: you cannot mix and match a dash and a comma together, for instance.

How to solve Supplements questions?

Step 1

Identify the Supplements questions: Since all Boundaries questions share the same question stem, being able to identify Supplements questions will help you understand the goal of the question. Answer options of Supplements questions will often vary in the use of commas, dashes, or the lack thereof. Basically, the question is asking you if an element should be set off with punctuation or not.

Step 2

Test for necessity: A quick test to determine if an element is essential is to remove it from the sentence. Try crossing it out entirely. If removal alters the sentence's fundamental meaning or leaves it incomplete as a dependent clause, the element is essential. If the sentence remains grammatically correct and coherent without the element, it is nonessential.

Step 3

Search for punctuation in the passage: Nonessential elements in the middle of a sentence require two punctuation marks to set it off from the rest of the sentence. When the passage includes such a nonessential element, one punctuation mark to set off nonessential information is almost always included in the passage directly. Your only job will be to match the same punctuation to fully set off the nonessential element!

Step 4

Check if you have identified the entire nonessential element: Some Supplements passages consist of long sentences with complex sentence structures to confuse you. In these cases, the answer options can differ very slightly, where one answer choice places a comma right before a word and another answer choice places a comma right after the same word instead. Make sure you are not accidentally setting off an incomplete nonessential element or setting off more than you need to. For example, examine this sentence:

"Elephants, the largest land mammal alive on Earth, retain memories for a long time."

One incorrect answer option may place the comma in this way: "Elephants, the largest land mammal alive, on Earth retain memories for a long time." Is "the largest land mammal alive" describing elephants? Yes. However, does it make sense to say that "elephants on Earth retain memories for a long time"? No, because elephants only exist on Earth. The sentence makes much more sense when you realize that the full nonessential element to set off is "the largest land mammal alive on Earth." Conducting an extra sanity check like we have done here never hurts!

Titles and proper nouns are essential information: When a title is used before a name, it is considered an essential part of the sentence. For instance, in the sentence "President John Adams visited the capital", "President" is a title that is an essential part of describing John Adams. Therefore, no commas are needed to separate it from the name.

 A Word of Caution

Do not mistake length for essential information: When a nonessential element is very long, you might think all of this description is necessary information to include. However, remember that "essential" does not refer to the importance of the information in understanding the full idea. "Essential" merely refers to whether or not the information is required for the sentence to be an independent clause on its own.

Let's solve a Supplements question now:

Environmental activists and biologists suspect that extreme heat waves and drought may have played roles in the deaths of 120 river dolphins in the Amazon. Although swift measures are needed to protect this threatened species, scientists must first eliminate other potential causes before moving the dolphins to areas of the river with cooler temperatures. Amazon river dolphins, one of the few remaining_____ been classified as a threatened species since 2018.

Which choice completes the text so that it conforms to the conventions of Standard English?

A) freshwater dolphin species have

B) freshwater dolphin species — have

C) freshwater dolphin, species have

D) freshwater dolphin species, have

First, we can identify this question as a Supplements question because all the same words are present across all the answer choices, but there is variation in the usage of commas and dashes.

Now let's focus solely on the last sentence of the passage as it is the sentence with the underlined blank.

Amazon river dolphins, one of the few remaining _____ been classified as a threatened species since 2018.

Notice that there is already a comma in the sentence after the word "dolphins":

This is a hint that there may be a nonessential element in the middle of the sentence that we need to fully set off with commas. Let's plug in the remaining words to evaluate which parts are essential or nonessential.

Amazon river dolphins, one of the few remaining freshwater dolphin species have been classified as a threatened species since 2018.

What has been classified as a threatened species? Amazon river dolphins. What is additional information that describes the dolphins? One of the few remaining freshwater dolphin species.

We can cross out the nonessential information and see if we still have an independent clause to test for necessity.

> Amazon river dolphins, ~~one of the few remaining freshwater dolphin species,~~ have been classified as a threatened species since 2018.

This is still a complete thought on its own. In this independent clause, "Amazon river dolphins" is the subject, and "have been classified" is the verb phrase. Through our test, we have identified a nonessential element in the middle of the sentence that can be removed without affecting the coherence or completeness of the sentence. For consistency, we need to add a comma (,) after the word "species" to set off the nonessential element, aligning with the comma used earlier in the sentence.

Choice A is incorrect because there is no comma used to fully set off the nonessential element "one of the few remaining freshwater dolphin species".

Choice B is incorrect because a dash is used rather than a comma, which is inconsistent with the comma used earlier in the sentence.

Choice C is incorrect because the comma is placed earlier than it is supposed to be and does not set off the full nonessential element "one of the few remaining freshwater dolphin species".

Choice D correctly sets off the full nonessential element "one of the few remaining freshwater dolphin species" using commas.

Exercises

For the following exercises, identify if the underlined portion of the sentence is an essential or non-essential supplement.

1. <u>In the novel *To Kill a Mockingbird*,</u> the character Atticus Finch, who is a lawyer, defends Tom Robinson, a black man wrongly accused of a crime.

2. The scientist <u>who discovered penicillin</u> was Alexander Fleming.

3. The novel *Pride and Prejudice,* <u>written by Jane Austen</u>, is a classic of English literature.

4. The building <u>that houses the museum</u> was designed by a famous architect.

5. The athlete <u>who trains rigorously every day</u> is expected to perform well in the upcoming competition.

6. <u>President</u> John F. Kennedy, who was assassinated in 1963, was known for his inspirational speeches.

7. The building, <u>designed by Frank Lloyd Wright</u>, is an architectural masterpiece.

8. The painting <u>created by Picasso</u> is on display at the museum.

For the following exercises, please cross out the non-essential element OR state if there are no non-essential elements in the sentence.

9. Orson Welles directed *Citizen Kane* — one of the greatest movies of all time for many critics — in 1941.

10. Philologist and academic J.R.R. Tolkien authored *The Lord of the Rings* series.

11. The study, which was published in a prestigious journal, has been widely criticized for its methodology.

12. Founded in 1998 by Jeff Bezos, the company revolutionized online shopping.

Answers

1. Non-essential

2. Essential

3. Non-essential

4. Essential

5. Essential

6. Essential

7. Non-essential

8. Essential

9. Orson Welles directed Citizen Kane — ~~one of the greatest movies of all time for many critics~~ — in 1941.

10. No non-essential element

11. The study, ~~which was published in a prestigious journal,~~ has been widely criticized for its methodology.

12. ~~Founded in 1998 by Jeff Bezos,~~ the company revolutionized online shopping.

Boundaries III: Coordination and Subordination

Coordination and Subordination questions are a subset of Boundaries questions that assess your command over sentence structure, coherence, and proper use of conjunctions. These questions evaluate your ability to create clear and logical relationships between clauses, ensuring that the sentence maintains coherence and conveys a complete thought.

> **Coordination involves connecting words, phrases, or clauses of equal importance within a sentence.** This is commonly achieved using a comma (,) and coordinating conjunctions such as *for, and, nor, but, or, yet, so.* Remember the acronym **FANBOYS** for these coordinating conjunctions.

Understanding how to appropriately use these conjunctions is crucial for constructing grammatically correct and logically coherent sentences. Examine the examples below.

The correct format is [**independent clause**] + [**comma (,)**] + [**coordinating conjunction**] + [**independent clause**]

- *She enjoys both playing the piano and singing, but she finds it challenging to balance both activities*

- *John went to buy groceries, and Sara decorated the house for the party.*

In the examples, the coordinating conjunctions "but" and "and" serve to connect each set of the two independent clauses, maintaining the equilibrium within the sentences. The comma before the coordinating conjunction emphasizes the separation between these distinct yet related ideas.

> **Subordination, on the other hand, deals with creating relationships between clauses by using subordinating conjunctions like *because, although, since, while, if, when,* etc, and a comma in some instances.** Subordination helps establish the hierarchy of ideas within a sentence, distinguishing between main and subordinate clauses.

One format is [**subordinating conjunction**] + [**independent clause**] + [**comma (,)**] + [**independent clause**]

- *After she finished her work, she went to the beach.*

- *Although she was tired, she continued working because she had a deadline to meet.*

Another format is [**independent clause**] + [**subordinating conjunction**] + [**independent clause**]

Note that this format where the subordinating conjunction is in the middle does not require any punctuation mark.

- *He went to the office because he had to print out a few files.*

- *Success is almost guaranteed if you work hard.*

Format 1 demonstrates a clear hierarchy with a comma separating the subordinate clause, while Format 2 seamlessly integrates the subordinating conjunction without the need for additional punctuation. Both are excellent ways to use subordination to connect two independent clauses.

How to solve Coordination and Subordination questions?

≫ Step 1

Identify coordination and subordination questions: Since all Boundaries questions share the same question stem, being able to identify coordination and subordination questions will help you understand what you should focus on. Answer choices in such questions will vary in the usage of conjunctions and other punctuation marks.

≫ Step 2

Label independent clauses, coordinating conjunctions, and subordinating conjunctions: The formats outlined above have specific structures related to clauses and conjunctions. Quickly labeling these components as you read will clarify the structure of the sentence. One way is to label independent clauses with an "I", coordinating conjunctions with a "C", and subordinating conjunctions with an "S".

≫ Step 3

Eliminate answer choices with a coordinating conjunction but no comma: As we have learned, coordinating conjunctions must be paired with a comma when linking independent clauses. Thus, if you see an answer choice using a coordinating conjunction without a comma, eliminate the choice.

≫ Step 4

Eliminate answer choices with run-on sentences or comma splices: While we learned correct sentence formats using coordinating and subordinating conjunctions, knowing incorrect formats helps eliminate incorrect answer choices quickly.

> When two independent clauses are linked without any punctuation, we have a run-on sentence error. When two independent clauses are linked without a coordinating conjunction, we have a comma splice error.

If you notice either of these in the answer choices, eliminate them.

⃝? Let's solve a Coordination and Subordination question now:

In our solar system, the outer planets typically have more moons than the inner planets. The outer planets, which include Jupiter, Saturn, Uranus, and Neptune, had more space and a lower level of gravity of the _____ each planet drew in masses of gas, dust, and ice during its formation. After the large outer planet was formed, the remaining material gathered together to form the outer planet's moons.

Which choice completes the text so that it conforms to the conventions of Standard English?

A) Sun, so

B) Sun

C) Sun,

D) Sun so

Let's break down and **label the components** of the sentence with the missing blank. We will substitute the words from the answer choices, but we won't analyze the punctuation yet.

1. The outer planets, which include Jupiter, Saturn, Uranus, and Neptune, had more space and a lower level of gravity of the Sun

2. each planet drew in masses of gas, dust, and ice during its formation

We know these are independent clauses because both stand as complete thoughts on their own. We can link two independent clauses together using either coordination or subordination conjunctions. Some of the answer choices include the coordinating conjunction "so", while there seems to be no subordinating conjunction in any of the answer choices. Hence, we can safely assume that we are dealing with coordination here.

Remember the correct format for coordination is **[independent clause] + [comma (,)] + [coordinating conjunction] + [independent clause]**. Therefore, the correct sentence should be:

> The outer planets, which include Jupiter, Saturn, Uranus, and Neptune, had more space and a lower level of gravity of the Sun, so each planet drew in masses of gas, dust, and ice during its formation.

The answer choice that matches this sentence format is **Choice A.**

Let's review the other answer choices to identify the errors.

Choice B creates a **run-on sentence error** because two independent clauses are linked without any punctuation. A coordinating conjunction is also missing.

Choice C includes a **comma splice error** because two independent clauses are linked without a coordinating conjunction.

Choice D creates a **run-on sentence error** because two independent clauses are linked without any punctuation.

To gain a more nuanced understanding of subordination and coordination, let's explore how subordination can replace coordination to link independent clauses in this sentence.

The first correct format for subordination is **[subordinating conjunction] + [independent clause] + [comma (,)] + [independent clause]**. Following this format, we can plug in the subordinating conjunction "since" to convey the premise-conclusion relationship between the independent clauses.

> Since the outer planets, which include Jupiter, Saturn, Uranus, and Neptune, had more space and a lower level of gravity of the Sun, each planet drew in masses of gas, dust, and ice during its formation.

In this format, the subordinating conjunction "since" establishes a cause-and-effect relationship between the two independent clauses. The clause introduced by "since" (which includes additional information about the outer planets) is subordinated to the main clause, creating a clear hierarchy and emphasizing the reason behind the subsequent action.

Another correct format is [**independent clause**] + [**subordinating conjunction**] + [**independent clause**].

> Each planet drew in masses of gas, dust, and ice during its formation because the outer planets, which include Jupiter, Saturn, Uranus, and Neptune, had more space and a lower level of gravity of the Sun.

In this format, the order of independent clauses is reversed, and the subordinating conjunction "because" is employed. This construction retains the meaning of the sentence, emphasizing the cause-and-effect relationship. The main clause, "Each planet drew in masses of gas, dust, and ice during its formation," is followed by the subordinate clause providing the reason for this action.

Exercises

Identify the coordinating conjunction in the sentences below.

1. She wanted to go play tennis outdoors, but it started raining heavily.

2. We could go to the beach, or we could go hiking in the mountains.

Identify the subordinating conjunction in the sentences below.

3. Since his alarm didn't go off, he was late and missed the bus.

4. She arrived early because she wanted to secure a good seat.

Correct the sentences below by adding the necessary punctuation.

5. She likes to sing and dance but she doesn't perform in public.

6. Although it was hot outside she decided to wear a jacket.

Combine the sentences below using a subordinating conjunction and any necessary punctuation.

7. Tom finished his homework. He watched TV.

8. It was late. He still wanted to watch the movie.

Pick the version that uses any necessary punctuation and conjunctions.

9. A) Sarah couldn't attend the meeting she had a doctor's appointment.

   B) Sarah couldn't attend the meeting because she had a doctor's appointment.

10. A) If tax continues to increase, many households will require some form of financial support.

    B) If tax continues to increase many households will require some form of financial support.

11. A) Despite the late hour, she continued working, because she had a deadline to meet.

B) Despite the late hour, she continued working because she had a deadline to meet.

Answers

1. But

2. Or

3. Since

4. Because

5. She likes to sing and dance, but she doesn't perform in public.

6. Although it was hot outside, she decided to wear a jacket.

7. After Tom finished his homework, he watched TV.

8. Although it was late, he still wanted to watch the movie.

9. B

10. A

11. B

1 ☐ **Mark for Review**

The fall of the Berlin Wall in 1989 was a pivotal event, and it marked the reunification of East and West Germany. This momentous occasion led to celebrations on both sides, and it represented a turning point in history. People from all walks of life came _____ a sense of unity and hope.

Which choice completes the text so that it conforms to the conventions of Standard English?

A) together, and the wall that once divided them crumbled fostering

B) together, and the wall that once divided them crumbled, fostering

C) together and the wall that once divided them crumbled, fostering

D) together and the wall that once divided them crumbled fostering

2 ☐ **Mark for Review**

Robert Hooke, a brilliant seventeenth-century scientist and polymath, significantly contributed to various fields of knowledge, including microscopy and physics._____ revealed a hidden world of minute structures, these discoveries were initially met with skepticism from some contemporaries. However, they ultimately laid the foundation for modern cell biology and microbiology.

Which choice completes the text so that it conforms to the conventions of Standard English?

A) While his microscopic observations particularly his study of cork cells under a microscope

B) While his microscopic observations, particularly his study of cork cells under a microscope,

C) While his microscopic observations, particularly his study of cork cells under a microscope

D) While his microscopic observations particularly his study of cork cells under a microscope,

3 ☐ **Mark for Review**

Throughout the course of human history, a fascinating tapestry woven with complex patterns of migration, isolation, and admixture, which is a term _____ from different populations, has left an indelible mark.

Which choice completes the text so that it conforms to the conventions of Standard English?

A) that, refers to gene flow between individuals

B) that refers to gene flow between individuals

C) that – refers to gene flow between individuals

D) that refers to gene flow between individuals,

4 ☐ **Mark for Review**

Environmental activists and biologists suspect that extreme heat waves and drought may have played roles in the deaths of 120 river dolphins in the Amazon. Although swift measures are needed to protect this threatened species, scientists must first eliminate other potential causes before moving the dolphins to areas of the river with cooler temperatures. Amazon river _____ been classified as a threatened species since 2018.

Which choice completes the text so that it conforms to the conventions of Standard English?

A) dolphins one of the few remaining freshwater dolphin species globally have

B) dolphins one of the few remaining freshwater dolphin species globally, have

C) dolphins, one of the few remaining freshwater dolphin species globally have

D) dolphins, one of the few remaining freshwater dolphin species globally, have

5   ◻ Mark for Review

Nudge: Improving Decisions About Health, Wealth and Happiness by Richard Thaler is a nonfiction book that argues that many "nudges", or subtle incentives or designs that push people to act in a certain way, affect people in their daily lives. Alternatively, "sludges" are inconspicuous ways that prevent or add friction to _____ people are pushed away from a specific choice or action.

Which choice completes the text so that it conforms to the conventions of Standard English?

A) decisions so

B) decisions, so

C) decisions

D) decisions,

6   ◻ Mark for Review

The Indian peacock displays iridescent blue and green plumage, _____ whereas the green peacock exhibits green and bronze body feathers. Both species feature slightly smaller females in terms of weight and wingspan, while males possess significantly longer tails, often referred to as "trains."

Which choice completes the text so that it conforms to the conventions of Standard English?

A) mostly metallic blue and green;

B) mostly metallic blue and green,

C) -mostly metallic blue and green

D) mostly metallic blue and green:

Answers & Explanations

1. **Level:** Easy | **Skill/Knowledge:** Boundaries

    Key Explanation: The convention being tested is punctuation use when linking two clauses by making one of the clauses dependent. **Choice B** is the best answer because it uses a comma after "together" to set it off from the rest of the sentence and a comma after "crumbled" to separate clauses properly. This choice follows the conventions of Standard English.

    Distractor Explanations: Choice A is incorrect because it separates "together" from the rest of the sentence with a comma, which disrupts the sentence's flow. The use of a comma or coordinating conjunction (like "and") is needed to connect them properly. **Choice C** is incorrect because it omits the necessary comma after "together." In Standard English, when "and" connects two independent clauses, a comma is typically used before it to separate them. **Choice D** is incorrect because it lacks the necessary commas to properly separate the clauses and phrases in the sentence. The sentence structure is not well-punctuated.

2. **Level:** Medium | **Skill/Knowledge:** Boundaries

    Key Explanation: The convention being tested is punctuation use when linking two clauses by making one of the clauses dependent. **Choice B** is the best answer because the passage talks about all of his microscopic observations, and how they revealed a hidden world of minute structures. The particular study of cork cells under a microscope wasn't the only observation that revealed that. Microscopic observations, by nature, reveal a hidden world. So, commas should be used to separate the inessential information, i.e., the "particularly...microscope" sentence.

    Distractor Explanations: Choice A is incorrect because it lacks commas after both "observations" and "microscope." Commas are needed to set off the introductory phrase and the non-essential information, making the sentence clearer and more grammatically correct. **Choice C** is incorrect because it does not use a comma after "microscope." **Choice D** is incorrect because it lacks a comma after "observations." Commas are needed to set off the introductory phrase "While his microscopic observations."

3. **Level:** Hard | **Skill/Knowledge:** Boundaries

Key Explanation: The convention being tested is punctuation use between a sentence and an essential element. **Choice B** is the best answer because it correctly uses "that" to introduce the relative clause and provide additional information about the term being discussed. It maintains a concise and grammatically correct structure, without any unnecessary punctuation.

Distractor Explanations: Choice A is incorrect because it includes a comma before "refers," creating a pause in the sentence. The comma suggests a break or interruption, which disrupts the flow of the sentence. Additionally, the use of a comma in this context is unnecessary because the relative clause "that refers to gene flow between individuals" directly modifies the term mentioned earlier in the sentence. **Choice C** is incorrect because it uses a hyphen ("-") after "that," suggesting a pause or interruption. Hyphens are not typically used to introduce relative clauses. **Choice D** is almost identical to Choice B, with the only difference being the presence of a comma after "individuals." While using a comma before the final comma in a series is generally accepted, it is not necessary in this sentence because there are no other items in the series. Therefore, the comma here is unnecessary and may create a pause that disrupts the flow of the sentence.

4. **Level:** Medium | **Skill/Knowledge:** Boundaries

Key Explanation: Choice D is the best answer. The convention being tested is the use of punctuation to mark boundaries between

nonessential supplements and clauses. The comma before and after the nonessential supplement ("one of the few remaining freshwater dolphin species globally") is used to set off the nonessential supplement from the main clause ("Amazon…2018") since this information can be removed without affecting the coherence of the sentence.

Distractor Explanations: Choice A is incorrect because there needs to be commas before and after the nonessential supplement ("one…globally") to set off the nonessential supplement from the main clause ("Amazon…2018") since this information can be removed without affecting the coherence of the sentence. **Choice B** is incorrect because there needs to be a comma before "one" to set off the nonessential supplement from the main clause ("Amazon…2018") since this information can be removed without affecting the coherence of the sentence. **Choice C** is incorrect because there needs to be a comma after "globally" to set off the nonessential supplement ("one…globally") from the main clause ("Amazon…2018") since this information can be removed without affecting the coherence of the sentence.

5. **Level:** Easy | **Skill/Knowledge:** Boundaries

Key Explanation: Choice B is the best answer. The convention being tested is the coordination of main clauses within a sentence. This choice correctly uses a comma and the coordinating conjunction "so" to join the first main clause ("alternatively…decisions") and the second main clause ("people…action").

Distractor Explanations: Choice A is incorrect because when coordinating two longer main clauses such as these, a comma is required before the coordinating conjunction. **Choice C** is incorrect because it results in a run-on sentence. The two main clauses are fused without punctuation and/or a conjunction. **Choice D** is incorrect because it results in a comma splice. Without a conjunction following it, a comma cannot be used in this way to join two main clauses.

6.　**Level:** Medium | **Skill/Knowledge:** Boundaries

Key Explanation: Choice B is correct. The convention being tested is punctuation for nonessential or non-defining clauses. Two commas are required to mark non-defining clauses in a sentence. Non-defining clauses give the reader extra information about the noun in the sentence. It is not necessary information, and the sentence will make sense even without the extra information.

Distractor Explanations: Choice A is incorrect because when using a semi-colon, it must be preceded and followed by independent clauses, meaning that both parts of the sentence must make sense independently. **Choice C** is incorrect because when using a dash to add extra information, if the main sentence resumes, a second dash must be added at the end of the added information. **Choice D** is incorrect because a colon is usually used to introduce a list or between sentences when the second sentence explains or justifies the first sentence.

Form, Structure, and Sense I: Subject-verb Agreement

Subject-verb Agreement questions on the SAT assess your ability to ensure grammatical consistency between the subject and verb within a sentence.

All questions in the Form, Structure, and Sense topic take the form of:

> *"Which choice completes the text so that it conforms to the conventions of Standard English?"*

The question will refer to a passage with a missing verb and the answer options will offer various verbs for you to fill in.

Your job is to ensure that the subject(s) and verb(s) in a sentence agree in terms of number.

Some Rules to Remember for Subject-verb Agreement

Rule	Example
A singular subject is paired with a singular verb.	The cat is sleeping on the couch.
Match plural subjects with plural verbs.	The dogs are barking loudly.
For compound subjects joined by "and", use a plural verb.	The teacher and the principal are attending the seminar.
For compound subjects joined by "or" or "nor", check each of the subjects. If the subjects are singular, use a singular verb. If at least one of the subjects is plural, use a plural verb.	Neither the book nor the magazines are on the shelf.
Some indefinite pronouns are always singular (e.g., everyone, somebody), and others are always plural (e.g., both, several).	Each of the students is responsible for completing their homework.
Treat collective nouns as singular unless the context implies individual actions.	The team is practicing for the upcoming match.

Since indefinite pronouns are a bit trickier, let's dive a little deeper into them.

1. **Indefinite pronouns are pronouns that do not refer to any specific person, thing, or amount. Instead, they refer to non-specific people, things, or amounts.** These pronouns are often used when the identity or quantity of the subject is unknown or irrelevant.

Singular Indefinite Pronouns	Plural Indefinite Pronouns	Singular or Plural Indefinite Pronouns (depending on context)
• Anyone • Someone • Nobody • Everybody • Anything • Something • Nobody • Each • Either • Neither	• All • Some • Many • Few • Both • Several	• All • Some • None • Any • Most
Example: Someone left their backpack in the classroom.	**Example:** All of the students submitted their assignments.	**Example 1:** None of the pizza has been eaten. (Singular) **Example 2:** None of the students have arrived. (Plural)

Another tricky part of subject-verb agreement questions is identifying the main subject because the SAT will include many additional words and phrases to distract you from the main subject. Cross out prepositional phrases and modifiers to focus on the main subject.

2. **Prepositions are words that show relationships between other words in a sentence** (e.g. before, in, below)

   • *On the table, the book is open.* In this example, "on the table" is a prepositional phrase. "On" is the preposition, and "the table" is its object.

3. **Modifier is a word, phrase, or clause that provides additional information about another word (usually a noun or a verb) in a sentence.** Modifiers add details to enhance the meaning of a sentence. Modifiers can be removed without affecting the coherence or completeness of an independent clause.

   • *With a smile, Sarah greeted her old friend at the airport.* "With a smile" is a modifier phrase that describes how Sarah greeted her friend. It adds a descriptive element to the action.

   • *Tired from work, Mark still decided to go to the gym.* "Tired from work" is a modifier clause expressing Mark's condition or state.

Finally, **sometimes the typical word order of a sentence is reversed, with the verb appearing before the subject. This inversion is often used for emphasis or to create a specific rhythm in writing.**

- *Underneath the tree stood a magnificent owl.*

In this example, the subject ("a magnificent owl") appears after the verb ("stood"). This is an inverted subject-verb order, placing emphasis on the owl.

How to solve a Subject-verb Agreement question?

⟫⟫ Step 1

Identify subject-verb agreement questions: Answer options of subject-verb agreement questions will include both singular and plural forms of the same verb.

⟫⟫ Step 2

Identify the main subject: Cross out modifiers and prepositional phrases to help identify the main subject. Underline the main subject and decide whether it requires a plural or singular verb.

⟫⟫ Step 3

Remember the different types of indefinite pronouns: Since indefinite pronouns can be plural or singular depending on the context, your best bet is to remember the different types of indefinite pronouns and their examples. The list is short enough for you to have a strong grasp of all indefinite pronouns.

⟫⟫ Step 4

Watch out for verbs that come before the subject: While the subject-verb agreement rules do not change, do not get flustered when a sentence does not match the usual format you are used to. Follow the same rules and tips advised in this chapter to identify the main subject and proceed as usual to determine whether it is singular or plural.

⟫⟫ Step 5

Think about the meaning of the sentence: When it is difficult to identify the main subject, simply think about the logical meaning of the sentence and which subject makes the most sense. For example, take this sentence: A cake made with organic flours (is/are) fluffy with a light crumb. Let's say you are not sure if "cake" or "flour" is the main subject. Would a cake be fluffy with a light crumb or would flour be fluffy with a light crumb? Clearly, it does not make sense for flour itself to be fluffy and have a crumb texture. Therefore, we can conclude that cake is the singular subject, which agrees in number with the singular verb "is".

⟫⟫ Step 6

Find the odd one out in the answer choices: If you encounter three answer options featuring singular verbs and one option with a plural verb, it is reasonable to assume that the correct answer is the one with the plural verb. But if the subject is singular, you may not be able to differentiate between the three singular verbs. Therefore, while this tip is helpful if you cannot identify the main subject, use this as a last resort.

Let's solve a Subject-verb Agreement question now:

Mah-jongg is a popular game originating from nineteenth-century China. The game can be played in various versions: Cantonese, American, Chinese, Japanese, and more. The game consists of decorated tiles that represent different numbers and ranks. The four players of the game, each with thirteen tiles and a poker face, _____ by drawing one more tile to replace an existing one. The game only ends when one player discards another player's winning tile or when one player picks their winning tile from the pile of tiles.

Which choice completes the text so that it conforms to the conventions of Standard English?

A) has started

B) is starting

C) start

D) starts

We know that this question is about subject-verb agreement because there are both singular and plural forms of the verb "start". The question does not seem to be about tense because all the answer options are in the present tense.

Now let's break down and **identify the main subject.**

> The four players of the game, each with thirteen tiles and a poker face

We can immediately notice there is a preposition "of". The full prepositional phrase is "of the game", which describes the relation between the four players and their participation in the game. There is also a modifier that describes the players: "each with thirteen tiles and a poker face." Prepositional phrases and modifiers can be crossed out.

> The four players ~~of the game, each with thirteen tiles and a poker face~~

We are left with our main subject: "four players" or "players". "Players" is a plural subject, so we should use the plural verb "start". The correct answer is **Choice C.**

To be safe, let's conduct a sanity check on the **meaning of the sentence.** Using Choice C, the four players are the ones starting the game, which makes sense.

Furthermore, let's try to **find the odd one out in the answer choices. Choice A, B, and D** are all singular verbs. Choice C is the only odd one out as a plural verb, and it indeed is the correct answer.

Using the tips and strategies we have learned, **Choice C** is confirmed to be the correct answer.

Exercises

For each of the following sentences, choose the correct subject or verb.

1. Each of the students <u>went/go</u> to the science fair last week.

2. Neither the teacher nor the students <u>is/are</u> interested in the movie.

3. The committee <u>hasn't/haven't</u> reached a decision yet.

4. Neither the cat nor the dog <u>is/are</u> awake at the moment.

5. Several of the students <u>is/are</u> unsure if they can complete the project before the tight deadline.

6. <u>Has/have</u> everybody finished their homework already?

7. None of the food <u>tastes/taste</u> good after being left out all night.

8. <u>Does/do</u> any of the pens <u>has/have</u> black ink?

9. The group of singers <u>is/are</u> performing at the concert next week.

10. The band's members, consisting of musicians from Mexico, Brazil, and India, <u>is/are</u> very talented.

11. Neither the manager nor his assistants <u>was/were</u> informed of the changes.

12. Some of the money <u>is/are</u> missing from the donation box.

Answers

1.	went	7.	tastes
2.	are	8.	Do/have
3.	hasn't	9.	is
4.	is	10.	are
5.	are	11.	were
6.	Has	12.	is

Form, Structure, and Sense II: Pronoun-antecedent Agreement

Pronoun-antecedent Agreement is a crucial concept, specifically under the Form, Structure, and Sense topic. This skill assesses your ability to ensure that pronouns match their antecedents in terms of number and gender.

1. First of all, **a pronoun is a word that takes the place of a noun or a group of words acting as a noun.** Pronouns are used to avoid repetition and make sentences less cumbersome.

   Examples of pronouns include: *he, she, it, they, we, us, you, me, him, her, them, I, you, myself, yourself, etc.*

2. **An antecedent is the noun or noun phrase to which a pronoun refers.** In other words, it is the word that the pronoun replaces or stands in for. In the sentence "John lost his keys," the noun "John" is the antecedent for the pronoun "his."

In sentences, pronouns and their antecedents work together to create clear and concise communication. Pronouns (e.g., he, she, it, they) must agree with their antecedents (the nouns they replace) to maintain clarity and correct grammar.

 Some Rules to Remember for Pronoun-antecedent Agreement

Rule	Example
Singular antecedents require singular pronouns, and plural antecedents need plural pronouns. (Recall the list of indefinite pronouns and the rules around plural and singular uses in the "Subject-verb Agreement" section)	Each of the students completed *his or her* homework. Both cats are very particular about *their* food.
Ensure that the pronoun matches the gender of its antecedent.	A person should take pride in *his or her* work. Bethany walked towards *her* car.
For people, use pronouns like *he, she, we, they.* For things, use pronouns like *it.*	The teacher gave *him* a book. The cat chased the mouse and caught *it.*
Differentiate between perspectives. First-person perspective requires pronouns like *me* or *our.* Second-person perspective requires pronouns like *you* or *your.* Third-person perspective uses pronouns like *his* or *their.*	This is *my* book. Are these *your* keys? I borrowed *her* umbrella.

How to solve Pronoun-antecedent Agreement questions?

⟫ Step 1

Identify pronoun-antecedent agreement questions: Answer options of pronoun-antecedent agreement questions will include both singular and plural forms of the same pronoun.

⟫ Step 2

Identify the antecedent: Underline the antecedent to help you clearly see what the pronoun should agree with in terms of number (singular or plural).

⟫ Step 3

Remember the different types of indefinite pronouns: Since indefinite pronouns can be plural or singular depending on the context, your best bet is to remember the different types of indefinite pronouns and their examples. The list, as given in the "Subject-verb Agreement" section, is short enough for you to have a strong grasp of all indefinite pronouns.

⟫ Step 4

Find singular or plural hints in the same sentence: Look for verbs associated with the pronoun. If the verb is singular, the corresponding pronoun should also be singular. This helps you make a connection between the verb and the correct pronoun form in terms of number agreement.

⟫ Step 5

Find the odd one out in the answer choices: If you encounter three answer options featuring singular pronouns and one option with a plural pronoun, it is reasonable to assume that the correct answer is the one with the plural pronoun. But if the antecedent is singular, you may not be able to differentiate between the three singular pronouns. Therefore, while this tip is helpful if you cannot identify the main antecedent, use this as a last resort.

⟨?⟩ Let's solve a Pronoun-antecedent Agreement question:

Past Lives is a 2023 American romantic drama film directed by Celine Song based on Song's personal experiences. The movie follows the story of Nora, a rising author living in New York who reconnects with her South Korean childhood love interest, Hae-sung. In the presence of Nora's husband Arthur, both Nora and Hae-sung grapple with _____ memories of the past and hopes for the future.

Which choice completes the text so that it conforms to the conventions of Standard English?

A) their

B) his

C) its

D) our

The **antecedent can be identified** as "both", which is a plural pronoun. In this passage, also notice that the plural verb "grapple" is associated with the pronoun phrase "both Nora and Hae-sung". We can safely confirm that the pronoun "both" is plural.

In the answer choices, there are two plural antecedents: "their" and "our". "Their" is a third-person perspective pronoun, while "our" is a first-person perspective pronoun. This passage is written from a third-person perspective, so the correct answer is **Choice A.**

Choice B is incorrect because the singular pronoun "his" doesn't agree in number with the plural antecedent "both".

Choice C is incorrect because the singular pronoun "its" isn't typically used to refer to a person and also doesn't agree with the plural antecedent "both".

Choice D is incorrect because the plural first-person pronoun "our" doesn't agree with the third-person perspective of the sentence.

Finally, attempting to **identify the odd one out among the answer choices** proves challenging in this case. The reason is that two choices (A and D) are plural, while the other two (B and C) are singular. Therefore, this particular strategy cannot be applied to distinguish the correct answer.

Exercises

For the following sentences, fill in the antecedent that matches the relevant pronoun to complete the sentence.

1. Bethany, after a long day at work, walked towards ____ car.

2. The committee members submitted ____ reports to the chairperson.

3. The company announced ____ decision to expand globally.

4. A teacher, respected by all, should conduct ____ self with professionalism.

5. The guard dog, known for ____ ferocity, was surprisingly gentle with the baby.

6. Each department handled ____ numerous tasks efficiently.

7. The students, excited about the trip, packed ____ bags early.

8. Both scientists conducted ____ experiments with precision and care.

9. You said you wanted to bring ____ tools to the workshop.

10. While the documents are shared, I am responsible for editing __ own mistakes.

11. The boy walked away before the teacher could give ____ the homework for the day.

12. The task will be time-consuming, so my parents are advising me not to commit to ____.

Answers

1. her

2. their

3. its

4. his or her

5. its

6. its

7. their

8. their

9. your

10. my

11. him

12. it

Form, Structure, and Sense III: Verb Forms

Verb Forms questions on the SAT typically assess your understanding of verb tenses and proper verb usage. You will be asked to choose among various verb forms to complete the sentence.

While you should already be familiar with past, present, and future tenses, there are more variations of each tense based on the particular scenario. These variations include simple, perfect, progressive, and perfect-progressive. Study the table below to understand the rules and examples. Memorizing the verb form name is neither required nor productive, but focus on understanding when to use each verb form. In general, **the more you read, the more intuitive and familiar it will be for you to identify the correct verb form.**

	Past	**Present**	**Future**
Simple	Describes completed actions in the past	Describes actions that are happening now, habitual actions, or general truths	Describes actions that will happen in the future
	They visited Paris last year.	*He plays the piano every day.*	*We will meet tomorrow.*
Perfect	Describes actions completed before another past action	Describes actions that were completed in the past but have relevance in the present	Describes actions that will be completed before a future point
	She had left by the time I arrived.	*I have watched that movie before.*	*We will have graduated by the end of the year.*
Progressive	Describes actions that were ongoing in the past	Describes actions that are currently in progress	Describes ongoing actions that will be happening at a specific point in the future
	I was cooking last weekend.	*She is studying now.*	*We will be celebrating the new year.*
Perfect-progressive	Describes ongoing actions that were happening before another past action	Describes ongoing actions that started in the past and continue into the present	Describes ongoing actions that will continue up to a future point
	When they arrived, I had been waiting for an hour.	*I have been working on the project for hours.*	*By the end of the month, he will have been working here for a year.*

In order to identify the correct verb form, you must first identify the subject the verb is corresponding to. Revisit the section on Subject-verb Agreement if needed to remember how to identify the main subject when there are several nouns in the sentence. Since the SAT can include many additional words and phrases to distract you from the main subject, cross out prepositional phrases and modifiers to focus on the main subject.

How to solve Verb Forms questions?

Step 1

Identify verb form questions: Answer options of verb forms questions will offer various verb tenses. Differentiating Subject-verb Agreement questions from Verb Forms questions is particularly valuable because it can be convoluting to think about both tense and singular or plural forms. Identifying the type of question right away will enable you to look out for specific clues and employ the relevant strategies.

Step 2

Identify the main subject: Cross out modifiers and prepositional phrases to help identify the main subject. Reference the Subject-verb Agreement section for definitions and examples of modifiers and prepositional phrases.

Step 3

Use the other verbs in the paragraph as clues: Most paragraphs will keep a consistent tense throughout the entire text. If you notice all the verb tenses are simple present tenses, you should most likely choose the simple present tense in the answer options. To easily identify the verb tenses, underline the verbs as you scan through the paragraph. Of course, there are paragraphs where there is a shift in time period or scenario, so read the paragraph carefully.

Step 4

Look for keywords to indicate shifts in timing: If the paragraph has a shift in timing, there will be words that convey this shift. Such words could be exact dates or timings, prepositions like "before" or "after", and phrases like "in the past" or "tomorrow". If you spot these keywords, pay attention to what sort of change is being indicated to choose the correct verb form.

Do not focus on choosing between singular or plural forms: Remember that verb form questions will test your knowledge of verb tenses, not singular or plural verbs. Do not get distracted and spend time trying to decide whether the verb should be singular or plural.

---

⑦ Let's solve a Verb Forms question:

DevOps stands for Development Operations. A DevOps team in a technology company consists of developers and IT operations professionals who enhance the efficiency and excellence of software deployment. In a DevOps model, the traditional separation between development and operations teams is dissolved. In some cases, these teams _____ into a unified entity, where engineers work across all stages of the application lifecycle, including development, testing, deployment, and operations.

Which choice completes the text so that it conforms to the conventions of Standard English?

A) merged

B) will merge

C) had merged

D) merge

Since the answer options consist of various verb tenses, we know we are being tested on verb forms here.

In this question, the **main subject** is quite clear since there are not many modifiers or prepositions thrown into the mix. The verb form we need to choose corresponds with the main subject "teams".

Now, let's scan through the paragraph so we can refer to the **other verb tenses** for consistency. The text includes verbs like "stands", "consists", "is", and "work", which are all simple present tenses. There are both singular and plural verbs included, but we do not need to focus on these details for verb forms questions.

While we have already identified simple present to be the predominant tense used throughout the paragraph, we should check if there are any **shifts in timing** in the paragraph to be sure because a part of the paragraph may discuss an event in the past or future. However, there do not seem to be any keywords or phrases that indicate a shift in timing. In fact, the whole paragraph is discussing the role and responsibilities of DevOps teams in the present tense.

To find the best answer, we can now label the verb tense of each of the answer options.

- **Choice A:** simple past tense to indicate that the merging of the teams occurred in the past.

- **Choice B:** simple future tense to indicate that the merging of the teams will happen in the future.

- **Choice C:** past perfect tense to indicate that the merging of the teams had already been completed before another action.

- **Choice D:** simple present tense to indicate that the merging of the teams is happening now or is a regularly occurring, habitual action.

Choice D is the correct tense that matches the context of the paragraph.

This question is a good example of why you often need to refer to the rest of the sentence or paragraph for context clues. Is it possible for the merging of the teams to happen in the future rather than being described as a habitual event? Absolutely. Imagine if the sentence below was used in the question.

> In some cases, these teams _____ into a unified entity, where engineers **will work** across all stages of the application lifecycle, including development, testing, deployment, and operations.

In this case, the correct answer would be **Choice B** (will merge) to match the simple future tense of "will work". Since logically thinking about the meaning of a sentence cannot help in eliminating answer choices, the point is to understand the specific context and timing of the paragraph.

Exercises

For the following sentences, pick the correct verb form to complete the sentence.

1. My grandfather builds/built this house in the 1950s.

2. By the time I finish my degree, I have studied/will have studied for four years.

3. We will not/would not start the meeting until everyone arrives.

4. Sarah travels/had traveled to many countries before she turned 25.

5. I had not seen/have not seen that movie yet, but I plan to watch it soon.

6. When the teacher came into the room, the students start/had already started the test.

7. The company does not make/did not make any profit until last year.

8. Domestic cats will have slept/sleep a lot during the day.

9. Will/would the team and I meet tomorrow or the day after that?

10. Despite his busy schedule, my father plays/played the guitar on a daily basis.

11. Throughout the last week, I cook/cooked at home every single day.

12. They will travel/travel to Europe next summer for two months.

Answers

1.	built	7.	did not
2.	will have studied	8.	sleep
3.	will not	9.	Will
4.	had traveled	10.	plays
5.	have not seen	11.	cooked
6.	had already started	12.	will travel

Form, Structure, and Sense IV: Subject-modifier Placement

Subject-modifier Placement questions assess your proficiency in recognizing and appropriately placing subject modifiers within a sentence. **Modifiers are words or phrases that provide additional information about the subject in a sentence.** We explored some examples of modifiers in the section on subject-verb agreement. This section is important because proper subject-modifier placement is crucial for maintaining clarity and coherence in the sentence.

 Remember

Modifiers must be placed **directly next** to the subject it modifies. In subject-modifier placement questions, the answer options mostly sound correct in terms of the meaning conveyed by the sentence. Therefore, since reading the sentence out loud or in your head may not help distinguish the correct answer, you must look at the sentence structure and the placement of the words.

Let's explore some incorrect examples and identify the errors. For each example, we will underline the modifier to help break down the sentence structure.

<u>Walking through the forest</u>, the old tree caught my attention. ✗

The subject directly following the modifier is "the old tree." In other words, the old tree is walking through the forest, which is logically incorrect. The subject that is actually walking through the forest should be the first-person subject "I."

<u>Walking through the forest,</u> I noticed the old tree. ✓

While the sentence could be rephrased in other ways, the subject "I" must be used after the modifier to follow the conventions of Standard English. Here is another example:

The cat slept on the warm laptop, <u>purring loudly.</u> ✗

Note that the modifier will not always be at the start of the sentence. In this case, the modifier "purring loudly" is placed directly after the subject of the "laptop". It doesn't make much sense for a laptop to be purring loudly, and the sentence clearly implies that the cat should be the one purring loudly. We can either move the modifier to the start of the sentence or rephrase the sentence so that the subject of the "cat" is directly before the modifier "purring loudly".

<u>Purring loudly,</u> the cat slept on the warm laptop. ✓

The warm laptop was covered by the cat, <u>purring loudly</u>. ✓

Both options are correct. Since the SAT is composed of multiple-choice questions, you will never have to rephrase a sentence on your own, but being able to do so through practice and repetition will enhance your expertise in subject-modifier placement.

How to solve Subject-modifier Placement questions?

⟫ Step 1

Identify subject-modifier placement questions: Answer options of subject-modifier placement questions will consist mostly of the same words placed in various orders.

⟫ Step 2

Focus on the sentence with the blank: Typically, all the information you need to answer subject-modifier placement questions will be contained within the sentence with the underlined blank. Therefore, do not waste time trying to read and understand the full paragraph unless you are unable to eliminate any answer option and need more context.

⟫ Step 3

Identify the modifier: Underline the modifier to help you clearly see what is being used to describe the subject. Understanding the modifier will allow you to easily eliminate the answer choices that are nonsensical. For example, if an inanimate subject is described to be physically moving, you can safely assume the subject-modifier placement is wrong.

⟫ Step 4

Identify the correct subject: In some difficult subject-modifier placement questions, it will be tricky to identify the subject in each answer option because of additional prepositions or possessive nouns. You can refer back to the tips on how to identify the main subject from the subject-verb agreement section and check the next section on plural and possessive nouns for additional tips.

⟫ Step 5

Plug in each subject: Each answer option should provide an option for the subject that should be modified. Try plugging in each subject one by one and evaluating which one makes the most logical sense based on the meaning conveyed by the sentence.

⑦ Let's solve a Subject-modifier Placement question now:

In a recent study, scientists have found that Caribbean box jellyfish are able to learn from past experiences and adjust their behavior accordingly. This finding may be surprising to those who know that jellyfish do not have a centralized brain like most animals and humans. In a tank with artificial markings to represent mangrove roots, _____ The results show that jellyfish are able to use visual and sensory information to mentally associate the dark "roots" with obstacles to be avoided.

Which choice completes the text so that it conforms to the conventions of Standard English?

A) the scientists observed how the jellyfish avoided colliding into the "roots" four times more than at the start of the experiment.

B) the observation that the jellyfish avoided colliding into the "roots" four times more than at the start of the experiment was made.

C) the jellyfish were able to avoid colliding into the "roots" four times more than at the start of the experiment

D) the experiment showed that the jellyfish avoided colliding into the "roots" four times more than at the start of the experiment.

First off, we can tell that this question is testing subject-modifier placement because the answer options consist of similar phrases placed in different orders.

Time to **focus on the sentence** in question and **underline the modifier.**

<u>In a tank with artificial markings to represent mangrove roots,</u> _____

Since the modifier is a bit long, we can focus on the key parts of the modifier. The subject we choose should be "in a tank" and have "artificial markings."

Now we can **plug in each subject** from the answer options, one at a time.

> **Choice A:** <u>In a tank with artificial markings to represent mangrove roots,</u> the scientists observed how the jellyfish avoided colliding into the "roots" four times more than at the start of the experiment.

The subject linked to the modifier here is the "scientists". Does it make sense for the scientists to be in a tank with artificial markings? Since we are not in a time crunch during practice, we can read the full paragraph to gain more context. You'll find that the paragraph describes an experiment being conducted by scientists to study jellyfish. With this context, it is more likely for the jellyfish to be in the tank as the subject being studied. For now, we can eliminate Choice A due to incorrect subject-modifier placement.

> **Choice B:** <u>In a tank with artificial markings to represent mangrove roots,</u> the observation that the jellyfish avoided colliding into the "roots" four times more than at the start of the experiment was made.

"The observation" is the subject the modifier is describing. This illogically suggests that the observation is the one in the tank. Since an observation is an abstract, nonphysical subject that likely cannot be in a tank, we can eliminate Choice B.

> **Choice C:** <u>In a tank with artificial markings to represent mangrove roots,</u> the jellyfish were able to avoid colliding into the "roots" four times more than at the start of the experiment.

We have finally found a choice with the subject "the jellyfish" placed right after the modifier. This seems like the best choice so far because the jellyfish are in the tank during the experiment.

> **Choice D:** <u>In a tank with artificial markings to represent mangrove roots,</u> the experiment showed that the jellyfish avoided colliding into the "roots" four times more than at the start of the experiment.

To be sure, we should check Choice D to safely eliminate all other choices. The subject being described by the modifier here is "the experiment." Again, an experiment is a nonphysical subject. Choice D also illogically suggests that the experiment is placed in a tank, so we can also eliminate this choice and conclude that Choice C is the best answer.

Exercises

For the following sentences, underline the modifier.

1. In a remote area of the jungle, the team of researchers discovered a new species of butterfly in the rainforest.

2. The city skyline, visible only on a clear night, glittered with a thousand lights.

3. The royal banquet was prepared by the chef, a well-known local celebrity.

4. After months of rigorous training, the hikers embarked on their month-long journey to South America.

For the following sentences, underline the subject being modified. Your answer should only be one word.

5. Lost in thought, the professor, a renowned expert in his field, failed to notice the students leaving the lecture hall.

6. The old house at the end of the street, abandoned for decades, was rumored to be haunted.

7. Overwhelmed by the sudden influx of orders, the small family-owned restaurant struggled to keep up with demand.

8. Hidden among the clutter on the desk, the key to the mysterious locked drawer remained elusive.

9. Surrounded by adoring fans, the actress, wearing an elegant gown, gracefully accepted her award.

10. At the top of the mountain, shrouded in mist, lay the ancient ruins of a civilization long forgotten.

11. In the center of the garden, surrounded by blooming flowers, stood a statue of a forgotten hero.

12. Despite the late hour, the CEO with a tireless work ethic was still in her office reviewing reports.

13. During the quarterly meeting, the head of the sales department announced a new company policy.

Answers

1. <u>In a remote area of the jungle,</u> the team of researchers discovered a new species of butterfly in the rainforest.

2. The city skyline, <u>visible only on a clear night,</u> glittered with a thousand lights.

3. The royal banquet was prepared by the chef, <u>a well-known local celebrity.</u>

4. <u>After months of rigorous training,</u> the hikers embarked on their month-long journey to South America.

5. Lost in thought, the <u>professor,</u> a renowned expert in his field, failed to notice the students leaving the lecture hall.

6. The old <u>house</u> at the end of the street, abandoned for decades, was rumored to be haunted.

7. Overwhelmed by the sudden influx of orders, the small family-owned <u>restaurant</u> struggled to keep up with demand.

8. Hidden among the clutter on the desk, the <u>key</u> to the mysterious locked drawer remained elusive.

9. Surrounded by adoring fans, the <u>actress</u>, wearing an elegant gown, gracefully accepted her award.

10. At the top of the mountain, shrouded in mist, lay the ancient <u>ruins</u> of a civilization long forgotten.

11. In the center of the garden, surrounded by blooming flowers, stood a <u>statue</u> of a forgotten hero.

12. Despite the late hour, the <u>CEO</u> with a tireless work ethic was still in her office reviewing reports.

13. During the quarterly meeting, the <u>head</u> of the sales department announced a new company policy.

Form, Structure, and Sense V: Plural and Possessive Nouns

The SAT includes questions related to **Plural and Possessive Nouns,** focusing on the accurate utilization of plural forms of nouns and possessive forms of nouns, with a specific emphasis on the correct use and placement of apostrophes.

1. **A plural noun refers to a word that indicates more than one person, place, thing, or idea.** In English, most plural nouns are formed by adding -s to the singular form. However, irregular nouns may have unique plural forms. In the context of grammar, recognizing and using the correct plural form is crucial for maintaining proper agreement within sentences.

2. **A possessive noun shows ownership or possession of something.** In English, possessive nouns are formed by adding an apostrophe and "s" to the singular form, and for plural nouns ending in -s, only an apostrophe is added.

In summary, there are distinct use cases for each noun; while plural nouns are used to indicate more than one entity, possessive nouns show ownership or possession. A comprehensive understanding of these principles is essential for success in navigating questions related to Plural and Possessive Nouns.

 Review and Remember the Different Types of Plural and Possessive Nouns below:

Type	Rule	Example
Plural nouns	To form regular plurals, add -s to the singular noun.	Book → Books
Irregular plural nouns	Some nouns have irregular plural forms that do not follow the typical -s rule.	Child → Children Foot → Feet
Singular possessive nouns	To form the possessive of a singular noun, add an apostrophe and -s.	Book → Book's
Plural possessive nouns	To form the possessive of a plural noun ending in -s, add only an apostrophe.	Books → Books'
Irregular plural possessive nouns	For irregular plural nouns, add an apostrophe and -s to the plural form.	Children → Children's Feet → Feet's
Possessive pronouns	Be aware that possessive pronouns do not use apostrophes.	Its His Hers Theirs Ours

If you are not confident in your knowledge of irregular plural forms, here are some additional helpful guidelines and examples to review. Note that these guidelines do not apply in all cases.

Rule	Singular	Plural
Words ending in -f or -fe change to -ves	knife	knives
	leaf	leaves
Words ending in -o take on extra -es	potato	potatoes
	hero	heroes
Words with oo vowels change to ee	goose	geese
	tooth	teeth
Words ending in -us change to -i	fungus	fungi
	cactus	cacti
Words ending in -is change to -es	analysis	analyses
	crisis	crises
Words ending in -on change to -a	phenomenon	phenomena
	criterion	criteria
Some words don't change at all	fish	fish
	sheep	sheep
	shrimp	shrimp

How to solve Plural and Possessive Nouns questions?

Step 1

Identify plural and possessive noun questions: Answer options of plural and possessive noun questions will include variations in the use of apostrophes.

Step 2

Determine if the noun(s) should be singular or plural: Assess whether the noun in question should be singular or plural. If the latter is the case, consider whether regular plural forms (typically formed by adding -s) or irregular plural forms are applicable.

Step 3

Determine if there is ownership or possession: Determine whether the context implies ownership or possession. Should one noun belong to the other? This is crucial in understanding whether a possessive noun is needed.

Step 4

Use the rest of the sentence for hints: For example, if you are having trouble deciding whether a noun should be plural or singular, check if there is a verb that matches the noun. Adhering to the principle of subject-verb agreement, if a plural verb is employed, it strongly suggests that the noun in question should also be in the plural form. The same logic goes for singular verbs matching with singular nouns.

Let's solve a Plural and Possessive Nouns question now:

The red-eyed tree frog is a tree frog native to the rainforests of Central and South America. Known for their red eyes, green color, and orange feet, red-eyed tree frogs lay their eggs on the underside of leaves that overhang pools or streams. After the _____ hatch, the tadpoles fall into the water where they continue to grow.

Which choice completes the text so that it conforms to the conventions of Standard English?

A) frogs eggs

B) frogs' egg's

C) frogs egg's

D) frogs' eggs

This is clearly a plural and possessive noun question because the answer options only differ in the use and placement of apostrophes.

For practice, let's decipher the meaning conveyed by each of the answer choices.

- **Choice A:** Multiple frogs and multiple eggs

- **Choice B:** Multiple frogs owning a single egg, which also holds possession of something else

- **Choice C:** Multiple frogs and a single egg, which holds possession of something else

- **Choice D:** Multiple frogs owning multiple eggs

While this breakdown is good practice in recognizing plural and possessive nouns, evaluating the answer choices in isolation is not as helpful as reading the paragraph to understand the context.

After reading the paragraph, we understand that there should be a **relationship of ownership** present for the word "frogs" because the paragraph is about the eggs belonging to the frogs. Since there are no pronouns present in the answer options, we know that we will need an apostrophe to indicate the possessive relationship of the eggs belonging to the frogs. Therefore, we can eliminate **Choices A** and **C** because they do not contain any apostrophe for the word "frogs". **Choices B** and **D** use the plural possessive form of "frogs'", keeping the -s to indicate the plural form and adding an apostrophe at the end after s to suggest possession.

Next, there should not be any **possession or ownership** for the word "eggs" because the word "hatch" is used as a verb, not a noun. Therefore, we can eliminate Choices B and C because they incorrectly attach an apostrophe in the word "eggs." The only remaining option D.

To recap, **Choice D** correctly indicates that there are multiple frogs that possess multiple eggs. An apostrophe is only required for "frogs'" to convey the frogs' ownership of the eggs. You may notice that in this question, we are not asked to choose between singular and plural forms because all the answer options include plural nouns with -s at the end. Thus, we solely focused on the usage of possessive nouns in this question.

Even though we are not being tested to discern singular or plural forms, observe that the verb "hatch" in this sentence serves as a crucial hint. "Hatch" is a plural verb. Therefore, the noun that is associated with the verb ("eggs") should be plural rather than singular.

Exercises

For the following sentences, choose the correct noun to follow the plural and possessive rules outlined in this chapter.

1. The childrens' toys/children's toys were scattered across the yard.

2. The cat's whiskers'/cat's whiskers, glistening in the sunlight, twitched with alertness and curiosity.

3. The boy's shoes/boys' shoes were thrown by the door in their haste to get outside and play.

4. My mother's house/mothers' house, nestled at the end of the street, was a grand old mansion in need of some loving care.

5. The squirrel decided to store the collection of nuts and seeds in its burrow/it's burrow.

6. Are the piles of books on the second shelf hers or ours/her's or our's?

7. The shoes were designed to support the feet's/feets' natural arches.

8. The dog wagged its/its' tail happily, anticipating the walk it knew was coming.

9. The horses/horse's mane, flowing in the wind, added to its majestic appearance.

10. The geeses'/geese's migration route took them over several countries.

11. The men's basketball games/mens basketball game's will take place over the next three days, with two games scheduled each day.

12. The car is ours/ours', a reliable companion on our many adventures.

Answers

1. children's toys	7. feet's
2. cat's whiskers	8. its
3. boys' shoes	9. horse's
4. mother's house	10. geese's
5. its burrow	11. men's basketball games
6. hers or ours	12. ours

1 🔖 **Mark for Review**

Chorus frogs, also referred to as swamp tree frogs or swamp cricket frogs, _____ a group of tree frogs within the *Hylidae* family. These frogs are primarily terrestrial and inhabit dense herbaceous growth and low shrubs. Unlike many other hylid frogs, they are not particularly skilled climbers. Chorus frogs are characterized by their trilling calls and a distinct light streak along the upper lip.

Which choice completes the text so that it conforms to the conventions of Standard English?

A) constitute

B) constitutes

C) have constituted

D) are constituting

2 🔖 **Mark for Review**

Fair Isle, one of_____, is situated between the mainland of Shetland and the Orkney Islands. This unique isle covers an area of 3 square miles and ranks as the 10th largest among the Shetland Islands. The majority of its population, approximately 60 islanders, live in crofting communities and engage in agricultural activities primarily in the southern part of the island.

Which choice completes the text so that it conforms to the conventions of Standard English?

A) the UK's most isolated inhabited islands

B) the UK's most isolated inhabited island

C) the UKs most isolated inhabited island

D) the UK's most isolated inhabited island's

3 🔖 **Mark for Review**

Residents and visitors in Singapore often complain about the high cost of living with an emphasis on food prices. This is not a surprising claim: the majority of food in Singapore has to be imported since the country has limited space for agriculture. However, since 2019, Singapore _____ on its goal to use less than 1% of its land to produce 30% of food locally by 2030.

Which choice completes the text so that it conforms to the conventions of Standard English?

A) has been progressing

B) progressed

C) had been progressing

D) will progress

4 🔖 **Mark for Review**

Work in the past few years by geologists and biologists show that the Amazonian drainage system, which includes some of the largest rivers in the world, is dynamic, and that _____ rearrangements lead to changes in the distribution ranges of species. Current species ranges thus hold information about how the Amazonian landscape has changed over time.

Which choice completes the text so that it conforms to the conventions of Standard English?

A) its

B) it's

C) their

D) they're

5 ▢ **Mark for Review**

One of the defining features of Renaissance literature was its newfound interest in human emotions and motivations. Writers _____ into the complexities of human nature, often through the lens of tragic heroes and complex characters, revealing the depths of the human psyche. There was a definite shift from the dominant religious themes of the Middle Ages to a greater focus on human experiences and exploration of the human potential.

Which choice completes the text so that it conforms to the conventions of Standard English?

A) will delve

B) are delving

C) delved

D) delve

6 ▢ **Mark for Review**

While women have often lacked cultural influence, they have consistently represented the most significant consumer demographic for recorded sound, from the rise of Emile Berliner's grooved shellac discs as the preferred medium in the 1890s, to other subsequent forms of physical media. As noted critic Isaac Goldberg once said, "Our popular song, in its industrial phase, _____ largely under the influence of women."

Which choice completes the text so that it conforms to the conventions of Standard English?

A) begin

B) is beginning

C) begins

D) are beginning

7 ▢ **Mark for Review**

All the Light We Cannot See is _____ that centers around two characters who meet during World War II. Marie-Laure Leblanc, a blind French girl, and Werner Pfennig, a German boy who ultimately becomes a soldier, are the protagonists of the novel.

Which choice completes the text so that it conforms to the conventions of Standard English?

A) one of Anthony Doerrs most recognized novel's

B) one of Anthony Doerr's most recognized novels

C) one of Anthony Doerr's most recognized novel's

D) one of Anthony Doerr's most recognized novel

8 ▢ **Mark for Review**

Artificial grass, commonly known as AstroTurf after its installation in the Astrodome in Houston, Texas, gained initial attention. However, naturalist Iolo Williams argues that artificial grass is highly detrimental to the environment due to the materials it utilizes, posing various ecological concerns. Often containing heavy metals, benzene, and other carcinogens, _____.

Which choice completes the text so that it conforms to the conventions of Standard English?

A) rubber granules from recycled tires are also used in the process of making artificial grass, the bane of environmentalists across the globe.

B) environmentalists across the globe despise the rubber granules from recycled tires also used in the process of making artificial grass.

C) artificial grass also uses rubber granules from recycled tires, the bane of environmentalists across the globe.

D) recycled tires are the bane of environmentalists across the globe.

9 ☐ Mark for Review

A research team has found that mushrooms and other fungi stay cooler than their surroundings. Some species, like the star-footed amanita, were just 1° C or 2° C cooler, but the mushroom Pleurotus ostreatus was almost 6° C cooler. Moreover, 19 other species, including Brewer's yeast, the mold that makes penicillin, were also cool, particularly near the center of _____ colonies.

Which choice completes the text so that it conforms to the conventions of Standard English?

A) its

B) they're

C) their

D) it's

10 ☐ Mark for Review

In 1958, Billboard introduced its Hot 100 chart, documenting the songs that were rapidly selling off record store shelves, dominating jukeboxes, and resonating through radio airwaves. Nearly six decades later, the methods of music consumption and tracking a song's popularity _____, but the enduring power of music in our culture remains unchanged.

Which choice completes the text so that it conforms to the conventions of Standard English?

A) is evolving

B) have evolved

C) has evolved

D) will evolve

Answers & Explanations

1. **Level:** Easy | **Skill/Knowledge:** Form, Structure, and Sense

    Key Explanation: Choice A is the correct answer. The convention being tested here is subject-verb agreement. The plural subject "Chorus frogs" agrees with the verb "constitute."

    Distractor Explanations: Choice B is incorrect because it uses the singular verb "constitutes," but the subject "Chorus frogs" is plural. Therefore, it does not agree with the subject in number. **Choice C** is incorrect because it implies a past action, but the context describes the general characteristics of chorus frogs, which is a general fact and not a specific event in the past. **Choice D** is incorrect because it uses the present continuous tense, "are constituting," which is not appropriate for describing the general characteristics of chorus frogs. It implies an ongoing or temporary action, which does not fit the context.

2. **Level:** Medium | **Skill/Knowledge:** Form, Structure, and Sense

    Key Explanation: Choice A is the correct answer. The convention being tested here is plurals and possessives. Choice A correctly uses an apostrophe in "UK's" to show possession and also uses the correct plural form "islands".

    Distractor Explanations: Choice B is incorrect because it uses the singular form "island," which does not accurately describe Fair Isle. It suggests that Fair Isle is the single most isolated inhabited island in the UK, which is not the intended meaning. **Choice C** is incorrect because it lacks the necessary apostrophe in "UK's." "UKs" is not a standard possessive form, so it does not convey the intended meaning. **Choice D** is incorrect because it introduces possessiveness unnecessarily with the additional "island's." The phrase "island's" is not needed to convey the intended meaning.

3. **Level:** Hard | **Skill/Knowledge:** Form, Structure, and Sense

    Key Explanation: Choice A is the best answer. The convention being tested here is verb forms. The present perfect-progressive verb form "has been progressing" correctly implies that Singapore's actions towards food security started in the past and continue into the present.

    Distractor Explanations: Choice B is incorrect because the simple past verb form "progressed" incorrectly suggests that Singapore's actions are already completed in the past. **Choice C** is incorrect because the past perfect-progressive verb form "had been progressing" incorrectly implies that the ongoing actions of Singapore were happening before in the past, but they are no longer in action anymore. **Choice D** is incorrect because the simple future verb form "will progress" incorrectly implies that Singapore's actions will happen in the future. However, they have started in the past and are ongoing.

4. **Level:** Medium | **Skill/Knowledge:** Form, Structure, and Sense

    Key Explanation: Choice A is the correct answer because the blank in the text needs to be a pronoun that explains whose arrangements led to changes. Since Choice A is the only pronoun in singular form that will point to the Amazonian drainage system, it is the correct answer.

    Distractor Explanations: Choice B is incorrect because it is a contraction for "it is," which does not explain whose arrangements led to changes. **Choices C** and **D** are both plural forms which cannot be used with a singular subject (the Amazonian drainage system).

5. **Level:** Medium | **Skill/Knowledge:** Form, Structure, and Sense

    Key Explanation: Choice C is the best option. The convention being tested is verb forms. In the context of the sentence, it is referring to past actions of writers during the Renaissance period.

The word "delved" is the past tense form of the verb "delve," which means to explore or investigate deeply. The sentence is describing how writers in the Renaissance delved into the complexities of human nature, indicating their past actions. Therefore, "delved" is the most appropriate choice to maintain tense agreement and ensure the sentence is grammatically correct.

Distractor Explanations: Choice A is incorrect because it suggests a future action, indicating that writers in the Renaissance will delve into the complexities of human nature. However, the sentence is discussing the past actions of Renaissance writers, so the use of "will" is incorrect. **Choice B** is incorrect because it uses the present progressive tense, indicating an ongoing action. However, the sentence is referring to the past actions of writers in the Renaissance, so the present tense is not appropriate. **Choice D** is incorrect because it uses the present simple tense form of the verb "delve". However, the sentence is discussing the past actions of Renaissance writers, and hence requires a past tense form of the verb.

6. **Level:** Medium | **Skill/Knowledge:** Form, Structure, and Sense

    Key Explanation: Choice C is the correct answer because it uses the simple present tense ("begins"), which is appropriate for a general statement of fact. The convention being tested is subject-verb agreement. Choice C creates a correct subject-verb agreement and accurately expresses that a popular song begins under the influence of women.

    Distractor Explanations: Choice A is incorrect because it creates a subject-verb agreement error. Since the subject is "popular song," which is singular, the verb should also be singular. "Begin" is not a singular verb. **Choice B** is incorrect because it uses the present continuous tense ("is beginning"), which suggests an ongoing action. However, the sentence is referring to a general statement about the influence of women on popular songs. **Choice D** is incorrect because it uses the present continuous tense ("are beginning") and denotes an ongoing action.

7. **Level:** Easy | **Skill/Knowledge:** Form, Structure, and Sense

   Key Explanation: Choice B is the correct answer. The convention being tested here is plurals and possessives. Plurals refer to nouns and pronouns that are more than one in number ("most recognized novels.") Possessives are nouns and pronouns that show possession and can usually be identified by the use of an apostrophe (Anthony Doerr's most recognized…). Choice B is correct because it correctly uses an apostrophe in the writer's name and uses the correct plural form of the word "novel."

   Distractor Explanations: Choice A is incorrect because it places an apostrophe after novel ("most recognized novel's"), which indicates an unnecessary possession. It also lacks the apostrophe in Anthony Doerr's name. **Choice C** is incorrect because there is an unnecessary use of an apostrophe in "novel's" (the correct plural of "novel" is "novels."). **Choice D** is incorrect because it does not use the plural form of the noun "novel," despite the text suggesting that *All the Light We Cannot See* is one of the many novels Anthony Doerr has written.

8. **Level:** Hard | **Skill/Knowledge:** Form, Structure, and Sense

   Key Explanation: Choice A is the best option. The convention being tested here is subject-modifier placement. Based on the information provided, it is the rubber granules from recycled tires that contain heavy metals, benzene, and other carcinogens. Therefore, the modifier ("Often containing heavy metals, benzene, and other carcinogens") is correctly placed next to the subject ("rubber granules".)

   Distractor Explanations: Choice B is incorrect because the modifier is incorrectly placed next to "environmentalists", therefore illogically suggesting that environmentalists contain heavy metals, benzene, and other carcinogens. **Choice C** is incorrect because it implies that artificial grass contains heavy metals, benzene,

   and other carcinogens. While this sentence does make grammatical sense, the previous sentence talks about the ingredients artificial grass uses. Therefore, we can reasonably infer that the subject of the next sentence would be an ingredient, aka, rubber granules. **Choice D** is incorrect because it is not the recycled tires that contain heavy metals, benzene, and other carcinogens.

9. **Level:** Hard | **Skill/Knowledge:** Form, Structure, and Sense

   Key Explanation: The correct answer is **Choice C.** The convention being tested here is pronoun-antecedent agreement. The noun/noun phrase in the sentence to be completed is a plural (19 other species). Therefore, a plural pronoun must also be used to correctly complete the sentence. Only Choice C uses the correct plural pronoun.

   Distractor Explanations: Choice A is incorrect because 'its' is a singular form that cannot be used with plural nouns. **Choice B** is incorrect because "they're" stands for "they are" and cannot be used with a plural noun (19 kinds of molds). **Choice D** is incorrect because "it's" is short for "it is", the usage of which does not make sense in this context.

10. **Level:** Medium | **Skill/Knowledge:** Form, Structure, and Sense

    Key Explanation: Choice B is the best choice. The convention being tested is verb forms. The sentence is referring to the past and present changes in the "methods" of music consumption and tracking song popularity. Therefore, the present perfect tense "have evolved" is more appropriate to use with the plural "methods."

    Distractor Explanations: Choice A is incorrect because "is" does not agree with the plural "methods." **Choice C** is incorrect because "has" does not agree with the plural "methods." **Choice D** is incorrect because the usage of "will" denotes an event in the future. However, the sentence mentions an event that has already occurred since the introduction of the Hot 100 chart.

Chapter 7
Introduction to Math Section

The Math section of the new Digital SAT Suite of Assessments is quite similar to the old paper-and-pencil test but with some differences. First, three out of the four domains were retained with slight changes in their names. The 'Heart of Algebra' was changed to just **'Algebra'**, 'Passport to Advanced Math' was changed to **'Advanced Math'**, and the domain name **'Problem-Solving and Data Analysis'** was kept the same. The fourth domain, 'Additional Topics in Math' has been renamed **'Geometry and Trigonometry'**. In this fourth domain, complex numbers are no longer a requirement.

Another difference is the weight/importance of each domain. The domain-wise breakup is provided in the table below.

Algebra	Advanced Math	Problem-Solving and Data Analysis	Geometry and Trigonometry
35%	35%	35%	15%

There were two sections for the old paper SAT Math: the calculator, and the non-calculator sections. On the new test, a **calculator is allowed** for the entire Math section, and a **digital graphing calculator powered by Desmos** is available to the test takers on the **Bluebook app**, the app on which you will take the test. You are also **allowed to bring your personal calculator.**

Another significant difference is the timing and the adaptivity of the test. The duration of the Math section was **reduced from 80 minutes to 70 minutes.** These 70 minutes are divided into **two equal parts: 35 minutes for each module.**

> **The Digital SAT is an adaptive test. Consequently, you will get a relatively easier or harder second module based on your performance on the first module.**

The College Board mentions that this change will affect your score, but specific details about the adaptive grading were not released.

Each Math module consists of **22 questions**, which is again different from the paper-and-pencil test. However, the scoring will still be done on a scale of 200 to 800. About 30% of questions are set in context, and you will see a variety of visuals that may accompany the questions. About 75% of the questions are multiple-choice, while 25% are student-produced response questions.

Multiple-choice questions have **four answer choices** and only **one correct answer.** Even if you do not have any idea about the answer, it's always better to guess than not answer the question.

> If you guess randomly, you will have a 25% chance of getting the correct answer. If you make an educated guess, you will have a higher chance of getting the correct answer which will raise your score.

Student-produced response questions contain blanks that need to be filled in by the test-taker. The guidelines for answering these questions are available on the Bluebook app.

- You should enter only one answer and no symbols ($, %, comma, etc.)

- You also **cannot enter a mixed number** like $4\frac{1}{5}$. You should enter it either as **an improper fraction** $\frac{21}{5}$ or as a **decimal** 4.2.

- If the answer is any number that does not fit in the available space, which is **5 characters for a positive answer** or **5 characters plus the negative sign** for a **negative answer,** you must either round off or cut (truncate) the decimal at the fifth character. Note that the **decimal point is counted as a character**.
For example, if the answer is 1.2446873, you should either enter 1.244 (truncating) or 1.245 (rounding off). If the answer is – 0.68492, you should either enter –0.684 (truncating with the leading zero), –0.685 (rounding off with the leading zero), or –0.6849 (truncating or rounding off without the leading zero).

What You Still Need to Know from High School Math

1. Starting with the **order of operations** commonly known as **PEMDAS**, you should first perform operations with **parentheses**, followed by **exponents** (including rational exponents known as roots), then proceed with **multiplication** and **division** from left to right, and finally **addition** and **subtraction** from left to right.

> **Note:** It is **critical** to **follow the order of operations** when performing calculations to get the correct answer.

P   Parentheses, Brackets, and Groupings

E   Exponents

M
D   Multiplication/Division
(perform left to right depending on which operation comes first)

A
S   Addition/Subtraction
(perform left to right depending on which operation comes first)

2. Secondly, you should also be familiar with the **commutative laws of addition and multiplication.** For any real numbers a and b, $a + b = b + a$, and $a \times b = b \times a$.

3. Another set of laws for addition and multiplication are the **associative laws**. For any real numbers a, b, and c, $(a + b) + c = a + (b + c)$, and $(a \times b) \times c = a \times (b \times c)$.

4. Another fundamental property is the distributive property which can be stated as follows: For any real numbers a, b, and c, $a(b \pm c) = ab \pm ac$, and $(a \pm b) \div c = a \div c \pm b \div c$. This property is commonly encountered in a fractional form $\frac{a \pm b}{c} = \frac{a}{c} \pm \frac{b}{c}$.

Basic properties of equalities

There are some basic properties of equalities that you need to know.

1. The **reflexive property of equality** states that any number is equal to itself. For any real number a, $a = a$.

2. The **symmetric property of equality** states that if two quantities are equal, it doesn't matter if you say that the first quantity is equal to the second, or the second quantity is equal to the first. For any a and b, if $a = b$, then $b = a$.

3. The **transitive property of equality** says that if a first quantity is equal to a second quantity, and this second quantity is equal to a third quantity, then the first quantity is equal to the third quantity. If $a = b$ and $b = c$, then $a = c$.

4. The **substitution property of equality** says that if two quantities are equal, you can substitute one for the other. If $a = b$ and $a = c$, then $b = c$.

Of course, you should be able to add, subtract, multiply, or divide any two real numbers, including fractions. Fractions are added or subtracted by finding the common denominator and combining the numerators. Fractions are multiplied straight across, with the numerator multiplied by the numerator and the denominator multiplied by the denominator. To divide one fraction by another, simply multiply the first fraction by the reciprocal of the second.

$$\text{Eg: } \frac{\left(\frac{1}{4} \right)}{\left(\frac{2}{5} \right)} = \frac{1}{4} \times \frac{5}{2} \quad (\frac{5}{2} \text{ is the reciprocal of the fraction } \frac{2}{5})$$

This rule can be applied to any division. Dividing by any number is the same as multiplying by its reciprocal.

From geometry, you need to know basic terms like a midpoint, acute angles (measuring less than 90°), right angles (measuring exactly 90°), obtuse angles (measuring more than 90°), straight angles (measuring exactly 180°), vertically opposite angles (any two opposite angles, equal in measure, created when two lines intersect) line, segment, ray, triangle, isosceles triangle (having two congruent sides and two congruent base angles), equilateral triangle (having three congruent sides and three congruent angles), and right triangle (having a 90° angle). You also need to know the segment addition and the angle addition postulate. If C is a point on $\overline{AB}$, then AC + CB = AB. If $\angle ACB$ and $\angle BCD$ share the same vertex C and the same leg $\overline{CB}$ but are on opposite sides of $\overline{CB}$, then $m\angle ACB + m\angle BCD = m\angle ACD$.

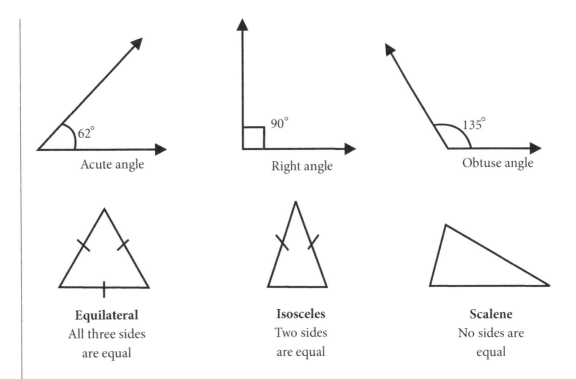

Acute angle	Right angle	Obtuse angle

Equilateral	**Isosceles**	**Scalene**
All three sides are equal	Two sides are equal	No sides are equal

Calculator

Throughout the Math section, you can access a built-in digital graphing calculator powered by Desmos. It has an input section on the left side and a coordinate plane display section (output) on the right side. This calculator is very powerful and can graph any function you enter into it. It also performs basic calculations.

There are hacks that can help you solve many questions quickly and correctly using the graphing calculator. For example, if you enter an equation or an inequality in the input section, the calculator will instantly display the solution, without you having to solve it algebraically.

Another powerful aspect of this calculator is that you don't need to manipulate the given information before entering it into the calculator. Even if the given expression is very complex with factors, roots, powers, and other terms, just enter it into the calculator as it is and let it work its charm!

The calculator is also able to graph parametric equations and functions. By this, we mean any expression that has an unknown quantity in addition to the variable. When you enter a letter such as 'm', 'a', or 'b', an option appears to create a slider for this quantity. You can then move the slider around to see how the expression on the display panel changes, as the quantity (m, a, or b) is varied. In many cases, you'll be able to choose the correct value for this quantity by simply moving the slider.

Familiarize yourself with the built-in graphing calculator well before the test day. Use it while you are solving practice questions. You can access a version of this calculator through the link: https://www.desmos.com/testing/cb-digital-Digital Digital SAT/graphing. You may also want to bring your personal hand-held calculator. Such calculators might be more convenient to perform basic calculations especially if you're already comfortable with using them. Ensure that your calculator is on the acceptable list of calculators from here: https://Digital Digital SATsuite.collegeboard.org/digital/what-to-bring-do/calculator-policy.

General Test-Taking Tips

For each Math question, the **average available time** is around a **minute and a half.** Some questions will require less than that, while others will require more. Nonetheless, try to **time yourself while practicing.** This will help you get used to solving the questions in the available time frame, so you don't rush the last set of questions when you realize you don't have much time left.

 Pro Tip -

If you encounter a question you don't feel confident solving, either mark it for review or simply pick one of the 4 answer choices and move on to the next one. Each question carries the same weightage and the time saved here can be better utilized elsewhere.

- -

There is no penalty for wrong answers, so even if you don't have any idea how to answer a specific question, it is always better to guess than to leave the answer blank. If you guess, you'll at least have a chance of getting the answer correct. Just remember not to spend too much time guessing, as managing your time is the key strategy to ensuring you get enough time to answer all questions.

When you encounter a difficult question, try to stay calm and do not panic! Stay positive and try to simplify the question by breaking it down into easier, more manageable parts. Use the process of elimination in the case of multiple-choice questions, and cross out choices that you know are incorrect. This will help you narrow down your focus to those options that might be correct. Finally, remember that it might make more sense to just skip the question if it's going to take a lot of time. This will help you keep going and reduce your stress. Keep in mind that you can always get back to the question if you have time available.

Another **important tool** that you might find useful is the provided **scratch paper. Writing down formulas** that you need, and **jotting down** any **notes** that come to your mind while solving a question might serve as a great memory aid. **Drawing down sketches** and annotating them can greatly help in solving geometry problems. Remember to keep your work on the scratch paper organized, as this will help you stay calm and maintain a positive mindset.

The key to getting your best score on the Digital SAT is to practice well before the exam. You learn Math by doing Math! If you dedicate enough time to practice solving Digital SAT-like questions, you'll feel more confident about tackling the real questions on the test day. That's why ample opportunities to practice are provided to you in this workbook. With the right guidance to supplement your efforts, we are confident you will achieve your target score!

Chapter 8
Algebra

Topics covered in this chapter:

- Linear Equations in One Variable
- Linear Equations in Two Variables
- Linear Functions
- Systems of Two Linear Equations in Two Variables
- Linear Inequalities in One or Two Variables

Algebra is one of the main topic domains tested in the Math section of the Digital SAT, accounting for about 35% of the total number of Math questions on the test. SAT Algebra tackles:

> Linear equations and Inequalities
> Systems of two linear equations in two variables
> Linear functions

Examples:

- If $3x + 18 = 27$, what is the value of x?

- If $12n < 49$ and $7n > 22$ and n is an integer, what is the value of n?

- If $y = 28.2 - 2.5x$, what are the coordinates of the y-intercept?

- If $p(n) = 2n - 2$ & $q(n) = 2 - p(n)$, what is the value of $q(2)$?

Algebra questions can be either multiple-choice or student-produced response questions. These questions range in difficulty and complexity. They can vary from basic drills and practice questions to complicated critical thinking questions with word problems.

> To nail this section, focus on developing a fundamental understanding of the frequently tested concepts, and strengthen your problem-solving skills.

Two strategies that are particularly helpful in solving many Algebra questions will be explained. Then, the details of different skills or knowledge points tested in this domain will be presented. Each skill will be broken down into bite-sized pieces to help you master the concepts gradually. It is recommended that you follow the order presented in the chapter and observe how your Mathematical knowledge builds upon itself as you progress.

 Rules to Remember while Solving Algebra Questions

- If $a = b$, then $a + c = b + c$ for any real numbers a, b, and c. This is known as the **Addition Property of Equality**.

- If $a = b$, then $a - c = b - c$ for any real numbers a, b, and c. This is known as the **Subtraction Property of Equality**.

- If $a = b$, then $ac = bc$ for any real numbers a, b, and c. This is known as the **Multiplication Property of Equality**.

- If $a = b$, then $ac = bc$ for any real numbers a, b, and non-zero c. This is known as the **Division Property of Equality**.

- For any real numbers a, b, and c, the following equality holds: $a(b \pm c) = ab \pm ac$. This is known as the **Distributive Property of Equality**.

- The **slope-intercept form** of the equation of a straight line is $y = mx + b$, where m **represents the slope** of the line and b **represents its y-intercept**.

- The **slope** of the **line**, $m = \dfrac{rise}{run} = \dfrac{y_B - y_A}{x_B - x_A}$ for **any two points A and B on the line**.

- The **point-slope form** of the equation of a straight line is $y - y_1 = m(x - x_1)$, where m represents the slope of the line, and the point $(x_1,\ y_1)$ is any point on the line.

- The **standard form** of the equation of a straight line is $ax + by = c$ where the slope $m = -\dfrac{a}{b}$ and the y-intercept is $\dfrac{c}{b}$.

- The **intercept form** of the equation of a straight line is $\dfrac{x}{a} + \dfrac{y}{b} = 1$, where a is the x-intercept of the line and b is the y-intercept.

- Any **vertical straight line** has an equation of the form $x = k$ where k is a constant.

- Any **horizontal straight** line has an equation of the form $y = k$ where k is a constant.

- If **two lines are parallel**, then they have the **same slope**.

- If **two lines are perpendicular,** then their **slopes are the opposite reciprocals** of one another. The product of the slopes of two perpendicular lines is −1.

- The **solution of a system of two linear equations** in two variables x and y, if it exists, is the **ordered pair** (x, y) which **represents the point of intersection** of the two straight lines representing the two system equations.

- If the **lines representing the system** of equations are **parallel**, then the system has **no solution**.

- If the **lines representing the system** of equations **coincide (same line)**, then the system has an **infinite number of solutions.**

- If $a < b$, then $a \pm c < b \pm c$ for any real numbers a, b, and c. The same rule applies to ≤, >, ≥ signs.

- If $a < b$, then $ac < bc$ if $c > 0$. The same rule applies to ≤, >, ≥ signs where the **inequality sign remains the same** when **both sides** are **multiplied** by the **same positive number.**

- If $a < b$, then $ac > bc$ if $c < 0$. The same rule applies to ≤, >, ≥ signs where the **inequality sign is flipped** when **both sides** are **multiplied** by the **same negative number.**

- The **previous two rules also apply** if you **divide both sides of an inequality** by a **non-zero number** c instead of multiplying.

- **Graphical solutions** of inequalities are shown on the screen of a graphing calculator as a **shaded region with either a solid limiting line** (in case of ≤ and ≥) or a **dashed limiting line** (in case of < and >). In the case of a **system of inequalities**, the **solution** is **represented by the overlapping region.**

Strategies

Two strategies that are particularly helpful in solving Algebra questions are **Going Backwards** and **Replacing**. These strategies will be explained and applied through solved examples in this chapter.

1. Going Backwards

This strategy is usually referred to as **"backsolving"**. It involves starting with the answer choices first. It is best utilized when the answer choices are numbers and the required calculations are clear to you.

Pro Tips -

Since the answer choices on the Digital SAT are usually arranged in ascending order, always start from the middle answer, choice B or C. Even if B or C is not the correct answer, it should give you a sense of whether you need to go higher or lower in many instances throughout this section.

- -

Let's take a look at some examples below:

 If $2(5x - 6) = -2(x + 3)$, what is the value of x?

A) 0

B) $\dfrac{1}{2}$

C) $\dfrac{3}{4}$

D) $\dfrac{5}{4}$

Solution: Of course, the above example can be solved mathematically, and the detailed solution will be shown later in this chapter. However, we will apply the **Going Backwards** strategy to solve this question.

Start by checking answer **Choice C.**

Substituting $\dfrac{3}{4}$ for x in the given equation yields $2\left(5 \times \dfrac{3}{4} - 6\right) = -2\left(\dfrac{3}{4} + 3\right)$.

Following the order of operations (**PEMDAS rule**), $2\left(\dfrac{15}{4} - 6\right) = -2\left(\dfrac{3}{4} + 3\right)$ can be rewritten as $2\left(\dfrac{-9}{4}\right) = -2\left(\dfrac{15}{4}\right)$.

This results in $\dfrac{-18}{4} = \dfrac{-30}{4}$, which is a **false statement** and thus $\dfrac{3}{4}$ **is not a solution** to this equation.

Nevertheless, you can see that the left-hand side $\dfrac{-18}{4}$ is greater than the right-hand side $\dfrac{-30}{4}$.

A little attention to the given equation $2(5x - 6) = -2(x + 3)$ allows you to notice that the left-hand side increases as x increases while the right-hand side decreases as x increases.

This gives you a sense of direction and you now know that the correct value of x is not $\frac{5}{4}$ because the left-hand side needs to be decreased and the right-hand side needs to be increased. Hence, you can **eliminate choice D**.

Now, you still have two choices to consider, 0 and $\frac{1}{2}$.

Since the number 0 is much easier to deal with in calculations, you should start by substituting 0 for x. This results in $2(0 - 6) = -2(0 + 3)$ or $-12 = -6$, which is again not true.

Therefore, **Choice A** is also **incorrect** and **Choice B** is the **correct answer.**

For practice, try substituting $\frac{1}{2}$ for x to verify that it is the solution to the given equation.

$$f(x) = 16x - 70$$

Given the function above, find the value of x when $f(x) = 90$.

A) -5

B) 3

C) 7

D) 10

Solution: Apply the **Going Backwards** strategy to solve this question by checking **Choice C** first.

It is given that $f(x) = 90$. Substituting this to the given function $f(x) = 16x - 70$ yields $90 = 16x - 70$.

Substituting x with 7 from Choice C results in $90 = 16(7) - 70$ or $90 = 42$. This is false and thus 7 is not the value of x.

Looking at this, you may notice that the right-hand side should be increased, hence, you can **eliminate Choices A and B** (Since -5 and 3 are less than 7).

The answer then should be **Choice D** and we can verify that by substituting 10 for x in the given function which yields $90 = 16(10) - 70$. This results in $90 = 90$, which is a true statement.

$$4x + 50 = 2(5x + 20)$$

Solve for the value of x.

A) $\dfrac{4}{3}$

B) $\dfrac{3}{2}$

C) $\dfrac{5}{3}$

D) $\dfrac{4}{2}$

Solution: Use the **Going Backwards** strategy to solve this question by checking the answer in **Choices B** or **C**. Start by checking **Choice B**.

Substituting $\dfrac{3}{2}$ for x in the given equation $4x + 50 = 2(5x + 20)$ yields

$4\left(\dfrac{3}{2}\right) + 50 = 2\left(5\left(\dfrac{3}{2}\right) + 20\right)$ and can be rewritten as $6 + 50 = 2\left(\dfrac{15}{2} + 20\right)$, following the order

of operations. Adding the left side and right side results in $56 = 2\left(\dfrac{55}{2}\right)$ or $56 = 55$, which is

incorrect, so 32 is not a solution to the given equation, and **Choice B** can be **eliminated**.

Looking at this result, you can see that the left-hand side is greater than the right-hand side and you may notice that both sides of the given equation increase as x increases and vice versa. But the right-hand side increases or decreases more than the left-hand side, therefore, **Choice A** can be **eliminated**.

You have 2 more choices to consider, $\dfrac{5}{3}$ and $\dfrac{4}{2}$. You can start by substituting **Choice C**, $\dfrac{5}{3}$ for x.

This results in $4\left(\dfrac{5}{3}\right) + 50 = 2\left(5\left(\dfrac{5}{3}\right) + 20\right)$ or $\dfrac{170}{3} = \dfrac{170}{3}$ which is the **correct answer**.

(?) The sum of three consecutive integers is 81. Find the product of the first two integers.

A) 702

B) 728

C) 756

D) 812

Solution: You should solve this question mathematically to save time and effort.

Let x represent the first integer. Consequently, $x + 1$ is the second integer and $x + 2$ is the third integer, since they are consecutive.

The equation will then become $x + (x + 1) + (x + 2) = 81$. Combining like terms yields $3x + 3 = 81$. Subtracting 3 from both sides results in $3x = 78$. Then divide both sides by 3 to get $x = 26$.

You have now found the value of the **first integer to be 26**. The **second integer** is $x + 1 = 26 + 1 = 27$ and the **third integer** is $x + 2 = 26 + 2 = 28$.

Now, to find the product of the first two integers, multiply 2627 which results in 702. The **answer**, therefore, is **702**.

It is better to solve this kind of question mathematically than using the Going Backwards strategy since it requires fewer steps compared to backsolving.

 A Word of Caution

There might be questions where simply solving the equation is a quicker and more efficient way of finding the answer. With extensive practice and some alertness, you should be able to determine which approach is more suitable for the given question.

2. Replacing

When all answer choices contain variables, and variables are also found in the question stem, a key strategy you might find useful is **replacing**. Simply **replace the variables with numbers that are easy to work with, and verify that all the conditions mentioned in the question are satisfied.** Beware of choosing numbers that might lead to incorrect conclusions such as 0 or 1. Moreover, do not choose numbers that contradict the conditions mentioned in the question stem. Check out the examples below:

$$3t - 4 \leq 23$$
Solve the given inequality.

A) $t \leq 3$

B) $t \leq 6$

C) $t \leq 9$

D) $t \leq 10$

Solution: To solve the inequality using the **Replacing** strategy, replace t with a positive value that will satisfy the given inequality. Replace t with 7 to get $3(7) - 4 \leq 23$ or $17 \leq 23$.

Since this satisfies the given inequality, you can eliminate **Choices A** and **B** which have values less than 7.

Choice D does not satisfy the given inequality since the value of t cannot be greater than or equal to 10.

Therefore, the **correct answer** is **Choice C**.

$$-\frac{5}{4} < \frac{1}{k}$$

In the given inequality, k is a non-zero real number. Which of the following must be true?

A) $k > -\dfrac{4}{5}$

B) $k < -\dfrac{4}{5}$

C) $k > -\dfrac{1}{4}$

D) $k \le -\dfrac{1}{4}$

Solution: To solve this question using the **Replacing** strategy, choose a value for k that satisfies the given inequality. Let's use $k = -1$.

Substituting -1 for k in the given inequality $-\dfrac{5}{4} < \dfrac{1}{k}$ yields $-\dfrac{5}{4} < \dfrac{1}{-1}$ or $-\dfrac{5}{4} < -1$ which is true.

Since $-1 < -\dfrac{4}{5} < -\dfrac{1}{4}$, then **Choices A and C can be eliminated.**

The equality sign for **Choice D** does not match the given inequality therefore **Choice D can be eliminated.**

The **correct answer** is **Choice B,** $k < -\dfrac{4}{5}$.

$$2(x + 5) - 5 < 19$$

What is the solution to the given inequality?

A) $x > 5$

B) $x < 5$

C) $x > 7$

D) $x < 7$

Solution: To solve this question using the **Replacing** strategy, choose a value for x that satisfies the given inequality $2(x + 5) - 5 < 19$.

Let's use $x = 6$.

Substituting 6 for x in the given inequality $2(x + 5) - 5 < 19$ yields $2(6 + 5) - 5 < 19$ or $17 < 19$ which is true.

Since $6 > 5$ and $6 < 7$, then **Choices B and C can be eliminated.**

You can already notice that **Choice D**, $x < 7$ satisfies the inequality but let us check choice A, if a value greater than 5 also satisfies the inequality.

Substitute $x = 8$ in the given inequality to get $2(8 + 5) - 5 < 19$ or $21 < 19$, which is false.

Consequently, **Choice A** can be **eliminated**.

Therefore, the **correct answer** is **Choice D**.

 Renting a car for a day costs $45 and a fee of $0.50 per mile driven. If a customer rented the car for a day and drove 180 miles, how much did they pay (in dollars)?

A) $100

B) $135

C) $155

D) $180

Solution: This is a question that should be solved **mathematically**, rather than using the **Replacing** strategy.

Let x be the number of miles driven and C be the total cost.

The given situation will be represented by the equation $C = 0.5x + 45$.

It is given that the customer drove 180 miles.

Substitute 180 for x in the equation to get $C = 0.5(180) + 45$ or $C = 135$.

Therefore, the **correct answer** is **Choice B**.

 A Word of Caution

There might be questions where replacing a variable with a particular value might satisfy more than one answer choice. In such cases, replace the variable with an alternative number and repeat the process.

Linear Equations in One Variable

Solving linear equations in one variable is a skill you should master for the Algebra section. While you still need to know the basic skills from your high school Algebra class like the order of operations (PEMDAS) and the basic laws of calculation, this part of the chapter will concentrate on solving linear equations in one variable using the laws of equality, and solving word problems that can be modeled into linear equations in one variable.

The Laws of Equality

The laws of equality include the **Addition, Subtraction, Multiplication,** and **Division Properties** of **Equality**. Simply put,

> You can add, subtract, multiply, or divide by the same number on both sides of an equation. **Beware that you CANNOT divide by zero,** which is an undefined operation.

In addition, other operations, like taking the square root on both sides, must be done very carefully keeping in mind that:

 Remember

Real square roots exist for **positive numbers only** and **every positive number** has **two square roots,** positive and negative.

Now, let's revisit the first example of this chapter which was previously solved using the **Going Backwards** strategy.

>   If $2(5x - 6) = -2(x + 3)$, what is the value of x?

A) 0

B) $\dfrac{1}{2}$

C) $\dfrac{3}{4}$

D) $\dfrac{5}{4}$

Solution: Applying the **Distributive Property of Multiplication** to the given equation yields $10x - 12 = -2x - 6$.

Adding $2x$ to both sides of this equation yields $12x - 12 = -6$.

Adding 12 to both sides of this equation results in $12x = 6$.

Dividing both sides of this equation by 12 yields $x = \dfrac{6}{12}$ which can be simplified into $x = \dfrac{1}{2}$.

Therefore, the correct answer is **Choice B.**

Choice A is incorrect and may result if the given equation is $2(5x - 6) = -2(x + 6)$.

Choice C is incorrect and may result if the given equation is $2(5x - 6) = -2\left(x + \dfrac{3}{2}\right)$.

Choice D is incorrect and may result if the given equation is $2(5x - 6) = -2\left(x - \dfrac{3}{2}\right)$.

Word Problems

As mentioned in the previous chapter, around 30% of the Math questions are written in context, which would be presented mostly as word problems. Some word problems can be modeled into linear equations in one variable. When tackling word problems on SAT Math, it is important to read the problem carefully, identify the quantities present, translate the given information into an equation, and sometimes solve the equation and interpret the results. Let's take a look at the student-produced response example below.

> Clara and Rana paid a **total of $1200 over 10 months** to get a fridge for their kitchen. **Clara paid twice as much as Rana did each month.** Supposing that the **monthly payments are equal,** how much did Clara pay, in dollars, for the fridge each month?

Solution: After reading the problem carefully, several quantities can be recognized. The total payment made by Clara and Rana is **$1200.** The duration of payment is **10 months. Identical payments** were made monthly, with **Clara paying twice as much as Rana each month.** The question is asking for the monthly payment made by Clara.

Let x represent the monthly payment made by Rana. Then $2x$ is the monthly payment made by Clara. The total monthly payment made by Rana and Clara is $x + 2x$.

A total payment of $1200 was made over a period of 10 months, then the equation $10(2x + x)$ = 1200 can be used to model the scenario.

Adding the terms inside the parentheses yields $10 \times 3x = 1200$, or $30x = 1200$.

Dividing both sides of this equation by 30 results in $x = 40$.

Thus, **Rana** paid **$40 monthly.**

Since the question asks for Clara's monthly payment, we need to find $2x$, or 2×40, which is equal to $80.

Therefore, **Clara** paid **$80** for the fridge **each month.**

The correct answer that you should enter is **80.**

If this example was a multiple-choice question with answer choices provided, you could use the **Going Backwards** strategy to solve it effectively.

Assume the given choices are 40, 60, 80, and 100.

Then, you can start by checking with 60. If Clara paid $60 monthly, Rana would have paid $30 monthly, and the total monthly payment would be $90. To pay the total of $1200, this would require $\dfrac{1200}{90}$ which is 13.33 months. This wrong choice trial would cause you to deduce that the monthly payment made by Rana should be greater than $60.

Then, you would eliminate the smaller choice 40, and try the values greater than 60, leading you to the correct answer **80.**

1   ◻ Mark for Review

Sarah's salary started at $800. It increases by $100 each year. Which of the following equations can be used to find the number of years, t, when her salary becomes $1500?

A) $800 + 100t = 1500$

B) $800 = 1500 + 100t$

C) $800t + 100 = 1500$

D) $800t + 100t = 1500$

2   ◻ Mark for Review

$$5fy - \frac{450}{9}y = -10$$

In the given equation, f is a constant. If the equation has no solution, what is the value of f?

3   ◻ Mark for Review

A customer orders 350 handmade beanies from Susan's online store. She already had 110 beanies in stock. She has two options, she can knit the remaining beanies by herself or she can ask her mother to help her knit the remaining beanies. If she can make 5 beanies per day and her mother can make 3 beanies per day, how many less days can she and her mother complete the order together than she can complete the order alone?

4   ◻ Mark for Review

In a lab, the number of rats is 5 times the number of rabbits. If there are 1600 more rats than rabbits, what is the number of rabbits in this lab?

A) 267

B) 320

C) 400

D) 600

5   ◻ Mark for Review

$$0.4tx + 0.07(300 - 100x) = -0.11(100x)$$

In the equation, t is a constant. Which of the following could not be the value of t for the equation to have only one solution?

A) -100

B) -10

C) 10

D) 100

Answers & Explanations

1. **Level:** Easy | **Skill/Knowledge:** Linear equations in one variable | **Testing Point:** Find a linear equation in one variable to represent a situation

   Key Explanation: Choice A is correct. It's given that Sarah's salary increases by $100 each year. Then after t years, her salary would have increased by $100t$. This increase in salary can be added to the original salary of $800 to find the salary after t years, yielding $800 + 100t$. Set this expression equal to $1500 to find the number of years when Sarah's salary becomes $1500, resulting in the correct equation $800 + 100t = 1500$.

   Distractor Explanations: Choice B is incorrect and may result from adding the total increase to her final salary instead of her starting salary. **Choice C** is incorrect and may result from multiplying the number of years to her starting salary instead of the yearly increase. **Choice D** is incorrect and may result from multiplying the number of years to her starting salary.

2. **Level:** Easy | **Skill/Knowledge:** Linear equations in one variable | **Testing Point:** Use the case of a linear equation in one variable having no solution to find an unknown quantity

   Key Explanation: $f = 10$ is the correct answer. The given equation has no solution, so the equation is false. Simplifying the equation $5fy - \dfrac{450}{9}y = -10$ yields $5fy - 50y = -10$. Factoring out the common factor of $5y$ results in $5y(f - 10) = -10$. Dividing both sides of the equation by $5(f - 10)$ to isolate y yields $y = -105(f - 10)$. This equation is false if and only if $5(f - 10) = 0$. Dividing both sides of $5(f - 10) = 0$ by 5 yields $f - 10 = 0$, or $f = 10$. Therefore, the given equation has no solution if and only if the value of f is 10.

3. **Level:** Medium | **Skill/Knowledge:** Linear equations in one variable | **Testing Point:** Create and use linear equations

   Key Explanation: The correct answer is **18**. Let x be the number of days.

   Since the customer ordered 350 beanies and she already had 110 beanies in stock, then she only needs $350 - 110 = 240$ beanies.

   Since she can make 5 beanies per day, then the equation that represents the situation when she complete the order alone is $5x = 240$. Dividing both sides of the equation by 5 yields $x = 48$. Hence, she can complete the order alone in 48 days.

   Since her mother can make 3 beanies per day, then the equation that represents the situation when she and her mother complete the order together is $8x = 240$. Dividing both sides of the equation by 8 yields $x = 30$. Hence, she and her mother can complete the order together in 30 days.

   Therefore, she and her mother can complete the order in $48 - 30 = 18$ less days than she can complete the order alone.

4. **Level:** Hard | **Skill/Knowledge:** Linear equations in one variable | **Testing Point:** Create and solve a linear equation in one variable

   Key Explanation: Choice C is correct. Let x represent the number of rabbits in the lab. It follows that there are $5x$ rats in the lab, which is $5x - x$, or $4x$, more than the number of rabbits. Then $4x = 1600$. Dividing both sides of the equation by 4 yields $x = 400$. Therefore, there are 400 rabbits in the lab.

   Distractor Explanations: Choice A is incorrect. It results from dividing 1600 by 6 instead of 4. **Choice B** is incorrect, and results from dividing 1600 by 5 instead of 4. **Choice D** is incorrect and may result from dividing the total number of rats and rabbits, which is 2400, by 4.

5. **Level:** Hard | **Skill/Knowledge:** Linear equations in one variable | **Testing Point:** Find the value of a constant for a linear equation to have one solution

Key Explanation: Choice B is correct.
Distribution on both sides of the given equation
$0.4tx + 0.07(300 - 100x) = -0.11(100x)$ yields $0.4tx$
$+ 21 - 7x = -11x$. Isolating the terms containing
the variable x on one side of the equation and the
constant on the other side results in $0.4tx + 11x$
$- 7x = -21$. Combining like terms and factoring
out x yields $(0.4t + 4)x = -21$. This equation has
one solution if the coefficient of x is different from
zero. It follows that $0.4t + 4 \neq 0$, or $t \neq \dfrac{-4}{0.4}$, or
$t \neq -10$. Therefore, for the given equation to have
one solution, the value of t could not be -10.

Distractor Explanations: Choice A is incorrect
because substituting -100 for t results in one
solution $x = \dfrac{21}{36}$ or $\dfrac{7}{12}$ for the equation. **Choice C**
is incorrect because substituting 10 for t results in
one solution $x = -\dfrac{21}{8}$ for the equation. **Choice D**
is incorrect because substituting 100 for t results
in one solution $x = -\dfrac{21}{44}$ for the equation.

Linear Equations in Two Variables

Linear equations in two variables represent straight lines when graphed in the xy-coordinate system. The equations of straight lines, their meanings, characteristics, and relationships to their corresponding graphs will be discussed in this part of the chapter.

Equations of Straight Lines

There are many forms of equations of straight lines, and each has its benefits.

> The **slope-intercept form $y = mx + b$, m represents the slope** of the line and b **represents its y-intercept**. The slope gives the inclination of the line in the xy-coordinate system. **It is positive if the line goes up as you move from left to right, and negative if the line goes down as you move from left to right. Horizontal lines have a slope of zero, and vertical lines have undefined slopes.**

To find the slope of a line, choose two points on the line and name them, for example, points A and B. You may either apply the slope formula $m = \dfrac{\Delta y}{\Delta x} = \dfrac{y_B - y_A}{x_B - x_A}$, or the ratio $\dfrac{rise}{run}$ as shown in the figure below. The y-intercept is the point where the line intersects the y-axis.

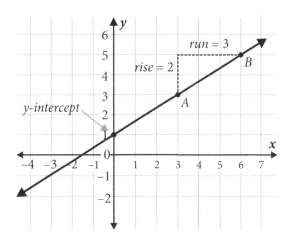

In the graphed line, the slope $m = \dfrac{rise}{run} = \dfrac{2}{3}$. Using points B (6, 5) and A (3, 3), the same result can be found using the slope formula $m = \dfrac{y_B - y_A}{x_B - x_A} = \dfrac{5-3}{6-3} = \dfrac{2}{3}$. The y-intercept is the point (0, 1). Consequently, the equation of the graphed line is $y = \dfrac{2}{3}x + 1$.

> A second form of equations of straight lines is the **point-slope form $y - y_1 = m(x - x_1)$**. This form is best used when the slope of the line is given and you know the coordinates of one point (x_1, y_1) on the line.

If we consider the graphed line having a slope of $\dfrac{2}{3}$ and passing through the point B(6, 5), the point-slope form would be $y - 5 = \dfrac{2}{3}(x - 6)$.

A third form of equations of straight lines is the **standard form** $ax + by = c$. When given, this form allows you to calculate the **slope** $m = -\dfrac{a}{b}$ and the **y-intercept** $\dfrac{c}{b}$.

For example, the standard form of the equation of the graphed line is $2x - 3y = -3$ where $a = 2$, $b = -3$, and $c = -3$. The slope can be easily found as $m = -\dfrac{2}{-3} = \dfrac{2}{3}$, and the y-intercept is $\dfrac{c}{b} = \dfrac{-3}{-3} = 1$. Let's learn more about linear equations in two variables through the word problem example below.

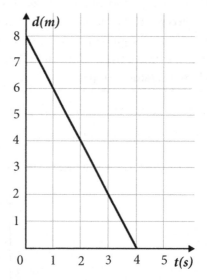

(?) The graph shows the distance from a reference point of a bicycle moving at a constant speed for 4 seconds. Which of the following equations could represent the graph?

A) $d = \dfrac{1}{2}t + 8$

B) $d = 2t + 8$

C) $2t + d = -8$

D) $\dfrac{t}{4} + \dfrac{d}{8} = 1$

Solution: Let's start by finding the slope and d-intercept of the graph. The graph is a line with a d-intercept of $(0, 8)$.

To find the slope, choose any two points on the line, for example, $A(2, 4)$ and $B(3, 2)$. Using the slope formula, $m = \dfrac{\Delta d}{\Delta t} = \dfrac{d_B - d_A}{t_B - t_A} = \dfrac{2 - 4}{3 - 2} = -2$.

As a result, you can **eliminate Choices A and B** since they have slopes of $-\dfrac{1}{2}$ and 2 respectively.

Rearranging the equation of **Choice C** to get the slope-intercept form gives $d = -2t - 8$. It has a slope of -2, but the d-intercept is -8 rather than 8. Thus, **Choice C is incorrect**.

Therefore, the **correct answer is Choice D**.

To verify this, substitute the coordinates of $A(2, 4)$ and $B(3, 2)$ into the equation $\dfrac{t}{4} + \dfrac{d}{8} = 1$, and check if they satisfy this equation.

Checking the coordinates of any two points on the line in the equation choices allows you to solve this question using the **'Going Backwards'** strategy.

Another thing to note in this question is that the equation $\dfrac{t}{4} + \dfrac{d}{8} = 1$ has the form of $\dfrac{x}{a} + \dfrac{y}{b} = 1$, which is known as the **'intercept form'**. The number a is the **x-intercept** (where the line intersects the x-axis), which is in this case 4, and the number b is the **y-intercept**, which is in this case 8.

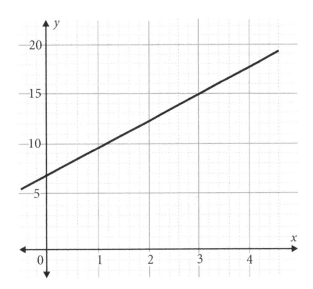

> (?) The graph shows a line passing through the points $(1, 9)$ and $(2, 12)$. Which of the following equations represents this graph?

A) $y = -3x - 5$

B) $y + 3 = 3(x + 4)$

C) $y - 6 = -3(2x + 2)$

D) $y = 3x + 6$

Solution: To find the equation of the line that passes through points $(1, 9)$ and $(2, 12)$, you can use the point-slope form $y - y_1 = m(x - x_1)$. Start by finding the slope using the slope formula,

$m = \dfrac{y_2 - y_1}{x_2 - x_1} = \dfrac{12 - 9}{2 - 1} = 3$. Looking at the choices, you can now **eliminate Choices A and C** as they have **negative slopes**.

Now, in order to check between **Choices B** and **D**, substitute the slope and the point $(1, 9)$ into the point-slope form to get: $y - 9 = 3(x - 1)$. Simplifying this results in $y = 3x - 3 + 9$ or $y = 3x + 6$ which is **Choice D**.

Hence, **Choice D** is the **correct answer**.

Choice B is **incorrect** since it has 9 as the y-intercept instead of 6.

$$y - 3 = -\frac{3}{2}(x - 7)$$

The straight line above passes through the point (7, 3) and has a slope of $-\frac{3}{2}$. What is the point where this line intersects the x-axis?

A) $(5, 3)$

B) $(0, \frac{27}{2})$

C) $(9, 0)$

D) $(8, 0)$

Solution: To find the point where the line intersects the x-axis, you need to find the x-coordinate of that point first.

The y-coordinate of any point on the x-axis is always 0.

Therefore, substitute $y = 0$ into the given equation and solve for x which will result in $0 - 3 = -\frac{3}{2}(x - 7)$.

Distributing the right-hand side yields $-3 = -\frac{3}{2}x + \frac{21}{2}$. Subtracting $\frac{21}{2}$ from both sides of the equation yields $-\frac{27}{2} = -\frac{3}{2}x$. Then, dividing both sides by $-\frac{3}{2}$ yields $9 = x$. Therefore, the point where the line intersects the x-axis is $(9, 0)$.

Therefore, the correct answer is **Choice C**.

Choice A is incorrect. The y-coordinate of any point on the x-axis is always 0, therefore this is incorrect.

Choice B is incorrect. The y-coordinate of any point on the x-axis is always 0, therefore this is incorrect.

Choice D is incorrect. This may result if the slope of the given equation is -3.

Line Relationships Based on Equations

As mentioned before, the slope gives the inclination of the line.

Thus, one can deduce that two distinct lines having the same slope would be parallel. In addition, if two lines have slopes that are opposite reciprocals of one another, then they are perpendicular. The opposite reciprocal of any fraction $\frac{a}{b}$ is $-\frac{b}{a}$.

For example, the opposite reciprocal of –2, which can also be written as $\frac{-2}{1}$, is $-\frac{1}{-2}$ or $\frac{1}{2}$. As a result, the product of the slopes of any two perpendicular lines is –1.

Of course, vertical lines are perpendicular to horizontal lines.

> The general equation of vertical lines is $x = k$, while the general equation of horizontal lines is $y = k$, where k is a constant real number.

Check out the examples below.

$$2x - 3y = 3$$

The equation $y = mx + b$ represents a line that is perpendicular to the given line and passes through the point (5, –3). What is the value of $m + b$?

Solution: First, find the slope of the line of the given equation. You may change the given equation from the standard form into the slope-intercept form, or you may use the formula $m = -\frac{a}{b}$ for calculating the slope directly from the standard form $ax + by = c$. Either way, the **slope of the given line** is $m = -\frac{2}{-3}$ or $m = \frac{2}{3}$.

The **slope of the line perpendicular to the given line** is the **opposite reciprocal of** $\frac{2}{3}$ which is $-\frac{3}{2}$.

It is also given that the **required line passes through the point** (5, –3). Using the point-slope form of the straight line $y - y_1 = m(x - x_1)$ yields $y - (-3) = -\frac{3}{2}(x - 5)$. This equation can be simplified into $y + 3 = -\frac{3}{2}x + \frac{15}{2}$. Subtracting 3 from both sides of this equation yields $y = -\frac{3}{2}x + \frac{9}{2}$.

It's given that this equation has the form $y = mx + b$. By comparison, $m = -\frac{3}{2}$ and $b = \frac{9}{2}$.

Therefore, the sum $m + b = -\frac{3}{2} + \frac{9}{2} = \frac{6}{2}$ or 3. The correct answer to this question is **3**.

Which of the following equations represents a line parallel to the line $y = -\frac{3}{4}x + 5$ passing through the point (– 4, 11)?

A) $y = -\frac{3}{4}x + 11$

B) $y = -\frac{3}{4}x + 8$

C) $y = 2x + 16$

D) $y = -\frac{4}{3} + 16$

Solution: To determine which equation represents a line parallel to $y = -\frac{3}{4}x + 5$, look at the slope. The slope of the given line is $-\frac{3}{4}$. Parallel lines have the same slope.

Among the choices given, you can **eliminate Choices C and D** since they **don't have the same slope.**

The remaining **Choices A** and **B** have the same slope making them parallel to the given line.

But we are looking at an equation parallel and passing through the point (– 4, 11).

To check if the line passes through the point (– 4, 11), substitute $x = -4$ in each equation and if we find $y = 11$, it is the correct answer.

For choice A: $y = -\frac{3}{4}(-4) + 11$ or $y = 14$

For choice B: $y = -\frac{3}{4}(-4) + 8$ or $y = 11$

Therefore, the **correct answer** is **Choice B**.

 Two lines are perpendicular. If the equation of a line that passes through the point (5, 6) is $y = x + 1$, what is the equation of a line that is perpendicular to it and also passes through the same point?

A) $y = -x + 11$

B) $y = -x + 7$

C) $y = -\frac{1}{2}x + 4$

D) $y = -\frac{1}{2}x + 3$

Solution: To find the equation of the perpendicular line, first, you need to determine the slope of the given line. The given line has the equation $y = x + 1$, the slope-intercept form $y = mx + b$, where m represents the slope. Then, the slope of this line is 1.

Since the two lines are perpendicular, the slope of the perpendicular line is the **opposite reciprocal** of 1 which is –1. Looking at the choices, **Choices C and D** can now be eliminated since their slope is $-\frac{1}{2}$.

Now, check between **Choices A** and **B**.

It is also given that the perpendicular line also passes through the point (5, 6).

Using the point-slope form $y - y_1 = m(x - x_1)$ to find the equation of the perpendicular line yields $y - 6 = -1(x - 5)$. Simplifying this results in $y - 6 = -x + 5$. Adding 6 to both sides yields $y = -x + 11$.

Therefore, the **correct answer** to this question is **Choice A**.

Choice B is incorrect since it has a y-intercept of 7 instead of 11.

1 ☐ **Mark for Review**

$$3x - 4y = 3$$
$$ax + 3y = 11$$

The two equations above are perpendicular. What is the value of *a*?

A) – 4

B) 3

C) 4

D) 5

2 ☐ **Mark for Review**

Two lines are perpendicular to each other. Line A has a *y*-intercept of (0, 8) and an *x*-intercept of (3, 0) while line B has a y-intercept of (0, 3). Which of the following coordinates is the intersection point of the two lines?

A) (1.64, 3.63)

B) (1.82, 3.15)

C) (1.96, 3.74)

D) (2.11, 3.08)

3 ☐ **Mark for Review**

Vivian bought 2 pineapples and 5 durians last month and paid $14. This month, the price of pineapples has increased by 20% while the price of durians has decreased by 10%. If Vivian buys the same number of pineapples and durians for only $13.5, how much is the price of one pineapple last month?

4 ☐ **Mark for Review**

$$\frac{5(x+4)+3y}{2} = 22$$

A line with the given equation is graphed in the *xy*-plane. Which of the following statements is true about the line?

A) The given line is parallel to the line whose equation is $y = -\frac{3}{5}x + 2$.

B) The given line is perpendicular to the line whose equation is $y = \frac{3}{5}x + 2$.

C) The given line has a slope of $\frac{5}{3}$.

D) The given line has a *y*-intercept of 24.

5 ☐ **Mark for Review**

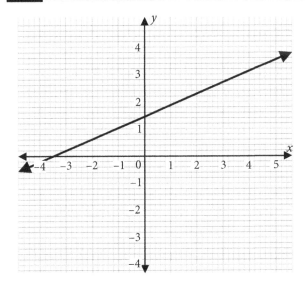

Given the graph of a line. Which equation represents the line perpendicular to the given line and passing through point (2, 1)?

A) $-5x + 2(y + 4) = 0$

B) $2x + 5\left(y - \frac{1}{5}\right) = 0$

C) $2x + 5\left(y - \frac{9}{5}\right) = 0$

D) $5x + 2(y - 6) = 0$

ALGEBRA

Answers & Explanations

1. **Level:** Easy | **Skill/Knowledge:** Linear equations in two variables | **Testing Point:** Perpendicular lines

   Key Explanation: Choice C is correct. The slope of the first equation is found by re-writing the equation in its slope-intercept form $y = mx + c$. The equation will become $y = 3/4x - 3/4$. Hence, the slope of the first line is 3/4. The slope of a line perpendicular to the first will be $-4/3$.

   Rewriting the second equation in slope-intercept form yields $y = -a/3x + 12/3$.

   Hence, the slope is $-a/3$.

   Equating the slope in terms of a and b with the actual value yields $-a/3 = -4/3$.

   Multiplying both sides of the equation by 3 yields $a = 4$

   Distractor Explanations: Choice A is incorrect and may result from assuming that the two lines are parallel to each other. **Choice B** is incorrect and may result from calculating the y coordinate value of the intersection. **Choice D** is incorrect and may result from calculating the x coordinate value of the intersection.

2. **Level:** Medium | **Skill/Knowledge:** Linear equations in two variables | **Testing Point:** Intersection point of two lines

   Key Explanation: Choice A is correct. Since line A has a y-intercept of $(0, 8)$ and an x-intercept of $(3, 0)$, then $0 = 3m + 8$. Subtracting $3m$ from both sides of the equation yields $-3m = 8$. Dividing both sides of the equation by -3 yields $m = -\frac{8}{3}$.

   Since the slope of line A is $-\frac{8}{3}$, then the equation for line A is $y = -\frac{8}{3}x + 8$.

   Since line B is perpendicular to line A, then the slope of line B is $\frac{3}{8}$.

Since the y-intercept of line B is $(0, 3)$, then the equation for line B is $y = \frac{3}{8}x + 3$.

Equating the two linear equations to find the intersection point yields $\frac{3}{8}x + 3 = -\frac{8}{3}x + 8$.

Adding $\frac{8}{3}x$ and subtracting 3 from both sides of the equation yields $3.042x = 5$. Dividing both sides of the equation by 3.042 yields $x = 1.64$.

Substituting the value of x to the equation of line A yields $y = -\frac{8}{3}(1.4) + 8 = 3.63$. Therefore, the intersection point is $(1.64, 3.63)$.

Distractor Explanations: Choice B is incorrect. This point lies only on line A and not on line B. **Choice C** is incorrect. This point lies only on line B and not on line A. **Choice D** is incorrect. This point does not lie on both lines.

3. **Level:** Medium | **Skill/Knowledge:** Linear equations in two variables

   Key Explanation: The correct answer is **$1.5**.

   Let p be the price of one pineapple last month and d be the price of one durian last month.

   Since Vivian bought 2 pineapples and 5 durians last month and paid $14, then $2p + 5d = 14$. Subtracting $2p$ from both sides of the equation yields $5d = 14 - 2p$. Dividing both sides of the equation by 5 yields $d = 2.8 - 0.4p$.

   Since the price of pineapples has increased by 20% while the price of durians has decreased by 10%, then the price of one pineapple this month is $1.2p$ and the price of one durian this month is $0.9d$.

   Since the same number of pineapples and durians only cost $13.5, then $2(1.2p) + 5(0.9d) = 13.5$. Simplifying the equation yields $2.4p + 4.5d = 13.5$.

   Substituting $d = 2.8 - 0.4p$ to $2.4p + 4.5d = 13.5$ yields $2.4p + 4.5(2.8 - 0.4p) = 13.5$. Using distributive property yields $2.4p + 12.6 - 1.8p = 13.5$. Subtracting 12.6 from both sides of the equation and combining like terms yields $0.6p = 0.9$. Dividing both sides of the equation by

0.6 yields $p = 1.5$. Therefore, the price of one pineapple last month is $1.5.

4. **Level:** Hard | **Skill/Knowledge:** Linear equations in two variables | **Testing Point:** Identify the characteristics of a line graphed in the xy-plane based on its equation

   Key Explanation: Choice B is correct. Multiplying both sides of the given equation $\dfrac{5(x+4)+3y}{2} = 22$ by 2 yields $5(x + 4) + 3y = 44$. Distribution on the left hand side of the equation results in $5x + 20 + 3y = 44$. Subtracting $5x + 20$ from both sides of the equation yields $3y = -5x + 24$. Dividing both sides of this equation by 3 results in $y = -\dfrac{5}{3}x + 8$. This line has a slope of $-\dfrac{5}{3}$. The slopes of two perpendicular lines are negative reciprocals of one another, then the slope of a line perpendicular to the given line is $\dfrac{3}{5}$. Therefore, the given line is perpendicular to the line whose equation is $y = \dfrac{3}{5}x + 2$.

   Distractor Explanations: Choice A is incorrect and may result if the equation of the given line is $\dfrac{3(x+4)+5y}{2} = 22$. **Choice C** is incorrect and may result if the equation of the given line is $\dfrac{5(x+4)-3y}{2} = 22$. **Choice D** is incorrect and may result if the equation of the given line is $\dfrac{5(x+4)+3y}{2} = 46$.

5. **Level:** Hard | **Skill/Knowledge:** Linear equations in two variables | **Testing Point:** Find the equation of the line perpendicular to a given line and passing through a given point

   Key Explanation: Choice D is correct. The slope of the given line can be found by using the coordinates of any 2 points on the line. Taking the points $(0, 1.5)$ and $(5, 3.5)$, the slope of the

graphed line is equal to $\dfrac{3.5 - 1.5}{5 - 0}$, or $\dfrac{2}{5}$. The slope of any line perpendicular to the given line must have a slope which is the negative reciprocal of $\dfrac{2}{5}$. It follow that the slope of the perpendicular line is $-\dfrac{5}{2}$. Then the equation of this perpendicular line has the form $y = -\dfrac{5}{2}x + b$, where b is a constant to be determined. It's given that the perpendicular line passes through the point $(2, 1)$. Substituting 1 for y and 2 for x in the equation $y = -\dfrac{5}{2}x + b$ yields $1 = -\dfrac{5}{2}(2) + b$. This equation can be simplified into $1 = -5 + b$. Adding 5 to both sides of this equation results in $6 = b$. Thus, the equation of the line perpendicular to the graphed line and passing through the point $(2, 1)$ is $y = -\dfrac{5}{2}x + 6$. Multiplying both sides of this equation by 2 yields $2y = -5x + 12$. Adding $5x - 12$ to both sides of this equation yields $5x + 2y - 12 = 0$. Factoring out 2 on the left hand side of the equation results in $5x + 2(y - 6) = 0$, which is the correct answer.

Distractor Explanations: Choice A is incorrect and may result if the given line had a slope of $-\dfrac{2}{5}$. **Choice B** is incorrect. This is the equation of the line parallel to the given line and passing through the point $(2, 1)$. **Choice C** is incorrect and may result if the given line had a slope of $\dfrac{5}{2}$.

Linear Functions

A function is a rule that assigns to each input, usually referred to as _x_, exactly one output, usually referred to as _y_ or _f(x)_. The graph of a function is the set of points having the input as their _x_-coordinates, and the corresponding outputs as their _y_-coordinates. You will learn more about functions in the Advanced Math chapter. The focus of this part is linear functions. **A linear function is a function whose graph is a straight line.** Characteristics of linear graphs were discussed in the previous part, so you will now learn more about translations of linear graphs and some instances of linear functions set in context.

Translations of Linear Graphs

Translation is another word for sliding. When you translate a straight line, its inclination is preserved while its position changes. Thus, translated lines have the same slope as the original line but they have different _y_-intercepts. There are two types of translation: vertical translation and horizontal translation. The graph of _f(x)_ + _a_ is the translation of the graph of _f(x)_ by + _a_ units vertically. The graph of _f(x + a)_ is the translation of the graph of _f(x)_ by –_a_ units horizontally. Moving negative units vertically is going down, while moving negative units horizontally is going left. To get a better understanding of the translation of straight lines, take a look at the example figures below.

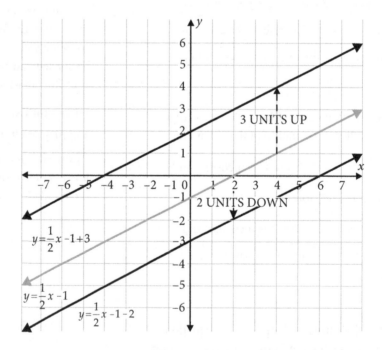

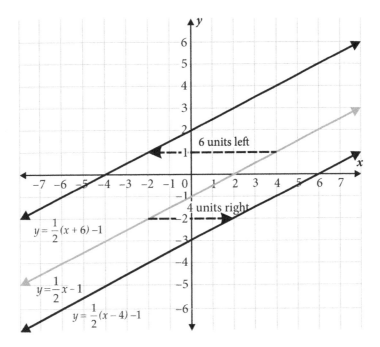

Check the examples below to see how you might encounter translation of linear functions graphs on the SAT Math.

x	f(x)
3	8
5	12

(?) The table represents a linear function f. The graph of function g is the result of translating the graph of function f 3 units to the right. What is the x-coordinate of the x-intercept of the function g?

A) −1

B) 1

C) 2

D) 3

Solution: The equation of the given linear function f can be written in slope-intercept form $f(x) = mx + b$, where m is the slope and b is the y-intercept.

It's given that the points $(3, 8)$ and $(5, 12)$ belong to the function graph, then the slope of f can be found using the slope formula as $\dfrac{12 - 8}{5 - 3}$, which is equal to $\dfrac{4}{2}$ or 2. Substituting 2 for m in $f(x) = mx + b$ yields $f(x) = 2x + b$.

Substituting 8 for $f(x)$ and 3 for x in this equation yields $8 = 2(3) + b$, or $8 = 6 + b$.

Subtracting 6 from both sides of this equation yields $2 = b$.

Thus, the equation representing the function f is $f(x) = 2x + 2$.

It's given that the graph of function g is the result of translating the graph of function f 3 units to the right. Then the equation of the function g is given by $g(x) = f(x - 3)$.

Substituting $x - 3$ for x in the expression $f(x) = 2x + 2$ yields $f(x - 3) = 2(x - 3) + 2$. Distribution on the right-hand side of this equation and replacing $f(x - 3)$ by $g(x)$ results in $g(x) = 2x - 6 + 2$, or $g(x) = 2x - 4$.

Substituting 0 for $g(x)$ in this equation to find the x-coordinate of the x-intercept of g yields $0 = 2x - 4$. Adding 4 to both sides of this equation yields $4 = 2x$. Dividing both sides of this equation by 2 results in $2 = x$. Therefore, the correct answer is **Choice C.**

Another method to find the correct answer would be to find the x-coordinate of the x-intercept of the function f, and add 3 to it since the graph of f was translated 3 units to the right.

Substituting $f(x) = 0$, we get $2x = -2$ or $x = -1$. The x-intercept of the function f is $(-1, 0)$ and therefore, the x-intercept of the function g would be $(-1 + 3, 0)$ or $(2, 0)$.

Choice A is incorrect. This is the x-coordinate of the x-intercept of the function f.

Choice B is incorrect and may result if the graph of f was translated 2 units to the right.

Choice D is incorrect and may result if the graph of f was translated 4 units to the right.

 A linear function $f(x) = 4x + 12$ is translated 4 units to the left and 5 units up. What is the equation of the translated function g?

A) $g(x) = 4x + 18$

B) $g(x) = 4x + 25$

C) $g(x) = 4x + 33$

D) $g(x) = 4x + 47$

Solution: To translate the given function $f(x) = 4x + 12$, you need to understand the translation that will be applied.

To translate the function 4 units to the left means replacing x with $(x + 4)$.

To translate the function 5 units up means adding 5 to $f(x)$.

The translated function will now have the form, $g(x) = f(x + 4) + 5 = 4(x + 4) + 12 + 5$.

Simplifying this function yields $g(x) = 4x + 16 + 12 + 5$ or $g(x) = 4x + 33$.

Therefore, the **translated function** is **Choice C**.

Choice A is incorrect. This may result if the function is translated 1 unit to the left and 2 units up.

Choice B is incorrect. This may result if the function is translated 2 units to the left and 5 units up.

Choice D is incorrect. This may result if the function is translated 4 units to the left and 12 units up.

Shift $x + 12y = 32$, 8 units to the right and 6 units down. What is the new equation?

A) $y = -\dfrac{1}{12}x + \dfrac{8}{3}$

B) $y = -\dfrac{1}{12}x - \dfrac{8}{3}$

C) $y = -\dfrac{1}{2}x - \dfrac{8}{3}$

D) $y = -\dfrac{1}{2}x + \dfrac{8}{3}$

Solution: To translate the given equation $x + 12y = 32$, you need to understand the translation that will be applied.

To translate 8 units to the right means replacing x with $(x - 8)$.

To translate 6 units down means subtracting 6 from the equation.

Since the choices are all in the slope-intercept form, let's express the given equation in slope-intercept form. Subtracting x from both sides yields $12y = -x + 32$. Dividing both sides by 12 yields $y = -\dfrac{1}{12}x + \dfrac{8}{3}$.

Now, the equation will have the form $y = -\dfrac{1}{12}(x - 8) + \dfrac{8}{3} - 6$.

Simplifying yields $y = -\dfrac{1}{12}x + \dfrac{2}{3} + \dfrac{8}{3} - 6$ or $y = -\dfrac{1}{12}x - \dfrac{8}{3}$.

Therefore, the new equation is **Choice B.**

Choice A is incorrect. This is the given equation in slope-intercept form.

Choice C is incorrect. This may result from a calculational error.

Choice D is incorrect. This may result from a calculational error.

Linear Functions Word Problems

Some in-context situations can be represented by linear functions. Linear functions can be used to solve several real-world problems like calculating the speed or distance of vehicles and calculating revenues, profits, rates, and expenses which yields a straight line. Check out the examples below.

An international shipping company charges a fixed rate of $1.4 per pound in addition to a fixed fee of $2 for shipping a package to a certain country. If the service charge is $6.9 for shipping a package to this country, what is the weight, in pounds, of the package?

A) 3

B) 3.5

C) 4

D) 4.5

Solution: After carefully reading the problem, you will notice that there are two variables in such a situation, the weight of a package and the amount of money charged by the shipping service.

Let x be the **weight of a package** in pounds, and let $f(x)$ represent the **charge** in dollars for shipping the package to the country. Then the given problem can be modeled by the linear function $f(x) = 1.4x + 2$.

It's given that the company charges $6.9 for shipping the package. Substituting 6.9 for $f(x)$ in the equation $f(x) = 1.4x + 2$ yields $6.9 = 1.4x + 2$.

Subtracting 2 from both sides of this equation yields $4.9 = 1.4x$ and dividing both sides of this equation by 1.4 results in $3.5 = x$.

Thus, the **weight of the package is 3.5 pounds** and the correct answer is **Choice B**.

Choice A is incorrect because the shipping service would charge $1.4 \cdot 3 + 2$, or $6.2 for shipping a package weighing 3 pounds.

Choice C is incorrect because the shipping service would charge $1.4 \cdot 4 + 2$, or $7.6 for shipping a package weighing 4 pounds.

Choice D is incorrect because the shipping service would charge $1.4 \cdot 4.5 + 2$, or $8.3 for shipping a package weighing 4.5 pounds.

The above example could be solved easily using the **'Going Backwards'** strategy. Starting with the answer **Choice C** (4 pounds), you will find that the charge for shipping this package is greater than the given charge.

Consequently, you should also eliminate **Choice D** as you know that the weight of the package must be less than 4.

Then, checking the weight of 3 pounds (**Choice A**) would also lead to an incorrect result which is less than the given charge, therefore, you can conclude that the correct answer is **Choice B**.

Store A sells scented candles. The store's revenue is given by $R(x) = 15x - 125$, where x is the number of candles sold. What does 125 represent?

A) The profit made by selling one candle.

B) The fixed cost incurred by the company.

C) The total revenue generated by selling one candle.

D) The cost of selling one candle.

Solution: In the given function $R(x) = 15x - 125$, 125 is the fixed cost incurred by the company. Fixed costs are expenses that a business incurs that do not change with the amount of goods produced or services provided. In this case, it is the costs that the store must pay regardless of how many candles were sold.

Therefore, the **correct answer is Choice B**.

Choice A is incorrect. The given term does not represent profit.

Choice C is incorrect. The total revenue generated by selling one candle can be solved by substituting 1 for x in the given function, resulting in $R(x) = 15(1) - 125$ or $R(x) = -110$.

Choice D is incorrect. The cost of selling one candle is 15.

 A dress rental shop charges a rental fee of $50 per dress and a fixed $10 reservation fee per customer. If you are charged $410, how many dresses did you rent?

A) 6

B) 7

C) 8

D) 9

Solution: To solve this, let x **be the number of dresses rented** and $C(x)$ **be the total cost of the rental.** Based on the given problem, a linear function can be modelled by $C(x) = 50x + 10$.

It is given that the total payment is $410. Substituting 410 for $C(x)$ in the equation yields $410 = 50x + 10$.

Subtracting 10 from both sides of the equation yields $400 = 50x$, then dividing both sides by 50 results in $8 = x$.

Therefore, the amount of dresses rented is **8**, which is **Choice C**.

Choice A is incorrect. This may result if the total amount paid is $310.

Choice B is incorrect. This may result if the total amount paid is $360.

Choice D is incorrect. This may result if the total amount paid is $460.

1 ☐ **Mark for Review**

If $f(2) = -1$ and $f(3) = -3$, what is the y-intercept of the function $f(x)$?

A) -2

B) $\dfrac{3}{2}$

C) 2

D) 3

2 ☐ **Mark for Review**

$$w(m) = 20 - 0.01m$$

The given function w models the volume of water, in cubic meters, remaining in a tank after m minutes of draining. According to the model, what is the volume of water, in cubic meters, that remains in the tank after 2.25 hours of draining?

3 ☐ **Mark for Review**

To model a car moving at a constant speed, a distance linear function d is used. d is a function of the time, t. It's given that $d(0) = 5$ and $d(3) = 185$. Which equation defines d?

A) $d(t) = 40t + 5$

B) $d(t) = 50t + 5$

C) $d(t) = 60t + 5$

D) $d(t) = 50t + 35$

4 ☐ **Mark for Review**

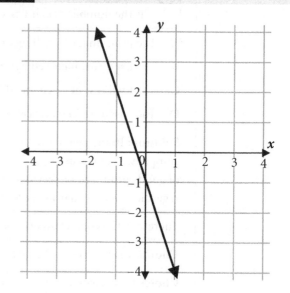

The graph represents a linear function f. The graph of the linear function g is the translation of the graph of f 3 units to the right after reflection over the x-axis. Which of the following equations represents g?

A) $g(x) = -3x - 1$

B) $g(x) = -3x + 8$

C) $g(x) = 3x + 1$

D) $g(x) = 3x - 8$

5 ⬚ **Mark for Review**

x	y
−7	8
7	20
14	26

The table of values represents a linear function *f*. This function is defined by the equation $c(x + 2) + 3(y - d) = -\dfrac{36}{7}$. What is the value of *cd*?

A) −36

B) $-\dfrac{18}{7}$

C) $\dfrac{80}{7}$

D) 14

Answers & Explanations

1. **Level:** Easy | **Skill/Knowledge:** Linear functions | **Testing Point:** Find the y-intercept of a linear function

   Key Explanation: Choice D is correct. To find the y-intercept of the function, we would first convert the function $f(x)$ to the slope intercept form $f(x) = mx + b$. First, rewrite $f(2) = -1$ and $f(3) = -3$ in their coordinate form: $(2, -1)$ and $(3, -3)$ respectively. The slope of the function, m, is calculated by $m = \dfrac{y_2 - y_1}{x_2 - x_1}$ which would result to $m = \dfrac{y_2 - y_1}{x_2 - x_1}$. Therefore, $f(x) = -2x + b$. To find b, the y-intercept, substitute the coordinates into the function and solve for b. Substituting $f(3) = -3$ in the equation yields $f(3) = -2(3) + b$ which is equivalent to $-3 = -2(3) + b$. The value of b would therefore be equal to 3.

   Distractor Explanations: Choice A is incorrect. This option represents the value of the slope of the function $f(x)$. **Choice B is incorrect.** This option represents the x-intercept of the function or the value of x when $f(x) = 0$. **Choice C is incorrect.** This option may be a result of conceptual or calculation errors.

2. **Level:** Medium | **Skill/Knowledge:** Linear functions | **Testing Point:** Use a linear function to find an unknown quantity

   Key Explanation: 18.65 is the correct answer. The given function gives the remaining volume of water after m minutes. As a result, 2.25 hours need to be converted into minutes. Multiplying 2.25 hours by the conversion factor $\dfrac{60\ minutes}{1\ hour}$ yields 135 minutes. Substituting 135 in the given function yields $w(135) = 20 - 0.01135 = 20 - 1.35 = 18.65$. Therefore, there remains 18.65 *cubic meters* of water in the tank after 2.25 hours of draining.

3. **Level:** Medium | **Skill/Knowledge:** Linear functions | **Testing Point:** Find the equation of a linear function with two values of the function given

   Key Explanation: Choice C is correct. Since d is a linear function, its equation can be written as $d(t) = at + b$, where a is the slope and b is the d-intercept. Since $d(0) = 5$, then $b = 5$. Substituting 5 for b in $d(t) = at + b$ yields $d(t) = at + 5$. It's also given that $d(3) = 185$. Thus, $d(3) = 3a + 5 = 185$. Subtracting 5 from both sides of this equation yields $3a = 180$. Dividing both sides of this equation by 3 results in $a = 60$. Therefore, the equation that defines d is $d(t) = 60t + 5$.

   Distractor Explanations: Choice A is incorrect and may result if $d(3) = 125$ and not 185. **Choice B is incorrect** and may result if $d(3) = 155$ and not 185. **Choice D is incorrect** and may result if $d(0) = 35$ and not 5.

4. **Level:** Hard | **Skill/Knowledge:** Linear functions | **Testing Point:** Find the equation of a linear function after translation

   Key Explanation: Choice D is correct. Using the slope formula and the points $(-1, 2)$ and $(0, -1)$, the slope of the graphed linear function f is equal to $\dfrac{-1-2}{0-(-1)}$, which is equal to -3. The graphed function has a y-intercept of -1, then the equation of the linear function f is given by $f(x) = -3x - 1$. Let h represent the function which is the reflection of the function f over the x-axis. The equation of the function h is given by $h(x) = -f(x) = 3x + 1$. The function g is the translation of the function h 3 units to the right. Then, the equation of the function g is given by $g(x) = h(x - 3)$. Substituting $x - 3$ for x in the equation $3x + 1$ results in $g(x) = 3(x - 3) + 1$. Distribution of 3 in the equation yields $g(x) = 3x - 9 + 1$, which simplifies into $g(x) = 3x - 8$.

   Distractor Explanations: Choice A is incorrect. This is the equation of the function f. **Choice B is incorrect.** This is the equation of the function which is the translation of the function f 3 units to the right. **Choice C** is incorrect. This is the equation of the reflection of the function f over the x-axis.

Distractor Explanations: Choice B is incorrect. This is the value of c. **Choice C** is incorrect. This is the value of $c + d$. **Choice D** is incorrect. This is the value of d.

5. **Level:** Hard | **Skill/Knowledge:** Linear functions | **Testing Point:** Find the equation of a linear function given a table of values

Key Explanation: Choice A is correct. The equation of the given linear function f can be written in slope-intercept form $y = mx + b$, where m is the slope and b is the y-intercept. It's given that the points $(7, 20)$ and $(14, 26)$ belong to the function graph, then the slope of f can be found using the slope formula as $\dfrac{26-20}{14-7}$, which is equal to $\dfrac{6}{7}$. Substituting $\dfrac{6}{7}$ for m in $y = mx + b$ yields $y = \dfrac{6}{7}x + b$. Substituting 20 for y and 7 for x in this equation yields $20 = \dfrac{6}{7}(7) + b$, or $20 = 6 + b$. Subtracting 6 from both sides of this equation yields $14 = b$. Thus, the equation representing the function f is $y = \dfrac{6}{7}x + 14$. Distributing the left hand side of the given equation $c(x + 2) + 3(y - d) = -\dfrac{36}{7}$ yields $cx + 2c + 3y - 3d = -\dfrac{36}{7}$. Adding $-cx - 2c + 3d$ to both sides of this equation yields $3y = -cx - 2c + 3d - \dfrac{36}{7}$. Dividing both sides of this equation by 3 results in $y = -\dfrac{c}{3}x - \dfrac{2}{3}c + d - \dfrac{12}{7}$, and it was shown that $y = \dfrac{6}{7}x + 14$. By comparison, $-\dfrac{c}{3} = \dfrac{6}{7}$ which gives $c = -\dfrac{18}{7}$, and $-\dfrac{2}{3}c + d - \dfrac{12}{7} = 14$. Substituting $-\dfrac{18}{7}$ for c in this equation yields $-\dfrac{2}{3}\left(-\dfrac{18}{7}\right) + d - \dfrac{12}{7} = 14$ or $\dfrac{12}{7} + d - \dfrac{12}{7} = 14$. Adding constants on the left hand side yields $d = 14$. Therefore, the value of cd is $-\dfrac{18}{7} \times 14$, which is equal to -36.

Systems of Two Linear Equations in Two Variables

Systems of two linear equations in two variables have been commonly used to solve Math riddles or real-world problems. In such cases, you would be given two pieces of information that relate 2 variables, and your job is to translate each piece of information into a linear equation in two variables. After that, you would need to solve the system of two equations to get the values of the unknown variables. You then have to carefully reread the question to identify the required quantity before you give your final answer.

Systems of two linear equations in two variables have 3 types of solutions according to their number. Such a system might have one unique solution, infinitely many solutions, or no solution. There are many different methods to solve a system of two linear equations in two variables. In this part of the chapter, you will learn about algebraic methods and graphical methods for solving a system.

Algebraic Methods

There are many algebraic methods to solve a system of linear equations in two variables. The focus of this part will be on the **elimination method** and the **substitution method.** Before we use each of the two methods to solve a real-world problem, it is important to note that the final equation you get after applying each of the methods tells you the number of solutions of the system.

> If you get a false statement (like $0 = 5$), then this signals that the system of equations has **no solutions.**
>
> If you get a statement that is true for any real value of x (like $0 = 0$), then this signals that the system has **infinitely many solutions.**
>
> Otherwise, you will get one specific solution in the form of an ordered pair (x, y) which would be the only solution of the system.

To learn more about the algebraic methods, let's look at the student-produced response example below.

 For using an app, Ameer has 3 times as many points as Malik. If Ameer transfers 5 points to Malik, then Ameer will have twice as many points as Malik. What is the sum of points that both Ameer and Malik have?

Solution: After reading the problem, you are aware of the two unknowns— the number of points that Ameer has and the number of points that Malik has.

Let's build the system by identifying the two pieces of information that relate the two unknown quantities. Let x represent the **number of points that Ameer has,** and let y represent the **number of points that Malik has.**

It's given that Ameer has 3 times as many points as Malik. Hence, $x = 3y$.

It's also given that Ameer will have twice as many points as Malik if he transfers 5 points to Malik.

After the transfer, Ameer will have $x - 5$ points, and Malik will have $y + 5$ points.

Then, the equation that models this piece of information is $x - 5 = 2(y + 5)$.

Now, the system is ready for you to solve.

$$x = 3y$$

$$x - 5 = 2(y + 5)$$

We will now use the **"elimination method"** to solve this system. Before using the elimination method, it's helpful to group the unknowns on one side of each equation and the constants on the other side. This results in the system below.

$$x - 3y = 0$$

$$x - 2y = 15$$

The elimination method requires the addition or subtraction of the two equations to eliminate one of the unknowns, resulting in a linear equation in one variable that you can easily solve.

> **Note:** You may multiply one or both equations by a convenient number before adding or subtracting.

In this system, you can directly subtract the second equation from the first equation.

> **Remember**
>
> Subtract the left-hand side from the left-hand side and the right-hand side from the right-hand side.

Subtracting $x - 2y$ from $x - 3y$ yields $-y$, and subtracting 15 from 0 yields -15. Thus, $-y = -15$, or $y = 15$.

Now, to find the value of x, substitute 15 for y in any of the equations. For this question, it seems easier to use the equation $x = 3y$. Substituting 15 for y in this equation yields $x = 3(15) = 45$.

Therefore, the given system has 1 solution which is $x = 45$ and $y = 15$.

This means that the number of points that Ameer has is 45, and the number of points that Malik has is 15.

The question asks for the **sum of points**, which is, **(45 + 15)** or **60**.

60 is the correct answer to enter.

The same system will be solved using the **substitution method.** Let's look at the original system again.

$$x = 3y$$

$$x - 5 = 2(y + 5)$$

Solution: The first equation says that x is equal to $3y$.

Substituting $3y$ for x in the second equation yields $3y - 5 = 2(y + 5)$. Distribution on the right-hand side of this equation yields $3y - 5 = 2y + 10$. Subtracting $2y$ from both sides of this equation yields $y - 5 = 10$. Adding 5 to both sides of this equation results in $y = 15$.

To find x, follow the same substitution procedure explained in the previous paragraph.

The following are some additional examples solved using the Elimination method:

$$8x + 3y = 7$$

$$4x - 4y = 9$$

Given the systems of equation, what is the sum of x and y?

A) $\dfrac{1}{8}$

B) $\dfrac{1}{4}$

C) $\dfrac{4}{5}$

D) $\dfrac{5}{4}$

Solution: Solve the system of equations using the elimination method.

First, multiply the first equation by 4 and the second equation by 3 to make the y terms in both equations opposite. This results in (1) $32x + 12y = 28$ and (2) $12x - 12y = 27$. Adding the equations together $(32x + 12y) + (12x - 12y) = 28 + 27$ yields $44x = 55$. Dividing by 44 on both sides yields $x = \dfrac{5}{4}$.

Now, substitute the value of x into the first equation to get $8\left(\dfrac{5}{4}\right) + 3y = 7$.

Simplifying yields $10 + 3y = 7$. Subtracting 10 from both sides yields $3y = -3$, and dividing by 3 results in $y = -1$.

Finally, finding the sum of x and y results in $\dfrac{5}{4} + (-1) = \dfrac{1}{4}$, which is **Choice B**.

Choice A is incorrect. This may result from a calculation error.

Choice C is incorrect. This is the reciprocal of x.

Choice D is incorrect. This is the value of x.

The school is trying to raise money by organizing a bake sale for charity. They plan to sell cupcakes and brownies. Each cupcake sells for $3 and each brownie sells for $2. If the school sold a total of 150 items and made $380 in sales. How many cupcakes and brownies did they sell?

A) 50 cupcakes and 100 brownies

B) 60 cupcakes and 90 brownies

C) 70 cupcakes and 80 brownies

D) 80 cupcakes and 70 brownies

Solution: From the given information, 2 equations can be identified.

First, **let x be the number of cupcakes** sold and y **be the number of brownies** sold.

The first equation is the total sales which is $3x + 2y = 380$.

The second equation is the total number of items sold which is $x + y = 150$.

Solve the system of equations using the elimination method. Multiplying the second equation by 2 results in $2x + 2y = 300$.

Subtracting the second equation from the first gives us:

$(3x + 2y) - (2x + 2y) = 380 - 300$ yields $x = 80$.

Now, substitute the value of x into the first equation will result in $3(80) + 2y = 380$. Simplifying yields $240 + 2y = 380$. Subtracting 240 to both sides yields $2y = 140$, then dividing by 2 results in $y = 70$. Therefore, the **school sold 80 cupcakes and 70 brownies,** which is **Choice D.**

Choice A is incorrect. This may result if the total sales is $350.

Choice B is incorrect. This may result if the total sales is $360.

Choice C is incorrect. This may result if the total sales is $370.

Now, let's go through some examples that have been solved using the Substitution method:

 In a fruit store, a customer buys some apples and oranges for a total of $20. The cost of each apple is $0.50, and the cost of each orange is $0.75. If they bought a total of 34 fruits, how many apples and oranges did the customer buy?

A) 14 oranges and 20 apples

B) 12 oranges and 22 apples

C) 20 oranges and 14 apples

D) 22 oranges and 12 apples

Solution: From the given word problem, 2 equations can be identified.

First, **let a be the number of apples** bought and o **be the number of oranges** bought.

The first equation is the total cost of apples and oranges which is $0.50a + 0.75o = 20$.

The second equation is the total number of fruits bought which is $a + o = 34$.

Solve the system of equations using the substitution method.

On the second equation, solve for a to get $a = 34 - o$. Substitute this for a into the first equation to get $0.50(34 - o) + 0.75o = 20$. Simplifying results in $17 - 0.50o + 0.75o = 20$.

Subtracting 17 to both sides yields $0.25o = 3$, then dividing by 0.25 results in $o = 12$.

Now, substituting the value of o into the second equation results in $a = 34 - 12$ or $a = 22$.

Therefore, the **customer bought 12 oranges and 22 apples.**

The correct answer is **Choice B.**

Choice A is incorrect. This may result if the total cost is $20.5.

Choice C is incorrect. This may result if the total cost is $22.

Choice D is incorrect. This may result if the total cost is $22.5.

$$3x + 3y = 12$$

$$5x - y = 8$$

Solve for the systems of linear equations above.

A) $(2, 2)$

B) $(2, 4)$

C) $(0, 2)$

D) $(4, 0)$

Solution: Solve the system of linear equations using the substitution method.

First, solve the second equation $5x - y = 8$ to get the value of y. This results in $y = 5x - 8$.

Now, substitute this equation for y into the first equation $3x + 3y = 12$ which results in $3x + 3(5x - 8) = 12$. Simplifying yields $3x + 15x - 24 = 12$. Adding 24 to both sides yields $18x = 36$, then dividing by 18 results in $x = 2$.

Substituting the value of x into the second equation $y = 5x - 8$ yields $y = 5(2) - 8$ or $y = 2$. Therefore, the solution for the system of equations is $(2, 2)$.

The correct answer is **Choice A.**

Choice B is incorrect. This may result if the given systems of equations are $3x + 3y = 18$ and $5x - y = 6$.

Choice C is incorrect. This may result if the given systems of equations are $3x + 3y = 6$ and $5x - y = -2$.

Choice D is incorrect. This may result if the given systems of equations are $3x + 3y = 12$ and $5x - y = 20$.

Graphical Methods

As discussed earlier, a linear equation in two variables represents a straight line when graphed in the xy-plane. Thus, a system of two linear equations in two variables can be visualized as a pair of straight lines. If these two lines intersect at a single point, the coordinates of this point of intersection form the unique solution for the system. If the two lines are parallel, the system has no solution. If the two lines overlap or are confounded, then the system has infinitely many solutions. Let's look at the system mentioned in one of the examples:

$$x = 3y$$

$$x - 5 = 2(y + 5)$$

In such cases, the Desmos graphing calculator can significantly reduce the time and effort required to solve these questions.

You don't need to expand or simplify any of the equations. Just enter them as they are, and the calculator will graph the two lines for you instantly. Click on the point of intersection and hover over it to see its coordinates, which are the actual values of x and y, the solution to the system.

Look at the calculator's image below.

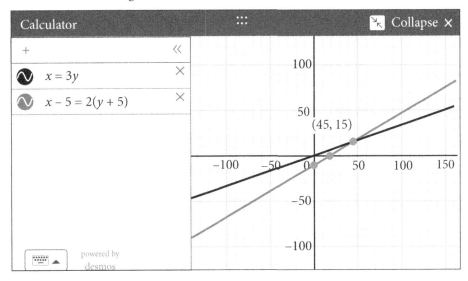

The following are additional examples that will be solved using the graphical method:

$$x + 2y = 5$$

$$2x - 3 = -4(y - 7/4)$$

Which of the following best describes the solution of the given system?

A) The system has one solution, (1, 2).

B) The system has one solution, (3, 1).

C) The system has no solution.

D) The system has infinitely many solutions.

Solution: To solve this problem, let's use the powerful bluebook calculator powered by Desmos.

Just enter the equations as they are given (see the figure below). You can see that the two lines overlap. This means that the system has **infinitely many solutions.** Therefore, the correct answer is **Choice D**.

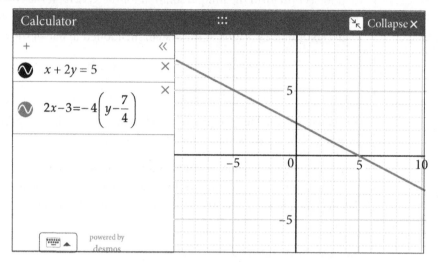

Choice A is incorrect and may result if the two graphed lines intersect at 1 point having the coordinates (1, 2).

Choice B is incorrect and may result if the two graphed lines intersect at 1 point having the coordinates (3, 1).

Choice C is incorrect and may result if the two graphed lines are parallel.

You could also use algebraic methods to solve this example, but it will take you a longer time. For practice, try to solve the system using algebraic methods and see if you can reach the same conclusion.

$$\frac{5}{2}y = 2x - 12$$

$$y = \frac{4}{5}x + 2$$

Which of the following describes the solution of the given systems of equations?

A) The system has one solution (11, 4).

B) The system has one solution (6, 2.5).

C) The system has no solution.

D) The system has infinitely many solutions.

Solution: Using the Desmos graphing calculator, enter the given equations in the input box.

Results will be displayed on the right side.

You can see that the **two lines are parallel** which implies that the **system has no solution.**

Therefore, the correct answer is **Choice C.**

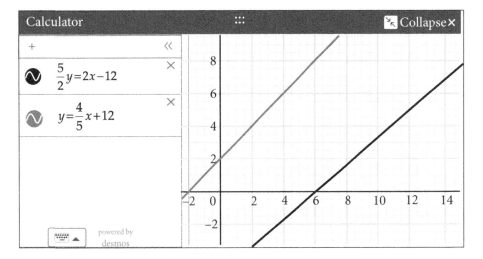

Choice A is incorrect. This may result if the two lines intersect at the coordinates (11, 4).

Choice B is incorrect. This may result if the two lines intersect at the coordinates (6, 2.5).

Choice D is incorrect. This may result if the two lines overlap.

$$x + \frac{2}{3}y = 12$$

$$\frac{5}{4}x - \frac{1}{2}y = 8$$

Which of the following describes the solution of the given systems of equations?

A) The system has one solution (8.50, 5.25).

B) The system has one solution (5.25, 8.50).

C) The system has no solution.

D) The system has infinitely many solutions.

Solution: Using the Desmos graphing calculator, enter the given equations in the input box.

Results will be displayed on the right side.

You can see that the **two lines intersect.** This means that the **system has one solution.**

The coordinates of the point of intersection can also be identified on the graph if you click on the point where the two lines intersect. Therefore, the correct answer is **Choice A.**

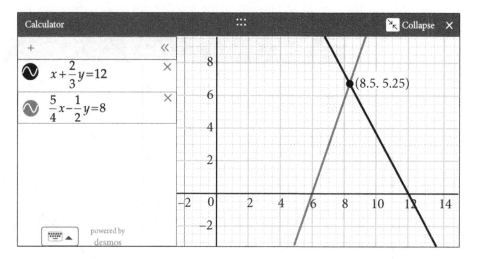

Choice **B** is incorrect. This may result if the two lines intersect at (5.25, 8.50).

Choice **C** is incorrect. This may result if the two lines are parallel.

Choice **D** is incorrect. This may result if the two lines overlap.

1 🔖 **Mark for Review**

$$y = 3x - 3 + 2x + 9$$
$$y = kx - 2 - 2x$$

If the system of equations above has no solution, what is the value of k?

2 🔖 **Mark for Review**

Jane has two electric fans in her house. One small fan uses 50 W per hour while the other big fan uses 80 W per hour. Last month, the two fans were used for a total of 315 hours and used a total of 19.68 kW. How many hours was the difference between the usage time of small and big fans last month?

3 🔖 **Mark for Review**

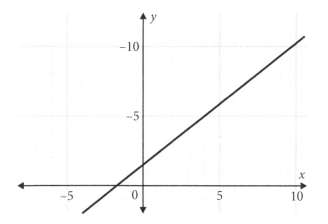

How many solutions will the line represented by the graph above and the equation $\frac{3}{7}y = \frac{x}{3} + \frac{2}{3}$ have?

A) 0

B) 1

C) 2

D) Infinite

4 🔖 **Mark for Review**

To supervise a children's school trip, it is estimated that 26 teachers and 33 helpers are needed. Knowing that the compensation of a teacher is $\frac{4}{5}$ more than 150% of a helper, what is a teacher's compensation if the total budget for supervising this trip is $2,580?

A) $25

B) $37.5

C) $45

D) $67.5

5 🔖 **Mark for Review**

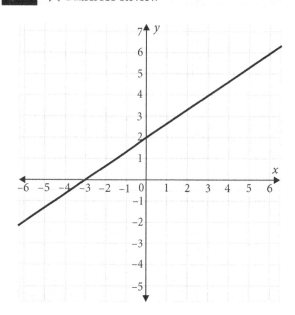

Line b (shown above) and line m (not shown) have no solution, which of the following equations would best represent line m?

A) $4y + 6x + 6 = 0$

B) $3y - 2x = 0$

C) $3y + 2x = 0$

D) $3y - 2x - 6 = 0$

ALGEBRA

1. **Level:** Easy | **Skill/Knowledge:** Systems of linear equations with two variables | **Testing Point:** Linear systems with no solutions

   Key Explanation: The correct answer is **7**. For a system of equations with no solution, the slope of the lines are equal.

   Using distribuive property to simplify the equations yields $y = 3x - 9 + 2x + 9$ and $y = kx - 2k - 2x$.

   Combining like terms yields $y = 5x$ and $y = (k - 2)x - 2k$.

   Hence, the slope of the 1st line is 5 and the slope of the 2nd line is $k - 2$.

   Equating the slopes of the two equations yields $5 = k - 2$.

   Adding 2 to both sides of the equation yields $7 = k$. Hence, the value of k will be 7.

2. **Level:** Medium | **Skill/Knowledge:** Systems of linear equations with two variables | **Testing Point:** Creating and using linear equations to solve a problem

   Key Explanation: The correct answer is **53 hours**.

   Let s be the usage time in hours of the small fan and b be the usage time in hours of the big fan.

   Since one small fan uses 50 W per hour while the other big fan uses 80 W per hour, then the expression that represents the total kW the two fans used is $50s + 80b$.

   Since the two fans are used for a total of 315 hours and used a total of 19.68 kW, then the two linear equations are $50s + 80b = 19.68(1000)$ and $s + b = 315$.

   Isolating s in the 2nd equation by subtracting b from both sides yields $s = 315 - b$.

   Substituting $s = 315 - b$ to $50s + 80b = 19.68 (1000)$ yields $50 (315 - b) + 80b = 19.68 (1000)$.

   Using distributive property yields $15750 - 50b + 80b = 19680$. Subtracting 15750 from both sides of the equation and combining like terms yields $30b = 3930$. Dividing both sides of the equation by 30 yields $b = 131$. Hence, the big fan was used for 131 hours last month.

   Substituting the value of b to $s = 315 - b$ yields $s = 315 - 131 = 184$. Hence, the small fan was used for 184 hours last month.

   Therefore, the difference between the usage time of small and big fans last month is $184 - 131 = 53$ hours.

3. **Level:** Medium | **Skill/Knowledge:** Systems of linear equations with two variables | **Testing Point:** Number of solutions of two linear equations

   Key Explanation: Choice D is correct. Looking at the graph, the line contains the points $(-2, 0)$ and $(7, 7)$. Using the formula $m = \dfrac{y_2 - y_1}{x_2 - x_1}$, the slope of the line is $\dfrac{7 - 0}{7 - (-2)} = \dfrac{7}{9}$. Substituting the point $(-2, 0)$ and the slope to the slope-intercept form equation yields $0 = \left(\dfrac{7}{9}\right)(-2) + b$. Simplifying the equation yields $0 = -\dfrac{14}{9} + b$. Adding $\dfrac{14}{9}$ to both sides of the equation yields $\dfrac{14}{9} = b$. Hence, the equation of the line represented by the graph is $y = \dfrac{7}{9}x + \dfrac{14}{9}$.

   Rewriting the given equation $\dfrac{3}{7}y = \dfrac{x}{3} + \dfrac{2}{3}$ to slope intercept form by multiplying $\dfrac{7}{3}$ to both sides yields $y = \dfrac{7}{9}x + \dfrac{14}{9}$.

   Since the two lines are the same, then they are collinear and have infinite solutions.

   Distractor Explanations: Choice A is incorrect. Only parallel lines with different y-intercepts will have no solutions. **Choice B** is incorrect. Since the lines have the same slope, then the system of linear equations cannot have one solution. **Choice C is incorrect.** Two lines cannot intersect at exactly two points. Hence, a system of two linear equations cannot have 2 solutions.

4. **Level:** Medium | **Skill/Knowledge:** Systems of two linear equations in two variables | **Testing Point:** Translate a word problem into a system of two linear equations in two variables and solve it

Key Explanation: Choice D is correct. Let t represent the compensation of a teacher in dollars for this trip, and let h represent the compensation of a helper in dollars for this trip. Since the total budget for supervising this trip is \$2,580 and there are 26 teachers and 33 helpers, then the equation $26t + 33h = 2580$ can be set up. It's given that the compensation of a teacher is $\frac{4}{5}$ more than 150% of a helper. This can be represented as

$$t = \left(1 + \frac{4}{5}\right) \times \frac{150}{100}h,$$ which can be simplified into

$t = \frac{9}{5} \times \frac{3}{2}h$, or $t = 2.7h$. Substituting $2.7h$ for t in the equation $26t + 33h = 2,580$ yields $26(2.7h) + 33h = 2,580$. This can be simplified into $70.2h + 33h = 2,580$. Combining like terms yields $103.2h = 2,580$. Dividing both sides of this equation by 103.2 results in $h = 25$. Substituting 25 for h in the equation $t = 2.7h$ yields $t = 2.725$, which is equal to 67.5. Therefore, the compensation of a teacher for this trip is \$67.5.

Distractor Explanations: Choice A is incorrect. This is the helper's compensation. **Choice B is incorrect.** This is 150% of a helper's compensation. **Choice C is incorrect.** This is 45 more than a helper's compensation.

5. **Level:** Hard | **Skill/Knowledge:** Systems of two linear equations in two variables | **Testing Point:** Linear systems with no solution

Key Explanation: The correct answer is B. A system of equations has no solution when the

graphs are parallel and with the same slope. Use the equation for the slope of the line b to find the slope. It is given from the graph that line b falls on the coordinates $(-3, 0)$ and $(0, 2)$. Substitute the coordinates to the equation $m = \dfrac{y_2 - y_1}{x_2 - x_1}$ yields $m = \dfrac{2 - 0}{0 - (-3)} = \dfrac{2}{3}$. The equation of line b is $y = \dfrac{2}{3}x + 2$ then line m would also have a slope of $\dfrac{2}{3}$. The equation $3y - 2x = 0$ rewritten in the form $y = mx + b$ is $y = \dfrac{2}{3}x$. The solution would therefore have no solution.

Distractor Explanations: Choice A is incorrect. This option is perpendicular to line b and would result in one solution. **Choice C is incorrect.** This option would result in a system of solutions with one solution. **Choice D is incorrect.** This option would result in a system of infinite solutions.

Linear Inequalities in One or Two Variables

In this part, the laws of solving linear inequalities will be stated. Also, the graphical solution of inequalities will be shown. This section will conclude with a word problem involving linear inequalities.

The Laws of Inequality

Similar to the laws of equality, you can add or subtract the same number from both sides of the inequality without worrying about the inequality sign. Also, multiplying or dividing by a positive number is permitted without changing the inequality sign, but you should pay attention when you multiply or divide by a negative number.

 Remember

Multiplying or dividing both sides of an inequality by a negative number is allowed but you need to swap the inequality sign. Of course, you may not divide by a zero or take the square root in case of inequalities too.

Let's go through some solved examples now:

$$2x - 8 < 2 \text{ and } 3x + 2 > 10$$

What is the solution set of the given inequalities?

A) $(\frac{8}{3}, 5)$

B) $(2, 5)$

C) $(2, 6)$

D) $(5, 8)$

Solution: Solve the given inequalities separately.

(1) $2x - 8 < 2$: Adding 8 to both sides yields $2x < 10$, then dividing by 2 on both sides results in $x < 5$.

(2) $3x + 2 > 10$: Subtracting 2 from both sides yields $3x > 8$, then dividing by 3 on both sides results in $x > \frac{8}{3}$.

To find the solution set of the given inequality, you need to find the intersection of the solution sets of both inequalities. The **intersection includes the values that satisfy both inequalities.** The value of x is greater than $\frac{8}{3}$ and less than 5 $\left(\frac{8}{3} < x < 5\right)$. Therefore, the solution set of the given inequalities is $\left(\frac{8}{3}, 5\right)$ which is **Choice A.**

This can also be solved using the Desmos graphing calculator. You can try solving it!

Choice B is incorrect. This may result if the given inequalities are $2x - 8 < 2$ and $4x + 2 > 10$.

Choice C is incorrect. This may result if the given inequalities are $2x – 8 < 4$ and $4x + 2 > 10$.

Choice D is incorrect. This may result if the given inequalities are $2x – 8 < 8$ and $2x + 2 > 12$.

$$4(2x – 7) –3(2x + 3) \leq 1$$

$$2x + 19 \leq 6x + 55$$

Which of the following is the solution set of the given inequalities?

A) $[–10, 19]$

B) $[–14, –5]$

C) $[–9, 19]$

D) $[9, –8]$

Solution: Solve the given inequalities separately.

(1) $4(2x – 7) –3(2x + 3) \leq 1$: Simplifying the equation yields $8x – 28 – 6x – 9 \leq 1$ or $2x – 37 \leq 1$. Adding 37 to both sides yields $2x \leq 38$, then dividing both sides by 2 results in $x \leq 19$.

(2) $2x + 19 \leq 6x + 55$: Subtracting $2x + 55$ from both sides yields $–36 \leq 4x$, then dividing both sides by 4 results in $–9 \leq x$.

To find the solution set of the given inequalities, you need to find the intersection of the solution sets of both inequalities. The intersection includes the values that satisfy both inequalities.

The **value of x is greater than or equal to –9 and less than or equal to 19** ($–9 \leq x \leq 19$). Therefore, the solution set of the given inequalities is $[–9, 19]$ which is **Choice C.**

This can also be solved using the Desmos graphing calculator. Give it a try!

Choice A is incorrect. This may result if the second inequality is $2x + 19 \leq 6x + 59$.

Choice B is incorrect. This may result from a calculation error.

Choice D is incorrect. This may result from a calculation error.

$$3x – 2y \leq 6$$

$$4x \geq y + 12$$

At which point does the given system of inequalities intersect?

A) $(3.6, 2.4)$

B) $(4, 4)$

C) $(4.2, 4.8)$

D) $(4.4, 5.6)$

Solution: First, rewrite both inequalities in slope-intercept form $y = mx + b$.

(1) $3x - 2y \leq 6$: Subtracting both sides by $3x$ yields $-2y \leq -3x + 6$. Dividing both sides by -2 results in $y \geq \frac{3}{2}x - 3$. Since the inequality was divided by a negative number, the inequality sign was flipped. This **inequality represents the area above the line** $y = \frac{3}{2}x - 3$.

(2) $4x \geq y + 12$: Subtracting 12 from both sides yields $4x - 12 \geq y$ or $y \leq 4x - 12$. This **inequality represents the area below the line** $y = 4x - 12$.

The point of intersection is where the lines intersect at a single point.

Set the equation of the two lines equal to each other.

This results in $\frac{3}{2}x - 3 = 4x - 12$.

Adding $-\frac{3}{2}x + 12$ on both sides of this equation yields $9 = \frac{5}{2}x$. Dividing both sides by $\frac{5}{2}$ results in $x = \frac{18}{5} = 3.6$.

To find y, substitute 3.6 for x in the first equation which results in $y = \frac{3}{2}(3.6) - 3$ or $y = 2.4$.

Therefore, the **point of intersection** for the given system of inequalities is (3.6, 2.4).

The correct answer is **Choice A**.

This can also be solved using the Desmos graphing calculator.

Choice B is incorrect. This may result if the first given equation is $3x - 2y \leq 4$.

Choice C is incorrect. This may result if the first given equation is $3x - 2y \leq 3$.

Choice D is incorrect. This may result if the first given equation is $3x - 2y \leq 2$.

Graphical Solutions of Linear Inequalities

Here lies another aspect of the power of the Desmos graphing calculator. You can enter inequalities into the input box of the calculator and it will graph the solution for you instantly. This works for both linear inequalities in one or two variables. The colored region indicates the solution of the inequality. The way to enter the sign $\leq$ is to enter <= on your keyboard. Also, if you want to solve the inequality $3 < -\frac{2}{k}$, which you saw in the previous example, graphically, you should enter $3 < -\frac{2}{x}$, and the calculator will depict the region between $-\frac{2}{3}$ and 0. Let's look at some examples that involves a system of two linear inequalities in two variables.

> (?)
>
> $$2x + 4y > 6$$
>
> $$3 - 2(x + 1) > y$$
>
> Which of the following points (x, y) is a solution to the given system of inequalities?

A) $(-5, -5)$

B) $(-5, 5)$

C) $(5, -5)$

D) $(5, 5)$

Solution: The traditional method of solving this question would be to substitute the coordinates of each point in the answer choices in both inequalities of the system, and check which point satisfies both inequalities.

However, with the presence of the Desmos graphing calculator, there is no need to waste precious testing time using this method.

Instead, just enter the inequalities into the input box of the calculator, and it will graph the solution.

> **Note:** The **solution to a system of inequalities** would be the **region where the two solutions of both inequalities overlap.**

In this example whose graph is shown below, it is the darker red region. The only answer choice that belongs to this region is the point $(-5, 5)$, thus the correct answer to this question is **Choice B**.

Choice A is incorrect. The point $(-5, -5)$ is a solution of the second inequality of the system but not the first.

Choice C is incorrect. The point $(5, -5)$ is not a solution of any of the two inequalities of the system.

Choice D is incorrect. The point $(5, 5)$ is a solution of the first inequality of the system but not the second.

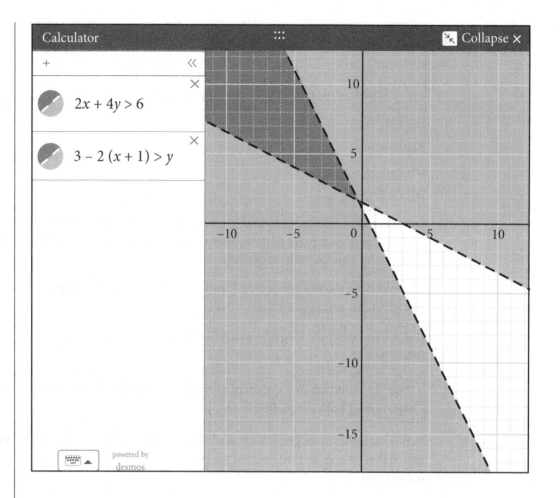

$$y \leq -3x + 7$$

$$5x \geq y + 8$$

Which of the following points satisfies the above system of inequalities?

A) $(-2, 2)$

B) $(4, -4)$

C) $(2, -4)$

D) $(-2, 4)$

Solution: Using the Desmos graphing calculator, we can solve this question easily.

Simply enter the given inequalities into the input box and the solution will be displayed on the right.

The solution to a system of inequalities is the region where both inequalities overlap.

The result of the graph is shown below. Going through the answer choices, the only acceptable answer is **Choice C.**

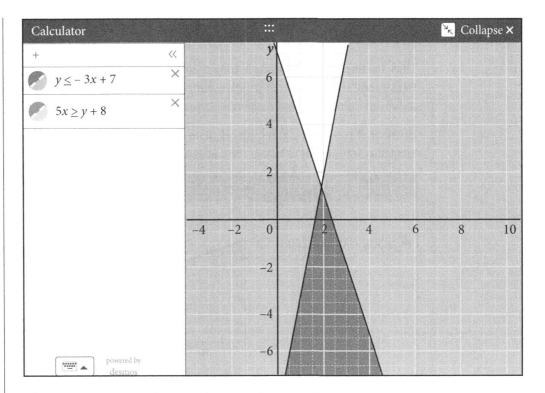

Choice A is incorrect. This is a solution to the inequality $y \leq -3x + 7$.

Choice B is incorrect. This is a solution to the inequality $5x \geq y + 8$.

Choice D is incorrect. This is a solution to the inequality $y \leq -3x + 7$.

Word Problem

Below is an example of how you might encounter linear inequalities in word problems on Digital SAT Math. As usual, there is more than one way of solving such problems. Let's take a look at some questions now.

> A 2000 m^2 plot of land is to be planted with orange and apple trees. On average, a fully grown orange tree occupies 36 m^2 of land, while a fully grown apple tree occupies 100 m^2 of land. Which combination can be planted on this plot?

A) 20 orange trees and 10 apple trees

B) 20 orange trees and 15 apple trees

C) 30 orange trees and 10 apple trees

D) 40 orange trees and 6 apple trees

Solution: The question asks for a possible combination of orange trees and apple trees to be planted on the 2,000 m^2 land.

It's given that each orange tree occupies 36 m^2 of land and each apple tree occupies 100 m^2 of land.

Let x represent the number of possible orange trees planted, and y represent the number of possible apple trees planted.

Then, a possible combination of orange and apple trees would have a total area of $36x + 100y$. This total area must be less than or equal to the area of the land which is 2,000 m^2.

Thus, the linear inequality $36x + 100y \leq 2000$ represents this situation. You can use the **'Going Backwards'** strategy and substitute x and y with the numbers given in the answer choices to see which numbers would make the inequality true.

However, if you use the graphing calculator, things will be easier and faster. Entering the inequality into the input box of the calculator results in the graph below.

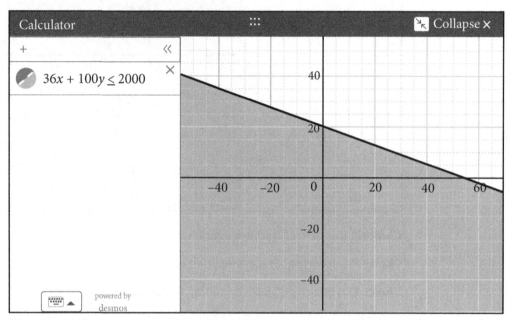

The only combination given in the answer choices that belongs to the shaded region is (20, 10), so a possible combination would be to plant 20 orange trees and 10 apple trees. Therefore, the correct answer is **Choice A**.

Choice B is incorrect. Planting 20 orange trees and 15 apple trees would result in an area $20 \times 36 + 15 \times 100 = 2{,}220 \ m^2$, which is greater than the given area of the land.

Choice C is incorrect. Planting 30 orange trees and 10 apple trees would result in an area of $30 \times 36 + 10 \times 100 = 2{,}080 \ m^2$, which is greater than the given area of the land.

Choice D is incorrect. Planting 40 orange trees and 6 apple trees would result in an area of $40 \times 36 + 6 \times 100 = 2{,}040 \ m^2$, which is greater than the given area of the land.

 A bakery sells doughnuts and cookies. The bakery makes a profit of at least $80 daily, selling doughnuts and cookies. If each doughnut sells for $2.5 and each cookie sells for $1.5, which of the following inequalities represents this situation?

A) $1.5d - 2.5c \geq 80$

B) $1.5d - 2.5c \leq 80$

C) $2.5d + 1.5c \geq 80$

D) $2.5d + 1.5c \leq 80$

Solution: To solve this problem, let d be the number of doughnuts sold and c the number of cookies sold.

From the given information, the profit by selling doughnuts can be represented by $2.5d$ and the profit by selling cookies can be represented by $1.5c$.

The bakery makes a profit of at least $80. The word **"at least"** indicates that the profit should be **greater than or equal to $80,** therefore the inequality sign for this situation is $\geq$.

The given information can also be represented as $2.5d + 1.5c \geq 80$ (**Choice C**).

Choice A is incorrect. This option subtracts the profit from selling cookies from the profit of selling donuts which does not reflect the combined profit of both items.

Choice B is incorrect. This option implies that the combined profit is less than or equal to $80.

Choice D is incorrect. This option implies that the combined profit is less than or equal to $80.

 A painter wants to buy art supplies but wants to spend no more than $40. If each paint cost $7 and each brush cost $4, how many paint and brushes can the painter buy?

A) 3 paints and 4 brushes

B) 3 paints and 5 brushes

C) 4 paints and 4 brushes

D) 4 paints and 5 brushes

Solution: Let's denote the number of paint as p and the number of brushes as b.

It is given that each paint costs $7 and each brush costs $4.

The total expenditure can be represented as $(7p + 4b)$.

The painter wants to spend no more than $40. The word **"no more than"** indicates that the cost should be **less than or equal to $40**, therefore the inequality sign for this situation is $\leq$.

The inequality can be written as $7p + 4b \leq 40$.

You can use the **"Going Backwards"** strategy and substitute the choices for p and b to determine which answer choice satisfies the inequality.

You can also use the graphing calculator and enter the inequality into the input box.

Before this, change the variables p to x and b to y since other variables will not be considered in the graphing calculator.

The result of the graph is shown below.

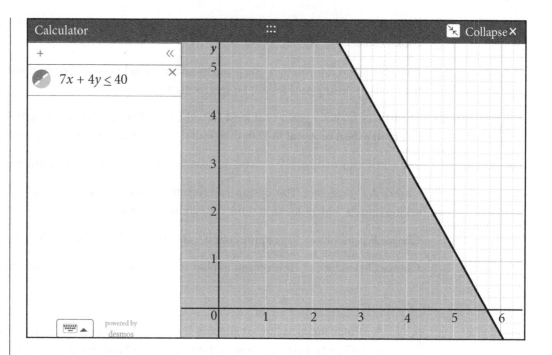

The only answer choice that belongs to the shaded region is (3, 4), **Choice A** which is 3 paints and 4 brushes.

Choice B is incorrect. This option is above the shaded region and therefore not a solution.

Choice C is incorrect. This option is above the shaded region and therefore not a solution.

Choice D is incorrect. This option is above the shaded region and therefore not a solution.

1 ⊓ **Mark for Review**

$$5x - 4y > 1$$

Which of the following points is a solution to the given inequality above?

A) $(-1, -1.4)$

B) $(0, -0.25)$

C) $(1.75, 1.9)$

D) $(2.2, 2.5)$

2 ⊓ **Mark for Review**

Lester needs to send his handmade pots and vases to his friend. He only wants to spend $30 for the shipping fee. In the $30 shipping fee rate, Lester can only ship up to 10 kg of package. A pot weighs 0.65 kg and a vase weighs 0.5 kg. If he decided to send only 5 pots, what is the maximum number of vases that he can add to his package?

A) 12

B) 13

C) 14

D) 15

3 ⊓ **Mark for Review**

$$3y \geq 5 - 2x$$

Which of the following points is not a solution to the given inequality above?

A) $\left(\frac{5}{2}, 0\right)$

B) $(2, 2)$

C) $(3, -1)$

D) $(-2, 4)$

4 ⊓ **Mark for Review**

$$\frac{3x - 5\left(\frac{7}{4}x + 1\right)}{2} < -2(3 - x)$$

The solution to the given inequality is $x > b$ where b is a constant. What is the value of b?

5 ⊓ **Mark for Review**

$$1.6tx > -1.2(10x) + 0.6(80 - 5x)$$

For what value of t is the solution to the given inequality $x < -48$?

Answers & Explanations

1. **Level:** Easy | **Skill/Knowledge:** Linear inequalities in one or two variables

   Key Explanation: Choice C is correct. To verify if a point is a solution, substitute the points to x and y in the inequality.

   Substituting $(1.75, 1.9)$ yields $5(1.75) - 4(1.9) > 1$. Simplifying the inequality yields $1.15 > 1$. Since the statement is true, then $(1.75, 1.9)$ is a solution.

   Distractor Explanations: Choice A is incorrect. Substituting the point $(-1, -1.4)$ to the inequality results in a false statement. Hence, it is not a solution. **Choice B is incorrect.** Substituting the point $(0, -0.25)$ to the inequality results in a false statement. Hence, it is not a solution. **Choice D is incorrect.** Substituting the point $(2.2, 2.5)$ to the inequality results in a false statement. Hence, it is not a solution.

2. **Level:** Medium | **Skill/Knowledge:** Linear inequalities in one or two variables | **Testing Point:** Creating and using a linear inequality

   Key Explanation: Choice B is correct. Let p be the number of pots and v be the number of vases.

   Since he can only send up to 10 kg, then the inequality that represents the situation is $0.65p + 0.5v \leq 10$.

   Since he only sends 5 pots, then $0.65(5) + 0.5v \leq 10$. Simplifying the inequality yields $3.25 + 0.5v \leq 10$. Subtracting both sides of the inequality by 3.25 yields $0.5v \leq 6.75$. Dividing both sides of the inequality by 0.5 yields $v \leq 13.5$. Therefore, he can add up to 13 vases in the package.

   Distractor Explanations: Choice A is incorrect. This is not the maximum number of vases that can be added since the total weight will only be 9.25 kg. Hence, one more vase can still be added. **Choice C is incorrect** and may result from rounding up 13.5. Adding 14 vases will result in a total weight of more than 10 kg. **Choice D is**

   incorrect. Adding 15 vases to the package will result in a total weight of more than 10 kg.

3. **Level:** Medium | **Skill/Knowledge:** Linear inequalities in one or two variables | **Testing Point:** Finding the solutions of an inequality

   Key Explanation: Choice C is correct. To verify if a point is a solution, substitute the points to x and y in the inequality.

   Substituting $(3, -1)$ yields $3(-1) \geq 5 - 2(3)$. Simplifying the inequality yields $-3 \geq -1$. Since the statement is false, then $(3, -1)$ is not a solution.

   Distractor Explanations: Choice A is incorrect. Substituting the point $(\frac{5}{2}, 0)$ to the inequality results in a true statement. Hence, it is a solution. **Choice B is incorrect.** Substituting the point $(2, 2)$ to the inequality results in a true statement. Hence, it is a solution. **Choice D is incorrect.** Substituting the point $(-2, 4)$ to the inequality results in a true statement. Hence, it is a solution.

4. **Level:** Hard | **Skill/Knowledge:** Linear inequalities in one or two variables | **Testing Point:** Solve a linear inequality in one variable

   Key Explanation: $\frac{28}{39}$ is the correct answer.

   Distribution on both sides of the given inequality $\dfrac{3x - 5\left(\dfrac{7}{4}x + 1\right)}{2} < -2(3 - x)$

   yields $\dfrac{3x - \dfrac{35}{4}x - 5}{2} < -6 + 2x$. Multiplying both sides of this inequality by 2 results in $3x - \dfrac{35}{4}x - 5 < -12 + 4x$. Combining like terms on the left hand side yields $-\dfrac{23}{4}x - 5 < -12 + 4x$. Subtracting $4x$ from both sides of the inequality results in $-\dfrac{23}{4}x - 4x - 5 < -12$. Combining like terms on the left hand side yields $-\dfrac{39}{4}x - 5 < -12$. Adding 5 to both sides of this inequality results in

$-\dfrac{39}{4}x < -7$. Dividing both sides of this inequality

by $-\dfrac{39}{4}$ (which flips the inequality sign) yields

$x > \dfrac{-7}{-\dfrac{39}{4}}$, which is equivalent to $x > \dfrac{28}{39}$.

Therefore, the value of b is $\dfrac{28}{39}$.

5. **Level:** Hard | **Skill/Knowledge:** Linear inequalities in one or two variables | **Testing Point:** Solve a linear inequality in one variable

Key Explanation: −10 is the correct answer. Distribution on the right hand side of the given inequality $1.6tx > -1.2(10x) + 0.6(80 - 5x)$ yields $1.6tx > -12x + 48 - 3x$. Combining like terms results in $1.6tx > -15x + 48$. Adding $15x$ to both sides of the inequality yields $1.6tx + 15x > 48$. Factoring out x results in $(1.6t + 15)x > 48$. Since the solution is $x < -48$ with the inequality sign flipped, then $1.6t + 15 < 0$ and $1.6t + 15 = -1$. Subtracting 15 from both sides of this equation yields $1.6t = -15 - 1$, which can be simplified into $1.6t = -16$. Dividing both sides of this equation by 1.6 results in $t = -10$.

This page is intentionally left blank

Chapter 9
Advanced Math

Topics covered in this chapter:

- Equivalent Expressions
- Nonlinear Equations in One Variable and Systems of Equations in Two Variables
- Nonlinear Functions

Advanced Math is another important topic tested on the Digital SAT Math, also spanning about 35% of the total number of questions. This domain prepares you for **higher-level math** and tests your **comprehension of nonlinear relationships,** such as **nonlinear functions** and their graphs (eg: **quadratic and exponential functions**).

Advanced Math questions can also be multiple-choice or student-produced response questions. In-context questions also appear in this domain, asking you to **interpret nonlinear functions, build functions to represent a problem,** and **define number solutions and characteristics of nonlinear graphs** in context.

Questions in the Advanced Math section also require procedural skills, such as the **ability to factorize and expand expressions, isolate variables,** and perform different types of **calculations with polynomials.** You may also be asked to solve **nonlinear equations** involving **exponents, square roots,** and **absolute values,** to mention a few, and **systems of equations in two variables,** where at least **one of the two equations is nonlinear.**

In this chapter, two helpful strategies will be explained with examples. Then, the different skills or knowledge points under Advanced Math will be analyzed into their subtopics. Many examples will be provided to help you master the concepts needed to get a high score on the Digital SAT Math.

 Rules to remember while solving Advanced Math questions

- $a^2 + 2ab + b^2 = (a + b)^2$

- $a^2 - 2ab + b^2 = (a - b)^2$

- $a^2 - b^2 = (a - b)(a + b)$

- If a and b are positive numbers, and m and n are real numbers, the following laws for exponents hold:

Product Rule	$a^m \times a^n = a^{m+n}$
Power of a Product Rule	$(ab)^m = a^m \times b^m$
Quotient Rule	$\dfrac{a^m}{a^n} = a^{m-n}$
Power of a Quotient Rule	$\left(\dfrac{a}{b}\right)^m = \dfrac{a^m}{b^m}$
Power of a Power Rule	$\left(a^m\right)^n = a^{m \times n}$
Negative Exponent Rule	$a^{-m} = \dfrac{1}{a^m}$
Zero Exponent Rule ($a \neq 0$)	$a^0 = 1$

- To solve a **radical equation, isolate the radical** and **square both sides.** Solve the resulting equation for the unknown, and **check for extraneous roots.**

- To solve a **rational equation with denominators not equal to zero, cross-multiply** and then solve the resulting equation.

- The solution of an absolute value equation $|ax + b| = |cx + d|$ is the set of solutions to the two equations $ax + b = cx + d$ and $ax + b = -(cx + d)$.

- The **graph of** $f(x) + a$ is the **translation of the graph of** $f(x)$ **by** $+a$ **units vertically.** Moving **negative units vertically** is **going down** while moving **positive units vertically is going up.**

- The **graph of** $f(x + a)$ is the **translation of the graph of** $f(x)$ **by** $-a$ **units horizontally.** Moving **negative units horizontally** is **going left** while moving **positive units horizontally** is **going right.**

- If $g(x) = -f(x)$, the graph of g will be the reflection of the graph of f over the x-axis.

- $ax^2 + bx + c = a(x - x_1)(x - x_2)$ where x_1 and x_2 are the zeros of the quadratic expression $ax^2 + bx + c$.

- The quadratic formula for finding the zeros x_1 and x_2 of the quadratic expression $ax^2 + bx + c$ is If the **discriminant** $b^2 - 4ac > 0$, then the **quadratic expression** $ax^2 + bx + c$ has **two zeros.** If $b^2 - 4ac = 0$, the **quadratic expression has one zero.** If $b^2 - 4ac < 0$, the **quadratic expression has no real zeros.** The **sum of the two zeros** is equal to and the **product of the two zeros** is equal to Graphically, the zeros are the x-intercepts of the function $f(x) = ax^2 + bx + c$.

- If $a > 0$, the **parabola** representing the function $f(x) = ax^2 + bx + c$ is **concave upwards** and we say that it **opens up.** If $a < 0$, the **parabola** is **concave downwards** and we say that it **opens down.**

- The quadratic function $f(x) = ax^2 + bx + c$ has a vertex at the point and a vertical axis of symmetry at

- The vertex form of the equation of a parabola having a vertex at the coordinates (h, k) is $f(x) = a(x - h)^2 + k$.

- The factored form of the equation of a parabola having two zeros x_1 and x_2 is $f(x) = a(x - x_1)(x - x_2)$.

- An exponential function has the form $f(x) = ab^x$, where b is a positive constant and x is a variable. The **number** $a = f(0)$ **is the initial value** of the exponential function.

- The **exponential function is increasing** (known as **exponential growth**) if $b > 1$, and it is **decreasing** (known as **exponential decay**) if $0 < b < 1$.

- The **general expression** of an **exponential function** involving a rate is written as $f(t) = a(1 \pm r)^t$, where a is the initial value and r is the constant rate (percent decrease or increase) by which the function changes every unit increase in the period of time t.

- In the **case of compound interest**, the future value F is given by where **P is the initial value of the deposit, r is the annual interest rate, t is the number of years, and k is the number of times the interest is compounded per year.**

- In the special case where the interest is compounded annually, the formula for the future value simplifies to $F = P(1 + r)^t$.

Strategies

In this part, you will learn more about **two strategies** that will help you find the correct answer to numerous questions in the Advanced Math section. One of the strategies involves 'Replacing', introduced in the previous chapter, which is very important in the Advanced Math domain, especially when dealing with equivalent expressions. Below you can find the strategies with examples of how to apply them.

1. Eliminating and Replacing

By careful analysis of the given question, one can sometimes eliminate choices that simply can't be true. This decreases the number of choices to be considered, resulting in a higher possibility of getting the correct answer. After limiting the number of choices, the **'Replacing'** strategy can be helpful, particularly if variables exist in the question stem and the answer choices. This is frequently encountered in questions about **equivalent expressions,** where this strategy can prove to be very useful. Choose simple numbers, avoiding 0 or 1, that also adhere to the given conditions in the question. Let's go through some examples below.

$$-2x^3 + 10(2x^2 - 5x)$$

Which of the following is equivalent to the given expression?

A) $-2x(x-5)^2$

B) $-2x(x - 5)(x + 5)$

C) $2x(x - 5)^2$

D) $2x(x - 5)(x + 5)$

Solution: The mathematical solution to this question will be presented later in the chapter. For now, we will use the **'Eliminating and Replacing'** strategy.

Looking at the given question: the first term is $-2x^3$. Expanding **Choice C**, we get $2x(x^2 + 25 - 10x)$. The first term is $2x^3$ instead of $-2x^3$. Hence, **Choice C** can be eliminated.

Similarly, expanding **Choice D**, we get $2x(x^2 - 25)$ and the first term is $2x^3$ instead of $-2x^3$. **Choice D** can be eliminated too.

To determine which of the two **Choices A** or **B** is correct, **choose a simple number,** for example $x = 2$.

Substituting **2 for x in the given polynomial expression** $-2x^3 + 10(2x^2 - 5x)$ yields $-2(2^3) + 10(2 \times 2^2 - 5(2))$, which can be simplified into $-16 + 10(8 - 10)$, or $-16-20$ which is equal to -36.

Now, try substituting 2 for x in **Choice A**, which yields $-2(2)(2-5)^2$, which is equal to $-4 \times (-3)^2 = -36$. This is the same result found when substituting 2 for x in the given expression, but we still **need to check the other choice** because there might be **instances where the number 2 gives the same result in both choices.** In that case, the substitution procedure should be repeated with a simple number **other than 2**.

Substituting 2 for x in **Choice B** yields $-2(2)(2-5)(2+5)$, which is equal to $-4(-3)(7)$, or 84. Since 84 is not equal to -36, the correct answer is **Choice A**.

---

⑦	$4x^5(x-1) - 2x(3x^2 + 5)$
	Which of the following is equivalent to the given expression?

A) $x(4x^4 - 4x^3 - 6x^2 - 10)$

B) $x(4x^5 - 4x^4 - 6x^3 - 10x)$

C) $2x(2x^5 - 2x^4 - 3x^2 - 5)$

D) $2x(-2x^5 - 2x^3 - 3x^2 - 5)$

Solution: Use the Eliminating and Replacing strategy to solve this question.

Looking at the given expression $4x^5(x-1) - 2x(3x^2 + 5)$, the first term when expanded is $4x^6$.

Expanding **Choice A** yields $4x^5 - 4x^4 - 6x^3 - 10x$. The first term should be $4x^6$ instead of $4x^5$. Therefore, **Choice A** is eliminated.

Expanding **Choice D** yields $-4x^6 - 4x^4 - 6x^3 - 10x$. The first term should be $4x^6$ instead of $-4x^6$. Therefore, **Choice D** is eliminated.

To determine between **Choices B** and **C**, substitute a number into the given expression to compare the results. Using $x = 2$ in the given expression yields $4(2)^5(2-1) - 2(2)(3(2)^2 + 5)$, which is equal to 60.

Substituting 2 for x into **Choice B** $x(4x^5 - 4x^4 - 6x^3 - 10x)$ yields $(2)(4(2)^5 - 4(2)^4 - 6(2)^3 - 10(2))$ which is equal to -8. Since -8 is not equal to 60, **Choice B** is eliminated.

Substituting 2 for x into **Choice C** $2x(2x^5 - 2x^4 - 3x^2 - 5)$ yields $2(2)(2(2)^5 - 2(2)^4 - 3(2)^2 - 5)$ which is equal to 60. Since 60 is equal to the result of the given expression, the **correct answer** is **Choice C**.

$$\frac{x-4}{3x^2+10x+8} \times \frac{3x+2}{x-4}$$

Which of the following is equivalent to the given expression?

A) $\dfrac{3x+2}{(3x+4)(x+2)}$

B) $\dfrac{(x-4)(3x+2)}{3x+4}$

C) $\dfrac{(x-4)(3x+2)}{(3x+4)(x+2)}$

D) $\dfrac{3x+2}{(3x+4)(x-4)}$

Solution: Use the eliminating and replacing strategy to solve this question.

Looking at the given expression $\dfrac{x-4}{3x^2+10x+8} \times \dfrac{3x+2}{x-4}$, you can see that the common factor

$x-4$ can be eliminated and only $3x+2$ will remain as the numerator.

Therefore, **Choices B** and **C** can be eliminated.

To determine between **Choice A** and **D**, substitute a number into the given expression

to compare the results. Using $x=2$ in the given expression $\dfrac{x-4}{3x^2+10x+8} \times \dfrac{3x+2}{x-4}$ yields

$\dfrac{2-4}{3(2)^2+10x+8} \times \dfrac{3(2)+2}{2-4}$, which is equal to $\dfrac{1}{5}$ or 0.2.

Substituting 2 for x into **Choice A** $\dfrac{3x+2}{(3x+4)(x+2)}$ yields $\dfrac{3(2)+2}{(3(2)+4)(2+2)}$ which is equal to $\dfrac{1}{5}$

or 0.2. Since 0.2 is equal to the result of the given expression, **Choice A** is the correct answer.

Let us make sure that **Choice D** does not give the same result as **Choice A**.

Substituting 2 for x into **Choice D** $\dfrac{3x+2}{(3x+4)(x-4)}$ yields $\dfrac{3(2)+2}{(3(2)+4)(2-4)}$ which is equal to

$-\dfrac{2}{5}$ or –0.4. Since –0.4 is not equal to 0.2, **Choice D** is incorrect.

So, even if you find factoring expressions difficult, you could still find the correct answer to such questions easily using the '**Eliminating and Replacing**' strategy.

⑦

$$\frac{S^8}{T} = m^6 r^4$$

Given the equation, find the expression of r in terms of S, T, and m.

A) $r = \dfrac{S^4}{m^3 \sqrt{T}}$

B) $r = m\sqrt[4]{\dfrac{S^8}{Tm^2}}$

C) $r = \dfrac{S^2}{T\sqrt[4]{m^6}}$

D) $r = \dfrac{S^2}{m\sqrt[4]{Tm^2}}$

Solution: This question can be solved more easily using mathematical solutions than a strategy.

To find the expression of r in terms of S, T, and m from the given equation $\dfrac{S^8}{T} = m^6 r^4$, isolate r^4 by dividing both sides by m^6. This results in $\dfrac{S^8}{Tm^6} = r^4$.

Taking the fourth root of both sides yields $r = \sqrt[4]{\dfrac{S^8}{Tm^6}}$.

Simplifying further results in $r = \dfrac{S^2}{m\sqrt[4]{Tm^2}}$. Therefore, the correct answer is **Choice D**.

Choice A is incorrect. This may result if $\dfrac{S^8}{T} = m^6 r^2$.

Choice B is incorrect. This may result from incorrectly placing m as a numerator instead of a denominator.

Choice C is incorrect. This may result if $\dfrac{S^8}{T^4} = m^6 r^4$.

2. Visualizing

Another strategy you might find helpful, especially when you're dealing with functions and extrema, is 'Visualizing'. Thanks to the built-in graphing calculator, you don't have to imagine or hand sketch your visualizations when you encounter real-life word problems on test day. Simply frame the equations based on the information provided or plug in the given equations directly into the input section and it will display the graph, instantly and error-free! Let's go through the word problem below.

$$y = -4.9t^2 + 30$$

A stone (initially at rest) falls from a height of 30 m. The equation shows the height y of the stone (in meters) relative to the ground after t seconds. After how many seconds does the stone reach the ground? (Round your answer to the nearest tenth)

Solution: You can find the detailed algebraic solution to this problem later in the chapter. For now, let's try visualizing. After replacing t by x, enter the given equation $y = -4.9x^2 + 30$ into the Desmos graphing calculator. Of course, the graph only makes sense for $x \geq 0$ and $y \geq 0$, that is in the first quadrant. Look at the figure below.

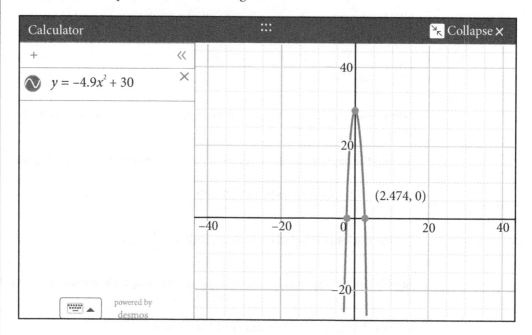

When the **stone reaches the ground,** the **height is zero.**

Thus, the value of **y is zero** and this is where the **function intersects the x-axis**.

Click on the graph and hover over the **positive x-intercept**. The coordinates are (2.474, 0). The **x-coordinate is the time** (in seconds) after which the stone reaches the ground.

Since the question asks you to round your answer to the nearest tenth, the **correct answer** that you need to enter is **2.5**.

Equivalent Expressions

Equivalent expressions are **different forms of the same expression.** These can be found by **factoring, expanding, or simplifying.** They can be different forms of rational expressions or expressions involving exponents. Additionally, when a certain quantity is isolated, the result is an equivalent expression.

Operations with Polynomials

Equivalent expressions can appear as **different forms** of the **same polynomial.** From your high school studies, you should be familiar with **adding and subtracting polynomials.** You should also be able to **factor** polynomials and **expand** factored **polynomials.**

To factor a polynomial, follow these steps.

 ### Step 1

Find a common factor: Look for a **common factor** among the different **terms of the polynomial.** If present, factor it out. For example, $3x^3 - 18x^2 + 27x = 3x(x^2 - 6x + 9)$.

 ### Step 2

Look for remarkable identities: By this, we mean the three formulae, $a^2 + 2ab + b^2 = (a + b)^2$ which is the **square of a sum,** $a^2 - 2ab + b^2 = (a - b)^2$ which is the **square of a difference,** and $a^2 - b^2 = (a - b)(a + b)$ which is the **difference of two squares.** For example, $3x(x^2 - 6x + 9) = 3x(x - 3)^2$.

 ### Step 3

Try alternatives: If the previous two steps didn't work and you need to factor a second-degree polynomial, try to use the **'trial and error'** method, the **quadratic formula**, or the **factor theorem.**

The quadratic formula will be discussed later in the chapter, but for now, if you know the two roots x_1 and x_2 of a quadratic expression of the form $ax^2 + bx + c$, the factored form of this expression will be $a(x - x_1)(x - x_2)$.

> **Note:** The factor theorem states that if a is a zero of a polynomial expression, then $(x - a)$ is a factor of this expression.

The **'trial and error'** method is generally used with **second-degree expressions** of the form $x^2 + sx + p$. You need to look for **two numbers** m and n whose **sum is** s and **product is** p. If you find these numbers, the **factored form** of $x^2 + sx + p$ would be $(x + m)(x + n)$.

For example, to factor the polynomial $x^2 - 3x + 2$, look for two numbers whose sum is -3 and product is 2. These two numbers are -1 and -2.

Thus, the factored form of $x^2 - 3x + 2$ is $(x - 1)(x - 2)$.

To **expand factored expressions,** simply **multiply each term in the first factor** by **each term in the second factor,** then simplify by **combining like terms,** which are terms with the same variable and exponent. For example,

$(2x^2 + 3x - 5)(x + 2) = (2x^2)(x) + (2x^2)(2) + (3x)(x) + (3x)(2) + (-5)(x) + (-5)(2)$.

This is equal to $2x^3 + 4x^2 + 3x^2 + 6x - 5x - 10$.

Combining like terms yields $2x^3 + (4 + 3)x^2 + (6 - 5)x - 10$, which can be simplified into $2x^3 + 7x^2 + x - 10$.

Go through the solved examples before using the **'Eliminating and Replacing'** strategy.

$$-2x^3 + 10(2x^2 - 5x)$$

Which of the following is equivalent to the given expression?

A) $-2x(x - 5)^2$

B) $-2x(x - 5)(x + 5)$

C) $2x(x - 5)^2$

D) $2x(x - 5)(x + 5)$

Solution: Expanding the expression $10(2x^2 - 5x)$ by multiplying 10 with each of the terms yields $20x^2 - 50x$.

Then the given expression $-2x^3 + 10(2x^2 - 5x)$ can be written as $-2x^3 + 20x^2 - 50x$. Factoring out the common factor $2x$ yields $2x(-x^2 + 10x - 25)$.

Factoring out -1 results in $-2x(x^2 - 10x + 25)$.

The expression $x^2 - 10x + 25$, which can be written as $x^2 - 2(x)(5) + 25$, has the form of $a^2 - 2ab + b^2$, which is equal to $(a - b)^2$. Thus, $x^2 - 10x + 25 = (x - 5)^2$.

Therefore, the factored form of the expression $-2x^3 + 10(2x^2 - 5x)$ is $-2x(x - 5)^2$.

The correct answer is **Choice A**.

Choice B is incorrect because $-2x(x - 5)(x + 5)$ is equal to $-2x(x^2 - 25)$. This expression can be expanded into $-2x^3 + 50x$ which is different from the given expression $-2x^3 + 20x^2 - 50x$.

Choice C is incorrect because $2x(x - 5)^2$ is equal to $2x(x^2 - 10x + 25)$. This expression can be expanded into $2x^3 - 20x^2 + 50x$ which is opposite to the given expression $-2x^3 + 20x^2 - 50x$.

Choice D is incorrect because $2x(x - 5)(x + 5)$ is equal to $2x(x^2 - 25)$. This expression can be expanded into $2x^3 - 50x$ which is different from the given expression $-2x^3 + 20x^2 - 50x$.

$$9(x + 2)^2 + 3(4x - 9) + 6$$

Which of the following is equivalent to the given expression?

A) $3(3x + 1)(x + 5)$

B) $9(3x + 1)(x + 5)$

C) $3(3x + 1)(x + 15)$

D) $3(3x + 5)(x + 1)$

Solution: Distributing the given expression $9(x + 2)^2 + 3(4x - 9) + 6$ yields $9(x^2 + 4x + 4) + 12x - 27 + 6$. Further distribution yields $9x^2 + 36x + 36 + 12x - 27 + 6$. Combining like terms results in $9x^2 + 48x + 15$.

Factor the expression by first looking for common factors among the coefficients which is 3.

This results in $3(3x^2 + 16x + 5)$. Factor the expression $3x^2 + 16x + 5$ by looking for two numbers that multiply to get $3 \times 5 = 15$ and add to get 16. The numbers are 1 and 15.

The expression inside the bracket can be rewritten as $(3x^2 + x + 15x + 5)$. Grouping the terms yields $x(3x + 1) + 5(3x + 1)$ or $(3x + 1)(x + 5)$.

Therefore, the expression equivalent to the given expression is $3(3x + 1)(x + 5)$, which is **Choice A.**

Choice B is incorrect. Expanding the expression $9(3x + 1)(x + 5)$ yields $27x^2 + 144x + 45$ which is different from the given expression.

Choice C is incorrect. Expanding the expression $3(3x + 1)(x + 15)$ yields $9x^2 + 138x + 45$ which is different from the given expression.

Choice D is incorrect. Expanding the expression $3(3x + 5)(x + 1)$ yields $9x^2 + 24x + 15$ which is different from the given expression.

 The expression $(x^3 - r)(x^3 - mx)$ is equivalent to $x^6 - 16x^4 + 22x^3 + tx$. What is the value of t?

A) -352

B) -22

C) 256

D) 484

Solution: To solve, first expand the given expression $(x^3 - r)(x^3 - mx)$ which yields $x^6 - mx^4 - rx^3 + rmx$. Comparing this expression to the given $x^6 - 16x^4 + 22x^3 + tx$ yields $m = 16$, $r = -22$, and $rm = t$. Substituting 16 for m and -22 for r in the equation $rm = t$ results in $(-22)(16) = t$ or $t = -352$. Therefore, the correct answer is **Choice A.**

Choice B is incorrect. This is the value of r.

Choice C is incorrect. This is the value of m^2.

Choice D is incorrect. This is the value of r^2.

Rational Expressions

The key to simplifying rational expressions, which are the quotients of two polynomials, is to obtain the factored form. Next, the common factors present in the numerator and the denominator should be canceled.

> **Note:** Canceling is just another term for dividing the numerator and denominator of the fractional expression by the same factor.

Since dividing by zero is an undefined operation, the condition of having the common factor not equal to zero should be satisfied before you perform the division. Look at the example below.

$$\frac{5x^2 - 10x}{x + 4} \cdot \frac{x^2 + 6x + 8}{x^2 - 4}$$

Which of the following expressions is equivalent to the given expression, given that x is not equal to -4, -2, and 2?

A) $5x$

B) $\dfrac{5x^2 - 10x}{x + 2}$

C) $\dfrac{5x(x^2 + 6x + 8)}{(x + 2)^2}$

D) $\dfrac{5x(x^2 + 6x + 8)}{(x + 4)^2}$

Solution: Your goal should be to get the factored form of the given expression.

The expression $5x^2 - 10x$ is equivalent to $5x(x - 2)$ by factoring out $5x$.

The expression $x^2 - 4$ is equivalent to $(x - 2)(x + 2)$ using the 'difference of two squares' identity.

The expression $x^2 + 6x + 8$ is equivalent to $(x + 4)(x + 2)$ using the **'trial and error'** method.

Thus, the expression $\dfrac{5x^2 - 10x}{x + 4} \cdot \dfrac{x^2 + 6x + 8}{x^2 - 4}$ is equivalent to $\dfrac{5x(x - 2)}{x + 4} \cdot \dfrac{(x + 4)(x + 2)}{(x - 2)(x + 2)}$.

Since x is not equal to -4, -2, or 2, you can cancel the common factors $(x - 2)$, $(x + 2)$ and $(x + 4)$.

Therefore, the simplified form of $\dfrac{5x(x - 2)}{(x + 4)} \cdot \dfrac{(x + 4)(x + 2)}{(x - 2)(x + 2)}$ is $5x$.

The correct answer is **Choice A.**

Choice B is incorrect and may result if the given expression is $\dfrac{5x^2 - 10x}{x + 4} \cdot \dfrac{x^2 + 6x + 8}{(x + 2)^2}$.

Choice C is incorrect and may result if the given expression is $\dfrac{5x^2 - 10x}{x + 2} \cdot \dfrac{x^2 + 6x + 8}{x^2 - 4}$.

Choice D is incorrect and may result if the given expression is $\dfrac{5x^2-10x}{x+4}\cdot\dfrac{x^2+6x+8}{(x+4)(x-2)}$.

You could also solve this question using the **'Replacing'** strategy. Remember that x is not equal to –4, –2, and 2.

Choosing 3 to substitute for x in the given expression yields $\dfrac{5(3)^2-10(3)}{3+4}\cdot\dfrac{(3)^2\,6(3)+8}{(3)^2-4}$, which is equal to 15.

Choice A yields the same result which is 15, while **Choices B, C,** and **D** result in the numbers 3, 21, and $\dfrac{75}{7}$, respectively.

Therefore, the correct answer is **Choice A**.

$$\dfrac{x^2-4}{2x^2+5x+2}$$

Which of the following is equivalent to the given expression?

A) $\dfrac{x+2}{2x+1}$

B) $\dfrac{(x-2)(x+2)}{2x+1}$

C) $\dfrac{x-2}{2x+1}$

D) $\dfrac{x-2}{2x-1}$

Solution: To find the equivalent expression, factor both the numerator and the denominator of the given expression $\dfrac{x^2-4}{2x^2+5x+2}$, which yields $\dfrac{(x+2)(x-2)}{(2x+1)(x+2)}$.

Canceling the common factor, $x+2$, results in $\dfrac{x-2}{2x+1}$.

Therefore, the correct answer is **Choice C**.

Choice A is incorrect. This results from an incorrect sign in the numerator.

Choice B is incorrect. This results from only canceling the denominator.

Choice D is incorrect. This results from an incorrect sign in the denominator.

(?)

$$\frac{3x^2 - 12}{x^2 - 4x + 4} \div \frac{3x^2 + 6x}{x^2 - 9}$$

Which of the following is equivalent to the given expression?

A) $\dfrac{(x^2 + 3)(x - 3)}{x(x - 2)}$

B) $\dfrac{(x + 3)(x - 3)}{x(x - 2)}$

C) $\dfrac{(x + 3)(x - 3)}{x^2(x - 2)}$

D) $\dfrac{x(x + 3)(x - 3)}{(x - 2)^2}$

Solution: To solve, simplify each fraction of the given expression $\dfrac{3x^2 - 12}{x^2 - 4x + 4} \div \dfrac{3x^2 + 6x}{x^2 - 9}$.

For the first fraction $\dfrac{3x^2 - 12}{x^2 - 4x + 4}$, factoring yields $\dfrac{3(x^2 - 4)}{(x - 2)(x - 2)}$ which simplifies to

$\dfrac{3(x + 2)(x - 2)}{(x - 2)(x - 2)}$. Canceling the common factor $x - 2$ yields $\dfrac{3(x + 2)}{x - 2}$.

For the second fraction $\dfrac{3x^2 + 6x}{x^2 - 9}$, factoring yields $\dfrac{3x(x + 2)}{(x + 3)(x - 3)}$.

The expression will now become $\dfrac{3(x + 2)}{x - 2} \div \dfrac{3x(x + 2)}{(x + 3)(x - 3)}$.

To simplify the fraction, multiply by the reciprocal of the second fraction

$\dfrac{3(x + 2)}{x - 2} \times \dfrac{(x + 3)(x - 3)}{3x(x + 2)}$ by canceling the common factors 3 and $(x + 2)$ results in

$\dfrac{(x + 3)(x - 3)}{x(x - 2)}$. Therefore, the correct answer is **Choice B**.

Choice A is incorrect. This may result from a calculation error.

Choice C is incorrect. This may result from a calculation error.

Choice D is incorrect. This may result from a calculation error.

Isolating Quantities

You may encounter questions on the Digital SAT that require you to **isolate a variable or a quantity.** You are generally required to **apply the properties of equality** to isolate the required quantity. This type of question also falls under the category of equivalent expressions. Check out the examples below.

⑦

$$S = 4\pi r^2$$

The given equation shows the surface area S of a sphere having a radius r. Which of the following expresses r in terms of S?

A) $r = \dfrac{S}{4\pi}$

B) $r = \sqrt{\dfrac{S}{2\pi}}$

C) $r = \dfrac{1}{2}\sqrt{\dfrac{S}{\pi}}$

D) $r = \sqrt{\dfrac{4\pi}{S}}$

Solution: The question asks to isolate the quantity r.

Dividing both sides of the given equation $S = 4\pi r^2$ by 4π yields $\dfrac{S}{4\pi} = r^2$.

Since r is a positive quantity (radius of the sphere), then it is equal to the positive square root

of $\dfrac{S}{4\pi}$. Thus, $r = \sqrt{\dfrac{S}{4\pi}}$. Since $\sqrt{4} = 2$, then $r = \dfrac{1}{2}\sqrt{\dfrac{S}{\pi}}$.

Therefore, the correct answer is **Choice C.**

Choice A is incorrect because $r^2 = \dfrac{S}{4\pi}$ and not r.

Choice B is incorrect because when taking the square root of 4, the number 2 should be placed outside the radical sign instead of inside.

Choice D is incorrect because $\dfrac{1}{r} = \sqrt{\dfrac{4\pi}{S}}$ and not r.

---

⑦

$$5a^2 + 2b = 30$$

What is the expression for a in terms of b, given the equation above, where a is a positive quantity?

A) $a = \sqrt{30 - \dfrac{2b}{5}}$

B) $a = \sqrt{6 - \dfrac{2b}{5}}$

C) $a = 6 - \sqrt{\dfrac{2b}{5}}$

D) $a = 30 - \sqrt{\dfrac{2b}{5}}$

Solution: To express a in terms of b, rearrange the equation to isolate a.

Subtracting $2b$ from both sides of the given equation $5a^2 + 2b = 30$ yields $5a^2 = 30 - 2b$.

Dividing both sides by 5 results in $a^2 = 6 - \dfrac{2b}{5}$.

Since there is a condition that a is a positive quantity, then a is the positive square root of $6 - \frac{2b}{5}$. Thus, $a = \sqrt{6 - \frac{2b}{5}}$.

Therefore, the correct answer is **Choice B**.

Choice A is incorrect. This may result from not dividing 30 by 5.

Choice C is incorrect. This may result from not taking the square root of 6.

Choice D is incorrect. This may result from not dividing 30 by 5 and not taking the square root.

(?)

$$V = \frac{1}{3}\pi r^2 h$$

The volume of a right circular cone is given by the equation above, where is the radius of the circular base and h is the height. Which of the following equations shows the radius of the circular base in terms of the height and volume of a right circular cone?

A) $r = \sqrt{\frac{3V}{\pi h}}$

B) $r = \sqrt[3]{\frac{3V}{\pi h}}$

C) $r = \sqrt{\frac{V}{3\pi h}}$

D) $r = \sqrt{3V\pi h}$

Solution: To solve for r in terms of volume and height, rearrange the given formula $V = \frac{1}{3}\pi r^2 h$ to isolate r.

Multiplying both sides by 3 and dividing both sides by h yields $\frac{3V}{\pi h} = r^2$.

Taking the square root of both sides yields $\sqrt{\frac{3V}{\pi h}} = r$. Therefore, the correct answer is **Choice A**.

Choice B is incorrect and may result from taking the cube root instead of the square root.

Choice C is incorrect and may result from dividing 3 instead of multiplying.

Choice D is incorrect and may result from multiplying h instead of dividing.

Exponents

There are many laws or rules for dealing with exponents that you should be familiar with from high school. In this part, the most frequently encountered laws will be stated. If a and b are positive numbers, and m and n are real numbers, the following laws hold true.

Product Rule	$a^m \times a^n = a^{m+n}$
Power of a Product Rule	$(ab)^m = a^m \times b^m$
Quotient Rule	$\dfrac{a^m}{a^n} = a^{m-n}$
Power of a Quotient Rule	$\left(\dfrac{a}{b}\right)^m = \dfrac{a^m}{b^m}$
Power of a Power Rule	$\left(a^m\right)^n = a^{m \times n}$
Negative Exponent Rule	$a^{-m} = \dfrac{1}{a^m}$
Zero Exponent Rule ($a \neq 0$)	$a^0 = 1$

Consider the example below:

 If $2s - 4r = 5$, which of the following is equivalent to $\dfrac{4^s}{16^r}$?

A) $\dfrac{1}{32}$

B) $\dfrac{1}{4}$

C) 4

D) 32

Solution: The number 4 can be written as 2^2 and the number 16 can be written as 2^4.

Then, $\dfrac{4^s}{16^r} = \dfrac{(2^2)^s}{(2^4)^r}$. This is equivalent to $\dfrac{2^{2s}}{2^{4r}}$, which is equal to 2^{2s-4r}.

It's given that $2s - 4r = 5$, then $2^{2s-4r} = 2^5 = 32$.

Therefore, the correct answer is **Choice D.**

Choice A is incorrect. This is the value of $\dfrac{16^r}{4^s}$.

Choice B is incorrect. This is the value of $\dfrac{16^r \times 2^3}{4^s}$.

Choice C is incorrect. This is the value of $\dfrac{4^s}{16^r \times 2^3}$.

You could also solve this question using the **'Replacing'** strategy. Choose convenient values for s and r such that $2s - 4r = 5$.

An example would be $s = 3$ and $r = \dfrac{1}{4}$.

Using your calculator or the Desmos graphing calculator, find the value of $\dfrac{4^3}{16^{\frac{1}{4}}}$. The result is 32.

Rational exponents are other forms of roots. If a is a positive real number, and m and n are strictly positive integer, the laws below hold.

$a^{\frac{1}{2}} = \sqrt{a}$
$a^{\frac{1}{n}} = \sqrt[n]{a}$
$a^{\frac{m}{n}} = \sqrt[n]{a^m}$
$\sqrt[n]{a} \times \sqrt[n]{b} = \sqrt[n]{ab}$
$\dfrac{\sqrt[n]{a}}{\sqrt[n]{b}} = \sqrt[n]{\dfrac{a}{b}} \ (b \neq 0)$

Let's try the example below:

> ⑦ If a and b are strictly positive numbers, which of the following is equivalent to
>
> $\sqrt[4]{81a^5} \cdot \sqrt[4]{\dfrac{a^7}{b^8}}$?

A) $\dfrac{3a^3}{b^2}$

B) $\dfrac{9a^3}{b^2}$

C) $\dfrac{9a^6}{b^4}$

D) $\dfrac{3a^{\frac{35}{4}}}{b^2}$

Solution: Applying the law $\sqrt[n]{a} \times \sqrt[n]{b} = \sqrt[n]{ab}$, the given expression $\sqrt[4]{81a^5} \cdot \sqrt[4]{\dfrac{a^7}{b^8}}$ is equivalent to $\sqrt[4]{81a^5 \times \dfrac{a^7}{b^8}}$.

Substituting 3^4 for 81 and a^{12} for $a^5 \times a^7$ yields $\sqrt[4]{3^4 \dfrac{a^{12}}{b^8}}$, which is equivalent to $\left(3^4 \dfrac{a^{12}}{b^8} \right)^{\frac{1}{4}}$.

Distributing the exponent over the factors yields $\left(3^4 \right)^{\frac{1}{4}} \dfrac{\left(a^{12} \right)^{\frac{1}{4}}}{\left(b^8 \right)^{\frac{1}{4}}}$, which can be simplified into

$3\dfrac{a^3}{b^2}$. Therefore, the given expression $\sqrt[4]{81a^5} \cdot \sqrt[4]{\dfrac{a^7}{b^8}}$ is equivalent to $\dfrac{3a^3}{b^2}$.

The correct answer is **Choice A**.

Choice B is incorrect and may result if the given expression is $\sqrt[4]{9^4 a^5} \cdot \sqrt[4]{\dfrac{a^7}{b^8}}$.

Choice C is incorrect and may result if the given expression is $\sqrt{81a^5} \cdot \sqrt{\dfrac{a^7}{b^8}}$.

Choice D is incorrect and may result if the given expression is $\sqrt[4]{81a^{28}} \cdot \sqrt[4]{\dfrac{a^7}{b^8}}$.

1 ▢ Mark for Review

$$2x^2 - 16x + 32 = 2(x + b)^2$$

For the equation above, what is the value of b?

A) -8

B) -4

C) 4

D) 8

2 ▢ Mark for Review

$$x^3 + 10x^2 + 17x - 28$$

If $(x - 1)(x + 4)(x + a)$ is equivalent to the expression above, what is the value of $2a$?

A) 4

B) 7

C) 8

D) 14

3 ▢ Mark for Review

$$2(3x - 2)(x + 1)$$

The expression above is equivalent to $ax^2 + bx + c$, what is the value of $a + b + c$?

4 ▢ Mark for Review

$$\frac{1 + 8xy}{8x^2y + 4xy} - \frac{y + 2}{2x + 1}$$

Which expression is equivalent to the given expression?

A) $\dfrac{1 - 4xy^2}{8x^2y + 4xy}$

B) $\dfrac{4xy^2 + 16xy + 1}{8x^2y + 4xy}$

C) $\dfrac{8x^2y + 4xy}{1 - 4xy^2}$

D) $\dfrac{-2xy^2 + 4xy + 1}{8x^2y + 4xy}$

5 ▢ Mark for Review

The expression $3x^2 + 8x + c$, where c is a constant, can be factored into $(3x + d)(x - 1)$, where d is a constant. What is the value of c?

Answers & Explanations

1. **Level:** Easy | **Skill/Knowledge:** Equivalent expressions | **Testing Point:** Identical equations

   Key Explanation: Choice B is correct. Factoring out 2 from the left side of the equation yields $2(x^2 - 8x + 16) = 2(x + b)^2$. Rewriting the equation to make it a binomial square results in $2(x - 4)^2 = 2(x + b)^2$. Therefore the value of b is -4.

   Distractor Explanations: Choice A is incorrect. This is the result if the left side of the equation is $2x^2 - 32x + 128$. **Choice C is incorrect.** This is the result if the left side of the equation is $2x^2 + 16x + 32$. **Choice D is incorrect.** This is the result if the left side of the equation is $2x^2 + 32x + 128$.

2. **Level:** Medium | **Skill/Knowledge:** Equivalent expressions | **Testing Point:** Matching the coefficients and constants

   Key Explanation: Choice D is correct. Using distributive property to multiply the first two binomials yields $(x^2 + 4x - x - 4)(x + a)$.

   Combining like terms yields $(x^2 + 3x - 4)(x + a)$.

   Using distributive property to multiply the trinomial with binomial yields $x^3 + 3x^2 - 4x + ax^2 + 3ax - 4a$.

   Combining like terms yields $x^3 + (3 + a)x^2 + (3a - 4)x - 4a$.

   Hence, $x^3 + (3 + a)x^2 + (3a - 4)\underline{x} - 4a = x^3 + 10x^2 + 17x - 28$.

   Matching the constants yields $-4a = -28$.

   Dividing both sides of the equation by -4 yields $a = 7$.

   Therefore, $2a = 2(7) = 14$.

   Distractor Explanations: Choice A is incorrect. This value of $2a$ makes the expression $(x - 1)(x + 4)(x + 2)$ which is equivalent to $x^3 + 5x^2 + 2x - 8$ and not the given expression. **Choice B is incorrect.** This the value of a and not $2a$. **Choice C**

   is incorrect. This value of $2a$ makes the expression $(x - 1)(x + 4)(x + 4)$ which is equivalent to $x^3 + 7x^2 + 8x - 16$ and not the given expression.

3. **Level:** Medium | **Skill/Knowledge:** Equivalent Expressions | **Testing Point:** Factoring (Difference of Squares)

   Key Explanation: The correct answer is **4**. Open the parentheses and combine like terms together to get $2(3x - 2)(x + 1) = 2(3x^2 - 2x + 3x - 2)$ or $2(3x^2 + x - 2) = 6x^2 + 2x - 4$, which is equivalent to $ax^2 + bx + c$. The value of a is 6, the value of b is 2 and the value of c is -4, therefore the value of $a + b + c = 6 + 2 - 4 = 4$.

4. **Level:** Hard | **Skill/Knowledge:** Equivalent expressions | **Testing Point:** Apply operations on rational expressions to find an equivalent expression

   Key Explanation: Choice A is correct. Factoring the denominator of the first term of the given expression results in $\dfrac{1 + 8xy}{4xy(2x + 1)} - \dfrac{y + 2}{2x + 1}$.

   Multiplying the second term by $\dfrac{4xy}{4xy}$ yields the expression $\dfrac{1 + 8xy}{4xy(2x + 1)} - \dfrac{4xy(y + 2)}{4xy(2x + 1)}$ with common denominators. Adding the two terms gives $\dfrac{1 + 8xy - 4xy(y + 2)}{4xy(2x + 1)}$. Distributing results in $\dfrac{1 + 8xy - 4xy^2 - 8xy}{8x^2y + 4xy}$. Combining like terms in the numerator of the expression yields $\dfrac{1 - 4xy^2}{8x^2y + 4xy}$.

   Distractor Explanations: Choice B is incorrect. This is the result if the given expression is $\dfrac{1 - 8xy}{8x^2y + 4xy} + \dfrac{y + 2}{2x + 1}$. **Choice C is incorrect and** may result from interchanging the denominator and numerator of the result. **Choice D is incorrect.** This is the result if the second term of the given expression is $\dfrac{y + 2}{4x + 2}$.

5. **Level:** Hard | **Skill/Knowledge:** Equivalent expressions | **Testing Point:** Use equivalent expressions to find unknown quantities

Key Explanation: –11 is the correct answer. Distributing $(3x + d)(x - 1)$ yields $3x^2 - 3x + dx - d$. Combining like terms results in $3x^2 + x(-3 + d) - d$. It's given that this expression is equal to $3x^2 + 8x + c$. Setting the like terms of these two expressions equal gives $-3 + d = 8$ and $-d = c$. Adding 3 to both sides of the equation $-3 + d = 8$ yields $d = 11$. Substituting 11 for d in $-d = c$ results in $-11 = c$. Therefore, the value of c is -11.

Nonlinear Equations in One Variable and Systems of Equations in Two Variables

In this section, you will learn how to solve nonlinear equations in one variable. These include **quadratic equations, square root equations, rational equations,** and **absolute value equations.** You will also learn how to deal with **systems of equations in two variables** where at least **one of the equations is nonlinear.**

Quadratic Equations

The general form of a quadratic equation is $ax^2 + bx + c = 0$ where $a \neq 0$. The **discriminant** of a quadratic equation or expression is $b^2 - 4ac$.

Note: The discriminant of a quadratic equation determines the number of real solutions to the equation.

If $b^2 - 4ac > 0$, the equation has 2 real and distinct solutions.

If $b^2 - 4ac = 0$, the equation has exactly 1 real solution.

If $b^2 - 4ac < 0$, the equation has no real solutions.

In case a quadratic equation $ax^2 + bx + c = 0$ has zeros, the formula used to find these zeros is known as the **'Quadratic Formula'**.

The **quadratic formula** is given by: $x = \dfrac{-b \pm \sqrt{b^2 - 4ac}}{2a}$

Notice the expression of the discriminant $b^2 - 4ac$ under the square root sign.

The **sum of the two solutions** is equal to $-\dfrac{b}{a}$, and the **product of the two solutions** is equal to $\dfrac{c}{a}$.

Let's look at some examples below:

$$x^2 + 13x + 40 = 0$$

What is one of the solutions to the given equation?

Solution: You could use many methods to solve this question.

Starting with the quadratic formula $x = \dfrac{-b \pm \sqrt{b^2 - 4ac}}{2a}$, substituting 1 for a, 13 for b and 40 for c yields $x = \dfrac{-13 \pm \sqrt{13^2 - 4(1)(40)}}{2(1)}$.

Performing the calculations results in $x = \dfrac{-13 \pm \sqrt{9}}{2}$ or $x = \dfrac{-13 \pm 3}{2}$.

This yields two solutions for x, $x = -5$ or $x = -8$.

Therefore, the correct answer to enter is either –5 or –8.

Remember to enter only one answer.

You could also search for the solutions by **finding the sum and the product** of the solutions. The **sum of the solutions** is $-\dfrac{b}{a}$ or –13, and the **product of the solutions** is $\dfrac{c}{a}$ or 40. Through the **"trial and error"** method, you can find the solutions –5 and –8, which have a sum of –13 and a product of 40.

$$3x^2 + 21x - 12 = 0$$

What is the sum of the solutions to the given equation?

A) –7.5

B) –7

C) –4

D) 0.5

Solution: For a quadratic equation in the form $ax^2 + bx + c = 0$, the sum of the solutions is given by the formula $-\dfrac{b}{a}$.

In the given equation $3x^2 + 21x - 12 = 0$, substituting 3 for a and 21 for b into the formula yields $-\dfrac{21}{3}$, or –7. Therefore, the correct answer is **Choice B**.

Choice A is incorrect. This is one of the solutions to the given equation.

Choice C is incorrect. This is the product of the solutions to the given equation.

Choice D is incorrect. This is one of the solutions to the given equation.

$$5x^2 - 18x - 34 = 0$$

What is the number of real roots of the given equation?

A) The equation has 2 real and distinct roots.

B) The equation has exactly 1 real root.

C) The equation has no real roots.

D) The equation has infinitely many roots.

Solution: For a quadratic equation in the form $ax^2 + bx + c = 0$, the discriminant is given by the formula $b^2 - 4ac$.

In the given equation $5x^2 - 18x - 34 = 0$, substituting 5 for a, –18 for b, and –34 for c into the discriminant formula yields $(-18)^2 - 4(5)(-34) = 1{,}004$.

If $b^2 - 4ac > 0$, the equation has 2 real and distinct roots. Since 1,004 is greater than 0, the given equation has 2 real roots. Therefore, the correct answer is **Choice A**.

Choice B is incorrect. This would be the case if the discriminant is equal to 0.

Choice C is incorrect. This would be the case if the discriminant is less than 0 or negative.

Choice D is incorrect. A quadratic equation can have at most 2 real roots.

Pro Tip --

The easiest and quickest method of solving this question would be to simply enter the quadratic equation into the built-in graphing calculator. Doing so will instantly display the 2 x-intercepts of the graph at $(-5, 0)$ and $(-8, 0)$.

Systems of Equations in Two Variables

You will sometimes encounter a system of two equations in two variables where **at least one of the equations is nonlinear.** The method for solving **most of these systems** is **substitution.**

Try to find **one variable from one equation** and **substitute its expression in the second equation.**

After that, solve the **resulting nonlinear equation in one variable.**

Consider the solved examples below:

$$y - m = 1$$

$$y = x^2 + 10x + 30$$

In the given system of equations, m is a real constant. If the system has only one solution, which of the following is the value of m?

A) -5

B) -4

C) 4

D) 5

Solution: To solve the given system, isolate y from the first equation and substitute its expression in the second equation.

Adding m to both sides of the equation $y - m = 1$ yields $y = m + 1$.

Substituting $m + 1$ for y in the second equation $y = x^2 + 10x + 30$ yields $m + 1 = x^2 + 10x + 30$.

Subtracting $m + 1$ from both sides of this equation results in $x^2 + 10x + 29 - m = 0$.

This is a quadratic equation.

Since the question states that the system has only one solution, the discriminant of this quadratic equation must be zero.

The discriminant is given by $b^2 - 4ac$.

Substituting 1 for a, 10 for b, and $(29 - m)$ for c in the equation $b^2 - 4ac = 0$ yields $10^2 - 4(1)(29 - m) = 0$.

Expanding the left-hand side of this equation yields $100 - 116 + 4m = 0$ or $-16 + 4m = 0$. Adding 16 to both sides of this equation results in $4m = 16$.

Dividing both sides of this equation by 4 yields $m = 4$.

Therefore, the correct answer is **Choice C.**

Choice A is incorrect. For $m = -5$, the discriminant of the equation $x^2 + 10x + 29 - m = 0$ is equal to -36 which is less than zero, and the system would have no solution.

Choice B is incorrect. For $m = -4$, the discriminant of the equation $x^2 + 10x + 29 - m = 0$ is equal to -32 which is less than zero, and the system would have no solution.

Choice D is incorrect. For $m = 5$, the discriminant of the equation $x^2 + 10x + 29 - m = 0$ is equal to 4 which is greater than zero, and the system would have two solutions.

You could also solve this question by using the **'Visualizing'** strategy. If you **enter the two equations** of the system into the **Desmos calculator,** and **'add slider'** for m when the button appears, a **line and a parabola** appear on the **graph**. Move the slider for m until the **line intersects the parabola at exactly one point.** This occurs for $m = 4$. Look at the graph below.

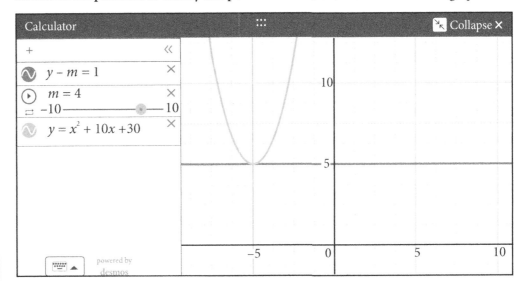

$$x^2 + 2 = 9$$

$$(x^2 + 2)^2 = y$$

The ordered pair (x, y) is a solution to the given system of equations. What is the value of y?

A) 9

B) 16

C) 36

D) 81

Solution: To solve this question, simply substitute 9 for $x^2 + 2$ from the first given equation $x^2 + 2 = 9$ into the second equation $(x^2 + 2)^2 = y$. This results in $(9)^2 = y$ or $y = 81$.

Therefore, the correct answer is **Choice D**.

Choice A is incorrect. This is the value of $x^2 + 2$.

Choice B is incorrect. This is the value of y if $x^2 + 2 = 4$.

Choice C is incorrect. This is the value of y if $x^2 + 2 = 6$.

$$y + 3 = 0$$

$$y = (x^2 - 6x + 8) - 3$$

The given equations intersect at two points. What are the values of x?

Solution: To solve for the values of x where the given equations intersect, first solve for y from the first equation $y + 3 = 0$.

Subtracting 3 from both sides of the equation yields $y = -3$.

Now, substitute the value of y into the second equation $y = (x^2 - 6x + 8) - 3$ to find x. This results in $-3 = (x^2 - 6x + 8) - 3$. Adding 3 to both sides of this equation yields $0 = x^2 - 6x + 8$.

This can be solved using the quadratic formula or factoring.

Using the quadratic formula $x = \dfrac{-b \pm \sqrt{b^2 - 4ac}}{2a}$, substitute 1 for a, -6 for b, and 8 for c,

which yields $x = \dfrac{-(-6) \pm \sqrt{(-6)^2 - 4(1)(8)}}{2(1)}$.

This results in $x = \dfrac{6 \pm 2}{2}$. The two solutions are $x = \dfrac{6 + 2}{2} = 4$ and $x = \dfrac{6 - 2}{2} = 2$.

Therefore, the values of x are 4 and 2.

Other Nonlinear Equations

Radical Equations

In the Math section, you may encounter questions asking you to solve equations involving radicals. The key to solving these equations is to **isolate the radical** on one side of the equation, **square both sides,** and then solve the resulting equation.

 A Word of Caution

You need to check your solutions in the original equation because squaring both sides sometimes introduces extraneous solutions that are not true.

Check out the examples below.

$$x + \sqrt{2x+1} = 1$$

What is the value of x which is a solution to the given equation?

Solution: First, isolate the radical.

Subtracting x from both sides of the given equation $x + \sqrt{2x+1} = 1$ yields $\sqrt{2x+1} = 1 - x$. Squaring both sides results in $2x + 1 = 1 - 2x + x^2$.

Subtracting $2x + 1$ from both sides of this equation yields $x^2 - 4x = 0$.

Factoring out x on the left-hand side of this equation yields $x(x - 4) = 0$.

Using the zero product property, $x = 0$ or $x = 4$.

Substituting 0 for x in the given equation $x + \sqrt{2x+1} = 1$ results in $1 = 1$, then zero is a valid solution.

Substituting 4 for x in the given equation $x + \sqrt{2x+1} = 1$ results in $7 = 1$, which is false. Then 4 is an extraneous solution.

Therefore, the correct answer to enter is **0**.

$$\sqrt{x+4} = x - 8$$

What is the value of x in the given equation?

A) 5

B) 7

C) 12

D) 17

Solution: To solve this equation, first, square both sides of the given equation $\sqrt{x+4} = x - 8$ to eliminate the square root.

This will result in $(\sqrt{x+4})^2 = (x-8)^2$ or $x + 4 = (x - 8)^2$.

Expanding the right-hand side yields $x + 4 = x^2 - 16x + 64$.

Subtracting $x + 4$ from both sides of this equation yields $x^2 - 17x + 60 = 0$.

Using the quadratic formula $x = \dfrac{-b \pm \sqrt{b^2 - 4ac}}{2a}$ to solve for x yields

$$x = \frac{-(-17) \pm \sqrt{(-17)^2 - 4(1)(60)}}{2(1)} \quad \text{or} \quad x = \frac{17 \pm 7}{2}.$$

The solutions for x are $x = \dfrac{17+7}{2} = 12$ and $x = \dfrac{17-7}{2} = 5$.

You need to check the solutions in the original equation to ensure they are valid.

Substituting 12 for x in the given equation yields $\sqrt{12+4} = 12-8$ or $4 = 4$, then 12 is a valid solution.

Substituting 5 for x in the given equation yields $\sqrt{5+4} = 5-8$ or $3 = -3$, then 5 is an extraneous solution. Therefore, the correct answer is **Choice C**.

Choice A is incorrect. This is the extraneous solution to the given equation.

Choice B is incorrect. This is the difference between the two solutions.

Choice D is incorrect. This is the sum of the two solutions.

Rational Equations

Rational equations have a **variable in the denominator** of a rational expression. After setting the condition that the **denominator** is **not equal to zero, cross-multiplication** and **factoring** can be useful to generate non-rational equations that you need to solve. Consider the examples below.

$$\frac{x+1}{7x+2} = \frac{1}{x+2}$$

Which of the following is a possible value of x such that the given equation is true?

A) 3

B) 4

C) 5

D) 6

Solution: First, set up the denominators of the two given fractional expressions different from zero. The condition $7x+2 \neq 0$ yields $x \neq -\frac{2}{7}$, and the condition $x+2 \neq 0$ yields $x \neq -2$. Applying **cross-multiplication** to the given equation $\frac{x+1}{7x+2} = \frac{1}{x+2}$ results in $x^2 + 3x + 2 = 7x + 2$.

Subtracting $7x + 2$ from both sides of this equation yields $x^2 - 4x = 0$.

Factoring out x on the left-hand side of this equation yields $x(x - 4) = 0$.

Using the zero product property, $x = 0$ or $x = 4$.

Therefore, the correct answer is **Choice B**.

Choice A is incorrect. Substituting 3 for x in the given equation $\frac{x+1}{7x+2} = \frac{1}{x+2}$ results in $\frac{4}{23} = \frac{1}{5}$ which is false.

Choice C is incorrect. Substituting 5 for x in the given equation $\frac{x+1}{7x+2} = \frac{1}{x+2}$ results in $\frac{6}{37} = \frac{1}{7}$ which is also false.

Choice D is incorrect. Substituting 6 for x in the given equation $\dfrac{x+1}{7x+2} = \dfrac{1}{x+2}$ results in $\dfrac{7}{44} = \dfrac{1}{8}$ which is also false.

(?)
$$\frac{2x-1}{x+1} = \frac{8}{x-8}$$

Which of the following is a possible value of x?

A) $\dfrac{25}{2}$

B) $\dfrac{26}{2}$

C) $\dfrac{28}{2}$

D) $\dfrac{29}{2}$

Solution: To solve the given equation $\dfrac{2x-1}{x+1} = \dfrac{8}{x-8}$, apply cross-multiplication to eliminate the fractions. This will result in $(2x-1)(x-8) = 8(x+1)$. Expanding both sides yields $2x^2 - 17x + 8 = 8x + 8$.

Subtracting $8x + 8$ from both sides yields $2x^2 - 25x = 0$.

Factoring out x on the left-hand side of this equation yields $x(2x - 25) = 0$.

The two possible solutions are $x = 0$ and $x = \dfrac{25}{2}$.

Substituting 0 for x in the given equation yields $\dfrac{2(0)-1}{(0)+1} = \dfrac{8}{(0)-8}$ or $-1 = -1$, then 0 is a valid solution.

Substituting 252 for x in the given equation yields $\dfrac{2\left(\dfrac{25}{2}\right)-1}{\left(\dfrac{25}{2}\right)+1} = \dfrac{8}{\left(\dfrac{25}{2}\right)-8}$ or $\dfrac{16}{9} = \dfrac{16}{9}$, then $\dfrac{25}{2}$

is also a valid solution. Therefore, the correct answer is **Choice A.**

Choice B is incorrect. Substituting $\dfrac{26}{2}$ for x in the given equation yields $\dfrac{25}{14} = \dfrac{8}{5}$, which is false.

Choice C is incorrect. Substituting $\dfrac{28}{2}$ for x in the given equation yields $\dfrac{9}{5} = \dfrac{4}{3}$, which is false.

Choice D is incorrect. Substituting $\dfrac{29}{2}$ for x in the given equation yields $\dfrac{56}{31} = \dfrac{16}{13}$, which is false.

Absolute Value Equations

For any real number a, the absolute value is denoted by $|a|$, the **distance from a to zero on the number line.** It follows that the **absolute value** is always a **positive number**. For example, $|5| = 5$, and $|-5| = 5$. You may encounter questions asking you to solve equations with absolute value having the form $|ax + b| = |cx + d|$ for any real numbers a, b, c, and d. You may square both sides of the equation to get $(ax + b)^2 = (cx + d)^2$, and then solve the resulting quadratic equation. Alternately, the solution of the equation $|ax + b| = |cx + d|$ is the set of solutions to the two equations $ax + b = +(cx + d)$ and $ax + b = -(cx + d)$. Let's go through the examples below.

$$3|x + 2| + 1 = 10$$

What is the smallest value of x that is a solution to the given equation?

Solution: The first thing you need to do is to isolate the absolute value on one side of the equation.

Subtracting 1 from both sides of the given equation $3|x + 2| + 1 = 10$ yields $3|x + 2| = 9$. Dividing both sides of this equation by 3 yields $|x + 2| = 3$.

The solution to this equation is the set of solutions to the two equations $x + 2 = 3$ and $x + 2 = -3$.

Subtracting 2 from both sides of the equation $x + 2 = 3$ yields $x = 1$, and subtracting 2 from both sides of the equation $x + 2 = -3$ yields $x = -5$.

Since -5 is less than 1, the smallest value of x that is a solution to the given equation is -5. The correct answer is -5.

$$3|2x - 9| = 15$$

What is the largest value of x that is a solution to the given equation?

A) 2

B) 5

C) 7

D) 9

Solution: To solve, first isolate the absolute value of the given equation $3|2x - 9| = 15$ by dividing both sides by 3 which yields $|2x - 9| = 5$.

The solution to this equation is the set of solutions to the two equations (1) $2x - 9 = 5$ and (2) $2x - 9 = -5$.

Solving the first equation $2x - 9 = 5$ by adding 9 to both sides yields $2x = 14$. Dividing both sides by 2 yields $x = 7$.

Solving the second equation $2x - 9 = -5$ by adding 9 to both sides yields $2x = 4$. Dividing both sides by 2 yields $x = 2$. Thus, the solutions to the equation are $x = 7$ and $x = 2$.

Therefore, the largest value x that is a solution to the given equation is 7, which is **Choice C.**

Choice A is incorrect. This is the smallest value of x to the given equation.

Choice B is incorrect. Substituting 5 for x in the given equation yields $3 = 15$, which is false.

Choice D is incorrect. Substituting 9 for x in the given equation yields $27 = 15$, which is false.

$$|2x + 4| \geq 16$$

What is the solution set to the given inequalities?

Solution: The given inequality $|2x + 4| \geq 16$ means that the expression inside the absolute value is either greater than or equal to 16 or less than or equal to -16.

Thus, the solution to this inequality is the set of solutions to the two equations (1) $2x + 4 \geq 16$ and (2) $2x + 4 \leq -16$.

Solving the first equation $2x + 4 \geq 16$ by subtracting 4 from both sides yields $2x \geq 12$. Dividing both sides by 2 yields $x \geq 6$.

Solving the second equation $2x + 4 \leq -16$ by subtracting 4 from both sides yields $2x \leq -20$. Dividing both sides by 2 yields $x \leq -10$.

Therefore, the solution set to the given inequality is $x \geq 6$ or $x \leq -10$.

1 ☐ Mark for Review

If $\dfrac{b}{3} - \dfrac{3}{b} = 0$ where $b \neq 0$, then which of the following could not be the value of b?

A) -3

B) 3

C) 9

D) All of the above

2 ☐ Mark for Review

If $3x + \sqrt{5 - x} = 5$, what is the value of $3x$?

A) 1

B) $\dfrac{20}{9}$

C) 3

D) $\dfrac{20}{3}$

3 ☐ Mark for Review

If $y = 2x^2 + 4x - 6$ intersects at exactly one point to the line $y = p$, what is the value of p?

A) -24

B) -8

C) -6

D) -2

4 ☐ Mark for Review

$$4y = 3x + 9$$

$$y = (2x + 10)^2 - (x - 1)^2$$

If (x_1, y_1) and (x_2, y_2) are solutions to the system of equations shown above and $x_1 < x_2$, what is the value of x_1?

A) $-\dfrac{43}{4}$

B) $-\dfrac{93}{16}$

C) -3

D) 0

5 ☐ Mark for Review

$$y = |x - 1|$$

$$x - 2y = -2$$

If (x_1, y_1) and (x_2, y_2) are solutions to the system of equations shown above and $y_1 < y_2$, what is the value of $x_2 - y_2$?

A) 0

B) 1

C) 3

D) 4

Answers & Explanations

1. **Level:** Easy | **Skill/Knowledge:** Nonlinear equations in one variable and systems of equations in two variables | **Testing Point:** Solving nonlinear equation in one variable

   Key Explanation: Simplifying the equation $\frac{b}{3} - \frac{3}{b} = 0$ by subtracting the fractions yields $\frac{b^2 - 9}{3b} = 0$.

   Multiplying both sides of the equation by $3b$ yields $b^2 - 9 = 0$.

   Factoring $b^2 - 9$ yields $(b + 3)(b - 3) = 0$.

   Equating both factors to zero and finding the values of b yields $b = -3$ and $b = 3$.

   Therefore, b cannot be 9.

   Distractor Explanations: Choices A and **B** are incorrect because both of them are values of b. **Choice D** is incorrect because only 9 is not the value of b.

2. **Level:** Medium | **Skill/Knowledge:** Nonlinear equations in one variable and systems of equations in two variables | **Testing Point:** Solving a radical equation

   Key Explanation: Choice C is correct. Subtracting $3x$ from both sides of the equation yields $\sqrt{5 - x} = 5 - 3x$. Squaring both sides of the equation yields $5 - x = (5 - 3x)^2$. Expanding the right side yields $5 - x = 25 - 30x + 9x^2$. Adding $x - 5$ to both sides of the equation yields $0 = 20 - 29x + 9x^2$. Rewriting the equation yields $9x^2 - 29x + 20 = 0$. Solving the value of x using the quadratic formula yields $x = \frac{-(-29) \pm \sqrt{(-29)^2 - 4(9)(20)}}{2(9)}$.

   Simplifying the equation yields $x = \frac{20}{9}$ and $x = 1$.

   Checking if each root is valid yields $\sqrt{5 - \frac{20}{9}} = 5 - 3\left(\frac{20}{9}\right)$ and $\sqrt{5 - 1} = 5 - 3(1)$.

   Simplifying the equations yields $\frac{5}{3} = -\frac{5}{3}$ and $2 = 2$. Since the first statement is false, then 1 is the only valid solution.

   Therefore, $3x = 3(1) = 3$.

   Distractor Explanations: Choice A is incorrect. This is the value of the real root. **Choice B** is incorrect. This is the value of the extraneous root. **Choice D** is incorrect. This is the value of 3 times the extraneous root.

3. **Level:** Medium | **Skill/Knowledge:** Nonlinear equations in one variable and systems of equations in two variables | **Testing Point:** System of quadratic and linear equation

   Key Explanation: Choice B is correct. Since $y = p$, then by substituting p to y the quadratic equation becomes $p = 2x^2 + 4x - 6$.

   Subtracting p from both sides of the equation yields $0 = 2x^2 + 4x - 6 - p$.

   Since the system of equations intersects at exactly one point, then the discriminant is equal to 0.

   The discriminant formula is $b^2 - 4ac$ where a and b are the coefficients of x^2 and x, respectively, and c is the constant.

   From $0 = 2x^2 + 4x - 6 - p$, $a = 2$, $b = 4$ and $c = -6 - p$.

   Substituting the values to the formula yields $(4)^2 - 4(2)(-6 - p) = 0$

   Simplifying the equation yields $64 + 8p = 0$.

   Subtracting 64 from both sides of the equation yields $8p = -64$.

   Dividing both sides of the equation by 8 yields $p = -8$.

   Distractor Explanations: Choice A is incorrect. The discriminant will be less than 0. **Choice C** is incorrect. The discriminant will be greater than 0. **Choice D** is incorrect. The discriminant will be greater than 0.

4. **Level:** Hard | **Skill/Knowledge:** Nonlinear equations in one variable and systems of equations in two variables | **Testing Point:** Solving system of quadratic and linear equations

   Key Explanation: Choice A is correct. Solve the system of equations by substitution method.

   Dividing both sides of the 1st equation by 4 yields $y = \frac{3}{4}x + \frac{9}{4}$.
   Substituting this equation to the 2nd equation yields $\frac{3}{4}x + \frac{9}{4} = (2x + 10)^2 - (x - 1)^2$. Expanding the square of binomials in the right side of the equation yields $\frac{3}{4}x + \frac{9}{4} = 4x^2 + 40x + 100 - x^2 + 2x - 1$. Combining like terms yields $\frac{3}{4}x + \frac{9}{4} = 3x^2 + 42x + 99$. Multiplying 4 to both sides of the equation yields $3x + 9 = 12x^2 + 168x + 396$. Subtracting $3x$ and 9 from both sides of the equation yields $0 = 12x^2 + 165x + 387$. Dividing 3 from both sides of the equation yields $0 = 4x^2 + 55x + 129$. Factoring the right side of the equation yields $0 = (x + 3)(4x + 43)$. Equating both factors to 0 yields $x + 3 = 0$ and $4x + 43 = 0$.

   Subtracting 3 from both sides of $x + 3 = 0$ yields $x = -3$.

   Subtracting 43 from both sides of $4x + 43 = 0$ yields $4x = -43$. Dividing both sides of the equation by 4 yields $x = -\frac{43}{4}$.
   Since $-\frac{43}{4} < -3$, then $x_1 = -\frac{43}{4}$.

   Distractor Explanations: Choice B is incorrect. This is the value of y_1. **Choice C is incorrect.** This is the value of x_2. **Choice D is incorrect.** This is the value of y_2.

5. **Level:** Hard | **Skill/Knowledge:** Nonlinear equations in one variable and systems of equations in two variables | **Testing Point:** Solving system of nonlinear and linear equations

   Key Explanation: Choice B is correct. Adding $2y$ to both sides of the 2nd equation yields $x = 2y - 2$.

Substituting this equation to the 1st equation yields $y = |2y - 2 - 1|$ or $y = |2y - 3|$.

Solving y using the positive value of the contents of the absolute value symbol yields $y = 2y - 3$. Adding 3 and subtracting y from both sides of the equation yields $3 = y$ or $y = 3$. Substituting the value of y to the modified 1st equation yields $x = 2(3) - 2$ or $x = 4$.

Solving y using the negative value of the contents of the absolute value symbol yields $y = -(2y - 3)$ or $y = -2y + 3$. Adding $2y$ to both sides of the equation yields $3y = 3$. Dividing both sides of the equation by 3 yields $y = 1$. Substituting the value of y to the modified 1st equation yields $x = 2(1) - 2$ or $x = 0$.

Since $1 < 3$, then $y^2 = 3$. Hence, $x^2 = 4$.

Therefore, $x^2 - y^2 = 4 - 3 = 1$.

Distractor Explanations: Choice A is incorrect. This is the value of x_1. **Choice C is incorrect.** This is the value of y_2. **Choice D is incorrect.** This is the value of x_2.

Nonlinear Functions

In this part, you will learn about the concept of **functions**, and more about **transformations of functions.** You will also get to focus on two important types of functions: the **quadratic function** and the **exponential function.**

Functions and Transformations

A function is sometimes compared to a machine that takes an input, commonly referred to as x, and gives an output, commonly referred to as $f(x)$ or y. For example, considering the function defined by $f(x) = 3x - 2$, this function takes any input x, multiplies it by 3, and then subtracts 2 from the result. Understanding what a function does is helpful in answering many questions. Let's say for the same function $f(x) = 3x - 2$, you were asked to find $g(x) = f(4x)$. The input is $4x$, and you know that function f takes the input, multiplies it by 3, and then subtracts 2. Then, $f(4x) = g(x) = (4x) \times 3 - 2$, or $g(x) = 12x - 2$.

Some transformations of linear functions were discussed in the previous chapter. The rules apply to all functions, not just linear functions.

 Remember

1. The graph of $f(x) + a$ is the translation of the graph of $f(x)$ by $+a$ units vertically

2. The graph of $f(x + a)$ is the translation of the graph of $f(x)$ by $-a$ units horizontally

3. Moving negative units vertically is going down, while moving negative units horizontally is going left

4. if $g(x) = -f(x)$, then the graph of g is the reflection of the graph of f over the x-axis

---

Consider the examples below.

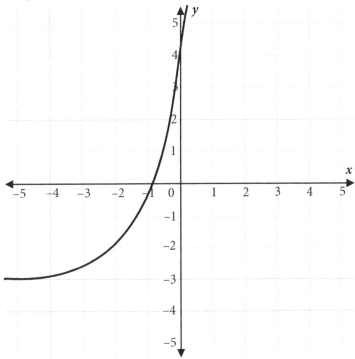

(?) The graph of $g(x) = f(x + 2) - 3$ is shown. What is the value of $f(0)$?

A) −3

B) −2

C) 0

D) 1

Solution: The question asks for the value of $f(0)$.

The expression of $g(x)$ contains $f(x + 2)$. To know the value of x which corresponds to $f(0)$, set $x + 2 = 0$. Subtracting 2 from both sides of this equation yields $x = -2$.

Substituting −2 for x in the equation $g(x) = f(x + 2) - 3$ yields $g(-2) = f(0) - 3$.

From the given graph, $g(-2) = -2$.

Substituting −2 for $g(-2)$ in the equation $g(-2) = f(0) - 3$ yields $-2 = f(0) - 3$. Adding 3 to both sides of this equation results in $f(0) = 1$.

Therefore, the correct answer is **Choice D**.

Choice A is incorrect and may result if $g(-2) = -6$.

Choice B is incorrect and may result if $g(-2) = -5$.

Choice C is incorrect and may result if $g(-2) = -3$.

(?)
$$f(x) = x^2$$

If the given function above is transformed by shifting it 3 units to the right and 4 units up, what is the equation of the transformed function?

A) $f(x) = (x + 3)^2 + 4$

B) $f(x) = (x - 3)^2 + 4$

C) $f(x) = (x + 3)^2 - 4$

D) $f(x) = (x - 3)^2 - 4$

Solution: To shift a function $f(x)$ to the right by 3 units, replace x with $x - 3$.

To shift up by 4 units, add 4 to the function.

Therefore, the transformed function is $f(x) = (x - 3)^2 + 4$ and the correct answer is **Choice B**.

Choice A is incorrect and may result if the function is shifted to the left instead of to the right.

Choice C is incorrect and may result if the function is shifted to the left instead of to the right and down instead of up.

Choice D is incorrect and may result if the function is shifted down instead of up.

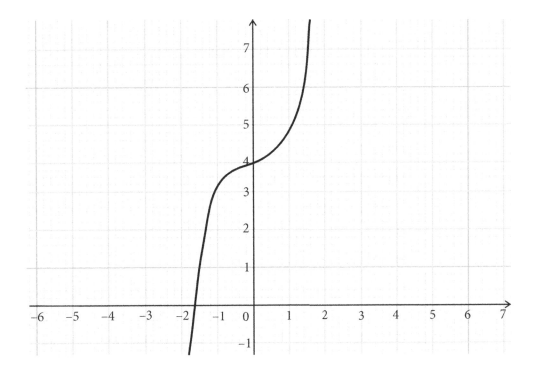

(?) The graph of the function $g(x) = x^3 + 4$ is shown above. If it is transformed by shifting it 5 units to the left and 6 units down, what is the equation of the transformed function?

A) $g(x) = (x + 5)^3 - 2$

B) $g(x) = (x - 5)^3 - 2$

C) $g(x) = (x + 5)^3 + 8$

D) $g(x) = (x - 5)^3 + 8$

Solution: To shift a function $g(x)$ to the left by 5 units, replace x with $x + 5$.

To shift down by 6 units, subtract 6 from the function.

Therefore, the transformed function is $g(x) = (x + 5)^3 + 4 - 6$, or $g(x) = (x + 5)^3 - 2$.

The correct answer is **Choice A**.

Choice B is incorrect and may result if the function is shifted to the right instead of to the left.

Choice C is incorrect and may result if the function is shifted up instead of down.

Choice D is incorrect and may result if the function is shifted to the right instead of to the left and up instead of down.

> ⑦
>
> $$f(x) = 7x - 9$$
>
> If $g(x) = f(6x)$, what is the value of $g(x)$?

A) $g(x) = 28x - 9$

B) $g(x) = 35x - 9$

C) $g(x) = 42x - 9$

D) $g(x) = 49x - 9$

Solution: The question asks for the function $g(x)$, given $g(x) = f(6x)$.

To find $g(x)$, replace x with $6x$ in the function $f(x)$, resulting in $f(6x) = 7(6x) - 9$.

Simplifying the expression yields $g(x) = f(6x) = 42x - 9$.

Therefore, the correct answer is **Choice C**.

Choice A is incorrect. This may result if the question states that $g(x) = f(4x)$ instead of $g(x) = f(6x)$.

Choice B is incorrect. This may result if the question states that $g(x) = f(5x)$ instead of $g(x) = f(6x)$.

Choice D is incorrect. This may result if the question states that $g(x) = f(7x)$ instead of $g(x) = f(6x)$.

Quadratic Function

> **Note:**
>
> For a quadratic function $f(x) = ax^2 + bx + c$;
>
> If $a > 0$, the parabola is concave upwards (Opens up)
>
> If $a < 0$, the parabola is concave downwards (Opens down)
>
> The coordinates of the vertex are $\left(-\dfrac{b}{2a}, f\left(-\dfrac{b}{2a} \right) \right)$
>
> The vertical line of equation $x = -\dfrac{b}{2a}$ passes through the vertex and is an axis of symmetry of the parabola

The x-intercepts of a parabola are the solutions to the equation $ax^2 + bx + c = 0$, and their number depends on the value of the discriminant $b^2 - 4ac$ as discussed earlier in this chapter. The y-coordinate of the y-intercept is the value of $f(0) = c$.

> **Note:**
>
> The **vertex form** of the equation of a parabola having a vertex of coordinates (h, k) is $f(x) = a(x - h)^2 + k$
>
> The factored form of the equation of a parabola having the two zeros x_1 and x_2 is $f(x) = a(x - x_1)(x - x_2)$

Look at the examples below.

$$y = -2(x - 1)(x - 3)$$

The given equation represents a parabola in the xy-plane. Which of the following is the correct vertex form of the equation of this parabola?

A) $y = -2(x - 1)^2 - 3$

B) $y = -2(x - 2)^2 - 2$

C) $y = -2(x - 2)^2 + 2$

D) $y = -2(x - 1)^2 + 3$

Solution: The given equation is in the factored form $y = a(x - x_1)(x - x_2)$. Thus, the two zeros of this parabola are $x_1 = 1$ and $x_2 = 3$.

Because of the symmetry of a parabola, the x-coordinate of the vertex is the average of the zeros of the parabola. Then, $x_V = \dfrac{1+3}{2} = 2$.

To find the y-coordinate of the vertex, substitute 2 for x in the given equation $y = -2(x - 1)(x - 3)$. This yields $y_V = -2(2 - 1)(2 - 3) = 2$.

Thus, the vertex has the coordinates (2,2).

The vertex form of the equation of a parabola having a vertex of coordinates (h,k) is $y = a(x - h)^2 + k$. Substituting –2 for a, 2 for h and 2 for k in this equation yields $y = -2(x - 2)^2 + 2$.

Therefore, the correct answer is **Choice C**.

You could also enter the given equation $y = -2(x - 1)(x - 3)$ into the Desmos graphing calculator to get the vertex (2,2), then substitute the coordinates of the vertex into the vertex form of the equation of a parabola to answer the question.

Choice A is incorrect and may result if the vertex of the parabola has the coordinates (1, –3). **Choice B** is incorrect and may result if the vertex of the parabola has the coordinates (2, –2). **Choice D** is incorrect and may result if the vertex of the parabola has the coordinates (1, 3).

$$f(x) = x^2 + 2x - 5$$

Which of the following are the roots of the given function?

A) 0 and 6

B) 3 and 9

C) 1.45 and –3.45

D) 0.37 and –5.37

Solution: To find the roots of the given function $f(x) = x^2 + 2x - 5$, solve for x when $f(x) = 0$.

Solve the quadratic equation $x^2 + 2x - 5 = 0$ using the quadratic formula $x = \dfrac{-b \pm \sqrt{b^2 - 4ac}}{2a}$.

Substituting 1 for a, 2 for b, and -5 for c yields $x = \dfrac{-2 \pm \sqrt{2^2 - 4(1)(-5)}}{2(1)}$, or $x = -1 \pm \sqrt{6}$.

Therefore, the roots of the function are $x = -1 \pm \sqrt{6} \approx 1.45$ and $x = -1 - \sqrt{6} \approx -3.45$. The correct answer is **Choice C.**

Choice A is incorrect. This may result if the given function is $f(x) = x^2 - 6x$.

Choice B is incorrect. This may result if the given function is $f(x) = x^2 - 12x + 27$.

Choice D is incorrect. This may result if the given function is $f(x) = x^2 + 5x - 2$.

$(?)$ $\qquad\qquad\qquad f(x) = 2x^2 - 10x + 20$

What is the vertex of the given function?

A) $\left(\dfrac{2}{5}, \dfrac{15}{2} \right)$

B) $\left(\dfrac{5}{2}, \dfrac{2}{15} \right)$

C) $\left(\dfrac{2}{5}, \dfrac{2}{15} \right)$

D) $\left(\dfrac{5}{2}, \dfrac{15}{2} \right)$

Solution: To find the vertex of the given quadratic function $f(x) = 2x^2 - 10x + 20$, use the vertex formula $x = -\dfrac{b}{2a}$ to find x.

Substituting 2 for a and -10 for b into the formula yields $x = -\dfrac{-10}{2(2)}$ or $x = \dfrac{5}{2}$.

Substituting the value of x into the function to find y yields $f\left(\dfrac{5}{2} \right) = 2\left(\dfrac{5}{2} \right)^2 - 10\left(\dfrac{5}{2} \right) + 20$ or $f\left(\dfrac{5}{2} \right) = \dfrac{15}{2}$.

Therefore, the vertex of the given function is $\left(\dfrac{5}{2}, \dfrac{15}{2} \right)$, which is **Choice D.**

Choice A is incorrect. This may result from interchanging the value of a and b during substitution.

Choice B is incorrect. This may result from a calculation error.

Choice C is incorrect. This may result from a calculation error.

Exponential Function

An exponential function has the form $f(x) = ab^x$, where b is a **positive constant** and x is a **variable.** The number $a = f(0)$ is the initial value of the exponential function.

> The graph of the function $g(x) = x^3 + 4$ is shown above. If it is transformed by shifting it 5 units to the left and 6 units down, what is the equation of the transformed function?

The power b^x is positive for any positive b and any real x. The **two most common scenarios** that can be modeled into an exponential function are **exponential change with a constant rate** (or percent change), and **compound interest.**

When a rate (or percent change) is involved, the **general expression of an exponential function is written as** $f(t) = a(1 \pm r)^t$, **where a is the initial value and r is the constant rate (percent decrease or increase) at which the function changes every one unit increase in the period of time t.** Such contexts are commonly seen on the Digital SAT when talking about a **depreciation (loss of value)** of an item, or an **exponential population growth.**

When talking about **compound interest,** the future value F is given by $F = P\left(1 + \dfrac{r}{k}\right)^{kt}$, where

P is the **initial value of the deposit,** r is the **annual interest rate,** t is the **number of years,** and k is the **number of times the interest is compounded per year.** If the **interest is compounded annually,** the formula for the future value simplifies to $F = P(1 + r)^t$.

Some questions ask for **changes in time units** of an exponential growth or decay function. You need to be **very careful** when dealing with such questions. The **base of the power does not change; what changes** is the **exponent.** To help you figure out what to do with the exponent, remember the following: If you're **converting from a smaller time unit to a larger time unit,** you need to **multiply the variable representing the larger unit to make it larger.** However, if you're **converting from a larger time unit to a smaller time unit,** you need to **divide the variable representing the smaller unit to make it smaller.** Also, make sure to **verify that the two functions give you the same value** after equal amounts of time. Consider the examples below.

> (?)
>
> $$P(m) = 120,000(1.003)^m$$
>
> The given equation models the population of a certain city m months after a demographic survey. Which of the following best represents the population of this city t years after the survey?

A) $Q(t) = \dfrac{120,000}{12}(1.003)^t$

B) $Q(t) = 120,000\left(\dfrac{1.003}{12}\right)^t$

C) $Q(t) = 120,000(1.003)^{\frac{t}{12}}$

D) $Q(t) = 120,000(1.003)^{\frac{t}{12}}$

Solution: This question asks you to convert from a smaller unit (months) to a larger unit (years). Hence, you need to multiply the variable t representing the larger unit to make it larger.

It is known that 1 year is equivalent to 12 months. Then, multiplying t by 12 in the exponent should give the correct function. The only choice that does this is **Choice D** where $Q(t) = 120,000(1.003)^{12t}$.

Remember that you still need to verify.

Substituting 1 for t in the equation $Q(t) = 120,000(1.003)^{12t}$ yields $Q(1) = 120,000(1.003)^{12}$ which is approximately equal to 124,392 (using the calculator).

Substituting 12 for m in the given equation $P(m) = 120,000(1.003)^m$ yields $P(12) = 120,000(1.003)^{12}$ which again gives the same result.

Thus, $Q(t)$ and $P(m)$ gave the same population number after 1 year and 12 months, respectively.

Therefore, the correct answer is **Choice D.**

Choice A is incorrect because it changes the initial number of the population at the time of the demographic survey (at $t = 0$).

Choice B is incorrect because it changes the rate of increase, while the base of the power of an exponential function won't change when time units are changed.

Choice C is incorrect because it makes the variable representing the larger unit smaller, which results in different population numbers after equivalent intervals of time. For example, after 1 year, $Q(t) = 120,000(1.003)^{\frac{t}{12}}$ results in approximately 120,030 which is smaller than the population number found using the given equation after 12 months.

 The population of a certain bacteria doubles every 4 hours. If the initial population is 250, what will be the population after 12 hours?

A) 2,000

B) 4,000

C) 16,000

D) 64,000

Solution: Since the population doubles every 4 hours, the number of times the population doubles in 12 hours with an initial population of 250 is represented by $P = 250(2)^{\frac{12}{4}}$ or $P = 2,000$. Therefore, the correct answer is **Choice A.**

Choice B is incorrect. This may result if the population doubles every 3 hours.

Choice C is incorrect. This may result if the population doubles every 2 hours.

Choice D is incorrect. This may result if the population doubles every 4 hours in 32 hours.

$$y = s(1 + t)^x$$

The exponential function above is given, where s and t are constants. If the function passes through the points $(0, 5)$ and $(3, 6)$, what is the value of the rate of growth?

Solution: It is given that the exponential function $y = s(1 + t)^x$ passes through the points $(0, 5)$ and $(3, 6)$.

Substituting 0 for x and 5 for y in the equation $y = s(1 + t)^x$ yields $5 = s(1 + t)^0$, or $s = 5$. Then, the equation of the exponential model can be written as $y = 5(1 + t)^x$.

Substituting 3 for x and 6 for y in the equation $y = 5(1 + t)^x$ yields $6 = 5(1 + t)^3$. Dividing both sides of the equation by 5 yields $1.2 = (1 + t)^3$. Taking the cube root on both sides yields $1.063 = 1 + t$. Subtracting 1 from both sides results in $t = 0.063$. Therefore, the rate of growth is 0.063.

An investment of \$2,000 in a savings account earns an annual interest rate of 5%. The interest is compounded annually. How many years will it take for the investment to triple?

A) 14

B) 19

C) 23

D) 28

Solution: The formula for compound interest is $A = P(1 + r)^t$, where A is the amount of money accumulated after t years, including interest, P is the principal amount, r is the annual interest rate, and t is the time (in years).

The given condition is for the investment to triple, which means $A = 3P$. Substituting this into the formula $3P = P(1 + 0.05)^t$ yields $3P = P(1.05)^t$. Dividing both sides by P yields $3 = (1.05)^t$ or $t \approx 23$. Therefore, the investment will triple in approximately 23 years, which is **Choice C.**

Choice A is incorrect. This may result if the question asks for the number of years it will take for the investment to double.

Choice B is incorrect. This may result if the given annual interest is 6%.

Choice D is incorrect. This may result if the question asks for the number of years it will take for the investment to quadruple.

1 🔖 **Mark for Review**

$$f(x) = 3^{2x} - 9$$

What is the y intercept of the function $f(x)$?

A) -9

B) -8

C) 1

D) 9

2 🔖 **Mark for Review**

A stone is thrown horizontally from the top of a cliff and undergoes a parabolic motion. The vertical distance, in feet, that the stone has fallen from the cliff is represented by the function $f(t) = 9t + 16.1t^2$ where t is the time lapsed in seconds after the stone was thrown. If the cliff is 250 ft high from the ground, how many seconds have lapsed when the stone is 40 ft high from the ground?

A) 2.58

B) 2.98

C) 3.34

D) 3.67

3 🔖 **Mark for Review**

$$f(x) = \frac{3x - 2}{x + 1}$$

Which of the following is the vertical asymptote of the function $f(x)$?

A) -5

B) -1

C) 23

D) 3

4 🔖 **Mark for Review**

A study was conducted in 2015 about the population growth and decline of two species of wild rabbits. According to the study, the population growth of species A can be represented by the function $f(t) = 450(1.1)^t$ where t is the number of years after 2015. On the other hand, the population decline of species B can be represented by the function $h(t) = 1120(0.99)^t$. What is the difference in population of the two species by the time the population of species A has doubled?

A) 38

B) 141

C) 419

D) 553

5 🔖 **Mark for Review**

$$f(x) = \frac{3^{|x-1|} - 5}{4}$$

What is the sum of the x-intercepts of the given function?

Answers & Explanations

1. **Level:** Easy | **Skill/Knowledge:** Nonlinear functions | **Testing Point:** y intercept of a function

   Key Explanation: Choice B is correct. The y intercept is found when the value of x is 0. Substituting x for 0 yields $f(0) = 3^{2(0)} - 9 = -8$. Therefore, the y intercept is -8.

   Distractor Explanations: Choice A is incorrect. This may be due to conceptual or calculation errors. **Choice C** is incorrect. This would represent the value of x when $f(x) = 0$. **Choice D** is incorrect. This may be due to conceptual or calculation errors.

2. **Level:** Medium | **Skill/Knowledge:** Nonlinear functions | **Testing Point:** Parabolic function

   Key Explanation: Choice C is correct. When the stone is 40 ft high from the ground, then it has fallen a distance of $250 - 40 = 210$ ft from the cliff.

   Substituting 210 to the function yields $210 = 9t + 16.1t^2$. Subtracting 210 from both sides of the equation yields $0 = -210 + 9t + 16.1t^2$. Rewriting the equation yields $16.1t^2 + 9t - 210 = 0$.

   Using quadratic formula to solve for t yields $t = \dfrac{-9 \pm \sqrt{9^2 - 4(16.1)(-210)}}{2(16.1)}$. Simplifying the equation yields $t = 3.34$ and $t = -3.9$. Since time can not be negative, then $t = 3.34$.

   Therefore, it took 3.34 seconds for the stone to be 40 ft high from the ground.

   Distractor Explanations: Choice A is incorrect. At 2.58 seconds, the stone is 120 ft high from the ground. **Choice B** is incorrect. At 2.98 seconds, the stone is 80 ft high from the ground. **Choice D** is incorrect. At 3.67 seconds, the stone hit the ground.

3. **Level:** Medium | **Skill/Knowledge:** Nonlinear functions | **Testing Point:** Vertical asymptote

   Key Explanation: Choice B is correct. The vertical asymptote is equivalent to the value of x for which the function becomes undefined.

   The function becomes undefined when the denominator is equal to 0.

   Equating the denominator to zero yields $x + 1 = 0$.

   Subtracting 1 from both sides of the equation yields $x = -1$.

   Therefore, the vertical asymptote is at $x = -1$.

   Distractor Explanations: Choice A is incorrect. This would be the value of the remainder when $3x - 2$ is divided by $x + 1$. **Choice C** is incorrect. This is the value of x when the numerator is equated to zero. **Choice D** is incorrect. This is the value of the horizontal asymptote.

4. **Level:** Easy | **Skill/Knowledge:** Nonlinear functions | **Testing Point:** Exponential growth and decay functions

   Key Explanation: Choice B is correct. Since the population growth of species A is under exponential growth function $f(t) = a(1 + r)^t$ where a is the initial population at the time of the study, then $a = 450$. To calculate the time when the population of species A doubles, solve for the value of t when $f(t) = 450 \cdot 2 = 900$. This yields $900 = 450(1.1)^t$. Dividing both sides of the equation by 450 yields $2 = (1.1)^t$. Getting the natural logarithm of both sides of the equation yields $ln(2) = ln(1.1^t)$. Applying the exponent rule in natural logarithm yields $ln(2) = t \, ln(1.1)$. Dividing both sides of the equation by $ln(1.1)$ yields $\dfrac{ln(2)}{ln(1.1)} = t$ or $t = 7.273$. Hence, the population of species A will become double in 7.273 years. Calculating the population of species B in 7.273 years yields $h(t) = 1120(0.99)^{7.273} = 1041$. Hence, the population of species B will be 1041 in 7.273 years.

   Therefore, the difference between the population of the two species is $1041 - 900 = 141$.

   Distractor Explanations: Choice A is incorrect and may result from calculating the difference in the population of the two species in 9 years. **Choice C** is incorrect and may result from calculating the difference in the population of the two species in 12 years. **Choice D** is incorrect and may result from calculating the difference in the population of the two species in 2 years.

5. **Level:** Easy | **Skill/Knowledge:** Nonlinear functions | **Testing Point:** Solving the x-intercepts of a nonlinear function

Key Explanation: The correct answer is **2**. To find the x-intercepts, set the function to 0 which yields $0 = \dfrac{3^{|x-1|} - 5}{4}$. Multiplying both sides of the equation by 4 yields $0 = 3^{|x-1|} - 5$. Adding 5 to both sides of the equation yields $5 = 3^{|x-1|}$. Getting the natural logarithm of both sides of the equation yields $ln(5) = ln(3^{|x-1|})$. Applying the rule for the exponent in natural logarithm yields $ln(5) = |x - 1|ln(3)$. Dividing both sides of the equation by $ln(3)$ yields $\dfrac{ln(5)}{ln(3)} = |x - 1|$.

To solve for the possible values of x, use the positive and negative values of the contents inside the absolute value symbol.

Solving for the 1st possible value of x yields $\dfrac{ln(5)}{ln(3)} = x - 1$. Adding 1 to both sides of the equation yields $\dfrac{ln(5)}{ln(3)} + 1 = x$.

Checking if the value of x is valid yields $0 = 3^{|\frac{ln(5)}{ln(3)}+1-1|} - 5$. Simplifying the equation yields $0=0$. Since the statement is true, then the value of x is valid.

Solving for the 2nd possible value of x yields $\dfrac{ln(5)}{ln(3)} - (x - 1)$ or $\dfrac{ln(5)}{ln(3)} = -x + 1$. Adding x and subtracting $\dfrac{ln(5)}{ln(3)}$ from both sides of the equation yields $x = 1 - \dfrac{ln(5)}{ln(3)}$.

Checking if the value of x is valid yields $0 = 3^{|\frac{ln(5)}{ln(3)}-1|} - 5$. Simplifying the equation yields $0=0$. Since the statement is true, then the value of x is valid.

Hence, the x-intercepts are $\dfrac{ln(5)}{ln(3)} + 1$ and $1 - \dfrac{ln(5)}{ln(3)}$.

Therefore, the sum of the x-intercepts is $\dfrac{ln(5)}{ln(3)} + 1 + 1 - \dfrac{ln(5)}{ln(3)} = 2$.

Chapter 10
Problem-Solving and Data Analysis

Topics covered in this chapter:

- Ratios, Rates, Proportional Relationships, and Units
- Percentages
- One-variable Data: Distributions and Measures of Center and Spread
- Two-variable Data: Models and Scatterplots
- Probability and Conditional Probability
- Inference from Sample Statistics and Margin of Error
- Evaluating Statistical Claims: Observational Studies and Experiments

The **Problem-solving and Data Analysis** domain **spans about 15%** of the questions and comprises many important topics. It assesses your **understanding of proportional relationships, percentages,** and **probability.** In this part, you will also encounter questions involving **ratios, rates,** and **unit conversions.**

Problem-solving and Data Analysis also **tests** your **ability to deal with statistical data.** This includes both **one-variable** and **two-variable data.** For **one-variable data,** you are expected to know how to **calculate measures of center,** and to **interpret measures of spread.** For **two-variable data,** you are expected to know **how to interpret scatterplots** and **lines of best fit,** and to use **models to deal with real-life problems.**

Another **important aspect** of this domain is **statistical inference** and **evaluation of statistical claims.** You will need to know how to make **simple inferences from sample statistics,** and to **interpret the margin of error.** You will also have to **evaluate claims based on statistical studies,** whether these studies are observations or experiments.

In this chapter, you will learn more about the subtopics mentioned in this introduction. As with the previous chapters, you will find two strategies that will help you tackle questions in this domain more effectively. Pay close attention to this chapter because the topics covered will be extremely helpful to you personally and academically, today and in the future!

The following is a comprehensive list of rules required to tackle questions in this chapter:

 Rules to remember while solving Problem-solving and Data Analysis questions

- The ratio $\frac{a}{b}$ is also written as $a:b$ or a to b.

- **Part-to-whole ratios relate** a **quantity to the total,** while **part-to-part ratios relate quantities to each other.** To find the part-to-whole ratios from part-to-part ratios, first **add the parts** to get the whole or the total.

- $speed = \dfrac{distance}{time}$, $time = \dfrac{distance}{speed}$ and $distance = speed \times time$

- In **linear functions,** the **unit rate** is the **slope** of the line graph representing the function.

- A **proportion** is **several equal ratios.** The **graph** of a **proportional relationship** $y = kx$ is a straight line passing through the origin, with a slope equal to k.

- To **convert between units,** you need to **use conversion factors** which are ratios that relate the units. Make sure to choose the conversion factor that makes the **units cancel properly.**

- When dealing with percentages, remember the proportion $\dfrac{part}{whole} = \dfrac{percentage}{100}$.

- percent change $= \dfrac{amount\ of\ change}{initial\ amount} \times 100\%$

- Mean or Average $= \dfrac{Sum\ of\ values}{Number\ of\ values}$

- Sum of values = Average × Number of values

- The **mode** is the **value that occurs most frequently** in a **data set**.

- The **median** is the **middle value** in an **ordered set**.

- The **range** is the **difference between the largest and smallest value** in a **data set**.

- The **standard deviation** would be **large if the data values are widely scattered** or dispersed around the mean, and would be **small if the data values are close to the mean with little variability**.

- **Scatterplots** are graphs of **ordered pairs** relating two variables in the *xy*-plane. A **line of best fit** is a line that is **closest to all the points** of the scatterplot. Lines of best fit are used to predict unknown values.

- $\text{probability} = \dfrac{number\ of\ favorable\ outcomes}{total\ number\ of\ possible\ outcomes}$

- The **value of a probability is between 0 and 1,** with a probability of **0 denoting an impossible event,** and a **probability of 1 denoting a certain event.**

- The **conditional probability** of an event is the probability that the **event occurs given that another event has occurred** (keywords: if, such that, given that).

- The conditional probability of an event A given that event B has occurred is the ratio of the number of outcomes favorable to both events A and B to the number of outcomes of event B.

- *Expected number = sample ratio × total population*

- In **observational studies and surveys, associations can be made** but no **cause-effect relationships** can be **concluded.**

- To **generalize the results** of **observational studies and surveys** to the **whole population,** the **sample must be chosen randomly** from a **well-defined population.**

- **Experiments** are **manipulated trials** with **controlled conditions.** To **conclude a cause-and-effect relationship,** subjects should be **chosen randomly** from a well-defined population to receive the treatment. The group **not receiving the treatment** is known as the **control group.**

Strategies

There are many topic-specific strategies for Problem-Solving and Data Analysis questions. These will be presented in their respective sections throughout the chapter. For now, we will discuss two **general strategies**.

1. Estimating

You are encouraged to estimate calculations to save precious testing time whenever possible. By **'Estimating'**, you may be able to **eliminate one or more choices** that don't make sense. Don't rush to the calculations before taking a moment to look and think. Consider the examples below.

The average of four numbers is 19. If the number 20 is introduced to the set of four numbers, what would be the average of all five numbers?

A) 18

B) 19

C) 19.2

D) 19.8

Solution: You will find the mathematical solution to this question using the average formula later in the chapter. However, trying to estimate and guess the answer might be the only thing you need to find the answer to this question.

First, since the average of the four numbers is given to be 19, and the number 20 (greater than 19) is introduced to the set of the other numbers, you should expect that the new average of the five numbers is greater than 19.

Thus, you could eliminate **Choices A** and **B**.

You still have to choose between 19.2 and 19.8. Since four numbers contribute to the average 19, and only one other number is 20, you can safely conclude that the new average must be closer to 19 than 20.

Therefore, the correct answer is **Choice C**. Actually, it makes perfect sense since the ratio of the distance from 19.2 to 19 (which is 0.2) to the distance from 19.2 to 20 (which is 0.8) is 1 to 4.

 78, 85, 92, 65, 78, 80, 78

The scores of 7 students in the exam are shown above. What is the mode of the test scores?

A) 65

B) 78

C) 85

D) 92

Solution: The **mode is the value** that **appears most frequently** in a dataset.

In the given dataset, scores in the 60s and 90s appear only once. Therefore, you can **eliminate Choices A** and **D**.

You can also **eliminate Choice C**, as 85 appears only once.

Therefore, the **correct answer** is **Choice B, 78**, which **appears thrice**.

> **(?)**   65, 68, 70, 71, 73, 75, 77
>
> The heights of 7 students are recorded above. What is the median height of the students?

A) 71

B) 72

C) 73

D) 74

Solution: The **median is the middle value** when a **dataset is ordered from least to greatest.**

Since the given dataset is already arranged in ascending order, it is easier to estimate the answer by looking for the middle value. In this case, the **median is the 4th value** which is **71**. Therefore, the **correct answer** is **Choice A.**

Choice B is incorrect and may result from incorrectly getting the median by finding the average of the 4th and 5th values.

Choice C is incorrect, it is the 5th value in the dataset.

Choice D is incorrect and may result from incorrectly getting the median by finding the average of the 5th and 6th values.

> **(?)** Out of 200 students, 118 students passed the Math exam. What percentage of students passed the test?

A) 55%

B) 59%

C) 62%

D) 68%

Solution: This question is easier to solve mathematically since the numbers are manageable for calculation.

To solve this question, simply divide the number of students who passed by the total number of students and multiply by 100.

This will result in percentage $=\dfrac{118}{200}\times100$ or 59%. Therefore, the **correct answer** is **Choice B.**

Choice A is incorrect and may result if 110 students pass the exam.

Choice C is incorrect and may result if 124 students pass the exam.

Choice D is incorrect and may result if 136 students pass the exam.

2. Looking Closely

You need to read the questions carefully and look closely at the given information and the required data. This is particularly important in the domain of 'Problem-Solving and Data Analysis'. Some of the reasons behind this are as follows:

1. The **titles of data graphs** can provide you with **insightful information** that is key to solving the question.

2. **Units** need to be **considered in comparison**. For example, you need to be careful while comparing a number (given in thousands) with another number (given in millions). Also, **quantities** need to be in the **same unit** to calculate ratios.

3. Some questions (especially student-produced response questions) might ask you to find the answer in a unit other than the unit you were using to get the result. Look closely for necessary unit conversions.

4. Percents are different from numbers. Some questions might ask you for the greatest percent change, for example, rather than the greatest change.

5. All the information you need to answer the question is found in the question. You are expected to adhere to the given information only, without using any of the external information you might already know about the question topic.

Consider as an example, the given question below on which many questions will be asked and solved later in the chapter.

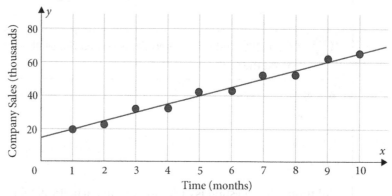

The given scatterplot shows the sales of a company Z, months after December 2022.

First, let's look at the graph titles.

The **horizontal axis** shows the **time in months,** while the **vertical axis** shows the **company sales in thousands**.

This means whenever you read 20, for example, as the y-coordinate of a point, it implies a sales of 20,000. A question might ask you to find the sales in a specific month in <u>hundreds</u>, and to enter that as a student-produced response. Be careful of the units. In addition, look closely for the required quantity. You would need to solve a question asking for the average yearly increase in sales differently than another question asking for the percent increase in sales between two months.

That's it for the general strategies for this chapter. Now let's dive deep into the subtopics of the 'Problem-solving and Data Analysis' domain.

Ratios, Rates, Proportional Relationships, and Units

You started learning about ratios, rates, proportional relationships, and units in middle school. You have learned the basics, in addition to reasoning and problem-solving skills with these topics. They are very important as they have a wide range of real-life applications.

Ratios

Ratios are used to compare quantities. For example, you might say that the ratio of chickens to cows on a farm is 33 to 2. This might also be expressed as 33:2 or $\frac{33}{2}$. You need to be able to differentiate between part-to-whole ratios and part-to-part ratios. Part-to-whole ratios relate a quantity to the total, while part-to-part ratios relate quantities to each other. To find the part-to-whole ratios from part-to-part ratios, first add the parts to get the whole or the total. If we go back to the **example about the chicken and the cows,** the ratio **33:2** is a **part-to-part ratio** because it **relates the number of chickens to the number of cows.** This ratio means that for every 33 chickens, there are 2 cows. To get the whole, add 33 to 2 to get 35. Thus, the **part-to-whole ratio for chickens would be** $\frac{33}{35}$, and the **part-to-whole ratio for cows would be** $\frac{2}{35}$. Check out the examples below.

 The tasks in a project were divided among Sam, Joe, and Diana in a ratio of 8:5:3. If there are a total of 320 tasks, how many tasks were assigned to Joe?

Solution: A part-to-part ratio is given.

To find the **number of tasks for each person,** you need to **multiply the part-to-whole ratio** for each person by **the total number of tasks.**

First, get the whole or the total number of parts. That is 8 + 5 + 3, or **16.**

Thus, the part-to-whole ratio of Joe's number of tasks is $\frac{5}{16}$.

Therefore, the number of tasks assigned to Joe is $\frac{5}{16} \times 320$, or 100 tasks.

The correct answer is **100.**

 To make a single cake, the ingredients are 3 cups of flour, 1.5 cups of sugar, 0.5 cup of milk, and 0.5 cup of butter. If a total of 27.5 cups are used in baking for the day, how many cups of sugar were used?

A) 2.5

B) 5.5

C) 7.5

D) 15

Solution: To solve this problem, find the total number of cups used in a single cake.

That is 3 cups of flour + 1.5 cups of sugar + 0.5 cup of milk + 0.5 cup of butter, or 5.5 cups total.

The part-to-whole ratio of the cups of sugar is $\dfrac{1.5}{5.5}$.

Multiply the part-to-whole ratio by the total number of cups used for the day.

This will result in $\dfrac{1.5}{5.5} \times 27.5 = 7.5$ 1.5/5.5×27.5=7.5. Therefore, the **correct answer** is **Choice C**.

Choice A is incorrect. This is the total cups of milk or butter used for the day.

Choice B is incorrect. This is the total cups of ingredients used in a single cake.

Choice D is incorrect. This is the total cups of flour used for the day.

Rates

Rates are **similar to ratios** in that they **relate two quantities**. However, **rates have units** that identify the quantities.

> For example, a speed of 60 kilometers per hour is a rate which can also be written as $\dfrac{60\ kilometers}{1\ hour}$. The rate units tell you that you should be dividing the distance (in kilometers) by the time (in hours) to get the speed (in kilometers per hour).

There are three useful forms of this speed formula $speed = \dfrac{ditance}{time}$, $time = \dfrac{distance}{speed}$ and

$distance = speed \times time$. In general, any **rate** can be expressed as the **amount of work done per unit of time**. In the case of **linear functions,** the **unit rate** is the **slope** of the **line graph** representing the function. Consider the example below.

 Sarah typed a 500-word page at an average rate of m words per minute. If she had typed 10 words per minute faster, she would have finished typing the page in 2.5 fewer minutes. Which of the following is the correct value of m?

A) 20

B) 40

C) 45

D) 50

Solution: In this question, there are 2 scenarios with two different rates.

In the first scenario, the rate is m words per minute, while in the second scenario, the rate is 10 words per minute faster, that is, $m + 10$ words per minute.

The rate is the number of words typed per unit time, then the time is the ratio of the number of words typed to the rate.

The number of words typed in both scenarios is 500.

Thus, the time for the first scenario is given by $\dfrac{500}{m}$, and the time for the second scenario is given by $\dfrac{500}{m+10}$.

It's given that if Sarah typed at a faster rate, she would finish 2.5 minutes earlier. Then, $\dfrac{500}{m} = \dfrac{500}{m+10} + 2.5$.

Taking the LCM on the right-hand side of this equation yields $\dfrac{500}{m} = \dfrac{500 + 2.5m + 25}{m+10}$, which can be simplified into $\dfrac{500}{m} = \dfrac{525 + 2.5m}{m+10}$.

Cross-multiplication results in $500m + 5000 = 525m + 2.5m^2$.

Subtracting $500m + 5000$ from both sides of this equation yields $0 = 2.5m^2 + 25m - 5000$. Dividing both sides of this equation by 2.5 yields $0 = m^2 + 10m - 2000$.

Using the quadratic formula:

$$m = \frac{-b \pm \sqrt{b^2 - 4ac}}{2a} = \frac{-10 \pm \sqrt{10^2 - 4(1)(-2000)}}{2(1)}$$ yields two roots for m, which are approximately –50 and 40.

Since m is a positive quantity (typing rate), then $m=40$.

Therefore, the correct answer is **Choice B**.

Choice A is incorrect because substituting 20 for m in the equation $\dfrac{500}{m} = \dfrac{525 + 2.5m}{m+10}$ yields $\dfrac{500}{20} = \dfrac{525 + 50}{20+10}$, or $25 = 19.1\overline{6}$ which is false.

Choice C is incorrect because substituting 45 for m in the equation $\dfrac{500}{m} = \dfrac{525 + 2.5m}{m+10}$ yields $\dfrac{500}{45} = \dfrac{525 + 112.5}{45+10}$, or $11.\overline{1} = 11.\overline{590}$ which is false.

Choice D is incorrect because substituting 50 for m in the equation $\dfrac{500}{m} = \dfrac{525 + 2.5m}{m+10}$ yields $\dfrac{500}{50} = \dfrac{525 + 125}{50+10}$, or $10 = 10.8\overline{3}$ which is false.

 A swimming pool can be filled by a garden hose in 18 hours. The hose pumps out 10 gallons of water per minute. How many gallons of water were used to fill the pool?

A) 1,080

B) 10,800

C) 36,800

D) 108,000

Solution: For this question, you need to find the amount of water the hose pumps out in 18 *hours.*

First, find the number of minutes in 18 hours. That is $18 \ hours \times \dfrac{60 \ minutes}{1 \ hour} = 1,080 \ minutes.$

Now, find the total volume of water that was pumped out in 1,080 minutes.

This can be expressed as $\dfrac{10 \ gallons}{1 \ minute} \times 1,080 \ minutes = 10,800 \ gallons.$

Therefore, **Choice B** is the **correct answer.**

Choice A is incorrect. This is the number of minutes in 18 *hours.*

Choice C is incorrect. This may result from incorrectly converting 60 *hours* instead of 18 *hours.*

Choice D is incorrect. This may result if the hose pumps 100 *gallons* of water instead of 10 *gallons.*

 A student riding a bike travels at a constant speed of 15 *miles* per hour and can reach home in 45 *minutes* from the school. What is the distance (in *kilometers*) from the school to the house (round up to the nearest tenths)? (1 *mile* = 1.609 *kilometers*)

A) 18.1

B) 72.4

C) 180

D) 675

Solution: To solve, first convert the time from minutes to hours since the given speed is in miles per hour.

Use the formula *distance = speed × time.*

It is given that the speed is 15 *miles* per hour and the time is 45 *minutes.*

Converting the time from minutes to hours yields $45 \ minutes \times \dfrac{1 \ hour}{60 \ minutes} = 0.75 \ hours.$

Substituting the given information in the formula yields

$distance = \dfrac{15 \ miles}{1 \ hour} \times 0.75 \ hours = 11.25 \ miles.$

To convert the distance to kilometers, use the given conversion factor to get

$11.25 \ miles \times \dfrac{1.609 \ kilometers}{1 \ mile} = 1810125 \ kilometers$ or 18.1 *kilometers.*

Therefore, the **correct answer** is **Choice A.**

Choice B is incorrect. This may result from incorrectly multiplying the time by the conversion factor of kilometers.

Choice C is incorrect. This may result from a calculation error.

Choice D is incorrect. This may result from directly multiplying speed and time without converting.

Proportional Relationships

When two quantities x and y vary in a proportional relationship, the ratio of y to x is a constant k known as the constant of proportionality. If one of the two quantities increases, the other quantity increases, and vice versa. The graph of a proportional relationship $y = kx$ is a straight line passing through the origin, with a slope equal to k. In simple terms, a proportion is a number of equal ratios. Let's study the student-produced response example below.

Distribution of Students in a High School According to Their Study of Foreign Languages

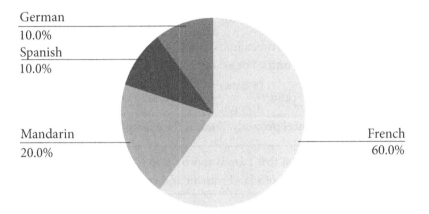

German
10.0%

Spanish
10.0%

Mandarin
20.0%

French
60.0%

> (?) The given pie graph shows the distribution of students in a high school according to their study of foreign languages. If 84 students are studying French, how many students are studying Mandarin?

Solution: There is a proportional relationship between the percentage shown on the pie graph and the corresponding number of students.

Let n represent the number of students studying Mandarin.

Setting up the proportion for students studying French and Mandarin yields $\frac{60\%}{84} = \frac{20\%}{n}$. Cross-multiplication results in $60n = 1680$.

Dividing both sides of this equation by 60 yields $n = 28$.

Therefore, the correct answer is **28**.

Here's another example:

> (?) An orchard grows pear trees. If 9 out of 16 pears are ripe, how many out of 32 pears would be ripe at the same rate?

A) 9

B) 16

C) 18

D) 57

Solution: To solve this question, let x represent the number of ripe pears.

The proportion for the ripe pears yields $\dfrac{9}{16} = \dfrac{x}{32}$.

Cross-multiplication results in 288 = 16x.

Dividing both sides by 16 yields $x = 18$. Therefore, the correct answer is **Choice C**.

Choice A is incorrect. This is the number of ripe pears in the original proportion.

Choice B is incorrect. This is the total number of pears in the original proportion.

Choice D is incorrect. This may result from incorrect cross-multiplication.

Conversion of Units

To convert between units, you need to use conversion factors. **Conversion factors** are **ratios** that **relate units**. For example, if 1 pound is equal to 16 ounces, then the conversion factors are

$\dfrac{1\ pound}{16\ ounces}$ and $\dfrac{16\ ounces}{1\ pound}$. Make sure to **choose the conversion factor** in such a way that the

units cancel properly. Look at the examples below.

 Given that 1 km is approximately equal to 0.62 $miles$, which of the following is the area in km^2 of a land with an area of 2,000 square miles to the nearest unit?

A) 769

B) 1,240

C) 3,226

D) 5,203

Solution: Given that 1 km is approximately equal to 0.62 $miles$, the resulting conversion factors

are $\dfrac{1\ km}{0.62\ miles}$ and $\dfrac{0.62\ miles}{1\ km}$.

The given area is in square miles or $miles^2$, and the required area is in km^2.

As a result, you need to cancel the unit $miles^2$ and introduce the unit km^2.

To achieve that, you need to multiply the given area of 2000 $miles^2$ by the conversion factor

$\dfrac{1\ km}{0.62\ miles}$ twice.

This yields $2000\ miles^2 \times \dfrac{1\ km}{0.62\ miles} \times \dfrac{1\ km}{0.62\ miles}$ which is equal to 5203 km^2.

Therefore, the correct answer is **Choice D**.

Choice A is incorrect and may result from incorrectly multiplying by the conversion factor

$\dfrac{0.62\ miles}{1\ km}$ twice.

Choice B is incorrect and may result from incorrectly multiplying by the conversion factor

$\dfrac{0.62\ miles}{1\ km}$ once.

Choice C is incorrect and may result from incorrectly multiplying by the conversion factor

$\dfrac{1 \ km}{0.62 \ miles}$ once.

 The weight of a sack of rice is 60 *kilograms*. If 28.6 *pounds* were used, how many pounds were left in the sack of rice, given that 1 *kilogram* is approximately equal to 2.2 *pounds*?

A) 28.6

B) 60

C) 103.4

D) 132

Solution: Since the given weight is in kilograms and the required answer is in pounds, convert

the weight of 60 kilograms into pounds using the conversion factor $\dfrac{2.2 \ pounds}{1 \ kilogram}$. This will

result in $60 \ kilograms \times \dfrac{2.2 \ pounds}{1 \ kilogram} = 132$ pounds.

Now, to find how many pounds were left in the sack of rice, subtract the pounds used from the total weight. This results in 132 *pounds* – 28.6 *pounds* = 103.4 *pounds*.

Therefore, the **correct answer** is **Choice C**.

Choice A is incorrect. This is the amount of rice used.

Choice B is incorrect. This is the original weight of the sack of rice in kilograms.

Choice D is incorrect. This is the conversion of the given weight of the sack of rice from kilograms to pounds.

1 ◫ **Mark for Review**

Roy runs at an average rate of 12 minutes per mile. Which function t models the number of minutes it will take Roy to run m miles at the same rate?

A) $t(m) = 12m$

B) $t(m) = \dfrac{12}{m}$

C) $t(m) = m + 12$

D) $t(m) = m - 12$

2 ◫ **Mark for Review**

The sum of x and y is 35.2. If $x - 2 = 18$, which of the following is equivalent to the ratio of y to x?

A) $\dfrac{5}{6}$

B) $\dfrac{19}{25}$

C) $\dfrac{25}{19}$

D) $\dfrac{6}{5}$

3 ◫ **Mark for Review**

What is a rate of 33 feet per hour in inches per second? (1 foot = 12 inches)

A) 0.11

B) 6.6

C) 396

D) 9900

4 ◫ **Mark for Review**

A small car consumes an average of 2.5 liters of gasoline per 50 km. If the car moves at an average speed of 72 km/h for 25 minutes, what is the average volume of gasoline it consumes in liters?

5 ◫ **Mark for Review**

m and n are natural numbers less than 100 such that m is a multiple of 2 and n is a multiple of 3. If the ratio of m to n is 5 to 7, which could be the value of $m + n$?

A) 42

B) 60

C) 72

D) 84

Answers & Explanations

1. **Level:** Easy | **Skill/Knowledge:** Ratios, rates, proportional relationships, and units | **Testing Point:** Use rates to write a function

   Key Explanation: Choice A is correct. Roy runs at an average rate of 12 minutes per mile. The number of minutes it will take Roy to run m miles can be determined by multiplying the average rate by the number of miles. This yields 12m. Therefore, the function $t(m) = 12m$ models the number of minutes it will take Roy to run m miles.

   Distractor Explanations: Choice B is incorrect and may result from conceptual errors. **Choice C** is incorrect and may result from conceptual errors. **Choice D** is incorrect and may result from conceptual errors.

2. **Level:** Medium | **Skill/Knowledge:** Ratios, rates, proportional relationships, and units | **Testing Point:** Find the ratio of two quantities

   Key Explanation: Choice B is correct. It's given that $x - 2 = 18$. Adding 2 to both sides of this equation yields $x = 20$. It's also given that the sum of x and y is 35.2, then the value of y is 20 less than 35.2, or 15.2. Thus, the ratio of y to x is $\frac{15.2}{20}$, or 0.76. The only fraction choice which is equivalent to 0.76 is $\frac{19}{25}$.

   Distractor Explanations: Choice A is incorrect. This is the ratio of x to y if $x + 2 = 18$. **Choice C** is incorrect. This is the ratio of x to y. **Choice D** is incorrect and may result if $x + 2 = 18$.

1. **Level:** Medium | **Skill/Knowledge:** Ratios, rates, proportional relationships, and units | **Testing Point:** Convert units between rates

   Key Explanation: Choice A is correct. It's given that 1 foot = 12 inches, then the corresponding conversion factors are $\frac{1\ foot}{12\ inches}$ and $\frac{12\ inches}{1\ foot}$.

   It's also known that 1 hour = 3600 seconds, then the corresponding conversion factors are $\frac{1\ hour}{3600\ seconds}$ and $\frac{3600\ seconds}{1\ hour}$. To convert from feet per hour into inches per second, using the correct conversion factors would cancel the units properly. Thus, the factors needed in this conversion are $\frac{12\ inches}{1\ foot}$ and $\frac{1\ hour}{3600\ seconds}$. To achieve the correct units, multiply the given rate by the conversion factors such that

   $$\frac{33\ feet}{1\ hour} \times \frac{12\ inches}{1\ foot} \times \frac{1\ hour}{3600\ seconds} = 0.11\ inches/second.$$

   Distractor Explanations: Choice B is incorrect. This is the rate in inches per minute. **Choice C** is incorrect. This is the rate in feet per hour. **Choice D** is incorrect and may result from using the wrong conversion factors.

4. **Level:** Hard | **Skill/Knowledge:** Ratios, rates, proportional relationships, and units | **Testing Point:** Use ratios, proportional relationships and conversion rates to solve a word problem

   Key Explanation: 1.5 is the correct answer. The traveled distance is the product of the speed by the time. It's given that the car moves at an average speed of 72 km/h for 25 minutes. 25 minutes is equivalent to $25\ min \times \frac{1\ hour}{60\ min}$, or $\frac{25}{60}$ hours. Then the distance traveled by the car is equal to $\frac{72\ km}{1\ hour} \times \frac{25}{60}\ hours = 30\ km$. It's also given that the car consumes an average of 2.5 liters of gasoline per 50 km. Then the following proportion can be set $\frac{2.5\ liters}{50\ km} = \frac{x\ liters}{30\ km}$. Cross-multiplication results in $75 = 50x$. Dividing both sides of this equation by 50 yields $1.5 = x$. Therefore, the average volume of gasoline the car consumes in this trip is 1.5 liters.

5. **Level:** Hard | **Skill/Knowledge:** Ratios, rates, proportional relationships, and units | **Testing Point:** Use ratios and proportions to find the value of an unknown quantity

    Key Explanation: Choice C is correct. It's given that the ratio of m to n is 5 to 7 where m is a multiple of 2 and n is a multiple of 3. Since there are no common factors between 2, 3, 5 and 7, then m and n must be multiples of 6 less than 100. Since $\dfrac{m}{n} = \dfrac{5}{7}$, then m should also be a multiple of 5, and n should also be a multiple of 7. It follows that m is a multiple of 65 = 30 and n is a multiple of 67 = 42. Multiples of 30 which are less than 100 are 30, 60, and 90, and multiples of 42 which are less than 100 are 42 and 84. Thus, the only pairs of numbers which could be the values of m and n and result in a ratio of 57 are respectively 30 and 42 or 60 and 84 since $\dfrac{30}{42} = \dfrac{60}{84} = \dfrac{5}{7}$. It follows that the possible values of $m + n$ are 30 + 42, or 72, and 60 + 84, or 144. Therefore, 72 could be the value of $m + n$.

    Distractor Explanations: Choice A is incorrect. This could be the value of n. **Choice B** is incorrect. This could be the value of m. **Choice D** is incorrect. This could be the value of n.

Percentages

Percentages is an important topic that you often encounter in daily life. You may not only see independent questions about percentages, but also questions incorporated with other topics and domains.

Working with Percentages

The basic equation one needs to remember when dealing with percentages is the proportion $\frac{part}{whole} = \frac{percentage}{100}$. You would also need to transform word problems into equations involving percentages. **Remember that the word percent just means a part of a hundred.** Look at the student-produced response example below.

 What percent of 164 is 19? (Round your answer to the nearest tenth)

Solution: Let x represent the unknown percentage.

Using the proportion $\frac{part}{whole} = \frac{percentage}{100}$, the given information can be modeled into the equation $\frac{x}{100} = \frac{19}{164}$.

Cross-multiplication yields $164x = 1900$.

Dividing both sides of the equation by 164 results in $x \approx 11.6$.

Therefore, the correct answer is **11.6**.

Here's another one:

 A store is offering a discount of $18 on a dress that costs $120. What is the percentage discount on the dress?

A) 15%

B) 17%

C) 19%

D) 21%

Solution: To solve, use the proportion $\frac{part}{whole} = \frac{percentage}{100}$. Let x represent the percentage discount. This results in the equation $\frac{18}{120} = \frac{x}{100}$. Cross multiplying yields $1,800 = 120x$.

Dividing both sides by 120 results in $x = 15$. Therefore, the **correct answer is Choice A**.

Choice B is incorrect. This may result if the discount is $20.

Choice C is incorrect. This may result if the discount is $23.

Choice D is incorrect. This may result if the discount is $25.

Percent Change

Asking for the percent change in a quantity is a common question on the SAT Math section. Percent change can be either a **percent increase** or a **percent decrease**.

Note: When dealing with percent change, you need to remember the formula,

$$percent\ change = \frac{amount\ of\ change}{initial\ amount} \times 100\%$$

 Remember

Always divide by the initial amount before multiplying by 100.

Consider the given question used in the introduction to this chapter with the first question about it.

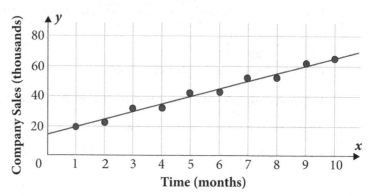

(?) The given scatterplot shows the sales of a company Z, months after December 2022. Which of the following is closest to the percent increase in sales between January 2023 and October 2023?

A) 5%

B) 69%

C) 200%

D) 225%

Solution: First, locate the points corresponding to the months of January 2023 and October 2023.

For January 2023, $x = 1$. This corresponds to the point (1, 20).

For October 2023, $x = 10$. This corresponds to the point (10, 65).

Thus, the sales have increased from 20,000 in January to 65,000 in October.

Applying the formula *percent change* $= \dfrac{amount\ of\ change}{initial\ amount} \times 100\%$ yields *percent change*

$= \dfrac{65,000 - 20,000}{20,000} \times 100\%$, which is equal to 225%.

Therefore, the correct answer is **Choice D.**

Choice A is incorrect because 5% is very small compared to the actual increase in sales between January 2023 and October 2023.

Choice B is incorrect because an increase of 69% is less than double the sales which contradicts the data represented in the graph.

Choice C is incorrect because an increase of 200% results in triple the sales in January 2023 which is 20,000. The triple of 20,000 is 60,000, and the graph shows a value of 65,000 which is greater than 60,000 for October 2023.

Let's go through another solved example:

 The price of a television, initially sold for $2,300, was reduced to $2,230. What was the percent decrease in the price of the television? (Round your answer to the nearest whole number)

A) 2%

B) 3%

C) 4%

D) 5%

Solution: To solve, calculate the decrease in price and express it as a percentage of the original price. Using the formula *percent change* $= \dfrac{amount\ of\ change}{initial\ amount} \times 100$ yields percent change

$= \dfrac{2,300 - 2,230}{2,300} \times 100$, which is equal to 3%. Therefore, the **correct answer** is **Choice B.**

Choice A is incorrect. This may result if the television cost is reduced to $2,254.

Choice C is incorrect. This may result if the television cost is reduced to $2,208.

Choice D is incorrect. This may result if the television cost is reduced to $2,185.

1 ⬜ **Mark for Review**

What is 15% of 164?

A) 10.93

B) 24

C) 24.6

D) 149

2 ⬜ **Mark for Review**

A square meter of land was priced at $20. If this price increased by 80% in the first 3 years, and by 104% in the next 3 years, what was its price after 6 years?

A) $37.44

B) $57.6

C) $73.44

D) $86.4

3 ⬜ **Mark for Review**

Cindy added 26 grams of sugar to 80 ml of water to make a drink. She then wanted to make a sweeter drink which is 7% more sugar concentrated. How many grams of sugar would she need to add to 120 ml of water to make the drink?

A) 31.6

B) 39.5

C) 39.6

D) 47.4

4 ⬜ **Mark for Review**

The line graph below shows the number of hours Sam worked in week 1 of September.

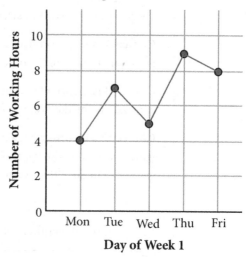

The following week, Sam worked 36 hours, x% more than week 1.

What is x to the nearest tenth?

5 ⬜ **Mark for Review**

The dimensions of a rectangle have been changed. If the length has increased by 150% but the area has decreased by 50%, what is the percentage increase in the perimeter?

Answers & Explanations

1. **Level:** Easy | **Skill/Knowledge:** Percentages | **Testing Point:** Calculating the percentage of a number

   Key Explanation: Choice C is correct. 15% of a quantity means $\frac{15}{100}$ times the quantity. Therefore 15% of 164 can be represented as $\frac{15}{100} \times 164$. Calculating it yields 15% of $164 = \frac{15}{100} \times 164 = 24.6$. Therefore, 15% of 164 is 24.6.

   Distractor Explanations: Choice A is incorrect and may result from dividing 164 by 15. **Choice B** is incorrect and may result from finding 15% of 160 instead of 164. **Choice D** is incorrect and may result from subtracting 15 from 164.

2. **Level:** Easy | **Skill/Knowledge:** Percentages | **Testing Point:** Find a quantity after a percent increase

   Key Explanation: Choice C is correct. To increase a number by 80%, it should be multiplied by 180%, or 1.8. Thus, after 3 years, the price of the square meter of land would be $20 \times 1.8 = 36$ dollars. To increase a number by 104%, it should be multiplied by 204%, or 2.04. Therefore, after 6 years, the price of the square meter of land would be $36 \times 2.04 = 73.44$ dollars.

   Distractor Explanations: Choice A is incorrect. This is the result of an increase by 4% in the next 3 years. **Choice B** is incorrect. This is the result of an increase by 60% in the next 3 years. **Choice D** is incorrect. This is the result of an increase by 140% in the next 3 years.

3. **Level:** Easy | **Skill/Knowledge:** Percentages | **Testing Point:** Use percentages to find an unknown quantity

   Key Explanation: Choice D is correct. The percentage of sugar in the initial drink was

   $\frac{26}{80} \times 100$, which is equal to 32.5%. It's given that the sweeter drink is 7% more concentrated, then it has a percentage of sugar equal to $32.5 + 7$, or 39.5%. Thus, the amount of sugar that needs to be added to 120 ml of water to make a 39.5% drink is $\frac{39.5}{100} \times 120$, which is equal to 47.4 grams.

   Distractor Explanations: Choice A is incorrect and may result from conceptual or calculation errors. **Choice B** is incorrect. This is the percentage concentration of sugar in the new drink. **Choice C** is incorrect and may result from conceptual or calculation errors.

4. **Level:** Hard | **Skill/Knowledge:** Percentages | **Testing Point:** Find the percent change

   Key Explanation: The correct answer is **9.1**. Using the line graph, the total number of working hours in week 1 is $4 + 7 + 5 + 9 + 8 = 33$ hours. x is the percent increase from 33 hours to 36 hours. Thus, $x = \frac{36-33}{33} \times 100 \approx 9.09$ which is rounded to 9.1 to the nearest tenth.

5. **Level:** Hard | **Skill/Knowledge:** Percentages | **Testing Point:** Applying percentages to solve a problem

   Key Explanation: The correct answer is **73.33%**.

   For easy calculation, the following variables will be used.

	Old	New
Length	L	L_N
Width	W	W_N
Area	A	A_N
Perimeter	P	P_N

   Assuming $L = 2$ and $W = 1$, then $A = 21 = 2$ and $P = 2(2) + 2(1) = 6$.

   Since the length has increased by 150%, then $L_N = 2(2.5) = 5$.

Since the area has decreased by 50%, then $A_N = 2(0.5) = 1$.

Calculating the new width yields

$$W_N = \frac{A_N}{L_N} = \frac{1}{5} = 0.2.$$

Calculating the new perimeter yields $P_N = 2(5) + 2(0.2) = 10.4$.

Therefore, the percentage increase in the perimeter is $\frac{10.4 - 6}{6} \times 100\% = 73.33\%$.

One-variable Data: Distributions and Measures of Center and Spread

There are two types of measures you should be familiar with when dealing with one-variable data. The **first type** is the **measures of center,** which include the **mean, mode,** and **median.** The **second type** is the **measures of dispersion,** which include the **range** and the **standard deviation.**

Measures of Center

The measures of the center are mean, median, and mode. The **most common measure of center is the mean or the average.**

> **Note:** The formula for the **average** of a **set of values** states that the average is the ratio of the sum of values to the number of values, and it can be written as
>
> $$Average = \frac{Sum\ of\ values}{Number\ of\ values}$$

Cross-multiplication of this equation results in another useful formula:

Sum of values = Average × Number of values

Look at the student-produced response example below.

Number Value	Frequency
2	3
3	2
5	3
7	x

 The table shows the values of a data set of numbers. If the mean of this data set is 4.1, what is the value of x?

Solution: Recall that the frequency is the number of occurrences of a certain value in a set.

In the given table, the frequency of the number 2 is 3. This means that the number 2 occurs 3 times in the set.

Thus to find the sum of values, add the products of the numbers with their respective frequencies.

Then, *sum of values* = 2 × 3 + 3 × 2 + 5 × 3 + 7*x*.

Simplification yields *sum of values = 27 + 7x.*

The sum of values is also equal to the product of the mean by the number of values which is the total frequency.

It's given that the mean is 4.1. Consequently, the sum of values is equal to 4.1 × (3 + 2 + 3 + *x*), or 4.1 (8 + *x*).

Setting the equation for the two expressions of the sum of values results in $27 + 7x = 4.1 (8 + x)$.

Distribution on the right-hand side of the equation yields $27 + 7x = 32.8 + 4.1x$.

Subtracting $4.1x$ from both sides of this equation yields $27 + 2.9x = 32.8$.

Subtracting 27 from both sides of this equation results in $2.9x = 5.8$.

Dividing both sides of this equation by 2.9 yields $x = 2$.

Therefore, the correct answer is **2**.

> The mode is the value that occurs most frequently in a data set. It is the value with the highest frequency.

Some data sets have more than one mode, while others have no mode. In the previous example involving the table, the number values 2 and 3 have the highest frequency (3). Thus, this data set has **two modes: 2 and 3.** Here's a solved example:

$$85, 90, 75, 85, 90, 80, 75, 85, 80, 95$$

The given data shows the scores obtained by students on a math test. What is the mode of the test scores?

A) 75

B) 84

C) 85

D) 95

Solution: To find the mode, you must identify the value that occurs most frequently in the set of scores.

The frequency of each score is shown in the table below.

Scores	Frequency
75	2
80	2
85	3
90	2
95	1

The score that appears most frequently is 85.

Therefore, the correct answer is **Choice C.**

Choice A is incorrect. This is the lowest score from the given data.

Choice B is incorrect. This is the mean of the given data.

Choice D is incorrect. This is the highest score from the given data.

The **median** is the **middle value in an ordered set.** An ordered set is one in which the data points have been arranged in an ascending order.

Consider a set with n values. **If n is odd, the median is the number in the $\left(\dfrac{n+1}{2}\right)th$ place in the ordered set.** For example, in the ordered data set {1, 1, 3, 4, 7}, there are 5 values, and 5 is odd. Then the median is the number with the $\left(\dfrac{5+1}{2}\right)th$ place or 3rd place. Thus, the median is 3. If n is even, the median is the average of the two numbers with places $\dfrac{n}{2}$ and $\dfrac{n}{2}+1$ in the ordered set. For example, in the ordered data set {1, 1, 3, 4, 5, 7}, there are 6 values, and 6 is even. Then the median is the average of the two numbers with the places $\dfrac{6}{2}$ and $\dfrac{6}{2}+1$, so it's the average of the numbers in the 3rd and 4th places. The median in this case is $\dfrac{3+4}{2}$ or 3.5.

When n is even, the median of an ordered dataset may or may not be a value in the set.

Check the example below.

 The median of a set of 5 strictly positive distinct integers is 19. Which of the following is the lowest possible mean of this set?

A) 12.2

B) 12.6

C) 13

D) 19

Solution: Since the number of values is 5 (odd), the median 19 is one of the values in the set, and it's the middle value.

Then 19 is the third number in the ordered set of the 5 strictly positive distinct integers.

As a result, there are two distinct positive integers less than 19, and two distinct positive integers greater than 19.

To achieve the lowest possible value for the mean, the sum of the 5 integers needs to be minimized.

Then the set of integers must be 1, 2, 19, 20, 21.

Then the lowest possible mean is equal to $\dfrac{1+2+19+20+21}{5}$ which is equal to 12.6.

Therefore, the correct answer is **Choice B**.

Choice A is incorrect. The number 12.2 is less than 12.6, and the lowest possible value of the mean is 12.6 given that the positive integers are distinct.

Choice C is incorrect because the mean can be any number greater than or equal to 12.6, so it could be less than 13.

Choice D is incorrect. The number 19 is the median, and the mean would also be equal to 19 if the other numbers are evenly distributed around the median which is not the case to achieve the lowest possible mean.

Measures of Dispersion

Measures of dispersion show the variability of the data around the mean.

> The measure of dispersion will be large if the data values are widely scattered or dispersed around the mean.
>
> The measure of dispersion will be small if the data values are close to the mean with low variability.

A simple measure of dispersion is the **range.** It is the **difference between the largest and smallest values** in a **data set.** For example, the range of the set {1, 1, 3, 4, 5, 7} is 7 – 1, which is equal to 6. Let's go through an example:

58, 60, 62, 64, 66, 68, 70, 72, 74, 76

In a class, the heights (in inches) of 10 students are given above. What is the range?

A) 12

B) 14

C) 16

D) 18

Solution: The range is the difference between the largest and smallest values in a data set.

Since the given data is already arranged in ascending order, you can determine the largest and smallest values as 76 and 58.

Therefore, range = 76 – 58 or range = 18. The correct answer is **choice D.**

Choice A is incorrect. This may result from incorrectly subtracting 64 from 76.

Choice B is incorrect. This may result from incorrectly subtracting 62 from 76.

Choice C is incorrect. This may result from incorrectly subtracting 60 from 76.

Another more informative measure of dispersion is the standard deviation. You are not expected to know how to calculate the standard deviation for the Digital SAT, since you won't be asked such a question. What you will need to know is the general interpretation of the standard deviation which is the same as the one mentioned at the beginning of this paragraph since it applies to any measure of dispersion. Another sort of question that you might encounter is comparing the standard deviation of multiple data sets based on the general structure of the data set. In this case, you need to decide which data set has a larger dispersion about the mean, and in turn, would have the larger standard deviation. Check out the examples below.

> (?) Which of the following sets has the greatest standard deviation?

A) {13, 13, 13, 13, 13}

B) {13, 14, 15, 16, 17}

C) {12, 12, 13, 14, 14}

D) {13, 13, 13, 14, 14}

Solution: You don't need to perform any calculations to answer this question. Just look at the sets and compare. If you look closely, you can see that the set that has the largest spread of numbers around the mean compared to the other sets is {13, 14, 15, 16, 17}. Therefore, the correct answer is **Choice B**.

Choice A is incorrect. It has no dispersion at all. In this case, the standard deviation is zero.

Choice C is incorrect. You can easily see that the mean is 13, and all the numbers are close to 13 with two pairs of repeated values.

Choice D is incorrect. Three of the values are the same, and the two other values are close, and thus you can expect a very low standard deviation.

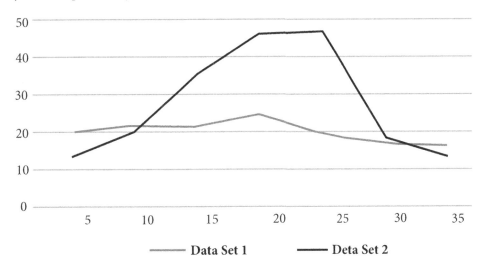

> (?) Which of the following statements is true about the standard deviation of the two data sets given on the graph?

A) Data Set 1 has a higher standard deviation than Data Set 2.

B) Data Set 1 has a lower standard deviation than Data Set 2.

C) Both Data Sets have almost the same standard deviation.

D) There is not enough information to draw a conclusion.

1 ▢ Mark for Review

Which of the following statement is true about the dataset above?

A) The mean of the data is greater than the median of the data.

B) The mean of the data is less than the median of the data.

C) The mean of the data is equal to the median of the data.

D) The mean and the median cannot be determined from the dataset.

2 ▢ Mark for Review

$$23, 34, 46, x, 52, 49, 32, 50, 38$$

The above data has a mean of 40, what is the value of x?

3 ▢ Mark for Review

$$80, 82, s, 81, 83$$

John's scores out of 100 on 5 tests are given. If John's average score is 83, what is his median score?

4 ▢ Mark for Review

Number of books read	3	5	9	12	15	18
Number of teenagers	15	19	$2n$	$n + 4$	10	5

A researcher surveyed teenagers about their reading habits in the past year. On average, each teenager read 8.5 books. Based on the table, how many teenagers were surveyed?

A) 62

B) 65

C) 68

D) 71

5 ▢ Mark for Review

Year	Price per ounce
2011	?
2012	$1,668.86
2013	$1,409.51
2014	$1,266.06
2015	$1,158.86
2016	$1,251.92
2017	$1,260.39

The table shows the average price per ounce of gold from 2011 to 2017. If the median price is $1,266.06, and the range is $510, which of the following options represents a possible price per ounce of gold in 2011?

A) $1,153.86

B) $1,258.25

C) $1,573.16

D) $1,671.86

Answers & Explanations

1. **Level:** Easy | **Skill/Knowledge:** One-variable data: distributions and measures of center and spread | **Testing Point:** Finding the mean and median of grouped data

   Key Explanation: Choice C is correct.
   The mean of the dataset is found by
   $\frac{The\ sum\ of\ the\ data\ values}{the\ value\ of\ frequency}$. The sum of the
   mean of the dataset is $(32 \times 2) + (34 \times 1) + (35 \times 4) + (36 \times 1) + (37 \times 3) = 385$. The value of the frequency is $2 + 1 + 4 + 1 + 3 = 11$. The mean of the dataset will be $\frac{385}{11} = 35$. The median of the dataset is the $\frac{11+1}{2} = $ 6th number. The sixth number is therefore 35. Hence, the mean of the dataset is equal to the median of the dataset.

   Distractor Explanations: Choice A is incorrect. This statement is false, the mean and median are both 35. **Choice B is incorrect.** This statement is false, the mean and median are both 35. **Choice D is incorrect.** The mean and the median can be determined from the dataset.

2. **Level:** Medium | **Skill/Knowledge:** One-variable data: distributions and measures of center and spread | **Testing Point:** Mean of ungrouped data

   Key Explanation: The correct answer is **36**. The mean of ungrouped data is given by mean $= \frac{Sum\ of\ the\ values}{Frequency\ of\ the\ values}$. The sum of the ungrouped data is $23 + 34 + 46 + x + 52 + 49 + 32 + 50 + 38 = 324 + x$.
   Since there are 9 data, then $40 = \frac{324+x}{9}$.
   Multiplying both sides of the equation by 9 yields $40 \times 9 = 324 + x$ or $360 = 324 + x$.

   Subtracting 324 from both sides of the equation yields $36 = x$.

   Therefore, $x = 36$.

3. **Level:** Easy | **Skill/Knowledge:** One-variable data: distributions and measures of center and spread | **Testing Point:** Find the median of a data set

   Key Explanation: 82 is the correct answer.
   The sum of the 5 scores is given by the average multiplied by 5, then the sum is equal to 83×5, or 415. To find s, subtract the sum of the 4 other numbers from 415. Then $s = 415 - (80 + 82 + 81 + 83)$, which is equal to 89. The median is the middle number in an ordered set. Sorting the numbers in ascending order results in the set 80, 81, 82, 83, 89. The middle number is the third number which is 82. Therefore, the median score is 82.

4. **Level:** Hard | **Skill/Knowledge:** One-variable data: distributions and measures of center and spread | **Testing Point:** Use the mean to find the total frequency

   Key Explanation: Choice C is correct.
   The average is given by the sum of values divided by the number of values. Based on the table, the average is equal to
   $$\frac{3 \times 15 + 5 \times 19 + 9 \times 2n + 12 \times (n+4) + 15 \times 10 + 18 \times 5}{15 + 19 + 2n + n + 4 + 10 + 5},$$
   which can be simplified into
   $$\frac{45 + 95 + 18n + 12n + 48 + 150 + 90}{15 + 19 + 2n + n + 4 + 10 + 5}, \text{ or } \frac{428 + 30n}{53 + 3n}.$$
   It's given that the mean is equal to 8.5, then $\frac{428 + 30n}{53 + 3n} = 8.5$. Cross-multiplication yields $428 + 30n = 450.5 + 25.5n$. Subtracting $25.5n$ from both sides of this equation yields $428 + 4.5n = 450.5$. Subtracting 428 from both sides of this equation results in $4.5n = 22.5$. Dividing both sides of this equation by 4.5 yields $n = 5$. Therefore, the total number of teenagers surveyed is $53 + 35$, which is equal to 68.

   Distractor Explanations: Choice A is incorrect and may result if the average is $\frac{259}{31}$. **Choice B** is incorrect and may result if the average is

$\dfrac{548}{65}$. **Choice D** is incorrect and may result if the average is $\dfrac{608}{71}$.

5. **Level:** Hard | **Skill/Knowledge:** One-variable data: distributions and measures of center and spread | **Testing Point:** Use information about the median and the range to find a possible value of an unknown quantity

    Key Explanation: Choice C is correct. Sorting the data given in the table in an ascending order results in 1,158.86, 1,251.92, 1,260.39, 1,266.06, 1,409.51,1,688.86. The range of this data is 1,688.86-1,158.86, or $530, which is the same as the given range. Then the unknown value must be between $1,158.86 and $1,688.86. It's also given that the median price is $1,266.06, which is a value in the set. Then $1,266.06 must be the fourth value in the ordered set, with three values less than or equal to it and three values greater than or equal to it. Since there are already 3 values less than $1,266.06, and only 2 values greater than $1,266.06, then the unknown value must be greater than $1,266.06. Out of the given options, the only value which is greater than $1,266.06 and less than $1,688.86 is $1,573.16. Therefore, a possible price per ounce of gold in 2011 is $1,573.16.

    Distractor Explanations: Choice A is incorrect. If the price per ounce of gold in 2011 is $1,153.86, the range would be $1,668.86 – $1,153.86 = $515. **Choice B** is incorrect. If the price per ounce of gold in 2011 is $1,258.25, the median price would be $1,260.39. **Choice D** is incorrect. If the price per ounce of gold in 2011 is $1,671.86, the range would be $1,671.86 – $1,158.86 = $513.

Two-variable Data: Models and Scatterplots

Analyzing data is an important skill that you need to master. On the Digital SAT Math, you may encounter models that represent two-variable data. The two most common models are the linear and exponential models. Sometimes, you will also come across questions based on scatterplots.

Models

You need to understand the differences between **linear and exponential models** representing **two-variable data**.

> If a variable increases or decreases by a constant value for every one unit increase in the other variable, then you are looking at a case of a **linear model.**
>
> On the other hand, if a variable is multiplied by a constant value for every one unit increase in the other variable, then you are looking at a case of an **exponential model.**

Equations of linear models are just equations of straight lines, and these have been covered in detail in the Algebra chapter. **A linear growth is represented by a straight line with a positive slope, while a linear decay is represented by a straight line with a negative slope.** Consider the examples below.

Hours of Studying, x	1	2	3	4
Score, y	80	85	90	95

 The table shows the relation between the average time, x, spent studying for a test and the corresponding test score, y. Which of the following equations best models this situation for $1 \leq x \leq 4$?

A) $y = 5x + 75$

B) $y = 20x + 60$

C) $y = 20(4)^x$

D) $y = 40(2)^x$

Solution: The table shows an **increase in the value of y** as the **value of x increases.** You need to first decide on the type of the increase. Is it a **linear increase** by the **addition of a constant value?** Or is it an **exponential increase** by the **multiplication of a constant value?** A little 'guess and check' allows you to conclude that there is a constant increase in y by 5 units for every 1 unit increase in x. This is a type of **linear growth.** Thus, the **equation representing this model** must be the **equation of a straight line.** Then you can **eliminate Choices C and D.** The slope of a straight line is the constant change in the value of y for every 1 unit increase in x. Based on the table, since the value of y increases by 5 units for every 1 unit increase in x, the slope is 5. Therefore, the correct answer is **Choice A**, and the equation for this linear growth model is $y = 5x + 75$. You can check your answer by substituting different pairs (x, y) from the table into the equation.

Choice B is incorrect. Although the equation $y = 20x + 60$ represents linear growth, the slope is 20, which means that the value of y increases by 20 units for every 1 unit increase in x. This contradicts the data given in the table.

Choice C is incorrect. The equation $y = 20(4)^x$ represents an exponential growth with an initial value of 20 and a constant factor of 4.

Choice D is incorrect. The equation $y = 40(2)^x$ represents an exponential growth with an initial value of 40 and a constant factor of 2.

 The cost of a car depreciates by $2,000 per year. If the car initially costs $25,000, which of the following equations represents the linear model for the cost (C) of the car (in dollars) t years after its initial value?

A) $C = 2,000t + 25,000$

B) $C = 25,000t - 2,000$

C) $C = -2,000t + 25,000$

D) $C = -25,000t - 2,000$

Solution: According to the given information, the price of the car depreciates with time and therefore, this is a case of linear decay. A linear decay is a straight line with a negative slope, hence **Choices A and B can be eliminated** since they have a positive slope.

The cost of the car decreases by $2,000 per year, so the **slope of the line is –2,000**.

The **initial cost** of the car is $25,000, so the y-intercept is 25,000.

Therefore, the equation representing the linear model is $C = -2,000t + 25,000$. The **correct answer** is **Choice C.**

Choice D is incorrect. This results if the initial cost of the car is interpreted as the slope of the line.

Now, let's move on to **exponential models.** The equations of exponential models are exponential functions which were explained in the Advanced Math chapter.

Recall that an exponential function has the basic form $f(x) = ab^x$, where b is a positive constant and $a = f(0)$ is the initial value. The exponential function is increasing (known as exponential growth) if $b > 1$, and it is decreasing (known as exponential decay) if $0 < b < 1$.

Look at the examples below.

 An electronics company studied a certain computer model. It was found that this computer loses 15% of its value per year after its manufacturing date. Which type of model best represents this scenario?

A) Linear growth

B) Linear decay

C) Exponential growth

D) Exponential decay

Solution: It's given that the computer **loses 15% of its value per year** after its **manufacturing date.**

To decrease a value by 15%, we multiply this value by (1-0.15). So, each year, the value of this computer should be multiplied by a constant value (0.85).

This is a case of an **exponential model.** Since 0<0.85<1, this is an **exponential decay model.**

Therefore, the correct answer is **Choice D**.

Choice A is incorrect because the value of the computer is decreasing, so it is a case of growth rather than decay.

Choice B is incorrect because the value of the computer is not decreasing by the same amount each year but rather by a certain percentage of its value that year.

Choice C is incorrect. Although it is an exponential model, it is a decay rather than a growth because the value of the computer is diminishing over time.

 The population of a bacterial colony is initially at 500 cells and triples every hour. Which of the following equations represents the exponential model for the population of the colony t hours after the initial count?

A) $P = 500 \times t^3$

B) $P = 3 + 500^t$

C) $P = (3 + t) \times 500$

D) $P = 500 \times 3^t$

Solution: It is given that the population of a bacterial colony triples its count every hour.

Let's use the form $P = ab^t$, where b is the growth rate and a is the initial population, to find the equation.

From the given information, $a = 500$ and $b = 3$.

Substituting the values yields $P = 500 \times 3^t$. Therefore, **Choice D** is the **correct answer**.

Choice A is incorrect. This may result from incorrect substitution of the given.

Choice B is incorrect. This may result from incorrect substitution of the given.

Choice C is incorrect. This may result from a conceptual error.

Scatterplots

Scatterplots are graphs of ordered pairs relating two variables in the *xy*-plane. The line of best fit is the line that is closest to all the points of the scatterplot. You won't be asked to find the equation of the line of best fit on the Digital SAT Math. You may be asked to choose the equation based on a provided scatterplot or to use the equation to predict unknown values. Consider the scatterplot presented at the beginning of this chapter with a new student-produced response question that follows.

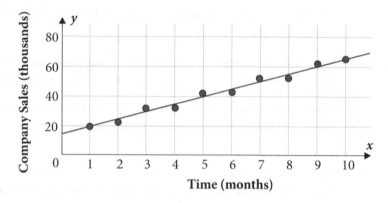

 The given scatterplot shows the sales of a company Z, months after December 2022. If this model continues its linear growth as represented by the line of best fit of the equation $y = 5x + 15$, what is the expected amount of sales in December 2023 in thousands?

Solution: To answer this question, you will first need to find the value of x corresponding to December 2023.

Since December 2023 is 12 months after December 2022, then $x = 12$.

Substituting 12 for x in the given equation of the line of best-fit yields $y = 5 \times 12 + 15$, which can be simplified as $y = 75$.

Thus, it is expected that the sales of the company Z in December 2023 will be 75,000. Since the question asks for the answer in thousands, the answer that you need to enter is **75**.

Here's another one:

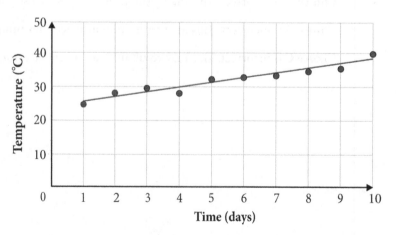

The scatterplot shows the data collected on the temperature over 10 days. If this model continues as represented by the line of best fit of the equation $y = 1.3x + 25$, what is the expected temperature on the 15th day?

Solution: First find the value of x that corresponds to the 15th day which is 15.

Substituting 15 for x to the given equation $y = 1.3x + 25$ yields $y = 1.3(15) + 25$.

This can be simplified to $y = 44.5$. Therefore, the **expected temperature** on the **15th day** is **44.5°C**.

PROBLEM-SOLVING AND DATA ANALYSIS

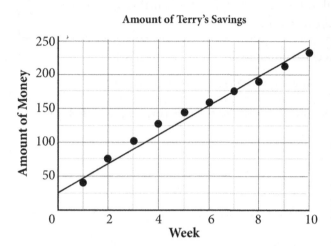

Amount of Terry's Savings

The scatterplot above shows the amount of Terry's savings. Using the given data, a line of best fit has been created. Which of the following is closest to the amount of money predicted by the line of best fit at week 5?

A) $126

B) $133

C) $148

D) $154

A company's marketing efforts cause the number of customers to double every half a year. If the company had 300 customers initially, how many customers would it have after 3 years?

A) 2,400

B) 4,800

C) 19,200

D) 90,000

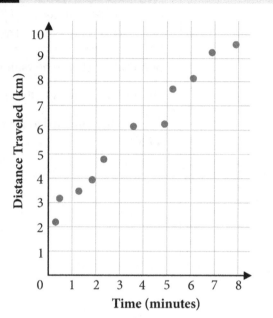

The scatterplot shows various distance readings in kilometers corresponding to different time intervals in minutes. Which of the following equations is the most appropriate linear model for the data shown?

A) $y = -x + 2$

B) $y = x + 2$

C) $y = \dfrac{5}{4}x - 2$

D) $y = -\dfrac{5}{4}x + 2$

4 ☐ **Mark for Review**

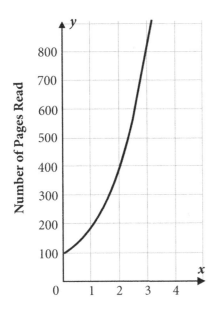

Joe starts tracking the number of pages he reads, and he aims to double the number each year. The model in the graph represents this situation. Based on this model, which is the best estimate of the number of pages that Joe is expected to read after 2.5 years?

A) 460

B) 492

C) 528

D) 566

5 ☐ **Mark for Review**

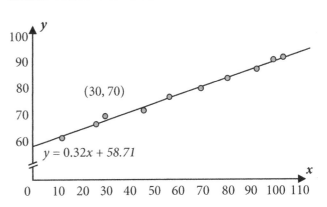

A scatterplot is shown with the line of best fit whose equation is shown. For $x = 30$, which of the following best approximates the percent decrease from the actual data value to the data value predicted by the line of best fit?

A) 1.69%

B) 2.41%

C) 2.47%

D) 68.31%

Answers & Explanations

1. **Level:** Easy | **Skill/Knowledge:** Two variable data: models and scatterplot | **Testing Point:** Analyze and interpret data in a scatterplot

   Key Explanation: Choice B is correct. In the line of best fit, week 5 corresponds to an amount between $125 and $150. **Choices A, B,** and **C** are the only options with values between $125 and $150.

   Since the amount of money represented in the line of best fit at week 5 is close to the middle of $125 and $150, then the correct answer is $133.

   Distractor Explanations: Choice A is incorrect. This is the actual amount of money that Terry saved in week 4. **Choice C** is incorrect. This is the actual amount of money that Terry saved in week 5 rather than the predicted value by the line of best fit at week 5. **Choice D** is incorrect. This is the amount of money predicted by the line of best fit at week 6.

2. **Level:** Easy | **Skill/Knowledge:** Two variable data: models and scatterplot | **Testing Point:** Set and use an exponential growth function based on a word problem

   Key Explanation: Choice C is correct. Let y represent the number of customers x years after the initial company observation. Since the number of customers doubles every half a year, the relationship between x and y can be represented by an exponential growth function of the form $y = a(b)^{\frac{x}{k}}$, where a is the number of customers during the initial observation and the number of customers increases by a factor of b every k years. Using the given information, set $a = 300$, $b = 2$ and $k = \frac{1}{2}$. Thus, $\frac{x}{k} = \frac{x}{\frac{1}{2}} = 2x$ and the exponential function becomes $y = 300(2)^{2x}$. The number of customers after 3 years is the value of y when $x = 3$. Substituting 3 for x in the equation $y = 300(2)^{2x}$

   yields $y = 300(2)^{2 \times 3} = 300(2)^6 = 300 \times 64 = 19{,}200$. Therefore, after 3 years, the company would have 19,200 customers.

   Distractor Explanations: Choice A is incorrect. This is the result of multiplying 300 by $(2)^3$ instead of $(2)^6$. **Choice B** is incorrect and it is the number of customers the company would have after 2 years. **Choice D** is incorrect and may result from incorrectly squaring 300.

3. **Level:** Medium | **Skill/Knowledge:** Two variable data: models and scatterplot | **Testing Point:** Choose the correct equation for the line of best fit for data shown in a scatterplot

   Key Explanation: Choice B is correct. The equation representing a linear model can be written in the form $y = bx + a$, where b is the slope of the line of the model and a is the y-intercept. The scatterplot shows that the points are getting higher as x increases, then the slope of the linear model must be positive. The scatterplot also shows data points near the y-axis at a positive value of y, then the y-intercept of the linear model is also positive. Thus, $b > 0$ and $a > 0$. Only Choice B of the given choices shows a positive slope and a positive y-intercept. Therefore, the most appropriate linear model for the data shown is $y = x + 2$.

   Distractor Explanations: Choice A is incorrect because it represents a linear model with a negative slope. **Choice C** is incorrect because it represents a line with a negative y-intercept. **Choice D** is incorrect because it represents a linear model with a negative slope.

4. **Level:** Hard | **Skill/Knowledge:** Two variable data: models and scatterplot | **Testing Point:** Model a real-life situation by an exponential function and use this function to predict unknown quantities

   Key Explanation: Choice D is correct. From the graph, the initial number of pages read is 100. An exponential function has the general form $y = ab^{\frac{x}{k}}$, where a is the initial number of pages read and the number of read pages increases by a factor of b every k years. Thus, the given situation can be modeled by the function $y = 100 \times 2^x$ because the number of pages is expected to double each year. The value of y for $x = 2.5$ is the expected number of pages read after 2.5 years. Substituting 2.5 for x in the equation $y = 100 \times 2^x$ yields $y = 100 \times 2^{2.5}$, which is approximately 566 pages.

Distractor Explanations: Choice A is incorrect. This is the approximate number of pages if $x = 2.2$. **Choice B** is incorrect. This is the approximate number of pages if $x = 2.3$. **Choice C** is incorrect. This is the approximate number of pages if $x = 2.4$.

5. **Level:** Medium | **Skill/Knowledge:** Two variable data: models and scatterplot | **Testing Point:** Find the percent change from the actual value on the scatterplot to the value predicted by the line of best fit

   Key Explanation: Choice B is correct. The point (30, 70) belongs to the scatterplot, so for $x = 30$, the actual y-value is 70. The predicted y-value can be found from the line of best fit having the equation $y = 0.32x + 58.71$. Substituting 30 for x in the equation $y = 0.32x + 58.71$ yields $y = 0.32(30) + 58.71$, which is equal to 68.31. The percent decrease is given by $\dfrac{amount\ of\ change}{actual\ value} \times 100$. The amount of change is equal to $70 - 68.31$, which is equal to 1.69. Thus, the percent decrease from the actual value to the predicted value for $x = 30$ is equal to $\dfrac{1.69}{70} \times 100$, or $2.4\overline{142857}$. Therefore, the percent decrease from the actual value to the predicted value for $x = 30$ is approximately equal to 2.41%.

   Distractor Explanations: Choice A is incorrect. The number 1.69 is the difference between the actual y-value and the predicted y-value for $x = 30$. **Choice C** is incorrect. This is approximately the percent increase from the predicted y-value to the actual y-value for $x = 30$. **Choice D** is incorrect. The number 68.31 is the predicted y-value for $x = 30$.

Probability and Conditional Probability

Probability is the chance of an event happening. A special type of probability question is one that is focused on finding conditional probability from two-way tables.

Probability

The probability of an event is the ratio of the number of outcomes for this event happening to the total number of possible outcomes of the whole experiment.

This can be written as $probability = \dfrac{total \ number \ of \ favorable \ outcomes}{total \ number \ of \ possible \ outcomes}.$

The value of a probability is between 0 and 1, with:

0 = impossible event
1 = certain event

To solve probability questions correctly, you need to read the question carefully and understand what the question is asking for. Look at the examples below.

	Positive Test	Negative Test	Total
Defective	25	4	29
Non-defective	1	164	165
Total	26	168	194

 The quality control department of a company performed a test on each item to detect if it was defective or not. The results are shown in the given table. What is the probability of choosing an item that was defective and received a negative test result?

A) $\dfrac{4}{194}$

B) $\dfrac{25}{194}$

C) $\dfrac{29}{194}$

D) $\dfrac{168}{194}$

Solution: The probability of an event is the number of favorable outcomes divided by the total number of possible outcomes.

From the table, the number of items that were defective and received a negative test result is 4 and the total number of items is 194.

Therefore, the probability of choosing an item that was defective and received a negative test result is $\dfrac{4}{194}$.

The correct answer is **Choice A.**

Choice B is incorrect. This is the probability of choosing an item that was defective and received a positive test result.

Choice C is incorrect. This is the probability of choosing a defective item.

Choice D is incorrect. This is the probability of choosing an item that received a negative test result.

 In a deck of cards, 2 cards are drawn at random without replacement. What is the probability that the first card drawn is a heart and the second card drawn is a diamond?

A) $\dfrac{2}{52}$

B) $\dfrac{1}{16}$

C) $\dfrac{13}{204}$

D) $\dfrac{169}{2,201}$

Solution: A deck of playing cards has 13 cards in each of the 4 suits of spades, hearts, diamonds, and clubs with a total of $(13 \times 4) = 52$ cards.

The probability of drawing a heart as the first card is $\dfrac{13}{52}$.

Since the card is drawn without replacement, 51 cards remain in the deck.

The probability of drawing a diamond as the second card is $\dfrac{13}{51}$.

The two events are independent as the outcome of drawing the first card does not affect the outcome of drawing the second card.

To find the probability of both events occurring, multiply the probabilities of the individual events.

This will result in a $probability = \dfrac{13}{52} \times \dfrac{13}{51}$ or $probability = \dfrac{13}{204}$. Therefore, the **correct answer** is **Choice C**.

Choice A is incorrect. This may result if the probability is to draw two consecutive cards of the same suit without replacement.

Choice B is incorrect. This may result from incorrectly multiplying $\dfrac{13}{52}$ twice.

Choice D is incorrect. This may result from incorrectly multiplying $\dfrac{13}{51}$ twice.

Conditional Probability

The conditional probability of an event is the probability that the event occurs *given that another event has occurred.*

Whenever you spot the words **"given that"**, **"such that"**, **"if"**, or a declarative statement in a question telling you that something has occurred, think about **conditional probability.**

The conditional probability of an event A given that event B has occurred is given by

$P(A/B) = \dfrac{P(A \cap B)}{P(B)}$. This means that the **numerator is the number of outcomes favorable to both events occurring,** and the **denominator is the number of outcomes satisfying the condition.** Let's take a look at the previous example but with a slightly different question.

	Positive Test	Negative Test	Total
Defective	25	4	29
Non-defective	1	164	165
Total	26	168	194

(?) The quality control department of a company performed a test on each item to detect if it was defective or not. The results are shown in the given table. Given that a chosen item was defective, what is the probability that it received a negative test result?

A) $\dfrac{4}{194}$

B) $\dfrac{4}{168}$

C) $\dfrac{4}{29}$

D) $\dfrac{168}{194}$

Solution: At first glance, you might think that this question is a duplicate of the previous question.

However, if you **look closely** and see the word **"given that"**, you should know that you are dealing with a **conditional probability example** here.

The event is choosing an item that received a negative test result with the condition that the item was defective.

From the table, the **number of items that were defective and received a negative test result** is 4.

Also, the **total number** of defective items is 29.

Therefore, the probability of choosing an item that received a negative test result given that it was defective is $\dfrac{4}{29}$.

The correct answer is **Choice C.**

Choice A is incorrect. This is the probability of choosing an item that was defective and received a negative test result.

Choice B is incorrect. This is the probability of choosing a defective item given that it received a negative test result.

Choice D is incorrect. This is the probability of choosing an item that received a negative test result with no condition.

Let's go through another one:

 There are 22 females and 11 of them have black hair in a group of 40 students in class. The number of black-haired students is 26. If a student is chosen at random from the group, what is the probability that the student is a male who has black hair?

Solution: The event is a probability of a student being male with the condition that he has black hair.

It is given that the total number of students is 40, the number of females is 22, the number of females with black hair is 11, and the total number of students with black hair is 26.

To find the number of males with black hair, subtract the number of female students with black hair from the total number of students with black hair. This will result in 26 – 11 = 15.

Therefore, the probability that a randomly chosen student from the group is a male and has black hair is $\dfrac{15}{40} = \dfrac{3}{8}$.

PROBLEM-SOLVING AND DATA ANALYSIS

1   ☐ Mark for Review

	No. of Red Balls	No. of Blue Balls
With Star	5	9
Without Star	6	6

The table above shows the number of red and blue balls inside a box. Some of the balls have stars on them. What is the probability of randomly picking a ball without a star?

2   ☐ Mark for Review

	Strawberry Flavor	Vanilla Flavor	Chocolate Flavor
With Almonds	6	5	5
Without Almonds	4	6	6

An ice cream store has only 32 ice cream sandwiches left. The table above shows the number of ice cream sandwiches for each flavor. If a customer will pick one random flavor without almonds, what is the probability of picking either a Vanilla or Chocolate flavor ice cream sandwich?

A) 0.375

B) 0.625

C) 0.688

D) 0.75

3   ☐ Mark for Review

A bag contains 4 red marbles with the letter A, 6 red marbles with the letter B, 7 green marbles with the letter A, and 3 green marbles with the letter B. What is the probability of selecting one marble, at random, having the letter A from this bag?

A) $\dfrac{1}{5}$

B) $\dfrac{7}{20}$

C) $\dfrac{1}{2}$

D) $\dfrac{11}{20}$

4   ☐ Mark for Review

	Basketball	Baseball	Football	Total
Freshman	33	24	25	82
Sophomore		20	23	
Junior	40	16		
Senior	48	7	25	80
Total		67		292

The table displays the distribution of students across school sports teams. If 25% of these students are sophomores, what is the probability that a student chosen at random is on the football team?

A) $\dfrac{57}{292}$

B) $\dfrac{67}{292}$

C) $\dfrac{37}{146}$

D) $\dfrac{151}{292}$

5   ⬚ **Mark for Review**

	Red	Orange	Blue	White	Total
First Class	73	70	72	71	286
Second Class	46	41	45	44	176
Third Class	80			85	325
Fourth Class	33	30	32		
Total	232	219		235	

The table displays the number of bricks in thousands owned by a construction company. If 24% of the third class bricks are orange, what is the probability of randomly selecting a third class blue brick from all the bricks?

A) $\dfrac{78}{917}$

B) $\dfrac{82}{917}$

C) $\dfrac{82}{325}$

D) $\dfrac{82}{231}$

Answers & Explanations

1. **Level:** Easy | **Skill/Knowledge:** Probability and Conditional Probability | **Testing Point:** Calculating the probability of an event

    Key Explanation: The correct answer is $\frac{6}{13}$. The formula to calculate the probability of an event is $\frac{number\ of\ favorable\ outcome}{total\ number\ of\ possible\ outcome}$. Since the favorable outcome is picking a ball without a star, then the number of favorable outcomes is $6 + 6 = 12$.

    The total number of possible outcomes is $5 + 9 + 6 + 6 = 26$.

    Therefore, the probability is $\frac{12}{26} = \frac{6}{13}$.

2. **Level:** Medium | **Skill/Knowledge:** Probability and Conditional Probability | **Testing Point:** Probability of an event

    Key Explanation: **Choice D** is correct. The formula to calculate the probability of an event is $\frac{Number\ of\ favorable\ outcomes}{Total\ number\ of\ outcomes}$.

    Since the customer will pick one random flavor without almonds, then the total number of outcomes is $4 + 6 + 6 = 16$.

    Since the probability of getting either a Vanilla or Chocolate flavor ice cream sandwich is being calculated and it is stated that the ice cream will not have almonds, then the number of favorable outcomes is $6 + 6 = 12$.

    Therefore, the probability is $\frac{12}{16} = 0.75$.

    Distractor Explanations: Choice A is incorrect and may result from calculating the probability of picking either a Vanilla or Chocolate flavor ice cream sandwich without almonds randomly. **Choice B** is incorrect and may result from calculating the probability of picking either a Vanilla or Chocolate flavor ice cream sandwich randomly from ice creams with almonds. **Choice**

C is incorrect and may result from calculating the probability of picking either a Vanilla or Chocolate flavor ice cream sandwich randomly.

3. **Level:** Medium | **Skill/Knowledge:** Probability and Conditional Probability | **Testing Point:** Calculate the probability of a random event

    Key Explanation: **Choice D** is correct. The probability of selecting one marble with the letter A is given by the number of favorable outcomes over the total number of possible outcomes. The number of marbles having the letter A is $4 + 7 = 11$. This is the number of favorable outcomes. On the other hand, the total number of possible outcomes is the total number of marbles in the bag, which is $4 + 6 + 7 + 3 = 20$, or 20 marbles. Therefore, the probability of selecting one marble with the letter A from the bag is $\frac{11}{20}$.

    Distractor Explanations: Choice A is incorrect. This is the probability of selecting one red marble with the letter A. **Choice B** is incorrect. This is the probability of selecting one green marble with the letter A. **Choice C** is incorrect. This is the probability of selecting one red marble from the bag.

4. **Level:** Hard | **Skill/Knowledge:** Probability and Conditional Probability | **Testing Point:** Find a probability from a table

    Key Explanation: **Choice C** is correct. It's given that 25% of the 292 students are sophomores. It follows that the total number of sophomores is $\frac{25}{100} \times 292$, which is equal to 73 students. Then the number of sophomores who are on the basketball team is $73 - 23 - 20$, which is equal to 30 students. It follows that the total number of students who are on the basketball team is $33 + 30 + 40 + 48$, or 151 students. Then the total number of students who are on the football team is $292 - 151 - 67$, which is equal to 74 students. Therefore, the probability that a student chosen at random is on the football team is $\frac{74}{292}$, or $\frac{37}{146}$.

Distractor Explanations: Choice A is incorrect. This is the probability of randomly choosing a student who is a junior. **Choice B** is incorrect. This is the probability of randomly choosing a student who is on the baseball team. **Choice D** is incorrect. This is the probability of randomly choosing a student who is on the basketball team.

5. **Level:** Hard | **Skill/Knowledge:** Probability and conditional probability | **Testing Point:** Find a probability from a table

Key Explanation: Choice B is correct. It's given that 24% of the third class bricks are orange, then $\frac{24}{100} \times 325$, or 78 bricks are third class orange. It follows that 325 – 80 – 78 – 85 or 82 bricks are third class blue. The probability of randomly selecting a third class blue brick from all the bricks is given by the total number of third class blue bricks divided by the total number of all the bricks. The total number of blue bricks is equal to 72 + 45 + 82 + 32 or 231 bricks. Thus, the total number of all the bricks is equal to 232 + 219 + 231 + 235 or 917 bricks. Therefore, the probability of randomly selecting a third class blue brick from all the bricks is equal to $\frac{82}{917}$.

Distractor Explanations: Choice A is incorrect. This is the probability of randomly selecting a third class orange brick from all the bricks. **Choice C** is incorrect. This is the probability of randomly selecting a third class blue brick from third class bricks. **Choice D** is incorrect. This is the probability of randomly selecting a third class blue brick from blue bricks.

Inference from Sample Statistics and Margin of Error

For the Digital SAT, you will need to know how to **estimate a population parameter** based on **sample statistics.** For this part, you would need to find the expected number in a population based on a sample proportion.

Expected Number

Finding the expected number of a population parameter based on sample statistics is a straightforward process. To do that, **simply multiply the sample ratio representing the parameter by the total number of individuals in the population.**

Consider the examples below.

 In a random sample of 460 residents of a city, 390 owned a car. Approximately how many of the city's 60,000 residents are expected to own a car?

A) 7,826 residents

B) 9,130 residents

C) 50,870 residents

D) 52,174 residents

Solution: It's given that **390 out of the 460** sampled **residents owned a car.**

It has also been given that the **total population** of the city is **60,000.**

Thus, the expected number of city residents who own a car is $\dfrac{390}{460} \times 60,000$, or 50,870 residents.

Therefore, the correct answer is **Choice C.**

Choice A is incorrect and may result if 60 of the 460 sample residents owned a car.

Choice B is incorrect and may result if 70 of the 460 sample residents owned a car.

Choice D is incorrect and may result if 400 of the 460 sample residents owned a car.

 A survey conducted in a library found that 45 students borrowed History books from a random sample of 150 students. How many of the 2,500 students are expected to borrow a History book?

A) 750

B) 1,000

C) 2,500

D) 7,500

Solution: The ratio representing the parameter is given by 45 out of 150 students who borrow History books.

It is also given that 2,500 is the total population of the students.

To find the expected number of students borrowing History books, multiply the two quantities.

This will result in $\dfrac{45}{150} \times 2,500 = 750$. Therefore, the correct answer is **choice A**.

Choice B is incorrect. This may result from conceptual or calculation errors.

Choice C is incorrect. This is the total number of students.

Choice D is incorrect. This may result from incorrectly multiplying 25,000 instead of 2,500.

Margin of Error

You won't be asked to calculate the margin of error on the SAT. However, you might be asked to interpret the margin of error in the context of the question.

This involves finding the interval that includes the parameter value based on the results of sample statistics. **You should find the lower limit and the upper limit of the interval using the estimated population parameter and the margin of error.** This interval is commonly referred to as the confidence interval, but keep in mind that the level of confidence does not affect the interval estimation. Consider the examples below.

 Based on the survey results of a random sample, a company estimated, with a 4% margin of error, that 85% of customers ask an artificial intelligence chatbot before deciding to buy a new smartphone device. Which of the following statements is true?

A) Exactly 85% of all customers ask an artificial intelligence chatbot before making a new smartphone purchase decision.

B) The company is 4% confident that 85% of all customers ask an artificial intelligence chatbot before making a new smartphone purchase decision.

C) The company is 96% confident that 85% of all customers ask an artificial intelligence chatbot before making a new smartphone purchase decision.

D) It is plausible that between 81% and 89% of all customers ask an artificial intelligence chatbot before making a new smartphone purchase decision.

From the given information, it is estimated that 85% of customers ask an artificial intelligence chatbot before deciding to buy a new smartphone device, and the margin of error for this estimation is 4%.

It is extremely unlikely that the percentage of customers in the population exactly matches the percentage from the survey, but the margin of error helps to construct an interval that one can be reasonably sure where the population percentage lies.

Then the lower limit of this interval is 85% – 4%, or 81%, and the upper limit of this interval is 85% + 4%, or 89%.

Therefore, it is plausible that between 81% and 89% of all customers ask an artificial intelligence chatbot before making a new smartphone purchase decision.

The correct answer is **Choice D**.

Choice A is incorrect. The word "exactly" signals a 0% margin of error which is not the case.

Choice B is incorrect. The margin of error does not relate to the confidence level of the company that has conducted the research.

Choice C is incorrect. There is no information about the confidence level of the company which has conducted the research.

 A survey was conducted to estimate the proportion of adults in a city who support a proposed new transportation system. The survey resulted in 62% of the adults supporting the new system, with a margin of error of 5%. What does the margin of error indicate in this context?

A) The proportion of adults who support the system is between 57% and 67%.

B) Exactly 62% of adult respondents support the new transportation system.

C) The result was not reliable as the survey was conducted on a small sample size.

D) A conclusion cannot be accurately drawn from the context.

Solution: From the given information, it is estimated that 62% of adults will support the new system with a 5% margin of error. The lower limit of this interval is 62% – 5%, or 57%, and the upper limit is 62% + 5%, or 67%.

Let's evaluate each conclusion.

Evaluating Choice A, this conclusion is valid. It correctly interprets the margin of error as indicating a range between 57% and 67% within which the true proportion is likely to fall. Therefore, **Choice A** is the **correct answer**.

Choice B is incorrect. The margin of error indicates that the true proportion of adults supporting the system could be slightly higher or lower than 62%. Therefore, it is not accurate to claim that **exactly** 62% of respondents support the system without considering the margin of error.

Choice C is incorrect. While sample size is an important consideration in survey reliability, the margin of error of 5% does not necessarily indicate that the sample size was small. The margin of error is affected by both the sample size and the level of confidence.

Choice D is incorrect. It is possible to draw conclusions based on the context. In this case, **Choice A** provides a valid interpretation of the margin of error.

1 ☐ **Mark for Review**

Questions	Yes	No
Does it still moisturize the skin after 4 hours?	45%	40%
Do you like the scent of the lotion?	64%	22%
Will you recommend the lotion to your friends?	71%	18%

A company conducted a survey about their new brand of skin lotion. The table above shows the results of the survey. During the survey, some customers did not answer some of the questions asked.

If 600 customers were asked if they would recommend the lotion to their friends, how many of them did not answer the question?

A) 66

B) 84

C) 90

D) 108

2 ☐ **Mark for Review**

32 employees at a company were surveyed about their favorite day to work half-day. 19 said that they prefer Saturday. If there are 408 employees at the company, what is the most reasonable estimate of the number of employees whose favorite day to work half-day is not Saturday?

A) 78

B) 131

C) 166

D) 242

3 ☐ **Mark for Review**

A study of 1,200 adults in a large city showed that 17% played games on their phones. If this percentage is consistent among all adults in the city which has a total population of 2.3 million, how many thousand adults in the city play games on their phones?

4 ☐ **Mark for Review**

Based on a survey, it was estimated that the average weight of a high school football player is 230 pounds with a margin of error of 14 pounds at the 90% confidence level. Which is the most reasonable claim about the average weight of a high school football player?

A) It is between 230 and 244 pounds.

B) It is between 216 and 244 pounds.

C) It is between 216 and 230 pounds.

D) It is between 207 and 244 pounds.

5 ☐ **Mark for Review**

A random sample of 345 residents of a city were asked if they preferred public transportation or not. If 120 didn't prefer public transportation, approximately how many of the city's 75,000 residents are expected to prefer public transportation?

A) 16,304 residents

B) 26,087 residents

C) 48,913 residents

D) 58,696 residents

Answers & Explanations

1. **Level:** Easy | **Skill/Knowledge:** Inference from sample statistics and margin of error | **Testing Point:** Inference from sample statistics

   Key Explanation: Choice A is correct. Since 71% answered Yes and 18% answered No, then 100 – 71 – 18 = 11% did not answer the question.

   Since 600 customers were asked if they would recommend the lotion to their friends, then 600 × 0.11 = 66 customers did not answer the question.

   Distractor Explanations: Choice B is incorrect and may result from finding the number of customers who did not answer the question "Do you like the scent of the lotion?". **Choice C is** incorrect and may result from finding the number of customers who did not answer the question "Does it still moisturize the skin after 4 hours?". **Choice D is incorrect** and may result from finding the number of customers who answered No to the question "Will you recommend the lotion to your friends?".

2. **Level:** Easy | **Skill/Knowledge:** Inference from sample statistics and margin of error | **Testing Point:** Make an inference from the results of a sample study

   Key Explanation: Choice C is correct. Finding the estimate of the number of employees who prefer Saturday yields estimate $= \dfrac{19}{32} \cdot 408 = 242.25$, which is approximately 242 employees. It follows that approximately 408 – 242, or 166 employees do not prefer the day Saturday to work half-day.

   Distractor Explanations: Choice A is incorrect. This is 19% of 408. **Choice B is incorrect.** This is 32% of 408. **Choice D is incorrect.** This is the estimated number of employees who prefer Saturday to work half-day.

3. **Level:** Easy | **Skill/Knowledge:** Inference from sample statistics and margin of error | **Testing**

Point: Make an inference from the results of a sample study

Key Explanation: 391 is the correct answer. If the percentage of adults in the city who play games on their phones is consistent with the results of the sample study, then 17% of adults in the city play games on their phones. Finding 17% of 2.3 million yields $\dfrac{17}{100} \times 2.3$ *million*, which is equal to 0.391 million. Each million is one thousand thousands. Therefore, 391 thousand adults in the city play games on their phones.

4. **Level:** Hard | **Skill/Knowledge:** Inference from sample statistics and margin of error | **Testing Point:** Make inferences from sample statistics and margin of error

   Key Explanation: Choice B is correct. It's given that the average weight of a high school football player is 230 pounds with a margin of error of 14 pounds. It is extremely unlikely that the average weight of a high school football player in the population exactly matches the average weight from the survey, but the margin of error helps to construct an interval that one can be reasonably sure where the average weight of the population lies. The lower limit of this interval is 230 – 14, or 216 pounds, and the higher limit of this interval is 230 + 14, or 244 pounds. The confidence interval does not affect the estimation. Therefore, the average weight of a high school football player is estimated to be between 216 and 244 pounds.

   Distractor Explanations: Choice A is incorrect. This option considers the upper level of estimation without the lower level. **Choice C is incorrect.** This option considers the lower level of estimation without the upper level. **Choice D is incorrect.** This option incorrectly uses the 90% confidence interval to calculate the lower level of estimation.

5. **Level:** Hard | **Skill/Knowledge:** Inference from sample statistics and margin of error | **Testing Point:** Make inferences from sample statistics

Key Explanation: Choice C is correct. It's given that 120 out of the 345 sampled residents didn't prefer public transportation. It follows that 345 − 120, or 225 out of the 345 sampled residents preferred public transportation. It's also given that the total population of the city is 75,000. Thus, the expected number of the city residents who prefer public transportation is $\frac{225}{345} \times 75,000$, or approximately 48,913 residents.

Distractor Explanations: Choice A is incorrect and may result if 75 out of the 345 residents preferred public transportation. **Choice B** is incorrect. This is the expected number of city residents that didn't prefer public transportation. **Choice D** is incorrect and may result if 75 out of the 345 residents didn't prefer public transportation.

Evaluating Statistical Claims: Observational Studies and Experiments

You are also expected to **test** the **reasonability of statistical claims** based on **observational studies and experiments.** You'll have to analyze the method of choosing the population and the sample to do that. You'll also have to **analyze the experiment conditions** that would allow you to **conclude a cause-effect relationship.**

Observational Studies

In observational studies, **relationships between factors and other characteristics are observed and studied,** but **no measures are taken** by the researcher that **affect the study.**

In surveys, **information is collected** from a sample of recipients **through answering questions.** In both **observational studies and surveys, associations can be made.** However, **no cause-effect relationships** can be concluded. To **generalize the results** of observational studies and surveys **to the whole population,** the **sample** must be **chosen randomly** from a **well-defined population.**

Consider the examples below.

 A poll of 700 university students chosen randomly from a certain state found that 67% agreed with the statement that owning a computer is essential for their studies. Based on the survey results, which of the following conclusions is valid?

I.   Of all university students in the state, about 67% would agree with the statement that owning a computer is essential for the life of a university student.

II. Of all university students in the state, exactly 67% would agree that owning a computer is needed for their studies.

III. If another poll is done with 700 university students randomly selected from another state, about 67% would agree with the statement that owning a computer is essential for their studies.

A) I only

B) III only

C) II and III only

D) None

Solution: Evaluating conclusion number I, the statement that owning a computer is essential for the life of a university student is different from the statement under study, so there is no information about the percentage of university students in the state who would agree with this statement based on the survey results alone. Consequently, conclusion number I is not valid.

Evaluating conclusion number II, even if the subjects were randomly selected and the results could be generalized to the entire population, the results would provide an estimate but not an exact percentage. As a result, conclusion number II is not valid either.

Evaluating conclusion number III, the subjects in the survey sample were randomly selected from a particular state, and thus the results may not apply to university students of another state. Hence, conclusion number III is not valid either.

Therefore, since none of the conclusions are valid, the correct answer is **Choice D.**

Choice A is incorrect. The statement that owning a computer is essential for the life of a university student is different from the statement under study which restricts the importance of the computer to the studies, so there is no information about the percentage of university students who would agree with this statement based on the survey results alone.

Choice B is incorrect. The subjects in the survey sample were randomly selected from a particular state, and thus the results may not apply to university students of another state.

Choice C is incorrect. Since conclusion number III is not valid, this choice is incorrect. Also, conclusion number II is not valid because even if the subjects were randomly selected and the results could be generalized to the entire population, the results would provide an estimate but not an exact percentage.

 A random sample of teenagers in a certain city were asked if they preferred to eat home-cooked meals or fast food meals. 72% said they preferred fast food meals. Based on this information, which of the following conclusions is valid?

A) 72% of all teenagers preferred fast food meals over home-cooked meals.

B) Home-cooked meals are preferred by most teenagers all over the world.

C) 72% of the teenagers in a certain city preferred eating fast food meals over home-cooked meals.

D) None of the conclusions is valid.

Solution: Evaluating Choice A, the information generalizes the sample data to all teenagers preferring fast food meals over home-cooked meals, which may not be accurate. Conclusion about all teenagers cannot be made based only on the sample from one city. Therefore, **Choice A** is incorrect.

Evaluating Choice B, the conclusion is too broad and cannot be inferred from the information provided. It extends beyond the scope of the data which is limited to a specific city rather than all over the world. Therefore, **Choice B** is incorrect.

Evaluating Choice C, the conclusion implies that 72% of all teenagers in a certain city prefer eating fast food meals, which is not necessarily supported by the survey of a random sample. Therefore, **Choice C** is not valid.

Evaluating Choice D, since none of the other conclusions accurately reflect the information provided by the survey of a sample, **Choice D** is the correct answer.

Experiments

Contrary to observational studies, **experiments are manipulated trials** with **controlled conditions,** whose **goal** is to **find a cause-and-effect relationship** between the **treatment** and the **characteristic under interest.**

A **treatment** is any **manipulation done by the researcher** to study its **effect on the characteristics.** To **conclude a cause-and-effect relationship, randomly chosen subjects** from a **well-defined population** must be **assigned to receive the treatment or not.** The group **not receiving the treatment** is known as the **control group.**

Check the examples below.

 A medical researcher studied the impact of a new herbal medicine on patients with hypertension. 100 patients with no history of hypertension were given placebo pills, while 100 patients with hypertension were given the new medicine. The hypertension patients reported improved symptoms with the new medicine. Which of the following conclusions is valid?

A) The new medicine will not help patients with no history of hypertension.

B) Patients with no history of hypertension will feel better if they don't take the new medicine.

C) The new medicine can only help improve the symptoms of patients with hypertension.

D) None of the conclusions is valid.

Solution: The population under study is not a well-defined one. It consists of **two populations** (**patients without hypertension** and **patients with hypertension**) instead of one. Also, the **sample subjects were not randomly chosen,** so the **results cannot be generalized to the population.** Furthermore, the treatment was not randomly assigned to participants in the study. As a result, **no cause-and-effect conclusions can be drawn** beyond the participants of the study.

Therefore, none of the conclusions are valid and the correct answer is **Choice D**.

Choice A is incorrect. The new medicine was only given to patients with hypertension. There is no information about the effect of the new medicine on patients with no history of hypertension.

Choice B is incorrect. The study did not include another group of patients without a history of hypertension who were given the new medicine, so such comparisons cannot be made.

Choice C is incorrect. The new medicine was not given to patients without hypertension, so no information is available about the effect of the new medicine on patients without hypertension.

A researcher wants to investigate the effect of the new fertilizer on plant growth. 50 out of 100 random plants were given the new fertilizer while the remaining plants were not given any fertilizer. The plants with the new fertilizer grow healthier compared to the ones without. Which of the following conclusions is valid?

A) Using the new fertilizer is the only factor contributing to the healthier growth of plants.

B) The new fertilizer leads to healthier plants compared to not using any fertilizer.

C) The new fertilizer is likely to have a negative effect on plant growth based on the observed results.

D) None of the conclusions is valid.

Solution: Evaluating Choice A, this conclusion is not valid. The observed results did suggest that the new fertilizer has a positive effect on plant growth but it is unlikely the only factor that contributes to healthier growth. There are other factors like soil quality, sunlight, and water. Therefore, **Choice A** is incorrect.

Evaluation **Choice B**, this conclusion is valid. The conclusion states the observed effect of the new fertilizer on plant health, which accurately reflects the result. Therefore, **Choice B** is correct.

Evaluating **Choice C**, this conclusion is not valid. This conclusion contradicts the observed result which indicates a positive effect on the plants treated with the new fertilizer rather than a negative one. Therefore, **Choice C** is incorrect.

Evaluating Choice D, since Choice B is the correct answer, then one conclusion is valid. Therefore, **Choice D** is incorrect.

1 🔖 **Mark for Review**

	Slept within 30 minutes	Slept after 30 minutes
Warm milk	68%	32%
Cold milk	56%	44%

A group of scientists wants to know which temperature of milk is effective in helping people to sleep at night. They conducted an experiment on two groups of people. One group was given warm milk and the other group was given cold milk. The result of the experiment is shown in the table above. If 55 people who drink cold milk during the experiment were not able to sleep within 30 minutes, how many people who drink cold milk were able to sleep within 30 minutes?

2 🔖 **Mark for Review**

Age 41-50
4.0%

Age 31-40
18.0%

Age 11-20
42.0%

Age 21-30
36.0%

A company made an observational study on the user demographics of their new social media app. The study took a random sample of app users and tallied their ages. Shown above is the result of their study. If there are 105 people from age 11-20 in the sample group, how many people are there in the group that is between 20 and 41 years old?

3 🔖 **Mark for Review**

In a study, half of 46 randomly selected grade 7 classes were randomly assigned to learn a lesson using a new educational method, while the other half used the traditional method. Students taught with the new method received higher grades on the same lesson assessment. Which is an appropriate conclusion?

A) The new educational method will likely raise the grades of grade 7 students in any lesson.

B) The new educational method will increase the level of understanding of grade 7 students.

C) The new educational method is better than all other methods in explaining the lesson to grade 7 students.

D) The new educational method is likely to improve grade 7 students' grades on this specific lesson.

4 ☐ **Mark for Review**

A poll of 670 adults chosen randomly from a city found that 58% agreed with the statement, "Children under 15 should be supervised by adults when walking by the river." Based on the survey results, which of the following conclusions is valid?

I. Of all adults in the city, about 58% would agree with the statement, "Children under 15 should always be supervised by adults."

II. Of all adults in the city, exactly 58% would recommend that children under 15 should be supervised by adults when walking by the river.

III. If another poll is done with 670 adults randomly selected from another city, about 58% would agree with the statement, "Children under 15 should be supervised by adults when walking by the river."

A) I only

B) III only

C) II and III only

D) None

5 ☐ **Mark for Review**

In a study on a fungal disease in frogs, 100 diseased frogs were randomly selected. Half were randomly assigned to receive a drug and 90% recovered, compared to 30% in the other half who did not receive the drug. Which conclusion is appropriate?

A) The drug has powerful antifungal properties.

B) The drug would likely help frogs with the fungal disease to recover.

C) The drug is better at treating the antifungal disease than other available drugs.

D) The drug would likely help newts with the fungal disease to recover.

Answers & Explanations

1. **Level:** Medium | **Skill/Knowledge:** Evaluating statistical claims: observational studies and experiments | **Testing Point:** Evaluating the result of a controlled experiment

   Key Explanation: The correct answer is **70**. Since 55 people were not able to sleep within 30 minutes which is 44% of all the people in the group, then the total number of people who drink cold milk is

   $$\frac{55}{0.44} = 125.$$

   Therefore, the number of people that drink milk who were able to sleep within 30 minutes is 125 − 55 = 70.

2. **Level:** Medium | **Skill/Knowledge:** Evaluating statistical claims: observational studies and experiments | **Testing Point:** Evaluating the result of an observational study

   Key Explanation: The correct answer is **135**. Since there are 105 people from age 11-20 in the sample group which is 42% of the whole sample, then there are a total of $\frac{105}{0.42} = 250$ people in that group.

   The total percentage of all the people in the sample group that is between 20 and 41 years old is 36% + 18% = 54%.

   Therefore, there are 2500.54 = 135 people in the sample group that is between 20 and 41 years old.

3. **Level:** Hard | **Skill/Knowledge:** Evaluating statistical claims: observational studies and experiments | **Testing Point:** Evaluate statistical claims based on an experiment

   Key Explanation: Choice D is correct. It's given that the study participants were selected from grade 7 students, which is a well-defined population. Also, the subjects in the sample were selected at random from the population, so results can be generalized to the entire grade 7 students

   population. Moreover, the subjects in the sample were randomly assigned to learn a specific lesson with the new educational method or not. Since the 3 conditions were met, conclusions about cause and effect can appropriately be drawn. Since the population is grade 7 students, and the study participants who learned the lesson using the new educational method reported better grades, an appropriate conclusion would be that the new educational method is likely to improve grade 7 students' grades on this specific lesson.

   Distractor Explanations: Choice A is incorrect. The participants were randomly selected from students of grade 7, and the treatment (new educational method) was applied to one specific lesson only, so the results of the study cannot be applied to other lessons. **Choice B** is incorrect. The study determined only the new educational method's effect on students' grades. Nothing was mentioned about evaluating the effect of this method on students' understanding. **Choice C** is incorrect. The study did not include other available educational methods, only the new and traditional method, so no conclusions can be drawn about the effectiveness of the new method relative to all other methods.

4. **Level:** Hard | **Skill/Knowledge:** Evaluating statistical claims: observational studies and experiments | **Testing Point:** Evaluate statistical claims based on an observational study

   Key Explanation: Choice D is correct. Evaluating conclusion number I, the statement "Children under 15 should always be supervised by adults." is different from the statement under study, so there is no information about the percentage of adults who would agree with this statement based on the survey results alone. Then, conclusion number I is not valid. Evaluating conclusion number II, even if the subjects were randomly selected and the results can be generalized to the entire population, the results would provide an estimate but not an exact percentage. Then, conclusion number II is not valid too. Evaluating conclusion number III, the subjects in the survey sample were randomly selected from a particular city, and thus the results may not apply to adults of another city. Then, conclusion number III is not valid too. Therefore, none of the conclusions is valid.

Distractor Explanations: Choice A is incorrect. The statement "Children under 15 should always be supervised by adults." is different from the statement under study which restricts adult supervision to walking by the river, so there is no information about the percentage of adults who would agree with this statement based on the survey results alone. **Choice B** is incorrect. The subjects in the survey sample were randomly selected from a particular city, and thus the results may not apply to adults of another city. **Choice C** is incorrect. Since conclusion number III is not valid, then this choice is incorrect. Also, conclusion number II is not valid because even if the subjects were randomly selected and the results can be generalized to the entire population, the results would provide an estimate but not an exact percentage.

5. **Level:** Hard | **Skill/Knowledge:** Evaluating statistical claims: observational studies and experiments | **Testing Point:** Evaluate statistical claims based on an experiment

    Key Explanation: Choice B is correct. It's given that the sample frogs were selected from frogs affected with the fungal disease, which is a well-defined population. Also, the subjects in the sample were selected at random from the population, so results can be generalized to the entire diseased frogs population. Moreover, the subjects in the sample were randomly assigned to receive the drug or not. Since the 3 conditions were met, conclusions about cause and effect can appropriately be drawn. Since the population is frogs with the fungal disease, and a higher percentage of the diseased sample frogs who received the drug recovered, an appropriate conclusion would be that the drug would likely help frogs with the fungal disease to recover.

Distractor Explanations: Choice A is incorrect. There is no information given about the antifungal properties of the drug. The drug might have helped frogs recover by boosting their immunity for example. **Choice C** is incorrect. The study did not include other available drugs, so no conclusions can be drawn about the effectiveness of this drug relative to other drugs. **Choice D** is incorrect. The study was done on frogs, and the sample is not representative of newts. Then, the results of the study cannot be generalized to other populations.

This page is intentionally left blank

Chapter 11
Geometry and Trigonometry

Topics covered in this chapter:

- Area and Volume
- Lines, Angles, and Triangles
- Right Triangles and Trigonometry
- Circles

Questions in the **Geometry and Trigonometry** domain also take up about 15% of the questions you will encounter in the Math section. You will be assessed on your **basic understanding of geometry** learned in middle and high school. You should also be familiar with **equations of circles** and know some **trigonometry**, mainly **right triangle trigonometry.**

Required geometry concepts span a wide range of topics from **angles and lines** to **triangles and circles.** You are also expected to know how to **calculate the areas and volumes** of **basic shapes**, and complex shapes built from basic shapes. Note that there are many geometry formulas provided to you in the reference sheet, accessible to you throughout the test. You would still need to choose the correct formula and know how to apply it.

You might remember many geometry concepts you learned while studying circles in middle and high school. You need to know the **relationships between segments, angles, and arcs in a circle.** You are also expected to comfortably use the formulas for the **length of an arc and the area of a sector.**

Trigonometry asked on the Digital SAT Math is confined to **basic trigonometry.** You would need to know right triangle trigonometry very well, and how to find the trigonometric functions of remarkable angles. All this can be done without a calculator, although a calculator can be helpful in some cases. Properties about the right triangle and special right triangles including the famous Pythagorean theorem are required. You are also expected to be able to **convert between degrees and radians** and know a bit about the **unit circle.**

As you may have noticed, there is a lot to cover in this chapter, so let's head straight to the meat of the aforementioned topics. You will also find in this chapter two strategies, which are particularly helpful in the geometry and trigonometry questions.

 ### Rules to remember while solving Geometry and Trigonometry questions

The first 8 area and volume formulas are available in the reference sheet throughout the test.

- Area of a **circle** = πr^2 where **r is the radius** of the circle.

- Area of a **rectangle** = lw where **l is the length** and **w is the width**. Note that a square is a special rectangle whose area is $s \times s$, or s^2.

- Area of a **triangle** = $\dfrac{1}{2}bh$ where **b is the base** and **h is the corresponding height.**

- Volume of a **rectangular prism** = lwh, where **l is the length**, **w is the width**, and **h is the height.**

- Volume of a **right circular cylinder** = $\pi r^2 h$, where r is the **radius of the circular base** and **h is the height.**

- When two parallel lines are cut by a transversal, the Z and F angles are congruent, while the C and U angles are supplementary.

- Similar figures including **similar triangles** have **congruent corresponding angles** and **proportional corresponding sides.**

- If **two triangles are congruent,** then their **corresponding angles and sides** are also congruent.

- Pythagorean theorem: $a^2 + b^2 = c^2$, where a and b are the respective lengths of the legs of the right triangle, and c is the length of the hypotenuse.

- Two common Pythagorean triples are the 3-4-5 triangle and the 5-12-13 triangle.

- SOH-CAH-TOA: For any acute angle α, $sin\ \alpha = \dfrac{opposite}{hypotenuse}$, $cos\ \alpha = \dfrac{adjacent}{hypotenuse}$, and $tan\ \alpha = \dfrac{opposite}{adjacent}$.

- $tan\ \alpha = \dfrac{sin\ \alpha}{cos\ \alpha}$ and $sin^2\ \alpha + cos^2\ \alpha = 1$

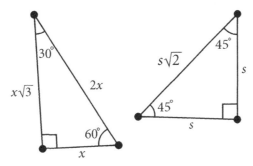

(also available in the reference sheet)

- If α + β = 90°, then sinα = cosβ and cosα = sinβ.

- To convert from **degrees to radians,** multiply by the **conversion factor** $\dfrac{\pi}{180}$. To convert from radians to degrees, multiply by the **conversion factor** $\dfrac{\pi}{180}$.

- The **standard form** of an equation of a **circle with center** (h, k) **and radius** r in the xy-plane is $(x - h)^2 + (y - k)^2 = r^2$.

- $\dfrac{central\ \alpha^{\circ}}{360^{\circ}} = \dfrac{central\ \beta\ radians}{2\pi\ radians} = \dfrac{length\ of\ an\ arc}{2\pi r} = \dfrac{area\ of\ a\ sector}{\pi r^2}$

- A central angle has its vertex at the center of the circle and it measures the same as the intercepted arc.

- An inscribed angle has its vertex at the circumference of the circle and measures half the measure of the intercepted arc.

- A **tangent to a circle** is a line that **touches the circle at exactly one point** called the point of tangency, and it is **perpendicular to the radius of the circle** at the point of tangency.

- Two chords intercepting equal arcs are congruent.

- Any line or segment passing through the center and perpendicular to a chord also bisects the chord.

Strategies

There are many strategies that might help you with geometry and trigonometry questions. Two strategies, that experts think are the most useful on the Digital SAT Math, were chosen to be a part of this chapter. These will be called '**drawing**' and '**redrawing**'. To help you understand, remember, and apply them, they will be explained below in detail.

1. Drawing

Whenever you are given a word problem as the question stem for a geometry or trigonometry question, you shouldn't think twice before drawing a sketch. This strategy is so critical that many questions that look difficult and intimidating when read, turn out to be easy after drawing a sketch. In addition, the sketch will help you avoid making careless mistakes. Consider the examples below.

 A parallelogram ABCD has the following measures for two of its interior angles; $m\angle ABC = 2(3x - 10)°$ and $m\angle BAD = 20°$. What is the value of x?

Solution: The first thing many students might do here is to set the expressions equal, thinking that opposite angles of a parallelogram are congruent, but hold on!

To solve this question, the first thing that you have to do is draw a sketch.

Look at the sketch below.

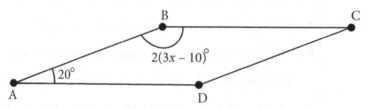

It turns out that the two given angles are **adjacent** and **not opposite**.

The **adjacent interior angles** of a **parallelogram** are **supplementary**.

Hence, $m\angle ABC + m\angle BAD = 180°$.

Substituting the given expressions into this equation yields $2(3x - 10) + 20 = 180$. Expanding and simplifying the left-hand side results in $6x = 180$.

Dividing both sides of this equation by 6 yields $x = 30$.

Therefore, the correct answer is **30**.

 A right triangle has one angle of 30° and the hypotenuse is 14 cm. What is the length of the side opposite the 30° angle?

A) 7

B) $7\sqrt{3}$

C) 14

D) $14\sqrt{3}$

Solution: To solve this problem, first sketch a right triangle with one angle of 30° and a hypotenuse of 14 cm.

In a 90-60-30 triangle, the side opposite the 30° angle is half the length of the hypotenuse. Then $BC = \dfrac{14cm}{2} = 7cm$. Therefore, the correct answer is **Choice A**.

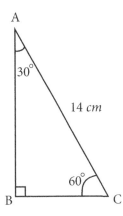

Choice B is incorrect. This is the length of the side adjacent to the 30° angle.

Choice C is incorrect. This is the length of the hypotenuse.

Choice D is incorrect. This is due to a calculation error.

(?) In a circle with radius of 5.3 cm, two chords AB and CD intersect at a point E inside the circle. If AE = 2.1 cm, EB = 4.4 cm, and CE = 3.2 cm, what is the length of ED? (Round to the nearest unit)

A) 1

B) 2

C) 3

D) 4

Solution: To solve this problem, first sketch the circle and draw two chords AB and CD intersecting at a point E inside the circle.

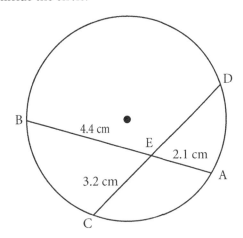

The intersecting chord theorem states that the products of the segments of each chord are equal. Therefore, AE × EB = CE × ED.

Substituting the given information yields 2.1 × 4.4 = 3.2 × ED or 9.24 = 3.2ED.

Dividing both sides by 3.2 yields 2.8875 = ED. Therefore, the length of ED is approximately 3 *cm*, which is **Choice C**.

Choice A is incorrect. This may result if CE = 9.2 *cm*.

Choice B is incorrect. This may result if CE = 4.6 *cm*.

Choice D is incorrect. This may result if CE = 2.3 *cm*.

 A triangle ABC has AB = 6 *cm*, BC = 10 *cm*, and is right angled at A. What is the length of AC?

A) 4

B) 6

C) 8

D) 10

Solution: This problem can easily be solved mathematically without drawing or sketching since all the data is given.

Since $\angle A = 90°$, the triangle ABC is a right triangle with sides AB and AC, and a hypotenuse BC.

Using the Pythagorean theorem to find the length AC yields $BC^2 = AB^2 + AC^2$. Substituting the given values into this formula yields $10^2 = 6^2 + AC^2$ or $100 = 36 + AC^2$.

Subtracting 36 from both sides yields $AC^2 = 64$.

Taking the square root of both sides results in AC = 8*cm*. Therefore, the correct answer is **Choice C**.

Choice A is incorrect. This is the difference between the length of BC and AB.

Choice B is incorrect. This is the length of AB.

Choice D is incorrect. This is the length of BC.

2. Redrawing

Sometimes, you will see a short note under a question saying, "Note: Figure not drawn to scale." Well, have you asked yourself why the test makers would draw a figure not to scale? The first thing that comes to mind is that maybe if the figure was instead drawn to scale, the question would be straightforward and you could easily find the answer. This is another strategy that you are encouraged to practice. Whenever a figure is not drawn to scale, try to **redraw it to scale**! Sometimes, you won't have enough information or tools to do that, but if you can do it, then go ahead and do it. Let's go through the example below.

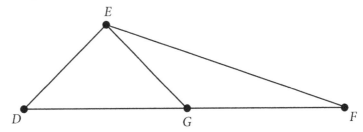

Note: Figure not drawn to scale

 The figure shows a triangle *DEF*, right-angled at *E*, with *G* being the midpoint of $\overline{DF}$. If *EG* = 4 cm, which of the following is the length of $\overline{GF}$ in *cm*?

A) 2

B) 3

C) 4

D) 5

Solution: Before rushing to choose D because in the figure $\overline{GF}$ looks longer than $\overline{EG}$, you need to pay attention to the statement saying that the **figure is not drawn to scale**.

This means that the lengths and angles shown in the figure might not be exact.

G looks like a midpoint but angle *E* does not look like a right angle.

Redraw the figure to scale.

It's given that triangle *DEF* is right-angled at *E*, so draw a right-angle triangle.

You can use the corners of the scrap sheet of paper that you have access to during the test to help you draw an almost perfect right angle.

Below is the redrawn sketch.

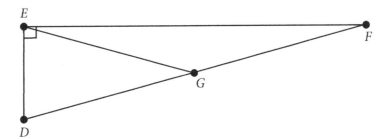

Now, if you didn't know how to solve this question mathematically, you could rely on the visual look of your sketch since it is drawn to scale.

It looks like GF = EG, and you can use your finger or the pen you're using to compare the lengths of the two segments.

Indeed, GF = EG = 4 cm, and the correct answer is **Choice C**.

The mathematical proof for this answer lies in this property: **The median drawn from the vertex of the right angle in a right triangle to the hypotenuse bisects it.**

The other choices are incorrect because they violate this property.

The two strategies '**drawing**' and '**redrawing**' are very important skills to master. They can lead you to the correct answer quickly if you get comfortable with them. It was mentioned that when figures are not drawn to scale, it's generally a good idea to redraw them to scale. On the other hand, if figures are drawn to scale (without a note under them), then you can trust the lengths and angle measures shown in the figure. That's it for the strategies in this chapter. Let's proceed with the subtopics of the domain 'Geometry and Trigonometry'.

Area and Volume

The formulas that you need for solving area and volume questions are available to you throughout the math section of the test. You just need to click on the reference button to display the reference sheet. The formulas will be restated here in each section for your convenience, but you don't need to memorize any of them.

Areas

The formulas of areas that are available in the reference sheet are the following:

- Area of a **circle** = πr^2 where **r is the radius of the circle**

- Area of a **rectangle** = lw where **l is the length** and **w is the width**. Note that a **square** is a **special rectangle** whose **sides have the same length** and the area is $s \times s$, or s^2.

- Area of a **triangle** $= \frac{1}{2}bh$ 1/2 bh where **b is the length of the base** and **h is the length of the corresponding height**

You might need to use multiple area formulae in one question to find areas of composite figures. Consider the student-produced response example below.

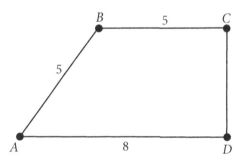

> ⑦   What is the area of the shown quadrilateral ABCD in square units?

Solution: The **given quadrilateral** is a **trapezoid,** and the area formula for such a quadrilateral is not provided in the reference sheet.

The key to solving similar questions is to **break down** the **given geometric figure into basic shapes.**

Draw the perpendicular issued from B to segment $\overline{AD}$.

This is another strategy that can be of great help in geometry problems. Feel free to add extra lines and name extra points to make your job easier.

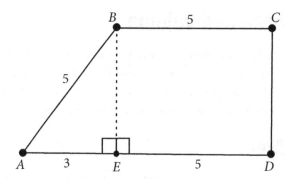

Now, the given trapezoid is simplified into a rectangle *EBCD* and a right triangle *ABE*.

The **right triangle *ABE* is the famous 3-4-5 triangle**, so *BE* = 4 (You can also use the Pythagorean theorem to find *BE*. This will be presented later in this chapter).

The **area of the triangle *ABE* is** $\frac{1}{2}bh = \frac{1}{2} \times AE \times BE = \frac{1}{2} \times 3 \times 4 = 6$ **square units.**

The **area of the rectangle *EBCD*** is $lw = 5 \times 4 = 20$ **square units.**

Therefore, the **area of the trapezoid *ABCD*** is 6 + 20 = **26 square units.**

The correct answer you should enter is **26**.

Let's go through some more examples:

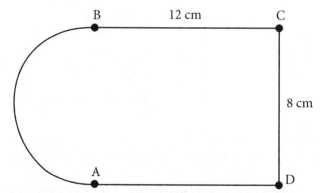

(?) The figure above is made up of a rectangle and a semicircle. The rectangle has a length of 12 cm and a width of 8 cm. If the diameter of the semicircle is equal to the width of the rectangle, what is the total area of the figure?

A) 103.24

B) 121.13

C) 139.81

D) 159.27

Solution: The key to finding areas of a composite figure is to break down the geometric figures into basic shapes.

For this question, break down the figure into a semicircle and a rectangle *ABCD*, then solve for the area. See the below figure.

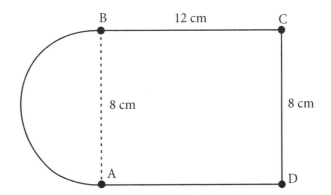

Find the area of the rectangle with the formula *length × width*. Substituting 12 cm for the length and 8 *cm* for the width yields 12 *cm* × 8 *cm* = 96 *cm²*.

The area of a semicircle is half the area of a full circle, thus the formula is $\frac{1}{2}\pi r^2$.

It is given that the diameter of the semicircle is the same as the width of the rectangle, which is 8 cm, then the radius is $r = \frac{8cm}{2} = 4cm$.

Substituting the radius into the formula of the area of a semicircle yields

$\frac{1}{2}\pi(4cm)^2 = 8\pi \ cm^2 \approx 25.13 \ cm^2$.

Adding the areas together yields 96 *cm²* + 25.13 *cm²* = 121.13 *cm²*. Therefore, the correct answer is **Choice B.**

Choice A is incorrect. This may result if the given width is 7 *cm*.

Choice C is incorrect. This may result if the given width is 9 *cm*.

Choice D is incorrect. This may result if the given width is 10 *cm*.

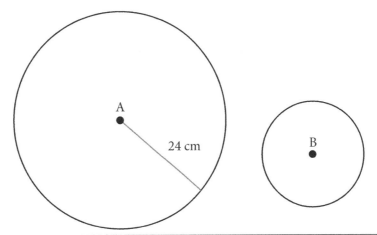

(?) Circle A has a radius of 24 cm. If the diameter of Circle B is equal to the radius of Circle A, what is the area of Circle B?

A) 24π

B) 72π

C) 144π

D) 576π

Solution: To solve for the area of Circle B, first find the radius of Circle B.

It is given that the diameter of Circle B is equal to the radius of Circle A, which is 24 cm, then the radius of Circle B is $\frac{24cm}{2} = 12cm$.

The formula for the area of a circle is πr^2. Substituting 12 cm for r into the formula yields $\pi(12cm)^2 = 144\pi \ cm^2$. Therefore, the correct answer is **Choice C.**

Choice A is incorrect. This is the circumference of Circle B.

Choice B is incorrect. This may result if the question asks for the area of a semicircle.

Choice D is incorrect. This is the area of Circle A.

Volumes

The formulas of volumes that are available in the reference sheet are the following:

- The volume of a **rectangular prism** = *lwh*, where *l* **is the length, *w* is the width, and *h* is the height**

- The volume of a **right circular cylinder** = $\pi r^2 h$, where *r* **is the radius of the circular base** and *h* **is the height**

- The volume of a **sphere** $= \frac{4}{3}\pi r^3$, where *r* **is the radius of the sphere**

- The volume of a **right circular cone** $= \frac{1}{3}\pi r^2 h$, where *r* **is the radius of the circular base** and *h* **is the height**

- The volume of a **rectangular pyramid** $= \frac{1}{3} lwh$, where *l* **and *w* are the length and width of the rectangular base respectively**, and *h* **is the height**

Again, a combination of these formulae might be required to answer a certain question. Let's go through the examples below.

 The radius of the circular base of a right circular cone is the same as the radius of a sphere having the same volume as the cone. If the height of the cone is 16 cm, what is the radius of the sphere?

A) 4 *cm*

B) 8 *cm*

C) 12 *cm*

D) 16 *cm*

Solution: Equating the volume formulas of a sphere and a right circular cone with the same r yields the equation $\frac{4}{3}\pi r^3 = \frac{1}{3}\pi r^2 h$.

Dividing both sides of this equation by πr^2 yields $\frac{4}{3}\pi r^3 = \frac{1}{3}h$.

Multiplying both sides of this equation by 3 results in $4r = h$.

Dividing both sides of this equation by 4 yields $r = \dfrac{h}{4}$.

Substituting 16 cm for h results in $r = \dfrac{16}{4}$, which is equal to 4 *cm*.

Therefore, the correct answer is **Choice A**.

Choice B is incorrect. This is the diameter of the circular base of the cone.

Choice C is incorrect. This is triple the radius of the sphere.

Choice D is incorrect. This is the height of the cone.

 A box in the shape of a rectangular prism has a length of 14 inches, a height of 6 inches, and a width that is half of the height. What is the volume of the box?

A) 252 *in*³

B) 504 *in3*

C) 588 *in*³

D) 1,008 *in*³

Solution: To solve for the volume of the box, use the formula for the volume of a rectangular prism: *volume = length × width × height*.

It is given that the width is half of the height, then the width is (6 in)/2=3 in.

Substituting the given values into the formula for the volume of a rectangular prism yields 14 in×3 in×6 in=252 in^3. Therefore, the correct answer is **Choice A.**

Choice B is incorrect and may result if the width is equal to the height.

Choice C is incorrect and may result if the width is half of the length.

Choice D is incorrect and may result if the width is double the length.

 A cylinder with a 10 cm diameter is drilled into a 20 cm cube. What is the remaining volume of the cube? (Round to the nearest unit)

Solution: To solve for the remaining volume of the cube, calculate the volume of the cube and cylinder and subtract the volume of the cylinder from the volume of the cube.

The volume of the cube is given by the formula a^3, where a is the side of the cube. Substituting the given information into the formula yields $(20\ cm)^3 = 8{,}000\ cm^3$.

The volume of the cylinder is given by the formula $\pi r^2 h$, where r is the radius of the cylinder, which is $\dfrac{10cm}{2} = 5cm$, and h is the height of the cylinder, which is the same as the height of the cube, 20 *cm*. Substituting the given information into the formula yields $\pi(5\ cm)^2\ (20\ cm) = 500\pi\ cm^3$.

The volume remaining in the cube after drilling of the cylinder is $V_{cube} - V_{cylinder} = 8{,}000 - 500\pi \approx 6{,}429\ cm^3$. Therefore, the remaining volume of the cube is approximately 6,429 *cm*³.

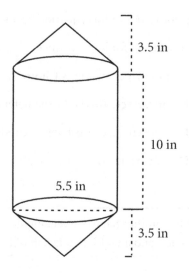

? What is the volume of the figure shown above?

A) 55 in^3

B) 238 in^3

C) 265 in^3

D) 293 in^3

Solution: The figure consists of two right circular cones and a right circular cylinder.

To find the total volume of the figure, add the volume of the cylinder and the cones, $V_{figure} = V_{cylinder} + 2V_{cone}$.

The volume of a right circular cylinder is given by the formula $V_{cylinder} = \pi r^2 h$, where r is the radius of the cylinder, which is $\dfrac{5.5\ in}{2} = 2.75\ in$, and h is the height of the cylinder, which is 10 in. Substituting the given information into the formula yields $V_{cylinder} = \pi(2.75\ in)^2 (10\ in) = 75.625\pi\ in^3$.

The volume of a right circular cone is given by the formula $V_{cone} = \dfrac{1}{3}\pi r^2 h$, where r is the radius of the cylinder, which is $\dfrac{5.5\ in}{2} = 2.75\ in$, and h is the height of the cone, which is 3.5 in. Substituting the given information into the formula yields $V_{cone} = \dfrac{1}{3}\pi(2.75\ in)^2 (3.5\ in) \approx 8.823\pi\ in^3$.

Substituting the volume of the cylinder and the cone into the volume of the figure yields $V_{figure} = 75.625\pi\ in^3 + 2(8.823\pi\ in^3) \approx 293\ in^3$. Therefore, the correct answer is **Choice D.**

Choice A is incorrect. This is the volume of one right circular cone.

Choice B is incorrect. This is the volume of the right circular cylinder.

Choice C is incorrect. This is the volume of the right circular cylinder and one right circular cone.

1   🔖 **Mark for Review**

Ricky has 10 cubes of similar size. He assembled it to make a structure as shown above. If the side length of the cube is 3 cm, what is the total surface area of the structure in cm^2?

2   🔖 **Mark for Review**

A square has a side of 4 and a circle has a diameter of 8. What is the ratio of the area of the circle to that of the square?

A) $\dfrac{1}{\pi}$

B) π

C) 16π

D) 64

3   🔖 **Mark for Review**

Circle A has a radius of 8 centimeters. The circumference of circle B is half the circumference of circle A. What is the area of circle B in square centimeters?

A) 8π

B) 16π

C) 64π

D) 80π

4   🔖 **Mark for Review**

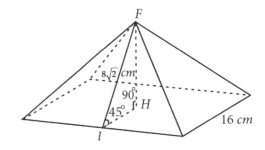

The pyramid has a square base with side length of 16 cm and a height $\overline{FH}$. The length of segment $\overline{FI}$ is $8\sqrt{2}\ cm$, and the measure of $\angle FIH$ is 45°. What is the volume of this pyramid in cubic centimeters? (Round your answer to the nearest unit)

A) 341

B) 512

C) 683

D) 853

5 ☐ **Mark for Review**

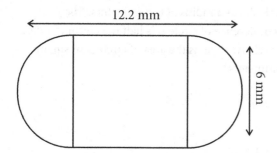

A capsule used by a pharmaceutical company is shown with its dimensions. This capsule is formed of a cylinder and two hemispheres. What is the volume of the capsule in cubic millimeters (mm^3)?

A) 55.8π

B) 73.8π

C) 91.8π

D) 295.2π

Answers & Explanations

1. **Level:** Easy | **Skill/Knowledge:** Area and Volume | **Testing Point:** Solving the surface area

   Key Explanation: The correct answer is 360 cm^2. The area of a single face of a cube is 33 = 9 cm^2.

   There are 40 cube faces on the whole surface.

   Therefore, the total surface area of the whole structure is 409 = 360 cm^2.

2. **Level:** Medium | **Skill/Knowledge:** Area and Volume | **Testing Point:** Compare the areas of two figures

   Key Explanation: Choice B is correct. The formula for the area of the square is $side^2$. It's given that $side = 4$ which yields $4^2 = 16$. The formula for the area of the circle is πr^2, where r is the radius, with a formula of $r = \dfrac{diameter}{2}$. It's given that $diameter = 8$ which yields $\pi\left(\dfrac{diameter}{2}\right)^2 = \pi\left(\dfrac{8}{2}\right)^2 = \pi(4)^2 = 16\pi$. The ratio of the area of the circle to that of the square is $\dfrac{16\pi}{16} = \pi$.

   Distractor Explanations: Choice A is incorrect. This is the ratio of the area of the square to that of the circle. **Choice C** is incorrect and is the area of the circle. **Choice D** is incorrect and may result from using the value of the diameter in calculating the area of the square.

3. **Level:** Medium | **Skill/Knowledge:** Area and Volume | **Testing Point:** Find the area of a circle

   Key Explanation: Choice B is correct. It's given that the circumference of circle B is half the circumference of circle A, then the radius of circle B is half the radius of circle A. Since the radius of circle A is 8 centimeters, then the radius of circle B is 4 centimeters. The area of a circle is given by πr^2, where r is the radius of the circle. Therefore, the area of circle B is equal to $\pi(4)^2$, or 16π.

   Distractor Explanations: Choice A is incorrect. This is the circumference of circle B. **Choice C** is incorrect. This is the area of circle A. **Choice D** is incorrect. This is the area of circle A and B when added.

4. **Level:** Medium | **Skill/Knowledge:** Area and Volume | **Testing Point:** Find the volume of a pyramid

   Key Explanation: Choice C is correct. The volume of a pyramid is given by $V = \dfrac{1}{3}lwh$, where l is the length of the base, w is the width of the base, and h is the height of the pyramid. It's given that the pyramid has a square base with side length of 16 cm, then $l = w = 16$, and $V = \dfrac{1}{3} \times 16 \times 16 \times h$ or $V = \dfrac{256}{3}h$. It's given that the height is $\overline{FH}$, then h is equal to the length FH. The right triangle FHI has $\angle FIH$ with a measure of 45°, then ΔFHI is a 90°-45°-45° triangle. From the reference section, if the side length of a 90°-45°-45° triangle is s, then its hypotenuse measures $s\sqrt{2}$. It's given that the length of hypotenuse $\overline{FI}$ is $8\sqrt{2}$ cm, then each of the sides $\overline{FH}$ and $\overline{HI}$ measures 8 cm. It follows that the height of the pyramid h is equal to 8 cm.

   Substituting 8 for h in the equation $V = \dfrac{256}{3}h$ yields $V = \dfrac{256}{3} \times 8$, or $V = \dfrac{2048}{3} \times 682.\overline{6}$. This is rounded to 683 to the nearest unit. Therefore, the volume of the pyramid is approximately 683 cubic centimeters.

   Distractor Explanations: Choice A is incorrect and may result if the length of segment $\overline{FI}$ is $4\sqrt{2}$ cm. **Choice B** is incorrect and may result if the length of segment $\overline{FI}$ is $6\sqrt{2}$ cm. **Choice D** is incorrect and may result if the length of segment $\overline{FI}$ is $10\sqrt{2}$ cm.

5. **Level:** Hard | **Skill/Knowledge:** Area and Volume | **Testing Point:** Find the volume of a solid formed of other solids

Key Explanation: Choice C is correct. The volume of a cylinder is given by $V_{cylinder} = \pi r^2 l$, where r is the radius of the circular cap of the cylinder, and l is the length of the cylinder. The volume of a sphere is given by $V_{sphere} = \frac{4}{3}\pi r^3$, where r is the radius of the sphere. It's given that the capsule is formed of a cylinder and two identical hemispheres. The two identical hemispheres sum up to a single sphere of the same radius. From the figure, the diameter of the circular cap of the cylinder or the sphere is 6 *mm*. It follows that the radius of the circular cap or the sphere is 3 *mm*. It's also shown on the figure that the length of the capsule is equal to 12.2 *mm*. The length of the capsule is the sum of the length of the cylinder and two radii of the hemispheres. Then the length of the cylinder is equal to 12.2 – 3 – 3, or 6.2 *mm*. Thus, the volume of the capsule can be found as $V_{capsule} = V_{cylinder} + V_{sphere} = \pi r^2 l + \frac{4}{3}\pi r^3$. Substituting 3 for r and 6.2 for l yields $V_{capsule} = \pi(3^2)(6.2) + \frac{4}{3}\pi(3^3) = 91.8\pi$. Therefore, the volume of the capsule is equal to 91.8 cubic millimeters.

Distractor Explanations: Choice A is incorrect. This is the volume of the capsule without the 2 hemispheres. **Choice B** is incorrect. This is the volume of the capsule without 1 hemisphere. **Choice D** is incorrect and may result if the radius of the capsule is 6 *mm* instead of 3 *mm*.

Lines, Angles, and Triangles

In this part, **three subtopics** will be discussed. The **first one** is about the **common case of two lines cut by a transversal.** The second subtopic will tackle the **similarity of triangles and other figures,** and the **third** one will be about the **cases of congruency of triangles.**

Parallel Lines Cut by a Transversal

When **two parallel lines** are **cut by a transversal, eight angles are formed.** You are expected to know the relationships between these angles. Look at the figure below.

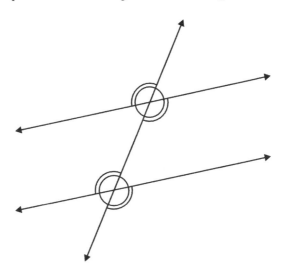

The 4 angles marked with one arc are congruent. The 4 angles marked by two arcs are also congruent. If you add an angle with one arc to an angle with two arcs, the sum is 180°. Check the examples below.

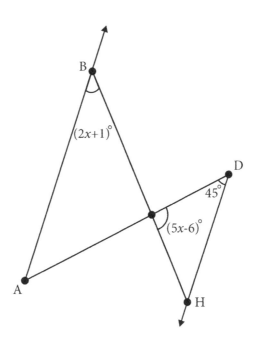

(?) In the figure, the rays $\overrightarrow{AB}$ and $\overrightarrow{DH}$ are parallel. What is the value of x?

Solution: It's given that the rays $\overrightarrow{AB}$ and $\overrightarrow{DH}$ are parallel.

Then $m\angle ABI = m\angle IHD$ because they are alternate-interior angles (Z angles). Consequently, $m\angle IHD = (2x + 1)°$.

In $\triangle IDH$, the sum of the interior angles is 180°. Thus, $(5x - 6) + (2x + 1) + 45 = 180$. Combining like terms on the left-hand side yields $7x + 40 = 180$.

Subtracting 40 from both sides of this equation yields $7x = 140$.

Dividing both sides of this equation by 7 results in $x = 20$.

The correct answer that you should enter is **20**.

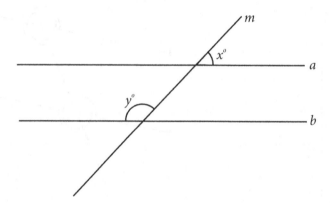

(?) In the figure, lines a and b are parallel. If $x = 3n - 10$ and $y = 7n + \dfrac{80n}{30}$, what is the difference between angles y and x?

A) 35°

B) 110°

C) 145°

D) 180°

Solution: To solve for the difference of y and x, first find the value of n.

It is given that the lines a and b are parallel, then the angles $x°$ and $y°$ are supplementary.

Thus, $x + y = 180°$. Substituting the values of x and y into this equation yields

$(3n - 10) + \left(7n + \dfrac{80n}{30}\right) = 180$. Combining like terms on the left-hand side results in

$10n + \dfrac{80n}{30} - 10 = 180$. Adding $10 - 10n$ to both sides yields $\dfrac{80n}{30} = 190 - 10n$.

Multiplying 30 to both sides results in $80n = 5{,}700 - 300n$. Adding $300n$ to both sides yields $380n = 5{,}700$. Dividing both sides by 380 yields $n = 15$.

Substituting the value of *n* into the values of *x* and *y* yields *x* = 3(15) – 10 = 35° and

$$y = 7(15) + \frac{80(15)}{30} = 145°.$$

The difference of *y* and *x* will therefore be 145 – 35 = 110°. Therefore, the correct answer is **Choice B.**

Choice A is incorrect. This is the value of x.

Choice C is incorrect. This is the value of *y*.

Choice D is incorrect. This is the sum of *x* and *y*.

Similar Triangles and Figures

Similar figures including similar triangles have congruent corresponding angles and proportional corresponding sides. Corresponding sides are the sides opposite to congruent angles. Questions about similarity are common on the Digital SAT. Consider the examples below.

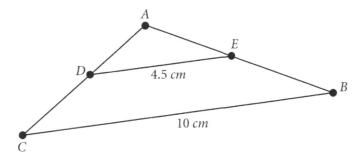

> (?) In the figure, $\overline{DE}$ is parallel to $\overline{CB}$. The lengths *EB*, *DE* and *CB* are 3.45 *cm*, 4.5 *cm* and 10 *cm* respectively. What is the length of $\overline{AE}$ in *cm*? [Round to the nearest tenth]

A) 1.8

B) 2.8

C) 3.5

D) 3.8

Solution: It's given that $\overline{DE}$ is parallel to $\overline{CB}$, then $m\angle AED = m\angle ABC$ because they are corresponding angles.

The 2 triangles *AED* and *ABC* also share a common angle at the vertex *A*. Then, $\triangle AED$ and $\triangle ABC$ are **similar triangles** having **two pairs of equal corresponding angles.**

It follows that their **corresponding sides are proportional.** $\overline{DE}$ corresponds to $\overline{CB}$, and $\overline{AE}$ corresponds to $\overline{AB}$.

Then the proportion can be written as $\dfrac{DE}{CB} = \dfrac{AE}{AB}$.

Using the segment addition postulate, AB = AE + EB.

Substituting the given values in the proportion yields $\dfrac{4.5}{10} = \dfrac{AE}{AE + 3.45}$.

Cross-multiplication results in 4.5AE+15.525=10AE.

Subtracting 4.5AE from both sides of the equation yields 15.525 = 5.5AE.

Dividing both sides of this equation by 5.5 yields $AE \approx 2.8$.

Therefore, the length of $\overline{AE}$ is approximately 2.8 cm, and the correct answer is **Choice B**.

Choice A is incorrect. This is approximately the length of $AB - DE$.

Choice C is incorrect. This is approximately the length of EB.

Choice D is incorrect. This is approximately the length of $CB - AB$.

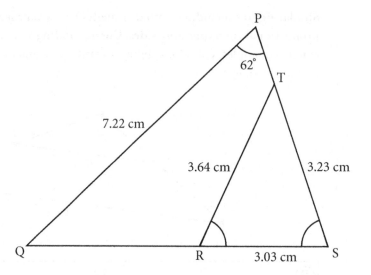

(?) In the figure, $TS = 3.23\ cm$, $RS = 3.03\ cm$, $RT = 3.64\ cm$, and $QP = 7.22\ cm$. If $m\angle QPS = m\angle SRT = 62°$, what is the length of $\overline{QS}$ in cm? (Round to the nearest hundredth)

A) 3.38

B) 3.58

C) 6.41

D) 9.90

Solution: It's given that $m\angle QPS = m\angle SRT = 62°$ and triangles PQS and TRS share a common angle at the vertex S. Then, these two triangles are similar and have two pairs of equal corresponding angles.

It follows that their corresponding sides are proportional, thus, $\overline{RT}$ corresponds to $\overline{QP}$, and $\overline{TS}$ corresponds to $\overline{QS}$.

The proportion can be written as $\dfrac{RT}{QP} = \dfrac{TS}{QS}$. Substituting the given values into the proportion

yields $\dfrac{3.64}{7.22} = \dfrac{3.23}{QS}$. Cross-multiplication yields $3.64QS = 23.3206$. Dividing both sides of the equation by 3.64 yields QS ≈ 6.41 cm. Therefore, the correct answer is **Choice C.**

Choice A is incorrect. This is the approximate length of *QR*.

Choice B is incorrect. This is the approximate length of *QP – RT*.

Choice D is incorrect. This is the perimeter of △*TRS*.

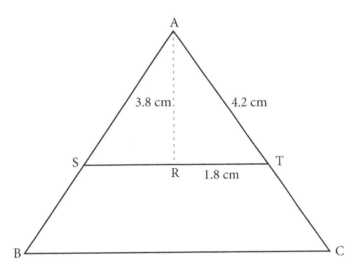

(?) Triangle *ABC* is similar to triangle *AST*. If the perimeter of triangle *ABC* is twice the length of the perimeter of triangle *AST*, what is the ratio of triangle ABC to the area of triangle *AST*?

A) 4:1

B) 3:1

C) 2:1

D) 1:1

Solution: It is given that the two triangles are similar and that the perimeter of the triangle *ABC* is twice that of the triangle *AST*. This means that each side's length and height of △*ABC* is twice as long as the corresponding side in △*AST* .

The formula for the area of a triangle is $\frac{1}{2} base \times height$.

The formula for the area of $\triangle AST = \frac{1}{2}(bh)$. Substituting the given information into this formula yields

$\triangle AST = \frac{1}{2}(1.8 \times 2)(3.8) = 6.84 cm^2$.

The formula for the area of $\triangle ABC = \frac{1}{2}(2b)(2h) = \frac{1}{2}4bh$. Substituting the given information into this formula yields $\triangle ABC = 2(1.8 \times 2)(3.8) = 27.35\ cm^2$. Therefore, the ratio of △*ABC* to the

area of △*AST* is 27.35:6.84 or 4:1, which is **Choice A.**

Choice B is incorrect. This may be due to a calculation error.

Choice C is incorrect. This is the ratio of the perimeters of the two triangles.

Choice D is incorrect. This may be due to a calculation error.

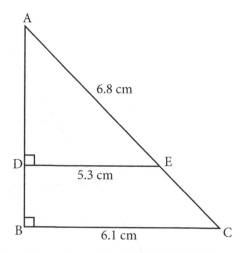

> (?) In the figure, what is the length of AC? (Round to the nearest hundredth)

Solution: From the figure, it is clear that triangles ABC and ADE share a common angle at the vertex A and a 90° angle. Consequently, the remaining angles are also equal. It follows that their corresponding sides are proportional, thus, $\overline{DE}$ corresponds to $\overline{BC}$, and $\overline{AE}$ corresponds to $\overline{AC}$.

The proportion can be written as $\dfrac{DE}{BC} = \dfrac{AE}{AC}$. Substituting the given values into the proportion yields $\dfrac{5.3}{6.1} = \dfrac{6.8}{AC}$. Cross-multiplication yields $5.3AC = 41.48$. Dividing both sides of the equation by 5.3 yields $AC \approx 7.83\,cm$. Therefore, the length of side AC is 7.83 cm.

There exists a **relationship** between the **perimeters, areas,** and **volumes of similar shapes**.

> The ratio of the perimeters of similar shapes is equal to the ratio of the corresponding sides.
>
> The ratio of the areas of similar shapes is equal to the square of the ratio of the corresponding sides.
>
> The ratio of the volumes of similar shapes is equal to the cube of the ratio of the corresponding sides.

Let's take a look at the example below.

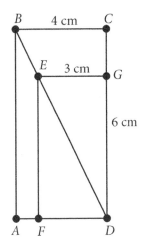

> (?) The figure shows 2 rectangles *ABCD* and *FEGD* where *D*, *E*, and *B* are collinear. What is the ratio of the area of rectangle *ABCD* to that of rectangle *FEGD*?

A) $\dfrac{4}{3}$

B) $\dfrac{3}{2}$

C) $\dfrac{16}{9}$

D) $\dfrac{9}{4}$

Solution: The **two rectangles** shown in the figure **are similar** figures because they have **congruent corresponding angles**, and thus would also have **proportional corresponding sides.**

The **ratio of the areas of the two similar rectangles** is **equal** to the **square of the ratios of their corresponding sides.** The side *BC* corresponds to the side *EG*.

Therefore, the **ratio** of the **area** of **rectangle *ABCD* to that of rectangle *FEGD*** is equal to $\left(\dfrac{4}{3}\right)^2$ or $\dfrac{16}{9}$.

The correct answer is **Choice C.**

Choice A is incorrect. This is the ratio of the perimeters or the corresponding sides of the two rectangles.

Choice B is incorrect. This is the ratio of *GD* to *BC*.

Choice D is incorrect. This is the square of the ratio of *GD* to *BC*.

Congruent Triangles

There are three cases of congruency for two triangles:

1. **SSS** (or 3 congruent corresponding sides)

2. **SAS** (or two congruent corresponding sides with a congruent included angle)

3. **AAS** (or two congruent corresponding angles and one congruent corresponding side)

Basically, congruent triangles are just similar triangles with congruent sides. It's enough to show that similar triangles have one pair of corresponding congruent sides for them to be congruent. If **two triangles are congruent, their corresponding sides and angles are also congruent**. This property is commonly referred to as **CPCTC (Corresponding Parts of Congruent Triangles are Congruent)**.

Look at the examples below.

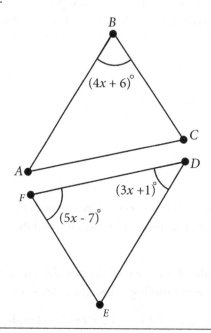

 In the figure, triangles BAC and EDF are congruent. Additionally, $m\angle BAC = m\angle EDF$ and $m\angle ACB = m\angle EFD$. What is the measure of $\angle DEF$ in degrees?

Solution: It's given that triangles BAC and EDF are congruent, as a result, corresponding angles are also congruent.

Since $m\angle BAC = m\angle EDF$ and $m\angle ACB = m\angle EFD$, then $m\angle ACB = m\angle DEF$.

Substituting $(4x + 6)°$ for $m\angle ABC$ yields $(4x + 6)° = m\angle DEF$. In ΔEDF, the sum of interior angles is $180°$. Thus, $(5x - 7) + (3x + 1) + (4x + 6) = 180$. Combining like terms on the left-hand side of this equation yields $12x = 180$.

Dividing both sides of this equation by 12 yields $x = 15$.

Substituting 15 for x in the equation $(4x + 6)° = m\angle DEF$ yields $66° = m\angle DEF$.

Therefore, the measure of $m\angle DEF$ is 66 degrees.

The correct answer that you should enter is **66**.

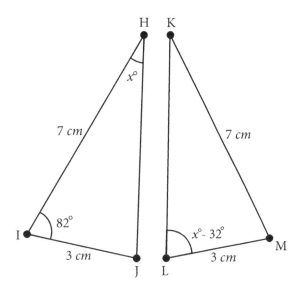

Figure not drawn to scale

(?) In the figure, triangles *HIJ* and *KLM* are congruent. What is the measure of $\angle MKL$?

A) 33°

B) 65°

C) 82°

D) 98°

Solution: It is given that triangles *HIJ* and *KLM* are congruent, hence corresponding angles are also congruent.

$m\angle HIJ = m\angle KML = 82°$

$m\angle HJI = m\angle KLM = x - 32°$

$m\angle IHJ = m\angle MKL = x°$

You need to find the value of $x°$.

In the triangle *HIJ*, the sum of the interior angles is 180°. Thus, $82 + (x - 32) + x = 180$.

Combining like terms yields $2x + 50 = 180$. Subtracting 50 from both sides yields $2x = 130$. Dividing both sides by 2 results in $x = 65$. Therefore, the correct answer is **Choice B.**

Choice A is incorrect. This is the measure of $\angle KLM$.

Choice C is incorrect. This is the measure of $\angle KML$.

Choice D is incorrect. This is the sum of the measure of $\angle KLM$ and $\angle MKL$.

1 ☐ **Mark for Review**

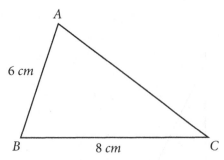

Note: Figure not drawn to scale.

Which could be the length of the side AC of the triangle?

A) 2 *cm*

B) 12 *cm*

C) 14 *cm*

D) 15 *cm*

2 ☐ **Mark for Review**

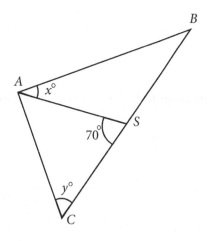

In the figure, $AS = SC = SB$. What is the sum of x and y?

A) 80

B) 90

C) 100

D) 110

3 ☐ **Mark for Review**

In the figure, what is the value of h?

A) $\dfrac{3}{8}$

B) 1.5

C) $\dfrac{8}{3}$

D) 4.86

4 ☐ **Mark for Review**

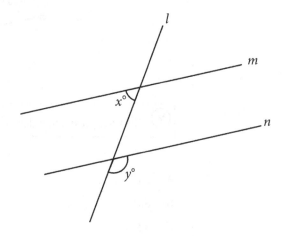

In the figure, lines m and n are parallel. If $x = 2(s - 10)$ $- 20$ and $y = \dfrac{11s - 2\left(-10 + \dfrac{3}{2}s\right)}{2}$, what is the value of s?

5 ☐ **Mark for Review**

The lengths of the sides of a triangle is 9 , 6 and $x +$ 2. If 9 is the longest side of the triangle, what are the possible integer values of x?

Answers & Explanations

1. **Level:** Medium | **Skill/Knowledge:** Lines, angles and triangles | **Testing Point:** Find the length of a side of a triangle

   Key Explanation: Choice B is correct. The length of a side of a triangle must be less than the sum of the lengths of the two other sides and greater than the absolute difference of the lengths of the two other sides. For the side AC, the sum of the lengths of the two other sides is $6 + 8$, or 14 and the absolute difference of the lengths of the two other sides is $8 - 6$, or 2. The only number choice which is less than 14 and greater than 2 is 12. Therefore, the length of AC could be 12.

   Distractor Explanations: Choice A is incorrect because 2 is equal to the absolute difference of 6 and 8. **Choice C** is incorrect because 14 is equal to the sum of 6 and 8. **Choice D** is incorrect because 15 is greater than the sum of 6 and 8.

2. **Level:** Easy | **Skill/Knowledge:** Lines, angles and triangles | **Testing Point:** Find the measure of an unknown angle in a triangle

   Key Explanation: Choice B is correct. It's given that $AS = SC = SB$. It follows that ΔASB and ΔASC are isosceles with a main vertex S. Thus, $m\angle SAB = m\angle SBA = x°$, and $m\angle SAC = m\angle SCA = y°$. See the figure below.

   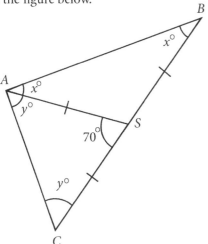

   The sum of interior angles in ΔABC is equal to 180°. Thus, $x + x + y + y = 180$. Combining like terms on the left side of this equation yields $2x + 2y = 180$. Taking 2 as a common factor results in $2(x + y) = 180$. Dividing both sides of this equation by 2 yields $x + y = 90$. Therefore, the sum of x and y is 90.

   Distractor Explanations: Choice A is incorrect and may result from conceptual or calculation errors. **Choice C** is incorrect and may result from conceptual or calculation errors. **Choice D** is incorrect. This is the measure of angle ASB.

3. **Level:** Medium | **Skill/Knowledge:** Lines, angles and triangles | **Testing Point:** Use proportional relationships in case of similar triangles to find an unknown quantity

   Key Explanation:

   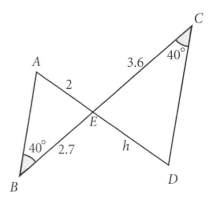

   Choice C is correct. The vertical angles $\angle AEB$ and $\angle CED$ are congruent. It's also given that $m\angle ABE = m\angle ECD = 40°$. It follows that ΔAEB and ΔCED are similar having 2 pairs of equal corresponding angles. Thus, the corresponding sides are proportional, and $\frac{2}{h} = \frac{2.7}{3.6}$. The fraction $\frac{2.7}{3.6}$ can be simplified into $\frac{3}{4}$ by dividing the numerator and denominator by 0.9. Therefore, $\frac{2}{h} = \frac{3}{4}$ and the value of h is equal to $\frac{2 \times 4}{3}$, or $\frac{8}{3}$.

   Distractor Explanations: Choice A is incorrect. This is the value of $\frac{1}{h}$. **Choice B** is incorrect and may result if $AE = h$ and $ED = 2$. **Choice D** is incorrect and may result if $CE = h$ and $ED = 3.6$.

4. **Level:** Hard | **Skill/Knowledge:** Lines, angles and triangles | **Testing Point:** Find the measure of a missing angle in case of two lines cut by a transversal

   Key Explanation: 35 is the correct answer. Since the lines m and n are parallel, then the angles $x°$ and $y°$ are supplementary. See the figure below for the visual reasoning of this conclusion. Thus, $x° + y° = 180°$. Substituting the given values for $x°$ and $y°$ into $x° + y° = 180°$ yields $2(s - 10) - 20 +$

   $$\dfrac{11s - 2\left(-10 + \dfrac{3}{2}s\right)}{2} = 180.$$ Distribution on the left

   hand side results in $2s - 20 - 20 + \dfrac{11s + 20 - 3s}{2}$

   $= 180$. Combining constants and like terms yields

   $2s - 40 + \dfrac{8s + 20}{2} = 180$. Dividing $8s + 20$ by 2 on

   the left hand side of the equation results in $2s - 40 + 4s + 10 = 180$. Combining like terms on the left hand side of this equation yields $6s - 30 = 180$. Adding 30 to both sides of this equation yields $6s = 210$. Dividing both sides of the equation by 6 results in $s = 35$. Therefore, the value of s is 35.

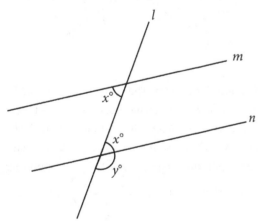

5. **Level:** Hard | **Skill/Knowledge:** Lines, angles and triangles | **Testing Point:** Triangle inequality theorem

   Key Explanation: The correct answer is **2, 3, 4, 5 and 6**. The third side of the triangle is given by a value greater than the difference and less than the sum of the other two sides.

This can be represented by the inequality $9 - 6 < x + 2 < 9 + 6$.

Simplifying the inequality yields $3 < x + 2 < 15$.

Subtracting 2 from the inequality yields $1 < x < 13$.

Hence, the minimum integer value of x is 2.

Since 9 is the longest side, then the maximum value of x can be obtained from $x + 2 < 9$ which is equivalent to $x < 7$.

Hence, the maximum integer value of x is 6.

Therefore, the possible values of x would be 2, 3, 4, 5 and 6.

Right Triangles and Trigonometry

The bulk of this part deals with trigonometry in right triangles. There will also be a section about angle unit conversion, and a brief part about the unit circle. If you pay close attention to the details and get comfortable with using the relevant rules, you will be able to master this topic.

Pythagorean Theorem

This is the well-renowned theorem according to which the **square of the length of the hypotenuse** of a **right triangle** is **equal to the sum of the squares of the lengths of the two legs of the right angle.** It is commonly written as $a^2 + b^2 = c^2$, where a and b are the respective lengths of the legs, and c is the length of the hypotenuse.

> When dealing with such questions, you will often come across the **Pythagorean triples.** The **most famous** among them are the **3-4-5 triangle** and the **5-12-13 triangle**. They provide a **quick way** to **find the lengths of the sides** of **some right triangles.** For example, for any **constant k**, if **one leg** of the right angle measures **$3k$** and the **other leg** measures **$4k$**, the **hypotenuse** would measure **$5k$**. As a result, the 3-4-5 triangle gives you the measures of many right triangles starting with 3-4-5, 6-8-10, 9-12-15, …

Consider the examples below.

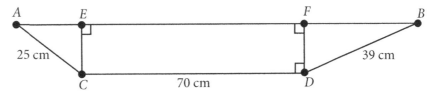

> ⑦ In the figure, what is the measure of $\overline{AB}$?

A) 36 *cm*

B) 90 *cm*

C) 106 *cm*

D) 126 *cm*

Solution: In the figure, **quadrilateral *CEFD* is a rectangle** because it has three right angles. Since the **opposite sides** of a **rectangle are congruent,** then DF = CE = 15 cm, and EF = CD = 70 cm.

The two triangles AEC and DFB are right triangles. Consequently, you can use the Pythagorean theorem to find the missing measures of AE and FB.

In triangle AEC, $AC^2 = AE^2 + EC^2$, then $AE^2 = AC^2 - EC^2$.

Substituting 25 for AC and 15 for EC yields $AE^2 = 25^2 - 15^2 = 400$.

Then, AE is the positive square root of 400 which is equal to 20.

Similarly, in triangle DFB, $FB^2 = DB^2 - DF^2$. Substituting 39 for DB and 15 for DF yields $FB^2 = 39^2 - 15^2 = 1296$.

Then, FB is the positive square root of 1,296 which is equal to 36.

Using the segment addition postulate, AB = AE + EF + FB. Substituting the values in this equation yields AB = 20 + 70 + 36 = 126 cm.

Therefore, the correct answer is **Choice D**.

Choice A is incorrect. This is the length of FB.

Choice B is incorrect. This is the length of AF.

Choice C is incorrect. This is the length of EB.

You could have saved some time had you noticed that the 15-20-25 triangle is a 3-4-5 triangle in disguise (with $k = 3$), and that the 15-36-39 triangle is a 5-12-13 triangle (also with $k = 3$).

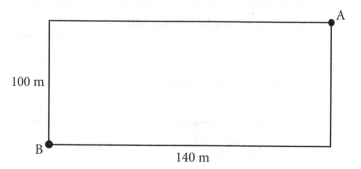

⑦ The figure above shows a rectangular-shaped soccer field 100 meters wide and 140 meters long. If the players run diagonally from point A to point B across the field, how far do they run?

A) 149 *m*

B) 156 *m*

C) 164 *m*

D) 172 *m*

Solution: It is given that the field is rectangular shaped, and if the players run diagonally, it creates two right triangles. See the figure below.

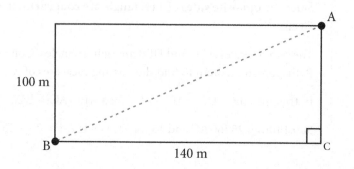

Use the Pythagorean theorem to find the measure of AB: $AB^2 = AC^2 + BC^2$.

Substituting AC=100 and BC=140 into this formula yields $AB^2 = 100^2 + 140^2 = 29,600$.

Taking the square root of both sides yields $AB = 20\sqrt{74} \approx 172\,m$. Therefore, the correct answer is **Choice D**.

Choice A is incorrect and may result if the field is 110 meters long.

Choice B is incorrect and may result if the field is 120 meters long.

Choice C is incorrect and may result if the field is 130 meters long.

The SOH-CAH-TOA Rule

The mnemonic SOH-CAH-TOA helps you to remember the formulas for finding the trigonometric functions of acute angles in a right triangle.

For any acute angle α, $sin\ \alpha = \dfrac{opposite}{hypotenuse}$, $cos\ \alpha = \dfrac{adjacent}{hypotenuse}$ and $tan\ \alpha = \dfrac{opposite}{adjacent}$

The **hypotenuse** is the **longest side of a right triangle.** It is the side facing the 90° angle. The side opposite to the angle is the side facing the angle. The side adjacent to the angle is the side next to the angle but not the hypotenuse. Check out the examples below.

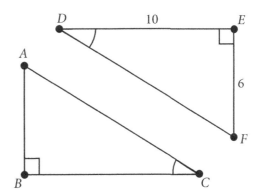

(?) The two right triangles *ABC* and *FED* are similar. Angle *C* corresponds to angle *D*. What is the value of *tan A*?

A) $\dfrac{3}{\sqrt{34}}$

B) $\dfrac{3}{5}$

C) $\dfrac{5}{\sqrt{34}}$

D) $\dfrac{5}{3}$

Solution: It's given that the two right triangles ABC and FED are similar, then the corresponding angles are congruent.

Since angle C corresponds to angle D, angle A corresponds to angle F. As a result, the two angles are congruent and $m\angle A = m\angle F$. Thus, $\tan A = \tan F = \dfrac{DE}{EF}$.

Therefore, $\tan A = \dfrac{10}{6} = \dfrac{5}{3}$ and the correct answer is **Choice D**.

Choice A is incorrect. This is the value of *cos* A.

Choice B is incorrect. This is the value of *tan* C.

Choice C is incorrect. This is the value of *sin* A.

 In a triangle, the angle A is a right angle. The length of the hypotenuse is 17, and the side adjacent to the angle B is 15. What is the value of *cos* (C)?

Solution: To solve, first draw a sketch of the triangle based on the given information. Look at the figure below.

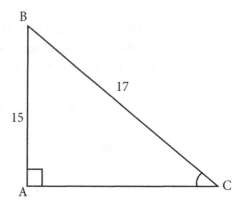

The formula to find *cos* (C) is $\cos (C) = \dfrac{adjacent}{hypotenuse} = \dfrac{AC}{BC}$.

Using the Pythagorean theorem to find AC yields $AC^2 = BC^2 - AB^2 = 17^2 - 15^2 = 64$.

Taking the square root of both sides yields $AC = 8$.

Substituting this information into the formula to find cos (C) yields $\cos (C) = \dfrac{8}{17}$. Therefore, the correct answer is $\dfrac{8}{17}$.

Note that the **tangent of an angle** can be **any value**. However, the **sine or cosine of an angle** is **always between –1 and 1**. You should also keep in mind that $\tan \alpha = \dfrac{\sin \alpha}{\cos \alpha}$ and that $\sin^2 \alpha + \cos^2 \alpha = 1$. It is advisable to know the exact values of the trigonometric functions of some remarkable angles, shown in the table below.

α	0°	30°	45°	60°	90°	180°
sin α	0	$\dfrac{1}{2}$	$\dfrac{\sqrt{2}}{2}$	$\dfrac{\sqrt{3}}{2}$	1	0
cos α	1	$\dfrac{\sqrt{3}}{2}$	$\dfrac{\sqrt{2}}{2}$	$\dfrac{1}{2}$	0	−1
tan α	0	$\dfrac{\sqrt{3}}{3}$	1	$\sqrt{3}$	undefined	0

Special Right Triangles

Whenever special right triangles are mentioned, you need to think of the relationships between the lengths of their sides.

The relationships between the lengths of the sides of the 90-45-45 triangle and the 90-60-30 triangle can be found in the reference sheet.

They are also shown in the figure below for your convenience.

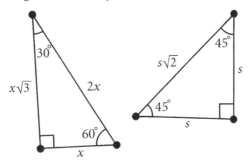

Consider the examples below:

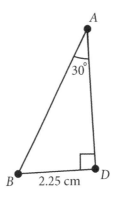

(?) In the given triangle, what is the length of $\overline{AD}$ to the nearest tenth of a *cm*?

Solution: Since triangle *ABD* is a right-angled triangle having a 30° angle, it's a 90-60-30 triangle.

Since tan 30° = opposite/adjacent = *BD/AD*, the length of $AD = BD\sqrt{3}$.

Then, $AD = 2.25 \times \sqrt{3} = 3.897$. To the nearest tenth, *AD* is approximately equal to 3.9 *cm*. The correct answer that you should enter is **3.9**.

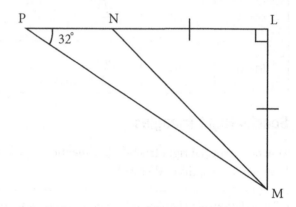

(?)   Based on the figure above, what is the measure of ∠*NMP*?

A) 13°

B) 32°

C) 45°

D) 135°

Solution: The given Δ*LMN* with two equal sides is a 90-45-45 triangle. Thus, ∠*LNM* = ∠*LMN* =45°.

The ∠*LMN* is an exterior angle to Δ*MNP*. Thus, ∠*LNM* is equal to the sum of its two remote interior angles, ∠*NPM* and ∠*NMP*, which yields the formula ∠*LNM* = ∠*NPM* + ∠*NMP*.

Substituting this information into the formula yields 45° = 32° + ∠*NMP*, or ∠*NMP* = 13°.

Therefore, the correct answer is **Choice A.**

Choice B is incorrect. This is the *m*∠*NPM*.

Choice C is incorrect. This is the *m*∠*LNM* and *m*∠*LMN*.

Choice D is incorrect. This is the *m*∠*MNP*.

    Triangle *DEF* is right at *E*. One leg has a length of $5\sqrt{3}$ and the hypotenuse is 10. What is the measure of the angle between the hypotenuse and the other leg?

A) 30°

B) 60°

C) 90°

D) 120°

Solution: Sketching the figure from the given information, it is clear that this is a 90-60-30 triangle.

This means that the length of the other leg is 5 and the angle between the hypotenuse and the other leg is 60°.

Solving it mathematically using the formula $sin(F) = \dfrac{opposite}{hypotenuse}$ yields $sin(F) = \dfrac{5\sqrt{3}}{10} = \dfrac{\sqrt{3}}{2}$, or $F = 60°$.

Therefore, the correct answer is **Choice B.**

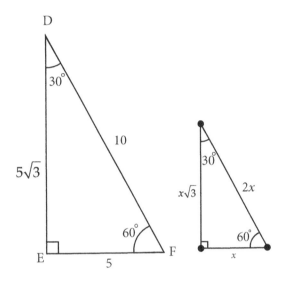

Choice A is incorrect. This is the angle between the hypotenuse and the leg with the length of $5\sqrt{3}$.

Choice C is incorrect. This is the measure of the angle E.

Choice D is incorrect. This may result from a calculation error.

Cofunction Identities

The **sine of an angle** is the **cosine of its complement,** and the **cosine of an angle** is the **sine of its complement.**

Two angles are called **complementary** if the **sum of their measures is 90°**. Look at the examples below.

(?)   For two acute angles α and β, $sin\ α = cos\ β$. If $α = (2x + 9)°$ and $β = (3x + 1)°$, what is the value of x?

A) 8

B) 16

C) 18

D) 34

Solution: It's given that $\sin \alpha = \cos \beta$, then $\alpha + \beta = 90°$.

Substituting the expressions for α and β yields $2x + 9 + 3x + 1 = 90$.

Combining like terms on the left-hand side results in $5x + 10 = 90$.

Subtracting 10 from both sides of the equation yields $5x = 80$.

Dividing both sides of the equation by 5 results in $x = 16$.

Therefore, the correct answer is **Choice B.**

Choice A is incorrect and may result from incorrectly setting $\alpha = \beta$.

Choice C is incorrect and may result from incorrectly setting $\alpha + \beta = 100°$.

Choice D is incorrect and may result from incorrectly setting $\alpha + \beta = 180°$.

 What is the value of $cot(30°)$?

A) $\dfrac{\sqrt{3}}{3}$

B) 1

C) $\sqrt{3}$

D) $2\sqrt{3}$

Solution: Cofunction identities state that $tan(90° - \theta) = cot(\theta)$.

Thus, $cot(30°) = tan(90° - 30°) = tan(60°)$, or $cot(30°) = \sqrt{3}$

Therefore, the correct answer is **Choice C.**

Choice A is incorrect. This is the value of $cot(60°)$

Choice B is incorrect. This is the value of $cot(45°)$

Choice D is incorrect and may be due to a calculation error.

 In a right triangle, one angle measures 25°, where $cos(25°) = \dfrac{3}{7}$. What is $sin(65°)$?

A) $\dfrac{3}{7}$

B) $\dfrac{2\sqrt{10}}{7}$

C) $\dfrac{2\sqrt{10}}{3}$

D) $\dfrac{7}{3}$

Solution: Cofunction identities state that $cos(90° - \theta) = sin(\theta)$.

Thus, $sin(65°) = cos(90° - 65°) = cos(25°)$.

It is given that $cos(25°) = \dfrac{3}{7}$, therefore, $sin(65°) = \dfrac{3}{7}$. The correct answer is **Choice A.**

Choice B is incorrect and may be due to a calculation error.

Choice C is incorrect and may be due to a calculation error.

Choice D is incorrect and may be due to a calculation error.

Conversion between Degrees and Radians

To convert from degrees to radians, multiply by the conversion factor $\dfrac{\pi}{180}$.

To convert from radians to degrees, multiply by the conversion factor $\dfrac{180}{\pi}$.

π radians is equivalent to 180°. It would be useful to memorize some remarkable angles. These are presented in the table below.

Degrees	0°	30°	45°	60°	90°	180°
Radians	0	$\dfrac{\pi}{6}$	$\dfrac{\pi}{4}$	$\dfrac{\pi}{3}$	$\dfrac{\pi}{2}$	π

Consider the following examples.

 It's given that the difference between angle A and angle B is $\dfrac{4\pi}{9}$ radians. If $m\angle A = \dfrac{11\pi}{12}$ radians, what is the measure of angle B in degrees?

A) 80

B) 85

C) 165

D) 330

Solution: It's given that $m\angle A - m\angle B = \dfrac{4\pi}{9}$ radians.

Substituting $\dfrac{11\pi}{12}$ for $m\angle A$ yields $\dfrac{11\pi}{12} - m\angle B = \dfrac{4\pi}{9}$.

Subtracting $\dfrac{11\pi}{12}$ from both sides of this equation yields $-m\angle B = -\dfrac{17\pi}{36}$.

Multiplying both sides of this equation by –1 results in $m\angle B = \dfrac{17\pi}{36}$ radians.

In degrees, $m\angle B = \dfrac{17\pi}{36} \times \dfrac{180}{\pi} = 85°$.

Therefore, the correct answer is **Choice B.**

Choice A is incorrect. This is the value of $\dfrac{4\pi}{9}$ in degrees.

Choice C is incorrect. This is the value of $\dfrac{11\pi}{12}$ in degrees.

Choice D is incorrect. This is double the measure of angle A in degrees.

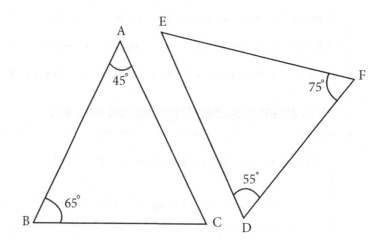

⑦ In the given figure, what is the sum of angles C and E in radians?

A) $\dfrac{11\pi}{16}$

B) $\dfrac{2\pi}{3}$

C) $\dfrac{13\pi}{18}$

D) $\dfrac{7\pi}{9}$

Solution: To solve, first find the measure of angles C and E.

In the triangle ABC, $A + B + C = 180°$. Substituting the given values from the figure yields 45° + 65° + C = 180, or C = 70°.

In the triangle DEF, $D + E + F = 180°$. Substituting the given values from the figure yields 55° + E + 75° = 180, or E = 50°.

Adding the angles C and E yields 70°+50°=120°.

Converting the degrees to radians results in $120 \times \dfrac{\pi}{180} = \dfrac{2\pi}{3}$. Therefore, the correct answer is **Choice B.**

Choice A is incorrect and may result if the question asks for the sum of angles A and B in radians.

Choice C is incorrect and may result if the question asks for the sum of angles D and F in radians.

Choice D is incorrect and may result if the question asks for the sum of angles B and F in radians.

Unit Circle

The unit circle allows you to compute the trigonometric functions of various angles. The unit circle is a circle with a radius of one and with the coordinate system dividing the circle into 4 equal quadrants. The origin of arcs is taken to be the point (1, 0). Once you draw any angle starting from (1, 0) with the origin of the coordinate system as its vertex, the x-coordinate of the endpoint, where the terminal side of the angle intersects the circle, is the value of the cosine of the angle, and the y-coordinate is the value of the sine of the angle. Look at the sketch below.

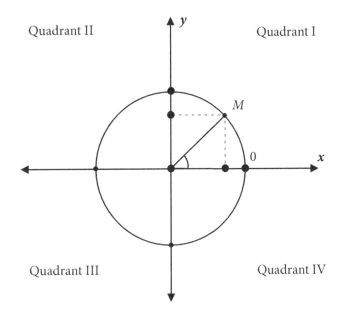

All angles in the **first quadrant** have **positive sine and cosine values.**

All angles in the **second quadrant** have **positive sine values** and **negative cosine values.**

All angles in the **third quadrant** have **negative sine and cosine values.**

All angles in the **fourth quadrant** have **positive cosine values** and **negative sine values.**

Let's look at the examples below.

(?) If $\pi < \alpha < \dfrac{3\pi}{2}$, and $cos\,\alpha = -\dfrac{1}{2}$, what is the exact value of $tan\,\alpha$?

A) $-\sqrt{3}$

B) $-\dfrac{\sqrt{3}}{2}$

C) $\dfrac{\sqrt{3}}{3}$

D) $\sqrt{3}$

Solution: Using the identity $\sin^2 \alpha + \cos^2 \alpha = 1$ and substituting -1/2 for cos α yield $\sin^2 \alpha + \left(-\frac{1}{2}\right)^2 = 1$.

Simplifying results in $\sin^2 \alpha = \frac{3}{4}$.

It's given that $\pi < \alpha < \frac{3\pi}{2}$, then α is in Quadrant III where the sine is negative.

Thus, $\sin \alpha = -\sqrt{\frac{3}{4}} = -\frac{\sqrt{3}}{2}$.

Substituting the values for sin α and cos α in the equation $tan\,\alpha = \frac{sin\,\alpha}{cos\,\alpha}$ yields

$tan\,\alpha = \dfrac{-\dfrac{\sqrt{3}}{2}}{-\dfrac{1}{2}} = \sqrt{3}$. Therefore, the correct answer is **Choice D.**

Choice A is incorrect. This is the value of –tan α.

Choice B is incorrect. This is the value of sin α.

Choice C is incorrect. This is the value of $\dfrac{1}{tan\,\alpha}$.

 What is the value of $\sin\left(\frac{5\pi}{6}\right)$?

Solution: To find the value of $\sin\left(\frac{5\pi}{6}\right)$, locate the angle $\frac{5\pi}{6}$ on the unit circle.

This angle is in the second quadrant where the sine function is positive.

The reference angle is $\pi - \frac{5\pi}{6} = \frac{\pi}{6}$. The sine of $\frac{\pi}{6}$ is $\frac{1}{2}$.

Therefore, the correct answer is $\frac{1}{2}$.

 If $sin(x) = \frac{3}{5}$ and x is in the second quadrant, what is $cos(x)$?

A) $-\dfrac{5}{4}$

B) $-\dfrac{4}{5}$

C) $\dfrac{4}{5}$

D) $\dfrac{5}{4}$

Solution: In the unit circle, for any angle x, the identity $sin^2\ x + cos^2\ x = 1$ holds true. Substituting the given value $sin(x) = \dfrac{3}{5}$ into this identity yields $\left(\dfrac{3}{5}\right)^2 + cos^2\ x = 1$ or $\dfrac{9}{25} + cos^2 x = 1$.

Subtracting both sides by $\dfrac{9}{25}$ yields $cos^2\ x = \dfrac{16}{25}$.

Taking the square root of both sides $\sqrt{cos^2\ x} = \sqrt{\dfrac{16}{25}}$ results in $cos(x) = -\dfrac{4}{5}$ or $cos(x) = \dfrac{4}{5}$.

Since x lies in the second quadrant, $cos(x)$ will be negative, therefore $cos(x) = -\dfrac{4}{5}$. The correct answer is **Choice B.**

Choice A is incorrect. This may result if the given is $sin(x) = \dfrac{5}{3}$.

Choice C is incorrect. This may result if x is in the first or fourth quadrant.

Choice D is incorrect. This may result if the given is $sin(x) = \dfrac{5}{3}$ and is in the first or fourth quadrant.

GEOMETRY AND TRIGONOMETRY

1 ☐ **Mark for Review**

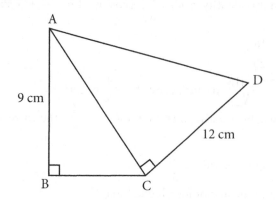

Triangle ABC is similar to CAD, angle BCA is equal to angle CDA, what is the length of AD in cm?

A) 15

B) 20

C) 21

D) 25

2 ☐ **Mark for Review**

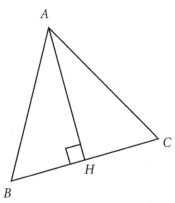

In the figure, $\triangle ABC$ is equilateral and $\overline{AH}$ is an altitude. What is the value of $\tan B$?

A) $\dfrac{1}{2}$

B) $\dfrac{\sqrt{3}}{3}$

C) $\dfrac{\sqrt{3}}{2}$

D) $\sqrt{3}$

3 ☐ **Mark for Review**

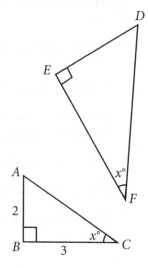

What is the value of $\sin D$?

A) $\dfrac{2\sqrt{13}}{13}$

B) $\dfrac{2}{3}$

C) $\dfrac{3\sqrt{13}}{13}$

D) $\dfrac{3}{2}$

4 ▢ **Mark for Review**

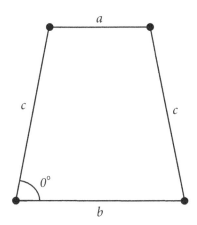

A road sign indicating a construction zone has the shape of an isosceles trapezoid as shown in the figure, where a, b and c are constant lengths. Which of the following represents the area of this road sign?

A) $c^2 \cdot sin\theta \cdot cos\theta$

B) $c \cdot sin\theta (b - c \cdot cos\theta)$

C) $c \cdot sin\theta (b - \dfrac{1}{2}c \cdot cos\theta)$

D) $b \cdot c \cdot sin\theta$

5 ▢ **Mark for Review**

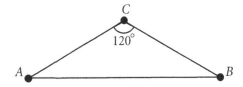

A house roof has the shape of an isosceles triangle as shown in the figure with $AC = BC$ and the angle $\angle ACB$ measuring 120°. If the distance from C to $\overline{AB}$ is 3 meters, what is the distance between A and B in meters?

A) $3\sqrt{3}$

B) 6

C) $6\sqrt{3}$

D) 12

Answers & Explanations

1. **Level:** Easy | **Skill/Knowledge:** Right triangles and trigonometry | **Testing Point:** Pythagoras theorem

    Key Explanation: The correct answer is **Choice D.** Find the hypotenuse of the triangle ABC using the Pythagoras theorem $a^2 + b^2 = c^2$, where c is the hypotenuse, $9^2 + 12^2 = c^2$ the value of c is therefore 15 *cm*. Since the two triangles are similar, $\dfrac{AC}{AB} = \dfrac{AD}{AC}$ or $\dfrac{15}{9} = \dfrac{AD}{15}$.
    Hence, the value of AD is 25 *cm*.

    Distractor Explanations: Choice A is incorrect. This option represents the value of the length of AC. **Choice B** is incorrect. This option represents the value of the length of CD. **Choice C** is incorrect. This option may be due to calculation or conceptual errors.

2. **Level:** Medium | **Skill/Knowledge:** Right triangles and trigonometry | **Testing Point:** Find the tangent of an acute angle in a right triangle

    Key Explanation: Choice D is correct. It's given that ABC is equilateral and AH is an altitude. Thus, AHB is a 90°-60°-30° triangle as shown in the figure below.

    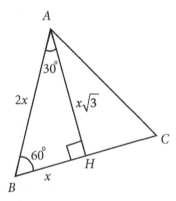

    $$\tan B = \frac{length\ of\ side\ opposite\ to\ B}{length\ of\ adjacent\ to\ B} = \frac{AH}{BH}.$$

    Using the relations between the sides of a 90°-60°-

    30° triangle, $\dfrac{AH}{BH} = \dfrac{x\sqrt{3}}{x} = \sqrt{3}$. Therefore, the value of *tan B* is $\sqrt{3}$. 3.

    Distractor Explanations: Choice A is incorrect. This is the value of *cos B*. **Choice B** is incorrect. This is the reciprocal of *tan B*. **Choice C** is incorrect. This is the value of *sin B*.

3. **Level:** Medium | **Skill/Knowledge:** Right triangles and trigonometry | **Testing Point:** Find the sine of an acute angle in a right triangle

    Key Explanation: Choice C is correct. The right angles $\angle ABC$ and $\angle DEF$ are congruent. It's also given that $m\angle ACB = m\angle DFE = x°$. It follows that $\triangle ABC$ and $\triangle DEF$ are similar having 2 pairs of equal corresponding angles. Angle A corresponds to angle D, then the two angles are congruent and $sin\ D = sin\ A$. The value of *sin A* is equal to $\dfrac{length\ of\ side\ opposite\ to\ A}{hypeotenuse}$, which is equal to $\dfrac{BC}{AC}$. Using the pythagorean theorem to find the length of the hypotenuse AC, $AC^2 = AB^2 + BC^2 = 2^2 + 3^2 = 4 + 9 = 13$. Thus, the length $AC = \sqrt{13}$. It follows that $sin\ A = \dfrac{BC}{AC} = \dfrac{3}{\sqrt{13}} = \dfrac{3\sqrt{13}}{13}$. Since $sin\ D = sin\ A$, therefore, $D = \dfrac{3\sqrt{13}}{13}$.

    Distractor Explanations: Choice A is incorrect. This is the value of *cos D*. **Choice B** is incorrect. This is the value of *tan x°*. **Choice D** is incorrect. This is the value of **tan D**.

4. **Level:** Hard | **Skill/Knowledge:** Right triangles and trigonometry | **Testing Point:** Use trigonometric functions to find the area of a trapezoid

    Key Explanation: Choice B is correct. Extending the trapezoid into a rectangle having a length of b and a width equal to the height of the trapezoid, drawing the heights of the trapezoid and labeling points and angles yield a figure as shown below.

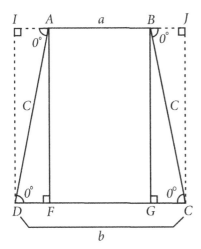

The area of the trapezoid *ABCD* is equal to the difference of the area of the rectangle *IJCD* and the combined area of the two right triangles *AID* and *BJC*. The area of the rectangle *IJCD* is equal to $DC \times DI$. It's given that $DC = b$ and $DI = FA$ due to the construction of the rectangle, then the area of the rectangle *IJCD* is equal to $b \times FA$. The length *FA* is the length opposite to angle θ in the right triangle *ADF* with a hypotenuse equal to *c*, then $FA = c \cdot \sin\theta$. It follows that the area of the rectangle *IJCD* is equal to $b \cdot c \cdot \sin\theta$. The four right triangles *AID*, *ADF*, *BGC* and *BJC* are congruent because they share the same length of the hypotenuse which is *c*, and have corresponding angles with an equal measure of $\theta°$. Then, the combined area of the two right triangles *AID* and *BJC* is equal to the area of the rectangle *AIDF* with a length $FA = c \cdot \sin\theta$, and a width *DF*. The width *DF* is the length of the side adjacent to angle θ in the right triangle *ADF* with a hypotenuse equal to *c*, then $DF = c \cdot \cos\theta$. It follows that the area of the rectangle *AIDF* is equal to $FA \times DF = c \cdot \sin\theta \times c \cdot \cos\theta$, which is equivalent to $c^2 \cdot \sin\theta \cdot \cos\theta$. Thus, the area of the trapezoid *ABCD* is equal to $b \cdot c \cdot \sin\theta - c^2 \cdot \cos\theta$. Factoring out $c \cdot \sin\theta$ yields $c \cdot \sin\theta (b - c \cdot \cos\theta)$ for the area of the trapezoid *ABCD*.

Distractor Explanations: Choice A is incorrect. This is the area of the rectangle having the dimensions $c \cdot \cos\theta$ and $c \cdot \sin\theta$. **Choice C** is incorrect. This is the sum of the area of the trapezoid and the area of a right triangle having

leg measures of $c \cdot \cos\theta$ and $c \cdot \sin\theta$. **Choice D** is incorrect. This is the area of the rectangle having the dimensions *b* and $c \cdot \sin\theta$.

5. **Level:** Hard | **Skill/Knowledge:** Right triangles and trigonometry | **Testing Point:** Use trigonometric functions in a right triangle to find a missing length

Key Explanation: Choice C is correct. Let *H* represent the foot of the perpendicular issued from *C* to $\overline{AB}$. It's given that the distance from *C* to $\overline{AB}$ is 3 meters, then $CH = 3\ m$. It's also given that $\triangle ACB$ is isosceles with $AC = BC$, then $\overline{CH}$ is a segment of the perpendicular bisector of $\overline{AB}$, and $\overline{CH}$ bisects $\angle ACB$ into two equal angles each measuring $\dfrac{120°}{2}$ or 60°. Let *x* represent the distance from *H* to *B*, then $x = \dfrac{AB}{2}$ or AB = 2x. See the completed figure below.

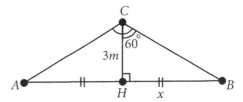

In the right triangle *CHB*, $tan(60°)$

$= \dfrac{length\ of\ side\ opposite\ to\ \angle HCB}{length\ of\ side\ opposite\ to\ \angle HCB} = \dfrac{HB}{CH} = \dfrac{x}{3}$.

Cross-multiplication yields $= 3 \times \sqrt{3} = 3\sqrt{3}\ m$. Substituting $3\sqrt{3}$ for *x* in the equation AB = 2x. results in $AB = 2 \times 3\sqrt{3} = 6\sqrt{3}$. Therefore, the distance between *A* and *B* is $6\sqrt{3}$ meters.

Distractor Explanations: Choice A is incorrect. This is half the length *AB*. **Choice B** is incorrect. This is the length *CB*. **Choice D** is incorrect. This is the sum of the lengths *AC* and *CB*.

Circles

Circle geometry comprises a wide range of topics. You may remember **tangents, chords, inscribed and central angles, arcs and sectors, and circle equations** from high school geometry lessons. The key to solving these types of questions correctly is to practice extensively. That is not to say that practice is needed only in this domain, as we learn math by doing math!

Circle Equations

> The standard form of an equation of a circle with center (h, k) and radius r in the xy-plane is $(x - h)^2 + (y - k)^2 = r^2$

You may be given the **equation of a circle in an expanded form,** for which you have to apply the strategy of **completing the square** to **change it into the standard form.** To make it easier, always keep in mind that you need to add to both sides of the equation the square of the half of the coefficient of x (not x^2) or y (not y^2). Consider the examples below.

>
>
> $$x^2 + 8x + y^2 - 6y + 23.31 = 0$$
>
> The given equation represents a circle in the xy-plane. What is the length of its radius?

Solution: The standard form of the equation of a circle with center (h, k) is $(x - h)^2 + (y - k)^2 = r^2$, where r is the radius of the circle.

The given equation can be expressed in the standard form by completing the square.

Using the associative property of addition, the given equation can be rewritten as $(x^2 + 8x) + (y^2 - 6y) + 23.31 = 0$.

To complete the square, add $\left(\dfrac{8}{2}\right)^2$ and $\left(\dfrac{-6}{2}\right)^2$ to both sides of this equation, which results in $(x^2 + 8x + 16) + (y^2 - 6y + 9) + 23.31 = 16+9$.

Subtracting 23.31 from both sides of this equation and combining the constants on the right-hand side yields $(x^2 + 8x + 16) + (y^2 - 6y + 9) = 1.69$.

Factoring results in $(x + 4)^2 + (y - 3)^2 = 1.69$.

Thus, the circle has a center $(-4, 3)$ and a radius equal to $\sqrt{1.69}$ or 1.3.

Therefore, the correct answer that you should input is **1.3**.

$$x^2 - 8x + y^2 + 10y + 6 = 0$$

The equation of a circle is given above. What are the coordinates of the center of the circle?

A) $(-4, 5)$

B) $(4, 5)$

C) $(-4, -5)$

D) $(4, -5)$

Solution: To find the coordinates of the center of the circle by the given equation $x^2 - 8x + y^2 + 10y + 6 = 0$, rewrite this equation in the standard form $(x - h)^2 + (y - k)^2 = r^2$, where (h, k) is the center of the circle, by completing the square.

To complete the square, take half of the coefficients of x and y, which are -8 and 10 respectively, square it, and add and subtract this value inside the equation.

This results in $(x^2 - 8x + 16) - 16 + (y^2 + 10y + 25) - 25 + 6 = 0$, or $(x - 4)^2 - 16 + (y + 5)^2 - 25 + 6 = 0$. Combining the constant terms yields $(x - 4)^2 + (y + 5)^2 - 35 = 0$. Adding 35 to both sides of this equation yields $(x - 4)^2 + (y + 5)^2 = 35$. Therefore, the circle has a center $(4, -5)$, which is **Choice D.**

Choice A is incorrect. This may be due to a calculation error.

Choice B is incorrect. This may be due to a calculation error.

Choice C is incorrect. This may be due to a calculation error.

A circle with the center $(5, 4)$ is tangent to the x axis. What is the radius of the circle?

A) 4

B) 5

C) 6

D) 7

Solution: For a circle to be tangent to the x axis, the distance from the center to the x axis must be equal to the radius of the circle. See below figure.

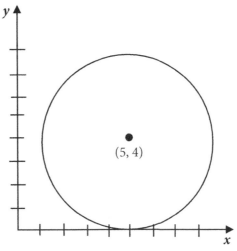

It is given that the center of the circle is (5, 4). Hence, the distance from the center (5, 4) to the x axis is 4. Consequently, the radius of the circle is 4, which is **Choice A.**

Choice B is incorrect and may result if the circle is tangent to the y-axis.

Choice C is incorrect and may result if the center of the circle is (5, 6).

Choice D is incorrect and may result if the center of the circle is (5, 7).

Arcs and Sectors

To find the length of an arc, or an area of a sector of a circle, keep this proportion in mind:

$$\frac{central\ \alpha^{\circ}}{360^{\circ}} = \frac{central\ \beta\ radians}{2\pi\ radians} = \frac{length\ of\ an\ arc}{2\pi r} = \frac{area\ of\ a\ sector}{\pi r^2}$$

Let's apply that concept with the help of examples.

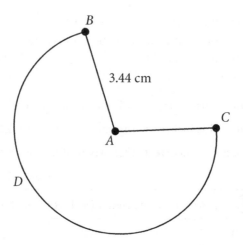

 The given circular sector has a center A, a radius of 3.44 *cm* and an area of 26 *cm²*. What is the length of the arc *BDC* to the nearest tenth of a centimeter (*cm*)?

A) 7.6 *cm*

B) 15.1 *cm*

C) 16.2 *cm*

D) 30.2 *cm*

Solution: Set the proportion $\frac{length\ of\ an\ arc}{2\pi r} = \frac{area\ of\ a\ sector}{\pi r^2}$.

Substituting the given values into this equation yields $\frac{length\ of\ arc\ BDC}{2\pi(3.44)} = \frac{26}{\pi(3.44)^2}$.

Multiplying both sides of this equation by $2\pi(3.44)^2$ yields $3.44 \times$ length of *arc* BDC = 52. Dividing both sides of this equation by 3.44 results in length of arc BDC = 15.1162.... Therefore, to the nearest tenth, the length of the arc BDC is 15.1 *cm*.

The correct answer is **Choice B.**

Choice A is incorrect. This is half the length of the arc *BDC*.

Choice C is incorrect and may result if the central angle *BAC* measures 270°.

Choice D is incorrect. This is double the length of arc *BDC*.

 A sector of a circle has a central angle of 120° and a radius of 6 cm. What is the area of the sector?

A) 6π cm²

B) 8π cm²

C) 10π cm²

D) 12π cm²

Solution: To find the area of a sector, set the proportion $\dfrac{Area\ of\ a\ sector}{\pi r^2}=\dfrac{central\ \alpha^\circ}{360^\circ}$, where α is the central angle and *r* is the radius.

Substituting 120° for α and 6 cm for r yields Area of the sector $=\dfrac{120^\circ}{360^\circ}\times\pi(6)^2=12\pi$ cm².

Therefore, the correct answer is **Choice D.**

Choice A is incorrect. This may result if the given central angle is 60°.

Choice B is incorrect. This may result if the given central angle is 80°.

Choice C is incorrect. This may result if the given central angle is 100°.

Angles and Segments in a Circle

Let's begin discussing **angles in a circle.** The two most commonly encountered angles in SAT circle questions are the **central angle** and the **inscribed angle**. A central angle has its vertex at the center of the circle and it measures the same as the intercepted arc. An inscribed angle has its vertex at the circumference of the circle and measures half the measure of the intercepted arc. This is why any inscribed angle in a semi-circle facing the diameter has a measure of $\dfrac{180^\circ}{2}$ or 90°, and any two inscribed angles intercepting the same arc are congruent. Consider the examples below.

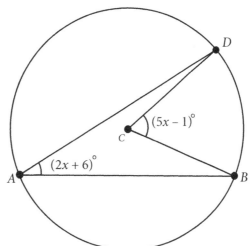

> (?) In the figure, what is the value of x?

A) $\dfrac{7}{3}$

B) 13

C) 32

D) 64

Solution: $\angle BAD$ is an inscribed angle that intercepts the arc BD.

Also, $\angle BCD$ is a central angle that intercepts the same arc BD. Thus, $m\angle BAD = \dfrac{1}{2} m\angle BCD$.

Substituting the given expressions for both angles yields $2x + 6 = \dfrac{1}{2}(5x - 1)$.

Multiplying both sides of this equation by 2 yields $4x + 12 = 5x - 1$.

Subtracting $4x$ from both sides of this equation results in $12 = x - 1$.

Adding 1 to both sides of this equation yields $13 = x$.

Therefore, the correct answer is **Choice B**.

Choice A is incorrect and may result if angles BAD and BCD are inscribed angles that intercept the same arc.

Choice C is incorrect. This is the measure of $\angle BAD$.

Choice D is incorrect. This is the measure of $\angle BCD$.

There are also some important properties that you need to know regarding segments, lines, and circles. A **tangent to a circle** is a **line that touches the circle at exactly one point** called the point of tangency. A **tangent** is **perpendicular to the radius** of the circle at the **point of tangency. A chord** is a **segment joining two points on a circle.** Two chords intercepting equal arcs are congruent. Any line or segment passing through the center and perpendicular to a chord also bisects the chord. Look at the examples below.

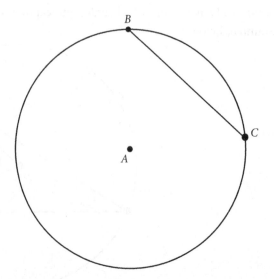

The figure shows a circle of circumference 6π *cm*, with the chord $\overline{BC}$ measuring 4 cm. What is the distance from point A to $\overline{BC}$ (to the nearest tenth of a centimeter)?

Solution: It's given that the circumference of the circle is 6π *cm*.

Substituting this value in the formula for the circumference $C = 2\pi r$ yields $6\pi = 2\pi r$.

Dividing both sides of this equation by 2π yields $3 = r$.

Then the radius of the circle is 3 *cm*, which is the length of $\overline{AB}$ and $\overline{AC}$.

The distance from point A to $\overline{BC}$ is the length of the perpendicular segment issued from A to $\overline{BC}$. This perpendicular segment from the center of the circle to the chord also bisects the chord.

See the sketch below.

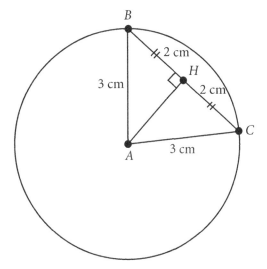

The required distance is the length of $\overline{AH}$.

Applying the Pythagorean theorem in $\triangle ABH$ yields $AH^2 = AB^2 - BH^2$.

Substituting 3 for the radius AB and 2 for half the chord BH yields $AH^2 = 9 - 4 = 5$.

Thus, the distance from A to $\overline{BC}$ is $\sqrt{5}$ cm. To the nearest tenth, this is equal to 2.2 cm. Therefore, the correct answer that you should enter is **2.2**.

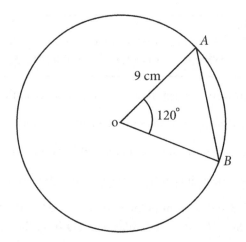

> ⑦ In a circle with center O, the measure of $\angle AOB$ is 120° and the radius is 9 *cm*. What is the length of the chord AB? (Round to the nearest tenth)

Solution: To find the length of the chord AB, use the relationship between the chord length, the radius, and the central angle.

The formula for the length of the chord is given by $2rsin\left(\dfrac{\theta}{2}\right)$.

Substitute 120° for θ and 9 cm for r into this equation yields chord length $= 2(9)\, sin\left(\dfrac{120°}{2}\right) = $ 18 $sin(60°)$.

From the SOH-CAH-TOA rules, we know that $sin(60°) = \dfrac{\sqrt{3}}{2}$. Substituting this to the formula yields chord length $= 18 \times \dfrac{\sqrt{3}}{2} = 9\sqrt{3}$. Therefore, the length of the chord is $9\sqrt{3}$ *cm* or approximately **15.6 *cm***.

This concludes the last math explanatory chapter of this SAT workbook. Now, it's your turn to practice working on as many questions as you can to master the concepts explained. With dedication and perseverance, you will reach your goal of getting the highest score on the Digital SAT. Best of luck to you!

1   ⚑ **Mark for Review**

$$x^2 + 6x + y^2 - 8y = 24$$

What is the value of the circumference of the circle with the equation above?

A) 7π

B) 14π

C) 49π

D) 98π

2   ⚑ **Mark for Review**

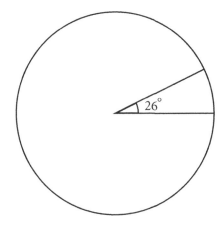

In the figure, the area of the sector is 0.65π. What is the radius of the circle?

A) 2

B) 3

C) 6

D) 9

3   ⚑ **Mark for Review**

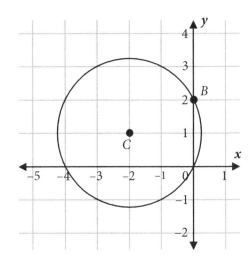

Choose the equation of the circle shown in the figure with center C and passing through point B.

A) $(x - 2)^2 + (y + 1)^2 = 5$

B) $(x + 2)^2 + (y - 1)^2 = 3$

C) $(x + 2)^2 + (y - 1)^2 = 5$

D) $(x + 2)^2 + (y - 1)^2 = 25$

4   ⚑ **Mark for Review**

$$3x^2 + 3y^2 - 8x + 7y - \frac{31}{12} = 0$$

The given equation represents a circle in the xy-plane. What is the y-coordinate of its center?

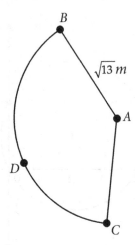

The figure shows the form of a curved seating area in a garden. This circular sector has a center A, a radius of $\sqrt{13}\,m$ and an area of $16\,m^2$. What is the length of the arc BDC to the nearest tenth of a meter (m)?

Answers & Explanations

1. **Level:** Easy | **Skill/Knowledge:** Circles | **Testing Point:** Equations of a circle in the xy plane

   Key Explanation: Choice B is correct. To solve for the circumference of the circle, find the radius/diameter of the circle. First, transform the given equation to standard form $(x - h)^2 + (y - k)^2 = r^2$, where (h, k) is the center of the circle and the radius of the circle is r.

   Completing the perfect square trinomials by adding 9 and 16 to both sides of the equation yields $x^2 + 6x + 9 + y^2 - 8y + 16 = 24 + 9 + 16$.

   This is equivalent to $(x + 3)^2 + (y - 4)^2 = 49$.

   The value of the radius for the above equation is $r = \sqrt{49} = 7$.

   Hence, the radius of the circle is 7.

   The circumference of the circle is given by $2\pi r$. Substituting the value of radius yields $2\pi(7) = 14\pi$.

   Distractor Explanations: Choice A is incorrect. This option could be calculated by assuming that 7 is the diameter of the circle. **Choice C is incorrect.** This option is calculated by finding the area of the circle above. **Choice D is incorrect.** This option could be calculated by assuming that the radius is 49.

2. **Level:** Medium | **Skill/Knowledge:** Circles | **Testing Point:** Use the area of a sector formula to find the radius of a circle

   Key Explanation: Choice B is correct. Substituting the given values in the formula $\dfrac{Area\ of\ a\ sector}{Area\ of\ the\ circle} = \dfrac{central\ angle\ measure}{360°}$ yields $\dfrac{0.65\pi}{\pi r^2} = \dfrac{26°}{360°}$. Canceling the common factor and cross multiplying results in $234 = 26r^2$. Dividing both sides of this equation by 26 yields $9 = r^2$. It follows that $3 = r$. Therefore, the radius of the circle is 3.

   Distractor Explanations: Choice A is incorrect and may result if the area of the sector is $\dfrac{13}{45}\pi$. **Choice C is incorrect** and may result if the area of the sector is $\dfrac{13}{5}\pi$. **Choice D is incorrect** and may result if the area of the sector is $\dfrac{117}{20}\pi$.

3. **Level:** Medium | **Skill/Knowledge:** Circles | **Testing Point:** Find the equation of a circle drawn in the xy-plane

   Key Explanation: Choice C is correct. The general equation of a circle is $(x - h)^2 + (y - k)^2 = r^2$, where (h, k) is the center and r is the radius of the circle. The center is $C(-2, 1)$ and the radius can be found using the distance formula. $r = CB = \sqrt{(0 - (2))^2} = \sqrt{4 + 1} = \sqrt{5}$. Substituting the coordinates of the center and the value of the radius in the general equation of a circle yields $(x -(-2))^2 + (y - 1)^2 = (\sqrt{5})^2$. Therefore, the equation of the circle is $(x + 2)^2 + (y - 1)^2 = 5$.

   Distractor Explanations: Choice A is incorrect. This is the equation of the circle with center $(2, -1)$ and radius $\sqrt{5}$. **Choice B is incorrect.** This is the equation of the circle with center $(-2, 1)$ and radius $\sqrt{3}$. **Choice D is incorrect.** This is the equation of the circle with center $(-2, 1)$ and radius 5.

4. **Level:** Hard | **Skill/Knowledge:** Circles | **Testing Point:** Find the center of a circle given its equation by completing the square

   Key Explanation: $-\dfrac{7}{6}$ is the correct answer. The standard form of the equation of a circle with center (h, k) is $(x - h)^2 + (y - k)^2 = r^2$, where r is the radius of the circle. The given equation can be written into the standard form by completing the square. First, divide both sides of the given equation $3x^2 + 3y^2 - 8x + 7y - \dfrac{31}{12} = 0$ by 3 yields $x^2 + y^2 - \dfrac{8}{3}x + \dfrac{7}{3}y - \dfrac{31}{36} = 0$, which can be grouped into $\left(x^2 - \dfrac{8}{3}x\right) + \left(y^2 + \dfrac{7}{3}y\right) - \dfrac{31}{36} = 0$.

To complete the square, add $\dfrac{64}{36}$ and $\dfrac{49}{36}$ to

both sides of this equation, which results in

$$\left(x^2 - \frac{8}{3}x + \frac{64}{36}\right) + \left(y^2 + \frac{7}{3}y + \frac{49}{36}\right) - \frac{31}{36} = \frac{64}{36} + \frac{49}{36}.$$

Adding $\dfrac{31}{36}$ to both sides of this equation and

adding the fractions on the right-hand side yields

$\left(x^2 - \dfrac{8}{3}x + \dfrac{64}{36}\right) + \left(y^2 + \dfrac{7}{3}y + \dfrac{49}{36}\right) = \dfrac{144}{36}.$ Factoring

results in $\left(x - \dfrac{8}{6}x\right)^2 + \left(y + \dfrac{7}{6}\right)^2 = 4.$ This equation

can be rewritten as $\left(x - \dfrac{4}{3}x\right)^2 + \left(y - \left(-\dfrac{7}{6}\right)\right)^2 = 2^2.$

Therefore, the y-coordinate of the center of the

circle is $-\dfrac{7}{6}.$

5. **Level:** Easy | **Skill/Knowledge:** Circles | **Testing Point:** Equations of a circle in the xy plane

Key Explanation: 8.9 is the correct answer. The area of any circular sector is given by

$A_{sector} = \dfrac{1}{2}\theta r^2,$ where is the measure of the

central angle in radians and r is the radius. It's given that the area of the circular sector is 16 m^2

and the radius is $\sqrt{13}\, m$, then $16 = \dfrac{1}{2}\theta\left(\sqrt{13}\right)^2$

or $16 = \dfrac{1}{2}\theta \times 13.$ Multiplying both sides of

this equation by 2 yields $32 = 13\theta.$ Dividing both sides of this equation by 13 results in

$\theta = \dfrac{32}{13}.$ The length of any circular arc is given

by $s = r\theta,$ thus the length of the arc BDC is

$s = \sqrt{13} \times \dfrac{32}{13} = 8.87520314.$ Therefore, to the

nearest tenth of a meter, the length of arc BDC is 8.9 m.

IMPORTANT

READ THE BELOW INSTRUCTIONS BEFORE BEGINNING THE TEST AND FOLLOW THEM AS YOU GO ALONG.

This full-length test consists of 3 modules. Module 1 is a mix of easy, medium and hard questions.

- Take Module 1 and note down your score on the sheet given at the end of the module.

- If your score is less than 15, attempt Module 2 (Easy).

- If your score is more than 15, attempt Module 2 (Hard).

Chapter 12
Digital SAT Supreme Guide - Test #1

Reading and Writing Test

27 QUESTIONS | 32 MINUTES

DIRECTIONS

The questions in this section address a number of important reading and writing skills. Each question includes one or more passages, which may include a table or graph. Read each passage and question carefully, and then choose the best answer to the question based on the passage(s). All questions in this section are multiple-choice with four answer choices. Each question has a single best answer.

---

1   ☐ **Mark for Review**

Recent research, led by Zita Laffranchi and Marco Milella at the University of Bern, sheds new light on the practices of prehistoric societies. The study looks into the modification of human bones found in prehistoric caves. These bones often exhibit cuts and marks, prompting the scientific community to _____ their potential use for human consumption. This work provides valuable insights into how prehistoric societies adapted and utilized human bones.

Which choice completes the text with the most logical and precise word or phrase?

A) inquire about

B) debate on

C) argue over

D) speculate about

2   ☐ **Mark for Review**

The utilization of metal as a form of currency has ancient origins dating back to Babylon before 2000 BCE. However, the concept of standardized and officially certified coinage may not have emerged until the seventh century BCE. According to the consensus among numerous historians, it was during this era that the kingdom of Lydia, situated in what is now modern-day Turkey, introduced the earliest forms of _____ coins.

Which choice completes the text with the most logical and precise word or phrase?

A) ancient

B) regulated

C) counterfeit

D) innovative

3 ☐ **Mark for Review**

A recent study has observed the problem-solving skills of individual wild Asian elephants as they _____ unlocked storage boxes to access food. This groundbreaking research marks the first time that variations in problem-solving willingness and abilities among wild elephants have been documented concerning food acquisition.

Which choice completes the text with the most logical and precise word or phrase?

A) successfully

B) reluctantly

C) uncertainly

D) rarely

4 ☐ **Mark for Review**

An academic journal serves as a platform for researchers to publish articles within a specific discipline, facilitating the transparent presentation of findings and enabling evaluation and discussion by the academic community. Prior to publication, research manuscripts undergo a peer-review or refereeing process. This means that experts in the field have thoroughly _____ the paper's quality and significance, ultimately determining its suitability for publication in the journal where the author submitted it.

What choice completes the text with the most logical and precise word or phrase?

A) reviewed

B) evaluated

C) scanned

D) read

5 ☐ **Mark for Review**

While clinical psychologists and psychiatrists both share the overarching goal of mitigating mental distress, their training, perspectives, and approaches diverge significantly. Notably, psychiatrists hold _____ medical doctors, and consequently, they tend to employ the medical model when evaluating mental health issues and often utilize psychotropic medications as a means of addressing these concerns. On the other hand, psychologists typically do not have prescription authority.

Which choice completes the text with the most logical and precise word or phrase?

A) permission for

B) licenses as

C) expertise in

D) affiliation with

6 ☐ **Mark for Review**

The tongue is an often-overlooked organ in both animals and humans. Without it, most terrestrial vertebrates could not survive as it gives them the ability to process a range of foods. Furthermore, its versatility is an astonishing example of adaptability, with snakes using their tongue for smell, chameleons using theirs at lightning-fast speed to catch an insect, and hummingbirds using their lengthy tongue to slurp nectar from deep within flowers. Though it is small, the tongue is truly mighty.

Which choice best states the main purpose of the text?

A) To argue that the human tongue is the most important organ in the body

B) To conclude that animals have adapted their tongue for survival

C) To demonstrate the importance of the tongue for many species

D) To inform about the versatility of the tongue for specific species

The following is an excerpt from *Dracula* by Bram Stoker.

> Sometimes the hills were so steep that, despite our driver's haste, the horses could only go slowly. I wished to get down and walk up them, as we do at home, but the driver would not hear of it. "No, no," he said; "you must not walk here; the dogs are too fierce"; and then he added, with what he evidently meant for grim pleasantry—for he looked round to catch the approving smile of the rest—"and you may have enough of such matters before you go to sleep." The only stop he would make was a moment's pause to light his lamps.

Which choice best states the function of the underlined sentence in the text as a whole?

A) It foreshadows a dangerous event that may occur later in the story.

B) It highlights the driver's concern about the steep hills in the area.

C) It emphasizes the passengers' eagerness to get out of the carriage.

D) It adds a sense of suspense and anticipation to the passage.

Passion has almost always been considered a positive attribute for any employee. However, it turns out that an employee and an employer may have very different definitions of what passion truly is. One might consider it the excitement and creativity put into a project, while the other would define it as late nights and weekends working on the job. If the two cannot get on the same page about what constitutes a passionate worker, conflicts will arise between unhappy workers and frustrated managers.

Which choice best states the function of the underlined sentence in the text as a whole?

A) It explores what employees and employers have in common.

B) It discusses what passion on the job is defined as.

C) It illustrates how employees and employers differ in their definition of passion.

D) It defines what it means to be a successful employee.

9 ☐ **Mark for Review**

Scientists at the Washington State University have recently conducted a study that claimed that <u>the intense urban lights in large cities may be driving an evolutionary adjustment towards smaller eyes in certain bird species.</u> The study further demonstrated that migratory birds are not adapting at the same rate as compared to residential birds adapting over time to urban areas.

Which finding from the above study, if true, would most directly support the underlined claim made by the scientists at Washington State University?

A) Two species of birds residing year-round in the urban heart of San Antonio exhibited 5% smaller eyes compared to their counterparts living in less illuminated outskirts.

B) The difference in eye size was not observed in two species of migratory birds, the Painted Bunting, and White-eyed Vireo, regardless of their urban residence for most of the year.

C) Since scientists were only able to compare a few species, both residing in urban and non-urban areas, a definite conclusion could not be reached, thus reflecting the need for more research.

D) Sensory pollution, including excess light, is one of the top challenges for birds to adapt to life in urban areas.

10 ☐ **Mark for Review**

"It Sifts From Leaden Sieves", a poem by Emily Dickinson, has winter at its heart. The poem sets the scene of a beautiful winter's day, where the falling snow has uniformly covered everything in sight. <u>The irony is that Dickinson never names the falling snow but only describes it such that the reader is able to guess the subject.</u> She also uses multiple metaphors, such as comparing the gray sky to a Leaden Sieve.

Which quotation from "It Sifts From Leaden Sieves" most effectively illustrates the underlined claim?

A) "It sifts from Leaden Sieves / It powders all the Wood/ It fills with Alabaster Wool/ The Wrinkles of the Road"

B) "To Stump, and Stack - and Stem / A Summer's empty Room / Acres of Joints, where Harvests were / Recordless, but for them"

C) "Of Mountain, and of Plain / Unbroken Forehead from the East / Unto the East again"

D) "It Ruffles Wrists of Posts / As Ankles of a Queen / Then stills it's Artisans - like Ghosts"

11   ☐ **Mark for Review**

Impacts of Meditation on Mental Health Outcome Types (categorized by the type of control group use)

Control Group	Outcome Type	SMD
Passive	Anxiety	−0.56
	Depression	−0.53
	Distress	−0.45
	Well-being	0.33
Active	Anxiety	0.07
	Depression	−0.17
	Distress	−0.01
	Well-being	0.04

Note: SMD reflects the post-meditation impact on each mental health outcome.

Numerous randomized controlled trials (RCTs) have attempted to study the impact of meditation and mindfulness on adverse mental health symptoms, such as anxiety and depression. A team of scientists has conducted a meta-analysis of 136 past studies across 29 countries. Among the studies, some focus on post-traumatic instances of anxiety and depression, while others examine anxiety and depression based on clinical factors. Based on the results, the scientists conclude that past studies demonstrate the beneficial impacts of meditation on _____

Which choice most effectively uses data from the graph to complete the statement?

A) depression, distress, and well-being across all control groups.

B) anxiety, depression, distress, and well-being across all control groups.

C) anxiety, depression, distress, and well-being for active control groups.

D) well-being for only passive control groups.

12   ☐ **Mark for Review**

Net number of migrants in China.

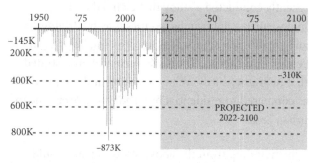

Net number of migrants is the number of immigrants into the country minus the number of emigrants out of the country. People may move into or out of a country to seek education, job opportunities, improved healthcare, or other perceived benefits. While China was the most populous country in the world in 2022, its title has been taken by another high-growth country, India. Furthermore, based on projections for 2022 to the year of 2100, _____

Which choice most effectively uses data from the graph to complete the statement?

A) more migrants will leave China than enter China compared to the early twentieth century.

B) more migrants will enter China than leave China compared to the early twentieth century.

C) China will experience a greater net outflow of migrants compared to the early twentieth century.

D) China will experience a greater net inflow of migrants compared to the early twentieth century.

13   🔖 **Mark for Review**

Emily Dickinson, an American poet, wrote "It Was Not Death, For I Stood Up" in the summer of 1862. The poem captures a haunting encounter with feelings of hopelessness and despair, rendering them even more formidable by their elusive nature, defying both identification and comprehension.

Which quotation from "It Was Not Death, For I Stood Up" most effectively illustrates this idea of despair?

A) "But, most, like Chaos—Stopless—cool—/ Without a Chance, or Spar—/Or even a Report of Land—/To justify—Despair."

B) "It was not Death, for I stood up /And all the Dead, lie down"

C) "As if my life were shaven / And fitted to a frame"

D) "It was not Night, for all the Bells/ Put out their Tongues, for Noon."

14   🔖 **Mark for Review**

"Mottainai", a modern Japanese expression that translates to "don't be wasteful" has ties back to civilization's mythology and rituals. For instance, there are many gods, spirits, and monsters associated with avoiding waste that are known as "yokai." The concept of "mottainai" is also closely tied to cleanliness as displayed in the ancient tradition of "oosouji" or "big cleaning" that is a yearly household ritual that provides a chance to not only clean up but also rid the dwelling of any negativity from the previous year. Clearly, _____.

Which choice most logically completes the text?

A) the Japanese place extreme importance on their mythology.

B) focus on monsters and creatures is a prominent part of ancient Japanese myths.

C) the idea of avoiding wastefulness and maintaining cleanliness is a chief principle in Japanese society.

D) waste and being unclean is looked upon as sinful in Japanese traditions.

15   🔖 **Mark for Review**

In British poet Carol Ann Duffy's *The World's Wife* (1999), she retells ancient myths and fairy tales through the perspective of liberated women. The themes explored include darkness, feminism, childhood, love, and murder. "Little Red Cap" transforms Little Red Riding Hood from a naive child eaten by a ferocious wolf to an attacker who kills the wolf in his sleep. Instead of "King Kong", she wrote "Queen Kong" focusing on a giant female gorilla who falls in love with a male film crew member. In "Herod's Wife" the three wise men who followed the star of finding Christ are imagined as three women who rely on friendship to succeed in a male-dominated world. Ultimately, _____

Which choice most logically completes the text?

A) themes in *The World's Wife* emphasize female equality including darkness, feminism, childhood, love, and murder.

B) in *The World's Wife* by Duffy, retellings like "Little Red Cap", "Queen Kong", and "Herod's Wife" take the power away from the original male protagonists and place them in the hands of females.

C) in Duffys's *The World's Wife,* retellings such as "Little Red Cap", "Queen Kong", and "Herod's Wife" allow female readers to see themselves in these stories and recognize their ability and power.

D) *The World's Wife* by Duffy contains the retelling of many classic fairy tales like "Little Red Riding Hood", "King Kong", and the story of the three wise men with female leads instead of male ones.

16   🔖 **Mark for Review**

Jupiter, the largest planet in our solar system, is a gas giant with a stunning appearance. Its towering size and powerful magnetic field make it a captivating celestial _____ its most famous feature is the Great Red Spot, a humongous storm that has raged for centuries. With 79 known moons, Jupiter's gravitational influence shapes our cosmic neighborhood.

Which choice completes the text so that it conforms to the conventions of Standard English?

A) body, but

B) body, and

C) body, yet

D) body, for

17   🔖 **Mark for Review**

The wood frog is notably recognized by the black marking spanning its eyes, often likened to a mask. Their adult bodies exhibit a range of colors, including brown, red, green, or gray, with females typically displaying brighter hues compared to males. In terms of size, adults of this amphibian species typically _____ between 1.5 to 3.25 inches (3.8 to 8.2 centimeters) in length.

Which choice completes the text so that it conforms to the conventions of Standard English?

A) measures

B) measure

C) is measuring

D) have measured

18 ☐ **Mark for Review**

The Indian Ocean, one of the world's major oceans, is renowned for its immense size and diverse cultures. It spans the regions of Asia, Africa, and Australia. This body of water is vital for _____ for the breathtaking beauty it offers along its shores. With its stunning coral reefs and myriad of marine life, the Indian Ocean is a treasure trove of natural wonders.

Which choice completes the text so that it conforms to the conventions of Standard English?

A) trade and transportation, or simply,

B) trade and transportation, or simply

C) trade and transportation or simply,

D) trade and transportation or, simply

19 ☐ **Mark for Review**

Bengali literature encompasses writings in the Bengali language of the Indian subcontinent. Its origins trace back to a collection of lyrics _____ the twelfth century, which mirror the beliefs and customs of the Sahajiyā religious sect.

Which choice completes the text so that it conforms to the conventions of Standard English?

A) predates

B) that will predate

C) that are predating

D) predating

20 ☐ **Mark for Review**

Employee turnover can pose a significant obstacle for businesses, particularly in industries where there is substantial demand for skilled labor. To mitigate employee turnover, it is critical to identify the underlying reasons for _____ is vital for developing effective strategies to retain skilled employees.

Which choice completes the text so that it conforms to the conventions of Standard English?

A) it (as understanding the root causes)

B) it, as understanding the root causes,

C) it, as understanding the root causes

D) it as understanding the root causes

21 ☐ **Mark for Review**

Over the course of his extensive life, which extended from 1840 to 1926, Monet _____ from sketching amusing caricatures of friends to skillfully capturing the subtle intricacies of natural landscapes in diverse expressions of light and color. Alongside fellow Impressionists, Monet dedicated his artistry to the pursuit of representing reality and dissecting the constantly shifting interplay of light and color.

Which choice completes the text so that it conforms to the conventions of Standard English?

A) evolved

B) has evolved

C) is evolving

D) will evolve

22　　☐ **Mark for Review**

Written by Benjamin Franklin from 1771 to 1788, *The Autobiography of Benjamin Franklin* saw partial publication as early as 1791 in French. A friend of Franklin's believed one of the _____ was to serve as a model for self-improvement, positioning it as one of the earliest examples of a "self-help" book and a significant contribution to the evolution of the autobiography genre.

Which choice completes the text so that it conforms to the conventions of Standard English?

A) autobiography's aim's

B) autobiographys aims

C) autobiography's aims

D) autobiography aim's

23　　☐ **Mark for Review**

The _____ is widely recognized as the Industrial Revolution. This era of advancement was characterized by a shift from an agrarian-based economy to one that was mechanized, leading to an extraordinary increase in efficiency and productivity.

Which choice completes the text so that it conforms to the conventions of Standard English?

A) innovation; that took place in the late eighteenth and early nineteenth centuries

B) innovation that took place in the late eighteenth and early nineteenth centuries

C) innovation, that took place in the late eighteenth, and early nineteenth centuries,

D) innovation (that took place in the late eighteenth and early nineteenth centuries)

24　　☐ **Mark for Review**

Stingless bees, also known as stingless honey bees or meliponines, form a diverse group of bees encompassing approximately 550 known species. They belong to the tribe Meliponini (or subtribe Meliponina, as stated by some researchers). While meliponines possess stingers, these stingers are significantly reduced and not used for defense. _____ despite the absence of a potent stinging mechanism, these bees employ alternative defensive behaviors and mechanisms to protect themselves.

Which choice completes the text with the most logical transition?

A) Furthermore,

B) Similarly,

C) Nevertheless,

D) Though,

25　　☐ **Mark for Review**

The field of algorithmic trading, utilizing computer algorithms to make investment decisions, made significant contributions with the development of high-frequency trading (HFT). This trading strategy, relying on ultra-fast computers and complex algorithms, has transformed financial markets by enabling lightning-fast transactions. _____ algorithmic trading's groundbreaking adoption of HFT has reshaped the landscape of modern finance.

Which choice completes the text with the most logical transition?

A) Therefore,

B) Moreover,

C) In a similar vein,

D) However,

26 ◻ **Mark for Review**

While researching a topic, a student has taken the following notes:

- The Gross Domestic Product (GDP) signifies the total worth of all products and services generated within a nation over a defined time span.

- The GDP growth rate is a significant indicator of the economic performance of a country.

- The inflation rate measures the percentage increase in the general level of prices for goods and services.

- Hyperinflation is an extremely high and typically accelerating inflation, rapidly eroding the real value of the local currency.

- An economic recession represents a substantial decrease in commercial operations that affects the entire economy and persists for an extended period, often exceeding several months.

The student wants to provide an appropriate synthesis of the information on inflation, GDP, and economic recession. Which choice most effectively uses relevant information from the notes to accomplish this goal?

A) As the total value of a nation's goods and services, GDP gauges economic performance, the inflation rate measures price increases, and a considerable, prolonged decline in commercial operations signifies an economic recession.

B) The GDP signifies a nation's total output of goods and services, and its growth rate serves as important measures of a country's economic health, while the inflation rate quantifies the percent increase in general price levels

C) Hyperinflation is an accelerating inflation that swiftly erodes a currency's real value, while an economic recession signifies a long-lasting, substantial reduction in commercial activity across the economy.

D) A recession occurs when there is a drop in commercial activities, unrelated to the inflation rate or the risk of hyperinflation.

While researching a topic, a student has taken the following notes:

- The advent of the Industrial Revolution ushered in an era of profound technological advancements, revolutionizing manufacturing processes and production methods.

- Correspondingly, these remarkable advancements led to a marked improvement in the overall standard of living, benefitting a substantial portion of the population.

- Amidst these triumphs, a dark underbelly emerged, characterized by deplorable working conditions and escalating environmental pollution as detrimental consequences.

- The Industrial Revolution fueled urbanization and population growth, transforming the societal landscape and prompting the rise of industrial cities.

- The Industrial Revolution sparked a paradigm shift in economic systems, transitioning from agrarian-based economies to industrial economies centered around factories and mass production.

The student wants to summarize the overall impact of the Industrial Revolution to an audience unfamiliar with the topic. Which choice most effectively uses relevant information from the notes to accomplish this goal?

A) The Industrial Revolution led to significant advancements in technology and improved the overall standard of living, but it also resulted in negative consequences such as poor working conditions and increased pollution.

B) The Industrial Revolution brought about transformative changes in manufacturing processes and technology, leading to an improved standard of living for many people, despite the negative consequences of poor working conditions and increased pollution.

C) The Industrial Revolution's positive impact on living standards was marred by negative consequences such as poor working conditions and increased pollution, even though it introduced significant advancements in technology and manufacturing processes.

D) The Industrial Revolution's advancements in technology and manufacturing processes positively affected the overall standard of living, although it came at the cost of negative consequences like poor working conditions and increased pollution.

Answer Key

Question Number	1	2	3	4	5	6	7	8	9	10	11	12	13	14
Correct Answer	D	B	A	B	B	C	A	C	A	A	A	C	A	C
Your Answer														

Question Number	15	16	17	18	19	20	21	22	23	24	25	26	27
Correct Answer	C	B	B	B	D	D	A	C	B	C	A	A	A
Your Answer													

IMPORTANT
READ THE BELOW INSTRUCTIONS BEFORE MOVING AHEAD.

- If you got less than 15 answers correct, turn to page 378 and take the easy module.

- If you got more than 15 answers correct, turn to page 392 and take the hard module.

Reading and Writing Test

27 QUESTIONS | 32 MINUTES

DIRECTIONS

The questions in this section address a number of important reading and writing skills. Each question includes one or more passages, which may include a table or graph. Read each passage and question carefully, and then choose the best answer to the question based on the passage(s). All questions in this section are multiple-choice with four answer choices. Each question has a single best answer.

---

1   ▢ **Mark for Review**

F. Scott Fitzgerald's *The Great Gatsby* is an American classic novel depicting the pursuit of the American Dream. The story is narrated by Nick Carraway, who moves to New York and becomes entangled in the lives of his wealthy and mysterious neighbor, Jay Gatsby, and his cousin Daisy Buchanan. The novel delves into themes of love, wealth, social class, and the decay of the American Dream, ultimately _____ in tragedy.

Which choice completes the text with the most logical and precise word or phrase?

A) evolving

B) culminating

C) resolving

D) emerging

2   ▢ **Mark for Review**

The prevalence of children witnessing or experiencing violence is not a new discovery, especially among those residing in inner-city areas. Studies by Campbell and Schwartz revealed that 88% of preadolescents in an urban middle school had been exposed to various acts of violence. Similarly, Taylor et al. found that 10% of 1- to 5-year-old children in an inner-city clinic had witnessed incidents involving knives or shootings. Considering the estimated 5 million children living in America's inner cities, the magnitude of children exposed to violence is _____.

What choice completes the text with the most logical and precise word or phrase?

A) inconsequential

B) sinister

C) difficult to understand

D) formidable

3   ☐ **Mark for Review**

Analyses were conducted for a sample of 308 subjects, both celiac (i.e., people who have serious negative autoimmune reactions to gluten such as that present in wheat) and non-celiac. Adherence to a gluten-free diet was measured considering two scales, self-declared adherence and scored adherence, in order to _____ possible inconsistencies between what subjects believe and what they really do.

What choice completes the text with the most logical and precise word or phrase?

A) value

B) express

C) discern

D) consider

4   ☐ **Mark for Review**

In the past two decades, the exploration of exoplanetary systems has offered scientists insights into the evolution of our solar system while enabling the search for habitable planets both within and beyond our solar neighborhood. Scientists have utilized advanced technology to detect a previously unknown exoplanet orbiting a distant star. This newfound exoplanet, located within the habitable zone, has _____ the interest of astronomers due to its potential to harbor life.

Which choice completes the text with the most logical and precise word or phrase?

A) piqued

B) unveiled

C) revealed

D) documented

5   ☐ **Mark for Review**

A recently unearthed pair of prehistoric logs near Kalambo Falls, Zambia is believed to be part of the earliest known wooden structure on Earth. Researchers now assert that this discovery is _____ established beliefs regarding the lifestyles of early human ancestors. During excavations along the banks of the Kalambo River, archaeologists uncovered a pair of wooden logs expertly connected by a carved notch, resting atop one another at a precise right angle.

Which choice completes the text with the most logical and precise word or phrase?

A) reinvigorating

B) excavating

C) underpinning

D) challenging

6   ☐ **Mark for Review**

The following text is an excerpt from Robert Frost's poem "The Road Not Taken"

> Two roads diverged in a yellow wood,
> And sorry I could not travel both
> And be one traveler, long I stood
> And looked down one as far as I could
> To where it bent in the undergrowth;

Which choice best describes the overall structure of the text?

A) The speaker describes a choice between two paths and then reflects on the consequences of that choice.

B) The speaker describes a forest scene and then considers the beauty of nature.

C) The speaker discusses the concept of regret and then offers advice on decision-making.

D) The speaker describes a journey and then contemplates the passage of time.

7   ⬚ **Mark for Review**

Text 1

Researchers allowed bumblebees into an area with access to pollen and sugar water. In order to reach the rewards, the bees had to pass by free-moving wooden balls or stationary wooden balls. Over numerous tries, the bees were 50% more likely to navigate through the free-moving balls and even pushed around the balls despite there being no reward for this action. Researchers speculate the bees may have just been having fun.

Text 2

While studies have demonstrated that bees may experience negative emotions, these insects lack cerebral cortexes, which regulate mood and motivation. However, a new study observing bumblebees pushing balls suggests that they may be capable of positive emotions as well. Nonetheless, these varying emotions are not as complex as human emotions.

Based on the texts, how would the author of Text 2 most likely respond to the study's conclusion presented in Text 1?

A) By qualifying that although bumblebees may not have complex emotions, it is likely that other special insects feel complex emotions

B) By stating that the "fun" the bees may have been experiencing constituted a very simple feeling

C) By arguing that the bees may have been feeling a negative emotion like stress rather than a positive, fun emotion

D) By speculating that there may be an incentive that the bees were striving for that could not be perceived by the researchers

8   ⬚ **Mark for Review**

For years, certain inhabitants of Taos, New Mexico, have been perplexed by a faint and enigmatic low-frequency hum pervading the desert atmosphere. Curiously, only a small fraction, approximately 2%, of Taos residents perceive this sound. Theories range from peculiar acoustics to mass hysteria or clandestine intentions. Regardless of whether it is described as a whir, hum, or buzz, and whether its source is psychological, natural, or supernatural, the origin of this sound remains elusive. Interestingly, a survey unveiled that those who report hearing it perceive a variety of sounds.

According to the text, what is true of the beliefs surrounding the mysterious hum in Taos, New Mexico?

A) Only a few select residents can hear the hum.

B) Many citizens believe that the hum has a sinister purpose.

C) The hum is a result of the hysteria surrounding supernatural events.

D) The hum is consistently described as a whir, hum, or buzz.

9 ☐ **Mark for Review**

The following text is adapted from an article written by Richard Saul that appeared in the National Geographic magazine.

In the fall of 1954, at the age of 18, I discovered the other half of the world. I began that journey through the eyes of an encyclopedic professor who guided me to China and the neighboring Altay Mountains, to Japan, and their elaborate methods of making swords. Then India, Tibet and the Potala Palace, Burma and the Burma Road, and, of course, the Khmer Empire and Cambodia. These places had all been hidden from my view by my Philadelphia suburban education.

Based on the text, what is most likely true about the author?

A) The author was transfixed by the world because he had not traveled before.

B) The author grew up in a small town of Philadelphia.

C) The author was helped by a professor.

D) The author had already traveled extensively.

10 ☐ **Mark for Review**

"Dulce et Decorum Est" is a poem written by Wilfred Owen that was published posthumously in 1920. In the poem, Owen highlights the physical violence and atrocities that occur during wartime.

Which quotation from "Dulce et Decorum Est" most effectively provides evidence for Owen's claim?

A) "Fitting the clumsy helmets just in time, / But someone still was yelling out and stumbling"

B) "And towards our distant rest began to trudge. / Men marched asleep."

C) "If you could hear, at every jolt, the blood / Come gargling from the froth-corrupted lungs"

D) "My friend, you would not tell with such high zest / To children ardent for some desperate glory"

11 ☐ Mark for Review

According to a study by the World Health Organization, flu season typically peaks during the fall and winter months in the Northern Hemisphere. It is characterized by the spread of influenza viruses, which can cause mild to severe respiratory illness. Annual flu vaccinations are recommended as the best preventive measure to reduce the risk of flu-related complications and transmission. Four types of influenza viruses — A, B, C, and D — exist. Influenza A and B viruses cause seasonal epidemics. Influenza A viruses, like A(H1N1) and A(H3N2), have subtypes based on surface proteins, while Influenza B viruses belong to B/Yamagata or B/Victoria lineages. Influenza C causes mild infections, and Influenza D primarily affects cattle.

Which finding, if true, would most directly support the claim made in the underlined sentence?

A) Flu-related hospitalizations increased by almost 3.5% in the winter months in multiple regions in the Northern Hemisphere.

B) The effectiveness of annual flu vaccinations varies depending on the predominant influenza virus strains circulating each flu season.

C) In the continental United States, districts with lower flu vaccination rates averaged 9 school closure days due to flu viruses, compared to 1 day in districts with higher flu vaccination rates.

D) Among populations studied, higher flu vaccination rates experienced a higher incidence of flu-related complications and transmission compared to regions with lower vaccination rates.

12 ☐ Mark for Review

Time to Reach Adult Stage for Larvae After Exposure to Plastic vs. Paper Leachates

		Days to reach adult stage
Water	Control	12.0
	Plastic cups	12.2
	Paper cups	13.5
Sediment	Control	13.0
	Plastic cups	14.0
	Paper cups	14.1

In an attempt to investigate whether certain types of cups are more toxic, scientists tested the effects of plastic cups and paper cups on larvae. To simulate how plastic and paper leach into the environment in real life, scientists extracted leachates from plastic and paper into water and sediment. Then, larvae were placed into the contaminated water and sediment. Scientists observed the time it took for the larvae to reach adult stage, treating a delay as a negative impact on growth due to contamination. They concluded that _____

Which choice most effectively uses data from the table to complete the statement?

A) it is inaccurate to say that plastic cups are less toxic than paper cups for the environment.

B) it is accurate to say that more leachates contaminated the water environment.

C) it is inaccurate to say that plastic cups are more toxic than paper cups for the environment.

D) it is accurate to say that more leachates contaminated the sediment environment.

13 🔖 **Mark for Review**

"The Applicant" is a poem by Sylvia Plath that explores themes of conformity, gender roles, and societal expectations. Through vivid imagery and sharp language, Plath critiques the commodification of marriage and the loss of individual identity within conventional gender roles. The poem presents a surreal scenario where marriage is reduced to a transactional process, emphasizing the dehumanizing effects of societal norms on women. <u>Plath uses this poem to highlight the absurdity of the expectations placed upon women in conforming to societal ideals.</u>

Which quotation from "The Applicant" most effectively illustrates the underlined claim?

A) "Now your head, excuse me, is empty / I have the ticket for that/ Come here, sweetie, out of the closet."

B) "First, are you our sort of a person? / Do you wear / A glass eye, false teeth or a crutch"

C) "It is waterproof, shatterproof, proof / Against fire and bombs through the roof/ Believe me, they'll bury you in it."

D) "A living doll, everywhere you look / It can sew, it can cook / It can talk, talk, talk / It works, there is nothing wrong with it."

14 🔖 **Mark for Review**

A study was conducted on 6,002 adults aged 40-85 in Germany to determine what risk factors contribute to loneliness and social exclusion. Because humans are very social, a lack of belonging is harmful to the individual and their society. Loneliness can contribute to lower a human's psychological well-being, quality of life, and health. It has also been found to contribute to lower levels of trust and cohesion within a social community. Risk factors include the level of education and income, participation opportunities, network structure (if one has a partner or child), and if emotional support is available. It can be determined that _____.

Which choice most logically completes the text?

A) individuals who experience loneliness and exclusion display a lack of trust and willingness to be a part of their communities.

B) humans experience higher rates of loneliness if they do not have a partner, child, or emotional support from others.

C) loneliness impacts not only society but an individual as it can lead to problems with heart health and a decline in mental well-being.

D) risk factors for loneliness and social exclusion were assessed in a group of individuals living in Germany of all ages.

15   ☐ **Mark for Review**

Listening to, singing, playing, or composing music has the ability to bring about many positive effects for those who take part in these musical activities. Research indicated that many aspects of life—like physical, emotional, and cognitive—can be supported by musical engagement. As a result, engaging in music is _____.

Which choice most logically completes the text?

A) shown to improve cognitive development in young children.

B) recommended for those looking to make a career from it.

C) the best medicine for people struggling with depression.

D) an ideal pastime for those looking to improve their outlook.

16   ☐ **Mark for Review**

From his backyard hut in Great Missenden, Buckinghamshire, prolific children's fiction author Roald Dahl crafted numerous tales, including *Matilda*, *James and the Giant Peach*, and *Fantastic Mr. Fox*. When he wrote *The Minpins*, he had already authored a total of 16 children's stories, which _____ into 68 languages and are enjoyed by readers worldwide. He undeniably remains one of the world's most revered storytellers.

Which choice completes the text so that it conforms to the conventions of Standard English?

A) has been translated

B) have been translated

C) are translated

D) translate

17   ☐ **Mark for Review**

According to some authorities, tattoos were deemed permissible unless they conveyed specific messages such as the name of God, the phrase "I am the Lord," or the name of a pagan deity. The Talmudic law, which emerged around 200 CE, states that tattoos are only forbidden if created _____ not if they serve to indicate a person's enslaved status.

Which choice completes the text so that it conforms to the conventions of Standard English?

A) "for the purpose of idolatry"– but

B) "for the purpose of idolatry" but

C) "for the purpose of idolatry", but

D) "for the purpose of idolatry"; but

18   ☐ **Mark for Review**

The native Australian Kakadu plum is known for its high nutritional value as it is packed with protein, dietary fiber, magnesium, calcium, phosphorus, and antioxidants. A wealth of aboriginal knowledge collected over 65,000 years _____ to the preservation of the rare fruit today, which is only found in specific national parks in Australia. While many international tourists may be interested in trying out the Kakadu plum, the availability of the fruit is limited due to ecological concerns.

Which choice completes the text so that it conforms to the conventions of Standard English?

A) contributes

B) contribute

C) have contributed

D) are contributing

19 ☐ **Mark for Review**

To the general public, excavation often appears as the primary and undoubtedly the most captivating facet of archaeology. However, fieldwork and excavation constitute just one aspect of an archaeologist's duties. The other crucial components involve interpreting the material remains of humanity's history, considering _____ cultural and historical contexts, and making sense of the facts uncovered—whether by chance discoveries, fieldwork, or excavations.

Which choice completes the text so that it conforms to the conventions of Standard English?

A) their

B) its

C) they're

D) it's

20 ☐ **Mark for Review**

The South African rand is the official currency of South Africa and its exchange rate is largely influenced by commodity prices, interest rates, and political developments in South Africa. Even though the rand has depreciated considerably against major global currencies in recent months, there remain certain _____ enjoy greater purchasing power.

Which choice completes the text so that it conforms to the conventions of Standard English?

A) destinations where, South Africans,

B) destinations, where South Africans

C) destinations where South Africans

D) destinations where, South Africans

21 ☐ **Mark for Review**

Fresh research _____ that the Amazon rainforest in South America conceals over 10,000, possibly even 23,000, yet-undiscovered pre-Columbian structures. Over five years, a team employed lidar technology, capturing intricate three-dimensional images of a 2,000-square-mile Amazon region. This aerial survey unveiled 24 previously unknown pre-Columbian earthworks, which may have held various functions like ceremonial, social, or defensive purposes.

Which choice completes the text so that it conforms to the conventions of Standard English?

A) suggest

B) have suggested

C) is suggesting

D) suggests

22 ☐ **Mark for Review**

Virginia Woolf's play *Freshwater: A Comedy* is a delightful departure from convention. It challenges norms, discards traditional _____ invites readers and audiences to embrace the unexpected. Woolf's whimsical storytelling and vivid characters create a world where art, identity, and creativity intertwine. *Freshwater* stands as a testament to Woolf's ability to push boundaries and captivate her audience.

Which choice completes the text so that it conforms to the conventions of Standard English?

A) structures, and

B) structures, and,

C) structures and,

D) structures and

23   ☐ **Mark for Review**

Researchers have finally understood how Peacock spiders, which range between just 2 to 5 millimeters and live in Australia, are able to produce vibrant colors on their bodies. The pigments that their barbed scales contain help to create the vivacious reds, whites, and yellows on the spiders, _____ tiny nanostructures found in their scales bend light to generate lustrous blues and purples.

Which choice completes the text with the most logical transition?

A) furthermore,

B) similarly

C) whereas

D) moreover

24   ☐ **Mark for Review**

The field of pet photography, dedicated to capturing stunning images of animals, made significant advancements with the introduction of creative lighting techniques. These lighting techniques, such as using natural light, off-camera flash, or studio lighting setups, have elevated the quality and aesthetics of pet portraits. _____ pet photography's groundbreaking lighting techniques have transformed the way we capture the essence and personality of our furry friends.

Which choice completes the text with the most logical transition?

A) Furthermore,

B) In addition,

C) Indeed,

D) Nevertheless,

⧄ **Mark for Review**

While researching a topic, a student has taken the following notes:

- Influenza (flu) viruses are typically transmitted through droplets (airborne respiratory aerosols) when people with the flu cough, sneeze or talk.

- COVID-19 is caused by a coronavirus named SARS-CoV-2 and spreads in similar ways to the flu.

- The incubation period for the flu is typically about 1 to 4 days, while for COVID-19 it is longer, typically around 2 to 14 days.

- While vaccines exist for both the flu and COVID-19, they function in different ways. The flu vaccine prepares the immune system to fight off the influenza virus, while the COVID-19 vaccines typically work by teaching cells to create a protein that triggers an immune response.

The student wants to highlight the similarities between the spread of the flu and COVID-19. Which choice most effectively uses relevant information from the notes to accomplish this goal?

A) Both the flu and COVID-19 are airborne diseases, typically transmitted through droplets when infected people cough, sneeze, or talk.

B) The flu generally has an incubation duration ranging from one to four days, in contrast to COVID-19, which usually necessitates a longer period, averaging between two and fourteen days.

C) Vaccines have been developed for both the flu and COVID-19, but they function in different ways.

D) Both the flu and COVID-19 are caused by viruses, specifically the influenza virus and SARS-CoV-2 respectively.

26   🔖 **Mark for Review**

While researching a topic, a student has taken the following notes:

- The invention of the internet has revolutionized communication and transformed the way we obtain information.

- It allows us to access a vast amount of knowledge, connect with people around the world, and engage in various online activities.

- The internet has bridged geographical barriers and made the world more interconnected than ever before.

- New opportunities for online learning, e-commerce including shopping online, entertainment (including online streaming services), and social interaction (including social media, gaming, blogging, etc.) are presented almost daily.

- The impact of the internet on society is undeniable and continues to shape the way we communicate, work, and navigate the world every day.

A student wants to emphasize the overall transformative impact internet has had on society. Which choice most effectively uses relevant information from the passage to accomplish this goal?

A) The internet has increased the availability of online shopping options and has made it easier to connect with people worldwide.

B) The invention of the internet has provided new opportunities for creative expression and entertainment through platforms like social media and streaming services.

C) Through the internet, people can now access a vast amount of information and engage in online activities such as gaming and blogging.

D) The internet has revolutionized communication, transformed information access, bridged geographical barriers, and continues to shape various aspects of society's functioning.

27   ⬚ **Mark for Review**

While researching a topic, a student has taken the following notes:

- Japanese businesses often use a system known as 'lifetime employment' wherein employees typically stay with a single company for their entire careers.

- Many Japanese firms implement a seniority-based pay scale, where employees' salaries rise gradually over time as they gain experience and seniority.

- The term "keiretsu" refers to a form of corporate structure common in Japan, where interconnected businesses own small portions of the shares in each other's companies to mutualize risk.

- Japanese companies tend to foster a culture of consensus decision-making, in which all members of a team are expected to agree before a decision is finalized.

- In comparison, Western companies frequently have a more hierarchical decision-making process and employees may change jobs more frequently.

The student wants to emphasize the unique characteristics of the Japanese business world compared to Western models. Which choice most effectively uses relevant information from the notes to accomplish this goal?

A) Japanese businesses, with their lifetime employment system and consensus decision-making, present a sharp contrast to Western companies, where employees change jobs more frequently and decisions are often made hierarchically.

B) The keiretsu system, a unique feature of the Japanese business world, is a stark departure from Western business models, underscoring the collaborative nature of Japanese businesses.

C) Lifetime employment and seniority-based pay scales are common in Japanese businesses, creating a work culture distinct from Western companies.

D) Japanese firms' culture of consensus decision-making and mutual risk-sharing through the keiretsu system underscores the uniqueness of their business practices.

Answer Key

Question Number	1	2	3	4	5	6	7	8	9	10	11	12	13	14
Correct Answer	B	D	C	A	C	A	B	B	C	C	C	C	D	B
Your Answer														

Question Number	15	16	17	18	19	20	21	22	23	24	25	26	27
Correct Answer	D	B	B	A	A	C	D	A	C	C	A	A	D
Your Answer													

IMPORTANT

READ THE BELOW INSTRUCTION BEFORE MOVING AHEAD.

- Turn to page 404 and start with Module 1 of the Math section.

No Test Material On This Page

Reading and Writing Test

27 QUESTIONS | 32 MINUTES

DIRECTIONS

The questions in this section address a number of important reading and writing skills. Each question includes one or more passages, which may include a table or graph. Read each passage and question carefully, and then choose the best answer to the question based on the passage(s). All questions in this section are multiple-choice with four answer choices. Each question has a single best answer.

---

1 🔖 **Mark for Review**

A. Mukherjee's *AI and Ethics* delves into diverse topics, including algorithmic decision-making, machine learning, regulation versus innovation, AI's role in information dissemination, and ethical considerations like individual rights and fairness. Unlike _____ approaches, the book adopts a computational lens, emphasizing the urgent moral and legal consequences of AI's prominence in society. By avoiding traditional philosophical or legal discussions, it aims to heighten awareness of AI's immediate impact on ethics and law.

Which choice completes the text with the most logical and precise word or phrase?

A) varied

B) diverse

C) predictable

D) conventional

2 🔖 **Mark for Review**

May Sarton, in her book *Journal of a Solitude*, beautifully expressed the contrasting nature of loneliness and solitude. She observed that loneliness signifies a lack within oneself, while solitude represents the abundance and fulfillment of one's own being. This <u>paradoxical</u> relationship between poetry and solitude is intriguing. Poets often cherish the seclusion necessary for their creative process, yet the ultimate goal of their work is to forge connections and foster a sense of community.

As it is used in the text, what does the word "paradoxical" most nearly mean?

A) Contradictory

B) Similar

C) Complicated

D) Unclear

3   ☐ **Mark for Review**

Vincent van Gogh, a renowned Dutch painter, is widely regarded as one of the greatest artists, following in the footsteps of Rembrandt van Rijn and leaving an indelible mark as a post-Impressionist. His art, characterized by vivid colors, bold and <u>emphatic</u> brushstrokes, and distinct forms, exerted a profound influence on the development of Expressionism in contemporary art. Remarkably, Van Gogh's artistic legacy surged in popularity after his demise, particularly during the latter half of the twentieth century.

As used in the text, what does the word "emphatic" most nearly mean?

A) Forceful

B) Successful

C) Hesitant

D) Indecisive

4   ☐ **Mark for Review**

Construction workers in Suffolk, England, made a startling discovery while preparing to build a housing development: they uncovered a cemetery dating back 1,400 years, from the seventh century. This ancient burial ground in Oulton, near Lowestoft in Suffolk, was used by an Anglo-Saxon farming community and contains the remains of around 200 individuals, including men, women, and children. What makes this find particularly eerie is that many of the skeletons have _____ time due to the acidic soil, leaving behind only "sand silhouettes" or dark outlines of the bodies that were once interred in the graves.

Which choice completes the text with the most logical and precise word or phrase?

A) eroded in

B) perished through

C) degraded over

D) dissolved in

5   ☐ **Mark for Review**

The Adventures of Tom Sawyer holds a dual charm; firstly, it enchants young adolescents with the _____ and thrilling escapades of an ordinary boy, which remain captivating and delightful, tapping into the universal instincts shared by youth across different eras and cultures. Secondly, the novel appeals to adult readers who fondly reminisce about their own childhoods when reading about Tom's wild exploits.

Which choice completes the text with the most logical and precise word or phrase?

A) energetic

B) eccentric

C) elaborate

D) exhilarating

6   ☐ **Mark for Review**

The following text is from Marjane Satrapi's 2000 graphic memoir *Persepolis*. The speaker is describing her departure from Iran to Austria.

> Before the revolution, my parents sent me to summer camp in Austria. My mother didn't want me to grow up like an only child. "We feel it's better for you to be far away and happy than close by and miserable. Judging by the situation here, you'll be better off somewhere else." At that point, I started to have my doubts. Why say those things if they were coming too? I repeated what they told me over and over in my head. I was pretty sure they weren't coming to Vienna. I stayed up all night and wondered if the moon shone as brightly in Vienna. The next day, I filled a jar with soil from our garden, Iranian soil. I took down all of my posters.

Which choice best describes the function of the underlined sentence in the text as a whole?

A) It represents the speaker's excitement to leave her home in Iran.

B) It presents a stark contrast to the actions of the speaker's parents.

C) It confirms the speaker's diligent and action-oriented nature during challenging times.

D) It manifests the speaker's understanding and acceptance of the upcoming departure.

7   ☐ **Mark for Review**

Text 1

Tropical mountain songbird species tend to inhabit narrow elevational ranges. For example, birds living on the west slope of the Peruvian Andes strictly conform to their elevational limits. If these birds were to go lower or higher than their usual elevation, they would struggle to survive due to the extreme hot or cold conditions.

Text 2

One dominant explanation for the limited elevational range of tropical mountain songbird species is competition. When each species inhabits a defined, small elevational range, each species is less likely to compete for resources with other species living at other elevations. Therefore, the birds may not be as sensitive to temperature as some believe, but they are extremely vulnerable to over-competition for food resources.

Based on the texts, how would the author of Text 2 most likely respond to the statements presented in Text 1?

A) By expressing that tropical mountain birds that live at lower elevations are more similar in their genetics

B) By agreeing that tropical mountain birds have narrow elevational ranges in which they live

C) By comparing the attributes of birds living at high elevations with those of birds residing in lower elevations

D) By confirming that tropical mountain birds have specific climatic conditions in which they can survive

8 ☐ **Mark for Review**

The following is an excerpt from *The Prince* by Nicolo Machiavelli.

> Men, walking almost always in paths beaten by others, and following by imitation their deeds, are yet unable to keep entirely to the ways of others or attain to the power of those they imitate. A wise man ought always to follow the paths beaten by great men, and to imitate those who have been supreme, so that if his ability does not equal theirs, at least it will savor of it. Let him act like the clever archers who, designing to hit the mark, and knowing the limits to which the strength of their bow attains, take aim much higher than the mark.

According to the text, which choice best describes the views of Machiavelli?

A) Wise men must carve their own ways to achieve success.

B) Imitation is the easiest way to succeed.

C) Archers aim higher because they know the limitations of their physical strength.

D) Most men are unable to succeed even after imitating others.

9 ☐ **Mark for Review**

Researchers at the Georgia Institute of Technology are studying cat locomotion to better understand how the spinal cord works to help humans with partial spinal cord damage walk and maintain balance. Using a mix of experimental studies and computational models, the researchers show that somatosensory feedback, or neural signals from specialized sensors throughout a cat's body, help inform the spinal cord about the ongoing movement and coordinate the four limbs to keep cats from falling when they encounter obstacles. Research suggests that with those motion-related sensory signals, the animal can walk even if the connection between the spinal cord and the brain is partially fractured.

According to the text, how did the researchers determine that cats would be able to walk even if the connection between the spinal cord and the brain is partially fractured?

A) They examined the somatosensory feedback a cat experiences when moving.

B) They watched how the cat coordinates all four limbs when they encounter obstacles.

C) They studied how a cat's spinal cord informs specialized sensors throughout the cat's body.

D) They monitored a cat with partial spinal cord damage and tracked its ongoing movement and coordination.

10   ⃞ **Mark for Review**

William Shakespeare, often hailed as the greatest playwright in the English language, remains an enigmatic figure whose life and works continue to intrigue scholars and enthusiasts alike. In a thesis on the plays of Shakespeare, a student asserts that Shakespeare's plays often feature intricate wordplay and nuanced character development.

Which quotation from a literary critic best supports the student's claim?

A) "Shakespeare's genius lies in his ability to infuse each character with a distinct voice and personality, creating a rich depiction of human experience."

B) "Through his masterful use of language, Shakespeare creates dialogues that are at once poetic and profound, inviting audiences to marvel at the complexities of the human condition."

C) "In Shakespeare's works, each character may be defined clearly but it is the interaction between characters, often characterized by complex wit and repartee, that shows the playwright's keen understanding of human nature."

D) "The depth of Shakespeare's characters is revealed not only through their actions but also through their soliloquies and asides, offering insight into their innermost thoughts and motivations."

11   ⃞ **Mark for Review**

In a recent study conducted by nutritionists at Johns Hopkins University, researchers investigated the impact of Mediterranean diet adherence on cardiovascular health among middle-aged adults. They found that individuals who adhered strictly to the Mediterranean diet experienced a significant reduction in their risk of developing heart disease compared to those who did not follow the diet. The researchers theorized that the diet's emphasis on whole grains, fruits, vegetables, and healthy fats like olive oil could contribute to its protective effects against cardiovascular issues.

Which finding from the study, if true, would most strongly support the researchers' claims?

A) Individuals who adhered to the Mediterranean diet reported higher levels of overall well-being and lower rates of depression compared to those on other dietary plans.

B) Regular consumers of olive oil exhibited lower levels of LDL cholesterol, commonly known as "bad" cholesterol, which is a major risk factor for heart disease.

C) Participants in the study who followed the Mediterranean diet experienced significant weight loss and reduced waist circumference throughout the study period, indicating improved metabolic health.

D) Despite adherence to the Mediterranean diet, some individuals in the study still developed heart disease, suggesting that factors beyond diet alone may influence cardiovascular health outcomes.

12 🔖 Mark for Review

% of 21-year-olds Who Have Reached Each Life Milestone

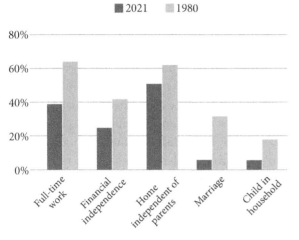

Annual U.S. census data tracks progress towards life milestones, such as financial achievements and changes in households. In the U.S. census, financial independence is defined as earning an annual income surpassing 150% of the poverty line. Additionally, a person is defined as having reached the "marriage" milestone if they are currently or have ever been married. If 21 years is used as a benchmark age by which one can reach certain life milestones, by comparing data from 1980 and 2010, _____

Which choice most effectively uses data from the graph to complete the statement?

A) young adults today are reaching life milestones earlier than young adults in the past.

B) young adults in the past are reaching life milestones earlier than young adults today.

C) young adults reach financial-related milestones earlier than family or house-related milestones.

D) young adults reach financial-related milestones later than family or house-related milestones.

13 🔖 Mark for Review

In the Phaidon book, *Co-Art: Artists on Creative Collaboration*, the renowned feminist art collective Guerilla Girls highlight a significant trend in the art world. They observe that there are numerous collaborative practices in various fields like film, theater, and music, further adding that the notion of solitary genius is now obsolete. In an essay about the advantages of artist collectives, a student claims that artist collectives hold several distinct advantages.

Which quotation from an art critic best illustrates the student's claims?

A) "Within art collectives, artists often wrestle with the intricacies of forging an autonomous artistic identity, as the gravitational pull of their peers' influences hinders their creative cores."

B) "Artists within collectives often engage in interdisciplinary collaborations, breaking down traditional boundaries between art forms and pushing the boundaries of creative expression."

C) "Individual artists frequently excel in art-making expeditiously, while art collectives often encumber the creative process with protracted debates."

D) "Art collectives, while fostering collaboration, often succumb to the chaos of creative differences, resulting in a fractured and discordant output."

14   ☐ **Mark for Review**

In some of the U.S.'s major critical states, voting reforms could significantly alter the way citizens can vote. While Republicans in Ohio are desiring stricter voter laws, Democrats in Michigan want to transform their constitution to allow early voting. Much of these changes are a result of the 2022 election and reformers are hoping to achieve these transformations before the upcoming 2024 November election. However, it is expected that _____.

Which choice most logically completes the text?

A) the upcoming election will play a major role in the enforcement of these reforms.

B) Democrat Michigan voters will have problems with voting for several election cycles.

C) many of these proposed voting reforms will take decades to fully come into effect.

D) Republicans in Michigan will also support early voting.

15   ☐ **Mark for Review**

In order to pay off their war debt, the British government enacted numerous tax laws upon the American colonists including taxes on newspapers, playing cards, paint, glass, lead, and tea. These acts, along with others that imposed British soldiers and their rule upon the colonists, enraged American patriots who desired to break away from British rule and laws that appeared tyrannical. As a result, on December 16, 1773, they committed the first major defiance against these laws by dumping 342 chests of tea imported by the British East India Company into the Boston Harbor, a rebellious act history remembers as the Boston Tea Party. Experts scholars have argued that _____.

Which choice most logically completes the text?

A) the colonists believed that their actions were appropriate since the tax laws were unjust.

B) the colonists planned on continuing to participate in more protests in order to attempt to change the laws.

C) the colonists argued that all laws stemming from British rule were unjust and should be broken.

D) the colonists felt that the only way to change the laws was to break them.

16 ☐ **Mark for Review**

Superhero Black Panther is a majestic and regal character with an intricate costume that references the superhero's African heritage and ancestry. The costume worn by the late Chadwick Boseman in the 2018 movie from Marvel Studios consists of multiple raised triangles, which the costume designer referred to as "sacred geometry of Africa" due to _____ significance in African symbolism and imagery.

Which choice completes the text so that it conforms to the conventions of Standard English?

A) its

B) it's

C) their

D) they're

17 ☐ **Mark for Review**

Jade Snow Wong's Cold War World Tour took her to places few could imagine. She traveled not only to the United States, where she was _____ solely to her ancestral homeland of China. Instead, her journey spanned continents, encompassing Europe and Asia. Wong's exploration of her heritage in the midst of Cold War tensions made her an inspiring figure who transcended borders and ideologies.

Which choice completes the text so that it conforms to the conventions of Standard English?

A) born, and

B) born, but

C) born, nor

D) born, yet

18 ☐ **Mark for Review**

Dr. Seuss' books are renowned in children's literature for their playful characters and witty rhymes. Among his most famous titles are *The Cat in the Hat*, *Green Eggs and Ham*, and *How the Grinch Stole Christmas*. These books have left a lasting impact, inspiring generations of readers, and his influence _____ through numerous adaptations and derivative works.

Which choice completes the text so that it conforms to the conventions of Standard English?

A) will endure

B) will have endured

C) had endured

D) endures

19 ☐ **Mark for Review**

A new generation of virtually noiseless, eco-friendly tractors _____ to liberate farmers from the limitations of traditional agriculture, going far beyond dependence on fossil fuels. These autonomous e-tractors, driven by electric vehicle (EV) and robotics innovations, enhance efficiency across farming tasks, from planting and weeding to harvesting and equipment maintenance. They have the potential to pave the way for improved labor, field management, and sustainability practices.

Which choice completes the text so that it conforms to the conventions of Standard English?

A) promise

B) promises

C) will be promising

D) have promised

20   ☐ **Mark for Review**

Solar electricity works by harnessing the power of the sun's rays. Solar panels, made up of photovoltaic cells, capture sunlight and convert it into electricity. These cells contain _____ and generate an electrical current. It's this clean and sustainable energy source that has the potential to transform our energy landscape and reduce our reliance on fossil fuels.

Which choice completes the text so that it conforms to the conventions of Standard English?

A) semiconductors, that absorb photons from the sun to, release electrons

B) semiconductors, that absorb photons from the sun to release electrons

C) semiconductors (that absorb photons from the sun to) release electrons

D) semiconductors, that absorb photons from the sun, to release electrons

21   ☐ **Mark for Review**

The Aasvik family _____ on a quest to locate a lost earring using a metal detector near their residence on Jomfruland, an isolated and scarcely populated island off the southeast coast of mainland Norway. They stumbled upon an intriguing discovery and uncovered two bronze brooches beneath a tree. Local archaeologists suggest these findings point to the burial of an aristocratic Viking woman around 1,200 years ago.

Which choice completes the text so that it conforms to the conventions of Standard English?

A) is

B) were

C) will be

D) was

22   ☐ **Mark for Review**

Banksy's artwork masterfully combines artistry with essential anti-war messages. His thought-provoking pieces not only captivate the eye but also challenge the mind. Through clever juxtapositions and vivid imagery, Banksy highlights the devastating consequences of armed _____.

Which choice completes the text so that it conforms to the conventions of Standard English?

A) conflict, reminding us, that the pursuit of peace is not just a choice but an imperative for humanity

B) conflict, reminding us that the pursuit of peace, is not just a choice but an imperative for humanity

C) conflict, reminding us that the pursuit of peace is, not just a choice, but an imperative for humanity

D) conflict, reminding us that the pursuit of peace is not just a choice but an imperative for humanity

23   ☐ **Mark for Review**

Teens involved exclusively in sports were the least likely to report depressive symptoms. _____ there was no difference in depressive symptoms between teens involved in the arts who also did sports and teens involved in the arts who did not also participate in sports. This suggests that arts participation rather than a lack of sports participation was associated with depression.

Which choice completes the text with the most logical transition?

A) Secondly,

B) Consequently,

C) Moreover,

D) However,

24   🔖 **Mark for Review**

The Battle of Marengo had a significant impact on Napoleon Bonaparte. Taking place on June 14, 1800, in northern Italy, it marked a crucial turning point in his military career. Despite facing initial setbacks, Napoleon's strategic brilliance and determination led to a decisive victory against the Austrian forces. This triumph not only secured his hold on power but also solidified his reputation as a military genius. _____ the Battle of Marengo bolstered Napoleon's confidence, enabling him to further expand his empire and shape European history for years to come.

Which choice completes the text with the most logical transition?

A) However,

B) Additionally,

C) Indeed,

D) Nevertheless,

25   🔖 **Mark for Review**

While researching a topic, a student has taken the following notes:

- The African gray hornbill belongs to the Hornbill family, a group of predominantly tropical birds found in the Old World.

- This species commonly breeds in a portion of sub-Saharan Africa and the southwestern parts of the Arabian Peninsula.

- African gray hornbills have escaped or have been intentionally released in Florida, USA. However, there is currently no evidence of a breeding population. Any existing individuals in the area are likely the result of ongoing releases or escapes.

- The African gray hornbill measures 45-51 cm (18-20 inches) in length, considered large for a hornbill species.

- African gray hornbills are widely distributed in sub-Saharan Africa, favoring open woodland and savannah habitats. However, their population has recently declined due to them being hunted down in large numbers.

The student wants to emphasize that it is unlikely that the African gray hornbill will rapidly multiply in Florida. Which choice most effectively uses relevant information from the notes to accomplish this goal?

A) The African gray hornbill is a larger hornbill and is easy to hunt down.

B) It seems likely that the presence of the African gray hornbill is due to a deliberate release or escape, with no proof of breeding.

C) The African gray hornbill is only commonly found in sub-Saharan Africa where the landscape includes open woodlands.

D) It is a tropical bird that is only widespread in open woodland and savannah areas.

26   ☐ Mark for Review

While researching a topic, a student has taken the following notes:

- The neocortex is the most evolved part of the human brain.

- It is responsible for higher functions such as sensory perception, generation of motor commands, and conscious thought.

- The hippocampus, another part of the human brain, is critical for learning and memory.

- In a 2018 study, it was found that the hippocampus and neocortex engage in dialogue when memories are being formed and consolidated.

- In a 2020 study, it was discovered that the same dialogue, involving the hippocampus and neocortex, occurs during the process of dream generation.

The student wants to emphasize a similarity in patterns involving the neocortex and hippocampus. Which choice most effectively uses relevant information from the notes to accomplish this goal?

A) Both the neocortex, responsible for higher functions such as sensory perception, and the hippocampus, critical for learning and memory, are components of the human brain.

B) Studies from 2018 and 2020 have illustrated a similar pattern of dialogue between the neocortex and hippocampus during both memory formation and dream generation.

C) As the most evolved segment of the human brain, the neocortex underpins higher functions, including conscious thought.

D) Research conducted in 2020 revealed that the dream-creation process runs concurrently with a consistent interaction between the hippocampus and the neocortex.

27   ☐ Mark for Review

While researching a topic, a student has taken the following notes:

- The "Thirty-by-thirty" initiative aims to protect 30% of the planet by 2030.

- In a new study, a group of researchers proposed a market-based system to boost conservation.

- Participants in the system can trade conservation credits to offset any negative environmental impacts.

- Their study combined data on marine species and fisheries revenue to create a model demonstrating significant cost savings through a conservation market.

- The results showed that allowing voluntary trade of conservation credits can lower conservation costs by up to 90%.

- This market system could help developing nations by providing flexibility that allows for both economic growth and conservation priorities.

The student wants to emphasize the new mechanism created to reduce conservation costs. Which choice most effectively uses relevant information from the notes to accomplish this goal?

A) To protect 30% of the planet by 2030, nations need a flexible method to support growing economies while conserving the environment.

B) A new study examined marine species levels and revenue from fisheries.

C) Conservation costs can be lowered by up to 90%, contributing to progress towards the "Thirty-by-thirty" initiative.

D) In a market-based system, nations can trade conservation credits to mitigate actions with negative environmental impacts.

Answer Key

Question Number	1	2	3	4	5	6	7	8	9	10	11	12	13	14
Correct Answer	D	A	A	C	D	D	B	A	A	C	B	B	B	C
Your Answer														

Question Number	15	16	17	18	19	20	21	22	23	24	25	26	27
Correct Answer	A	C	C	D	B	B	D	D	D	B	B	B	B
Your Answer													

IMPORTANT
READ THE BELOW INSTRUCTION BEFORE MOVING AHEAD.

- Turn to page 404 and start with Module 1 of the Math section.

Math

22 QUESTIONS | 35 MINUTES

The questions in this section address a number of important math skills. Use of a calculator is permitted for all questions.

Unless otherwise indicated: • All variables and expressions represent real numbers • Figures provided are drawn to scale • All figures lie in a plane • The domain of a given function is the set of all real numbers x for which $f(x)$ is a real number

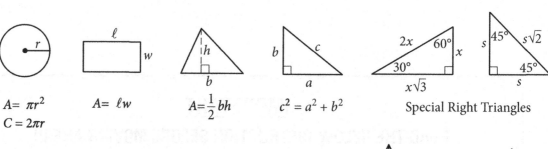

$A = \pi r^2$
$C = 2\pi r$

$A = \ell w$

$A = \frac{1}{2}bh$

$c^2 = a^2 + b^2$

Special Right Triangles

$V = \ell wh$

$V = \pi r^2 h$

$V = \frac{4}{3}\pi r^3$

$V = \frac{1}{3}\pi r^2 h$

$V = \frac{1}{3}\ell wh$

The number of degrees of arc in a circle is 360.

The number of radians of arc in a circle is 2π.

The sum of the measures in degrees of the angles of a triangle is 180.

For **multiple–choice questions,** solve each problem, choose the correct answer from the choices provided, and then circle your answer in this book. Circle only one answer for each question. If you change your mind, completely erase the circle. You will not get credit for questions with more than one answer circled, or for questions with no answers circled.

For **student–produced response questions,** solve each problem and write your answer next to or under the question in the test book as described below.

- Once you've written your answer, circle it clearly. You will not receive credit for anything written outside the circle, or for any questions with more than one circled answer.

- If you find more than one correct answer, write and circle only one answer.

- Your answer can be up to 5 characters for a positive answer and up to 6 characters (including the negative sign) for a negative answer, but no more.

- If your answer is a fraction that is too long (over 5 characters for positive, 6 characters for negative), write the decimal equivalent.

- If your answer is a decimal that is too long (over 5 characters for positive, 6 characters for negative), truncate it or round at the fourth digit.

- If your answer is a mixed number (such as $3\frac{1}{2}$), write it as an improper fraction $\left(\frac{7}{2}\right)$ or its decimal equivalent (3.5).

- Don't include symbols such as a percent sign, comma, or dollar sign in your circled answer.

1 ☐ **Mark for Review**

Kelly had 50 flowers on her balcony. She picked 12% of them to put in a vase. How many flowers did Kelly pick to put in the vase?

A) 4

B) 6

C) 8

D) 12

2 ☐ **Mark for Review**

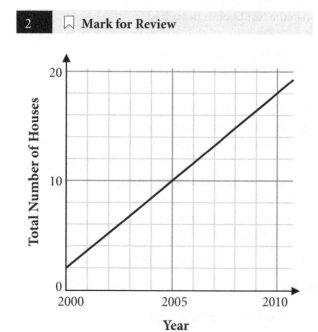

Year

The number of houses designed by an architect from 2000 to 2010 is represented by the graph above. If x represents the number of years after 2000, which expression best represents the total number of houses?

A) $\dfrac{5}{8}x$

B) $\dfrac{8}{5}x$

C) $\dfrac{5}{8}x + 2$

D) $\dfrac{8}{5}x + 2$

3 ☐ **Mark for Review**

$$x + 2 \le -2x + 5$$

What is the greatest integer solution for the equation above?

4 ☐ **Mark for Review**

$$f(x) = (x - 5)^2 - 4$$

What is the minimum value of the function above?

A) −5

B) −4

C) 3

D) 7

5 ☐ **Mark for Review**

	Yes	No
Parent		21
Teacher	2	

In a Parent Teacher meeting a vote to remodel the library was cast unanimously as shown on the given table. There were 36 parents and 7 teachers in the meeting. What is the probability that a parent chosen at random voted yes to the remodeling of the library?

6   🔖 **Mark for Review**

The ratio of Grade 7 students to Grade 8 students is $\frac{3}{4}$. If there are 240 Grade 8 students, how many are Grade 7 students?

A) 160

B) 180

C) 200

D) 320

7   🔖 **Mark for Review**

Week	Total savings
0	$120
1	$145
2	$170
3	$195

Janine is saving the same amount of money on a weekly basis. The table above shows her total savings. If x represents the number of weeks, which function below best represents her total savings?

A) $f(x) = 25x$

B) $f(x) = 20x + 120$

C) $f(x) = 25x + 120$

D) $f(x) = 120x + 25$

8   🔖 **Mark for Review**

$$mx + ny + 2 = 0$$

The given equation represents a line passing through the point $(3, 5)$ and having an x-intercept of -2. What is the value of n?

A) $-\dfrac{11}{5}$

B) -1

C) 1

D) $\dfrac{11}{5}$

9   🔖 **Mark for Review**

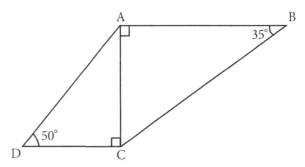

If $\triangle ABC$ and $\triangle ACD$ are right triangles, which of the following is true?

A) $\dfrac{\overline{AB}}{\overline{AD}} < 1.1$

B) $\dfrac{\overline{BC}}{\overline{AD}} > 1.4$

C) $\dfrac{\overline{AB}}{\overline{DC}} > 1.8$

D) $\dfrac{\overline{BC}}{\overline{DC}} < 1.9$

10 🔖 **Mark for Review**

Tom and Paul spend the same amount of money to buy items from a store. Tom buys 4 pieces of item A and 5 pieces of item B while Paul buys 6 pieces of item A and 2 pieces of item B. If a piece of item A and a piece of item B costs $2, how much do 3 pieces of item A and 2 pieces of item B cost?

A) $4.8

B) $5.2

C) $6.4

D) $8.8

11 🔖 **Mark for Review**

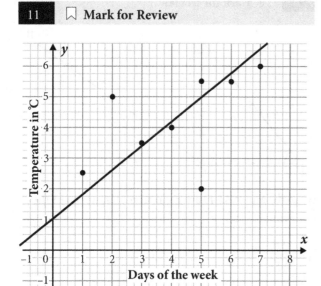

The above scatter plot shows the temperature in °C in city Y which is recorded over a period of 7 days. What is the percentage increase from the predicted temperature to the actual temperature on day 5?

A) 10%

B) 40%

C) 60%

D) 175%

12 🔖 **Mark for Review**

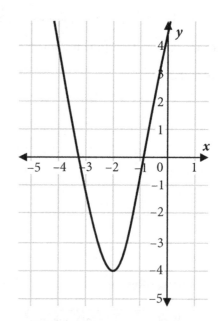

The graph of a function f is shown. Which of the following equations defines f?

A) $f(x) = 2x^2 + 8x + 8$

B) $f(x) = 2x^2 + 8x - 4$

C) $f(x) = 2(x + 2)^2 - 4$

D) $f(x) = 2(x - 2)^2 - 4$

13 🔖 **Mark for Review**

David can solve 10 math questions per hour. He aims to increase this rate by 3 questions per hour monthly. How many months will it take for him to be able to solve 28 questions per hour, following this plan?

A) 3

B) 6

C) 12

D) 18

If $y = -qx^2 + 3x + 7$ and $y = 5$ have two distinct real roots, what is the possible value of q?

A) -9

B) -8

C) $-\dfrac{9}{8}$

D) $\dfrac{9}{8}$

$$f(x) = (x - 1)^2 + 20$$

What is the minimum value of the given function?

A) -2

B) -1

C) 19

D) 20

The magnitude of the electrostatic force F between 2 point charges q_1 and q_2 separated by a distance r is given by $F = k\dfrac{q_1 \cdot q_2}{r^2}$, where k is a constant equal to $\dfrac{1}{4\pi\varepsilon_0} \cdot \varepsilon_0$ is the permittivity of free space. Find the expression of r in terms of F, q_1, q_2 and ε_0.

A) $r = \dfrac{1}{2}\sqrt{\dfrac{q_1 \cdot q_2}{\pi\varepsilon_0 F}}$

B) $r = 2\sqrt{\dfrac{\pi\varepsilon_0 q_1 \cdot q_2}{F}}$

C) $r = \sqrt{\dfrac{\varepsilon_0 q_1 \cdot q_2}{F}}$

D) $r = \dfrac{q_1 \cdot q_2}{4\pi\varepsilon_0 F}$

$$2x + ay = 3$$

Given the equation where a is a constant less than -2. Which could be the graph of this equation in the xy-plane?

A)

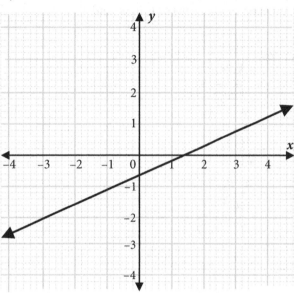

B)

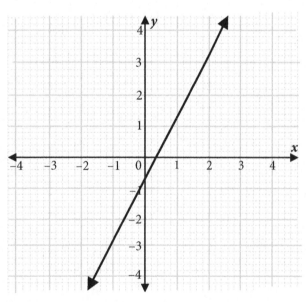

C)

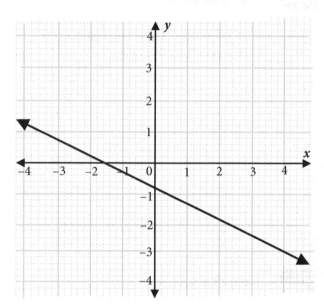

D)

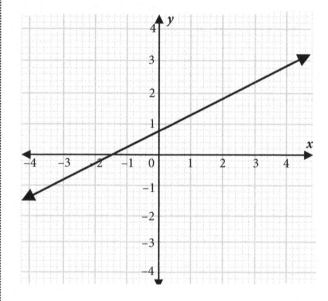

18 ⬚ **Mark for Review**

$$3(x - 2) = \frac{4y - 8}{2}$$

$$2x - 3y = 3$$

Given the equations of two lines, which statement is true regarding the graphs of the two lines in the xy-plane?

A) The two lines are parallel.

B) The two lines are perpendicular.

C) The two lines have the same x-intercept.

D) The two lines have the same y-intercept.

19 ⬚ **Mark for Review**

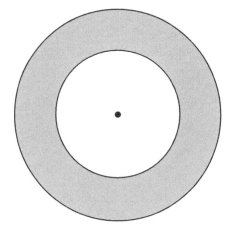

In the figure, the ratio of the circumference of the smaller circle to that of the larger circle is 0.6. What is the ratio of the area of the shaded region to that of the larger circle?

A) $\dfrac{9}{25}$

B) $\dfrac{3}{5}$

C) $\dfrac{16}{25}$

D) $\dfrac{16}{9}$

20 ⬚ **Mark for Review**

The mean of 7 numbers is a. The mean of 4 of these numbers is b. What is the expression of the mean of the 3 remaining numbers?

A) $\dfrac{a - 4b}{3}$

B) $\dfrac{7a - b}{3}$

C) $\dfrac{7a - 4b}{3}$

D) $7a - 4b$

21 ⬚ **Mark for Review**

$$12x^2 + 12y^2 + 3x - 9y - 10 = 0$$

The given equation represents a circle in the xy-plane. What is the length of its radius to the nearest hundredth?

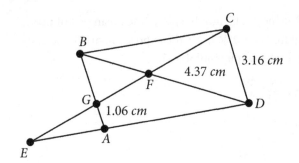

In the figure, $ABCD$ is a parallelogram, $AG = 1.06$ *cm*, $CD = 3.16$ *cm*, and $FD = 4.37$ *cm*. Also, E, G, F and C are collinear. What is the length of BF to the nearest tenth of a *cm*?

A) 1.5 *cm*

B) 2.9 *cm*

C) 3.1 *cm*

D) 3.3 *cm*

Answer Key

Question Number	1	2	3	4	5	6	7	8	9	10	11
Correct Answer	D	B	1	B	$\frac{5}{12}$	B	C	B	A	B	A
Your Answer											

Question Number	12	13	14	15	16	17	18	19	20	21	22
Correct Answer	C	B	D	D	A	A	D	C	C	0.99	B
Your Answer											

IMPORTANT

READ THE BELOW INSTRUCTIONS BEFORE MOVING AHEAD.

- If you got less than 15 answers correct, turn to page 414 and take Module 2 (Easy).

- If you got more than 15 answers correct, turn to page 422 and take Module 2 (Hard).

Math

22 QUESTIONS | 35 MINUTES

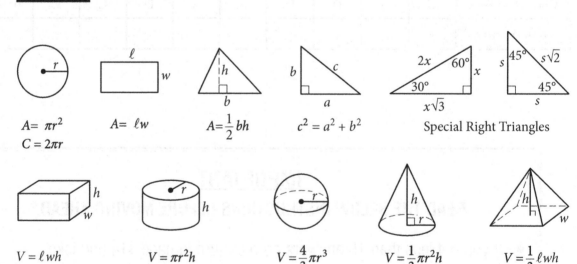

For **multiple–choice questions,** solve each problem, choose the correct answer from the choices provided, and then circle your answer in this book. Circle only one answer for each question. If you change your mind, completely erase the circle. You will not get credit for questions with more than one answer circled, or for questions with no answers circled.

For **student–produced response questions,** solve each problem and write your answer next to or under the question in the test book as described below.

- Once you've written your answer, circle it clearly. You will not receive credit for anything written outside the circle, or for any questions with more than one circled answer.

- If you find more than one correct answer, write and circle only one answer.

- Your answer can be up to 5 characters for a positive answer and up to 6 characters (including the negative sign) for a negative answer, but no more.

- If your answer is a fraction that is too long (over 5 characters for positive, 6 characters for negative), write the decimal equivalent.

- If your answer is a decimal that is too long (over 5 characters for positive, 6 characters for negative), truncate it or round at the fourth digit.

- If your answer is a mixed number (such as $3\frac{1}{2}$), write it as an improper fraction $\left(\frac{7}{2}\right)$ or its decimal equivalent (3.5).

- Don't include symbols such as a percent sign, comma, or dollar sign in your circled answer.

1   ☐ **Mark for Review**

Wendy can walk 1 mile in 45 minutes, how many miles can she walk in 1 hour?

A) $\dfrac{1}{45}$

B) $\dfrac{10}{9}$

C) $\dfrac{4}{3}$

D) $\dfrac{20}{9}$

2   ☐ **Mark for Review**

The function f is defined by the equation $f(x) = 5x - 8$. What is the value of $f(x)$ when $x = 2$?

A) −1

B) 2

C) 17

D) 18

3   ☐ **Mark for Review**

Tori and Kelly went to the bookstore. Tori bought 4 pens and 2 books which came to a total of $8.30 and Kelly bought 1 pen and 4 books which came to a total of $8.20. What is the price of a pen at the bookstore? (Ignore the $ sign)

4   ☐ **Mark for Review**

$$4x = 8$$
$$4x + y = 13$$

4 chocolate bars cost $8, and 4 chocolate bars plus a sandwich cost $13. This situation is represented by the given system. What is the price of a sandwich, y, in dollars?

5   ☐ **Mark for Review**

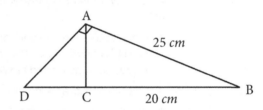

The figure ABD above is a right triangle. If line AC perpendicularly bisects line DB, what is the length of line AD in cm?

6   ☐ **Mark for Review**

Today, Ben is four times as old as John. In four years, Ben will be twice as old as John will be. How old is John now?

A) 2

B) 6

C) 8

D) 12

7   🔖 **Mark for Review**

The equation $h(x)=1,200(1.25)^x$ represents the number of pencils used by students at a certain school, where x is the number of years since the school opened. Which of the following statements is true?

A) There were 1,200 pencils used one year after the school was opened.

B) The number of pencils used increases by 125% every year.

C) There were 2,344 pencils used 3 years after the school was opened.

D) The number of pencils used increases by 25% every two years.

8   🔖 **Mark for Review**

In 1950, there were 5 houses in a certain residential area. If 3 new houses are built every year, which of the following functions represents the total number of houses in that residential area where x is the number of years after 1950?

A) $f(x) = 5x + 3$

B) $f(x) = 3x + 5$

C) $f(x) = 5x$

D) $f(x) = 3x$

9   🔖 **Mark for Review**

The gold reserve of Country A in 1995 is 150 tons. Since then, the reserve is decreasing exponentially at a rate of 2% every 10 years. If t represents the number of years after 2015, which function best represents the situation?

A) $h(t) = 150(0.98)^{\frac{t}{10}}$

B) $h(t) = 150(0.98)^{10t}$

C) $h(t) = 150(1.02)^{\frac{t}{10}}$

D) $h(t) = 150(1.02)^{10t}$

10   🔖 **Mark for Review**

$$x^2 + 3 = 4$$
$$(x^2 + 3)^3 = y$$

The ordered pair (x, y) is a solution to the given system of equations. What is y?

A) -1

B) 1

C) 27

D) 64

11   🔖 **Mark for Review**

$$16x^2 - 64$$

Which of the following is an equivalent form of the expression above?

A) $(4x - 8)^2$

B) $4(2x + 4)(2x - 4)$

C) $2(8x - 32)$

D) $(2x - 4)^2$

12   🔖 **Mark for Review**

$$4^4 + 4^4 + 4^4 + 4^4 = 2^t$$

In the equation above, what is the value of t?

A) 6

B) 8

C) 10

D) 12

13   🔖 **Mark for Review**

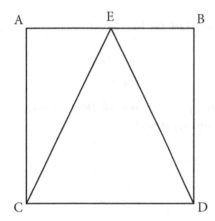

In the image shown above, figure ABCD is a square. If $\overline{CE}$ is equal to $\overline{ED}$, what is the value of $\angle ECD$?

A) 45°

B) 53.14°

C) 60°

D) 63.43°

14   🔖 **Mark for Review**

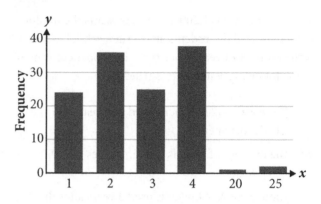

The bar chart shows the frequency of the numbers in a data set. Looking at the shape of the bar chart, which statement is true about the median and the mean?

A) The median is greater than the mean.

B) The median is approximately equal to the mean.

C) The median is less than the mean.

D) There is not enough information to conclude which quantity is greater.

15 ☐ Mark for Review

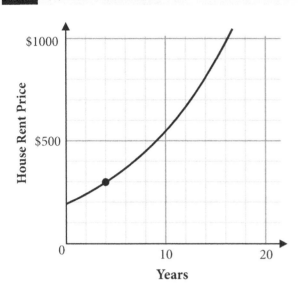

The growth of house rent price from the year 2000 is shown on the graph above. The house rent price in 2004 is represented by the green dot on the graph. If x is the number of years after 2000, which equation below represents the growth model for house rent price?

A) $f(x) = 200(2)^{\frac{x}{4}}$

B) $f(x) = 200(1.5)^x$

C) $f(x) = 200(2)^x$

D) $f(x) = 200(1.5)^{\frac{x}{4}}$

16 ☐ Mark for Review

$$h(t) = -5t^2 + 2t + 3$$

Kenny threw a ball across a field. The function $h(t)$ represents the height of the ball in meters in the air during its trajectory, where t is time in seconds. What is the maximum height the ball reached during its trajectory?

17 ☐ Mark for Review

X	−5	0	1	2	3
F(x)	2	2.2	3	7	27

Which of the following represents the function $f(x)$ shown in the table above?

A) $f(x) = 5^x + 2.2$

B) $f(x) = 5^x + 2$

C) $f(x) = 5^{x-1} + 2$

D) $f(x) = 5^{x-1} + 2.2$

18 ☐ Mark for Review

$$g(t) = 8t^2 - 27$$
$$f(t) = g(t - 1)$$

What is the value of $f(4)$?

A) −27

B) 45

C) 101

D) 173

19 ☐ Mark for Review

$$x^3 - 5x^2 + 3x + 2 = (x + b)^2 (x + 1) + c$$

For the equation above, what is the value of c?

20 ☐ **Mark for Review**

$$2(-3x+2)-1 > \frac{9x}{2}$$

The solution to the given inequality is $x < a$ where a is a constant. What is the value of a?

21 ☐ **Mark for Review**

$$2y = x - 1$$
$$y = (2x - 1)^2 - (x - 1)^2$$

If (x_1, y_1) and (x_2, y_2) are solutions to the system of equations shown above and $x_1 < x_2$, what is the value of $\frac{y_2}{y_1}$?

A) -1

B) $-\frac{1}{2}$

C) $\frac{3}{4}$

D) $\frac{3}{2}$

22 ☐ **Mark for Review**

The total surface area of a hemispheric lidless plastic bowl is given by $A_{bowl} = 2\pi r^2$, where r is the radius of the imaginary straight cap. If the radius r is decreased by 26%, what happens to the surface area of the bowl?

A) The surface area decreases by 26%.

B) The surface area decreases by 45.24%.

C) The surface area decreases by 54.76%.

D) The surface area decreases by 74%.

Answer Key

Question Number	1	2	3	4	5	6	7	8	9	10	11
Correct Answer	C	B	1.20	5	18.7	A	C	B	A	D	B
Your Answer											

Question Number	12	13	14	15	16	17	18	19	20	21	22
Correct Answer	C	D	C	D	3.2	C	B	−7	$\frac{6}{21}$	C	B
Your Answer											

CONGRATULATIONS!

You completed a full-length SAT test. Now, turn to page 430 to calculate your scaled score for the test.

Math

22 QUESTIONS | 35 MINUTES

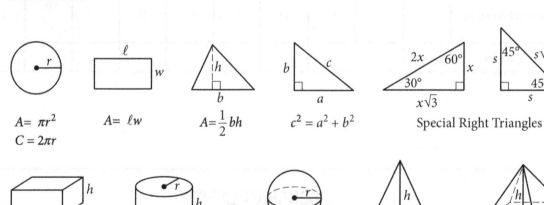

For **multiple–choice questions,** solve each problem, choose the correct answer from the choices provided, and then circle your answer in this book. Circle only one answer for each question. If you change your mind, completely erase the circle. You will not get credit for questions with more than one answer circled, or for questions with no answers circled.

For **student–produced response questions,** solve each problem and write your answer next to or under the question in the test book as described below.

- Once you've written your answer, circle it clearly. You will not receive credit for anything written outside the circle, or for any questions with more than one circled answer.

- If you find more than one correct answer, write and circle only one answer.

- Your answer can be up to 5 characters for a positive answer and up to 6 characters (including the negative sign) for a negative answer, but no more.

- If your answer is a fraction that is too long (over 5 characters for positive, 6 characters for negative), write the decimal equivalent.

- If your answer is a decimal that is too long (over 5 characters for positive, 6 characters for negative), truncate it or round at the fourth digit.

- If your answer is a mixed number (such as $3\frac{1}{2}$), write it as an improper fraction $\left(\frac{7}{2}\right)$ or its decimal equivalent (3.5).

- Don't include symbols such as a percent sign, comma, or dollar sign in your circled answer.

1   ☐ **Mark for Review**

The ratio of the number of chickens to turkeys on a farm is 6:4. If there are 18 turkeys on the farm, how many chickens are on the farm?

2   ☐ **Mark for Review**

The number of cars sold by a company is represented by the function $f(x) = 22x + 835$ where x is the number of years after 2003. In what year will the company achieves a total of 1,495 cars sold?

3   ☐ **Mark for Review**

Beebe is paid 30% commission on sales of dresses and 10% commission on sales of shirts. In her first week, she sells 5 dresses and 20 shirts and earns $65 in commission. In the second week, she sells 3 dresses and 30 shirts and earns a commission of $57. What is the price of one dress?

A) $10

B) $20

C) $30

D) $40

4   ☐ **Mark for Review**

Hannah and Jane made similar designs of bracelets and necklaces using beads. Hannah used 252 beads to make 4 bracelets and 4 necklaces. Jane used 381 beads to make 3 bracelets and 7 necklaces. How many beads does a single necklace require?

5   ☐ **Mark for Review**

In triangle ABC, angle B is a right angle. Knowing that $sin(A) = \dfrac{4}{5}$, what is the value of $cos(C)$?

A) $\dfrac{9}{25}$

B) $\dfrac{16}{25}$

C) $\dfrac{3}{5}$

D) $\dfrac{4}{5}$

6   ☐ **Mark for Review**

The sum of three consecutive numbers is 12 less than four times the largest number. What is the value of the smallest number?

7 ☐ **Mark for Review**

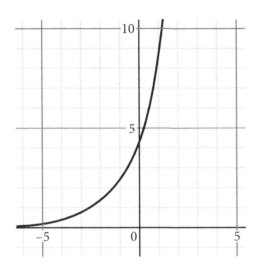

The $p(t) = gh^t$ represents the graphs above, what is the value of g?

8 ☐ **Mark for Review**

A resort charges $50 to rent a boat plus an additional fee of $20 per kilometers traveled. If Vincent rented the boat and went to an island 6 kilometers away from the resort, how much will he have to pay for the whole trip, going to the island and back to the resort?

A) $105

B) $145

C) $240

D) $290

9 ☐ **Mark for Review**

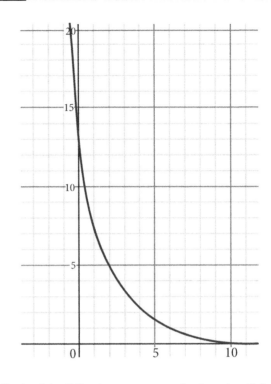

Which of the following represents the function $f(x)$ depicted in the above graph?

A) $f(x) = 14(2)^x$

B) $f(x) = 14(0.5)^x$

C) $f(x) = 7(2)^x$

D) $f(x) = -x + 14$

10 ☐ **Mark for Review**

If $y = 8x^2 - 2x + 9$ intersects at exactly one point to the line $y = p$, what is the value of $8p$?

11 🔖 **Mark for Review**

$$4x^4 + 16x^2 + 16$$

Which of the following is equivalent to the expression above?

A) $(2x^2 + 2x + 4)^2$

B) $(x + 2)^4$

C) $4(x^2 + 2)^2$

D) $4(x + 2)^2$

12 🔖 **Mark for Review**

$$f(x) = \frac{x + 3}{2x^2 - 9x - 5}$$

For what positive value of x does the function $f(x)$ become undefined?

A) -3

B) 0.5

C) 4.5

D) 5

13 🔖 **Mark for Review**

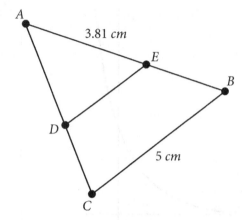

In the figure, $\overline{DE}$ is parallel to $\overline{CB}$. The lengths AE, DE and CB are 3.81 cm, 3 cm and 5 cm respectively. What is the length of $\overline{EB}$?

A) 1.35 cm

B) 2.54 cm

C) 3.35 cm

D) 6.35 cm

14 🔖 **Mark for Review**

The median of a set of 7 negative integers is −26. What is the greatest possible value of the mean of this set?

A) $-\dfrac{116}{7}$

B) $-\dfrac{107}{7}$

C) -1

D) 25

15   🔖 **Mark for Review**

Consider two functions f and g defined by

$f(x) \dfrac{3x}{x^2 - 2x - 1}$ and $g(x) \dfrac{1}{e^{x-2} + 3}$ respectively. What is the value of $f(g(2) - 1)$?

16   🔖 **Mark for Review**

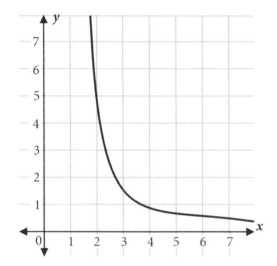

Shown is the partial graph of a rational function f defined by $f(x) = \dfrac{a}{2x + b}$ where a and b are constants. If $h(x) = f(x) - 2$, which equation could define function h?

A) $h(x) = \dfrac{-4x + 11}{2x - 3}$

B) $h(x) = \dfrac{4x + 1}{2x - 3}$

C) $h(x) = \dfrac{10}{2x - 2}$

D) $h(x) = \dfrac{10}{2x + 2}$

17   🔖 **Mark for Review**

Function h is defined by $h(x) = a^x + b$, where a and b are constants and $b = a + 1$. In the xy-plane, the graph of $f(x) = 3\,h(x) + 2$ passes through the point $(0, 14)$. What is the value of a?

A)   2

B)   3

C)   9

D)   14

18   🔖 **Mark for Review**

$$f(t + 1) = 5^t + 3$$

The function $f(t + 1)$ is shown above, what is the y-intercept of the function $f(t)$?

A)   3

B)   3.2

C)   4

D)   8

19

$$\frac{2x(x - 14)}{(3x + 2)(4x - 1)}$$

If the expression above is equivalent to $\dfrac{4ax}{3x + 2} + \dfrac{2bx}{4x - 1}$, what is the value of $b - a$?

20　　☐ **Mark for Review**

$$(k + 2)x - 6x < -12 - 2(3.5x + 5)$$

For what value of k does the inequality above have no real solution?

21　　☐ **Mark for Review**

The volume of a cube of clay decreases in dimensions as it dries. If the volume decreases by 26 *ml* and the length of each edge decreases by 0.15 *cm*, which is closest to the original edge length of the cube? (Given 1 *ml* = 1 *cm³*)

A) 6.7 *cm*

B) 7.7 *cm*

C) 9.1 *cm*

D) 9.4 *cm*

22　　☐ **Mark for Review**

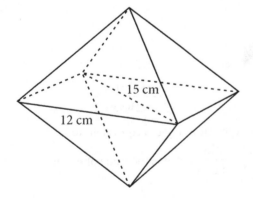

Two identical pyramids are attached at their rectangular bases of length 12 *cm* and diagonal 15 *cm*. If the height of each pyramid is 6 *cm*, what is the total volume of the combined solid in cubic *cm*?

Answer Key

Question Number	1	2	3	4	5	6	7	8	9	10	11
Correct Answer	27	2033	C	48	D	7	4	D	B	71	C
Your Answer											

Question Number	12	13	14	15	16	17	18	19	20	21	22
Correct Answer	D	B	B	$-\dfrac{36}{17}$	A	A	B	-7	-3	B	432
Your Answer											

CONGRATULATIONS!

You completed a full-length SAT test. Now, turn to page 430 to calculate your scaled score for the test.

Know Your Scaled Score

This table can be used to calculate your scaled score. Use a pencil to note down your scores for Module 1 and Module 2 (Easy or Hard).

Input the number of questions you got right for both modules and add them in the adjacent columns. To get your scaled score for each section, refer to the table on page 431. Lastly, add both sections' scaled scores to get your total score for Test #1.

If you attempted the Easy Modules, check your scaled scores in the "Reading and Writing (Easy)" and "Math (Easy)" columns.

If you attempted the Hard Modules, check your scaled scores in the "Reading and Writing (Hard)" and "Math (Hard)" columns.

	Module 1 (Number of correct answers)	Module 2 (Number of correct answers)	Total (Module 1 + Module 2)	Scaled Score
Reading and Writing				
Math				
			Total Score	

SCALED SCORE TABLE

Score	Reading and Writing (Easy)	Reading and Writing (Hard)	Math (Easy)	Math (Hard)
0	200		200	
1	200		200	
2	200		200	
3	200		200	
4	200		200	
5	200		200	
6	200		200	
7	200		200	
8	200		250	
9	200		290	
10	200		310	
11	200		330	
12	200		340	
13	220		340	460
14	240		350	470
15	260		360	480
16	280		370	490
17	300	480	380	500
18	300	490	380	510
19	320	490	390	520
20	340	500	400	530
21	360	500	410	530
22	360	510	410	550
23	380	510	420	560
24	400	520	430	580
25	420	530	440	590
26	430	540	450	600
27	450	550	460	610
28	460	550	470	620
29	470	560	480	620
30	480	560	500	630

SCALED SCORE TABLE

Score	Reading and Writing (Easy)	Reading and Writing (Hard)	Math (Easy)	Math (Hard)
31	490	570	510	630
32	500	580	530	640
33	500	580	540	640
34	510	590	550	650
35	510	590	550	650
36	520	600	550	670
37	520	610	550	690
38	530	620	550	710
39	530	630	550	730
40	540	640	550	750
41	540	640	550	770
42	550	650	550	780
43	550	660	550	790
44	550	680	550	800
45	550	700		
46	550	710		
47	550	730		
48	550	740		
49	550	750		
50	550	760		
51	550	770		
52	550	780		
53	550	790		
54	550	800		

1. **Domain:** CRAFT AND STRUCTURE
    Skill/Knowledge: Words in Context

    Key Explanation: Choice D is correct. "Speculate about" means to form theories or conjectures about something based on available evidence. This choice is the most fitting because it accurately conveys that the scientific community is considering and discussing possible uses for the marked human bones, leading to new light being shed on the practices of prehistoric societies.

    Distractor Explanations: Choice A is incorrect because to "inquire about" means to seek information or ask questions about something. However, the sentence is discussing the scientific community's response to the discovery of marked human bones, which involves more than just asking questions. **Choice B** is incorrect because it implies a more formal or structured discussion or argument, often involving differing opinions and arguments. It suggests a more extended and potentially contentious exchange of ideas. However, the context is that the scientific community is considering and discussing possible uses for the marked human bones instead. **Choice C** is incorrect because it suggests a dispute among scientists regarding the potential use of the bones, which is not implied by the original sentence.

2. **Domain:** CRAFT AND STRUCTURE
    Skill/Knowledge: Words in Context

    Key Explanation: Choice B is the correct answer. The text focuses on "the concept of standardized and officially certified coinage." Therefore, the text must be completed with a word that supports this focus. Choice B is the closest to this, since "regulated" accurately conveys the idea that the coins of Lydia were among the earliest forms of standardized and officially certified coinage.

    Distractor Explanations: Choice A is incorrect because it does not convey the idea that the coins of Lydia were among the first standardized and officially certified coinage. It merely describes the coins as old. **Choice C** is incorrect because it does not fit the context as it suggests that the

coins were fake or fraudulent, which is not the intended meaning. The text focuses on "the concept of standardized and officially certified coinage." **Choice D** is incorrect because it does not specifically convey the idea of standardized and officially certified coinage, which is the focus of the text.

3. **Domain:** CRAFT AND STRUCTURE
    Skill/Knowledge: Words in Context

    Key Explanation: Choice A is the correct answer. The text focuses on the "problem-solving skills of individual wild Asian elephants," where the study observed these elephants as they attempted to unlock storage boxes to access food. The use of "successfully" indicates that the elephants were able to achieve their goal of unlocking the boxes to obtain the food. It reflects a positive and effective outcome, which aligns with the idea that the elephants were able to solve the problem presented to them.

    Distractor Explanations: Choice B is incorrect because it implies that the elephants unlocked the storage boxes with some hesitation or unwillingness. It does not fit the context, as the text does not suggest reluctance at any stage; instead it focuses on the problem-solving skills of the elephants. **Choice C** is incorrect because "uncertainly" suggests a lack of confidence, hesitancy, or doubt in one's actions. When describing the problem-solving skills of the wild Asian elephants, especially in the context of unlocking storage boxes to access food, this option does not accurately reflect their actions, especially since the text implies that the problem was solved successfully. **Choice D** is incorrect because using "rarely" would suggest that the elephants almost never or very infrequently unlocked storage boxes to access food. However, the sentence discusses a recent study that observed the problem-solving skills of individual wild Asian elephants. The study indicates that these elephants did, in fact, engage in problem-solving activities by unlocking storage boxes to access food. Therefore, this choice would not accurately describe their behavior as documented in the study.

4. **Domain:** CRAFT AND STRUCTURE
    Skill/Knowledge: Words in Context

    Key Explanation: Choice B is the best answer. The passage describes the process of peer review, where fellow researchers closely assess a research manuscript to determine its suitability for publication in an academic journal. The missing word should accurately reflect this process. "Evaluated" better captures the depth and comprehensive nature of the process, where researchers critically analyze and make judgments about the manuscript.

    Distractor Explanations: Choice A is incorrect because reviewing a manuscript does not necessarily mean that its quality is being assessed. **Choice C** is incorrect because "scanned" indicates a rapid and cursory examination of the manuscript, without delving into the finer details or conducting an in-depth evaluation. **Choice D** is incorrect because "read" does not fully capture the comprehensive analysis and evaluation involved. "Read" alone does not convey the depth of scrutiny and judgment that researchers employ during peer review.

5. **Domain:** CRAFT AND STRUCTURE
    Skill/Knowledge: Words in Context

    Key Explanation: Choice B is the correct answer as it is the most appropriate choice given the context. "Licenses as medical doctors" accurately conveys that psychiatrists hold medical licenses, which is the key point in the text.

    Distractor Explanations: Choice A is incorrect because "permission for medical doctors" doesn't convey the intended meaning, as the sentence discusses the professional qualifications of psychiatrists, not their need for permission. **Choice C** is incorrect because while "expertise in medical doctors" is grammatically correct, it doesn't make sense in the context of the sentence. "Expertise" is usually used in the context of a topic

or subject. The sentence discusses the professional status of psychiatrists, not their expertise. **Choice D** is incorrect because "affiliation with medical doctors" changes the text's intended meaning. It suggests a different relationship between psychiatrists and medical doctors, which is not the focus of the text.

6. **Domain:** CRAFT AND STRUCTURE
    Skill/Knowledge: Text Structure and Purpose

    Key Explanation: Choice C is the best answer because the passage is providing overall information about the tongue in both human and animal species. It uses specific examples in humans to illustrate that the tongue has helped both humans and animals survive and adapt. The passage also demonstrates that it is a significant organ often overlooked.

    Distractor Explanations: Choice A is incorrect because the author never argues that the tongue is the "most" important organ, merely that it is important. Furthermore, the author is not only focusing on the human tongue. **Choice B** is wrong because it is too narrow. While it does detail the adaptability of the tongue in certain animal species, it does not only focus on the animal tongue. **Choice D** is wrong because it focuses on how versatile the tongue is, which is demonstrated in the passage. However, it ignores the overall point that the tongue is a very important organ that is usually unnoticed.

7. **Domain:** CRAFT AND STRUCTURE
    Skill/Knowledge: Text Structure and Purpose

    Key Explanation: Choice A is the correct answer. The driver's comment about encountering "such matters before you go to sleep" creates a feeling of anticipation and curiosity, which aligns with the passage's overall tone of mystery. It is as if he is hinting at a sinister event that will occur before the author goes to sleep. This makes Choice A the most likely answer.

    Distractor Explanations: Choice B is incorrect because while the underlined sentence does indicate the driver's caution, it does not directly highlight his concern about the steep hills. Instead, it focuses on his refusal to stop for anything but to light his lamps. **Choice C** is incorrect because the underlined sentence does not emphasize the passengers' eagerness to leave the carriage; it primarily emphasizes the driver's warning and eagerness to continue the journey unstopped. **Choice D** is incorrect because the underlined sentence is actually hinting at a sinister event and it is as if the driver is trying to warn the author in an indirect way. The entire passage has a tone of suspense but the underlined sentence does not specifically add to the anticipation in particular.

8. **Domain:** CRAFT AND STRUCTURE
    Skill/Knowledge: Text Structure and Purpose

    Key Explanation: Choice C is the best choice because the previous sentence states that the definition of passion differs for employees and employers. This sentence then shows that with an example of how people in this position can interpret the word "passion" differently.

    Distractor Explanations: Choice A is inaccurate because this sentence demonstrates a contrasting opinion on the definition of passion. Furthermore, the passage as a whole focuses on how this different opinion can create a conflict between employers and their employees. **Choice B** is wrong because it does not consider the rest of the passage. While passion is defined in two different terms in this sentence, this answer choice does not take into account the context of how employees and employers differ in their opinions. **Choice D** is incorrect because that is not the reason this sentence is included. While it does discuss some elements that would make a good employee, the sentence shows a difference of opinion between employers and employees..

9. **Domain:** INFORMATION AND IDEAS
    Skill/Knowledge: Command of Evidence (Textual)

    Key Explanation: Choice A is correct because it provides direct evidence of the difference in

eye size in residential birds living in urban areas compared to those in less illuminated outskirts, supporting the scientists' claim about the impact of intense urban lights on birds eye size.

Distractor Explanations: Choice B is incorrect because while it provides information about two species of migratory birds not exhibiting the same eye-size difference as residential birds, it does not directly support the claim being made. It mentions that the two species of migratory birds (the Painted Bunting, and White-eyed Vireo) did not show the same eye-size difference, but it does not directly compare them to any other groups or populations. **Choice C** is incorrect because it does not provide direct evidence supporting the claim, as it mentions that scientists only made comparisons between limited species, thus requiring further research to reach a definite conclusion. **Choice D** is incorrect because it does not directly address the claim that urban light causes smaller eye size, but instead discusses a challenge faced by birds in urban areas.

10. **Domain:** INFORMATION AND IDEAS
    Skill/Knowledge: Command of Evidence (Textual)

    Key Explanation: Choice A is the correct answer. The passage has already given us a hint that Dickinson is comparing the gray sky to a Leaden Sieve. Therefore, "it" sifts (like flour) from the gray sky, and it also powders (unlike rain) the wood while covering the road. Taking these hints into consideration, it makes it easier to guess that the poet is describing snow.

    Distractor Explanations: Choice B is incorrect because it does not give us many clues as to the subject of the poem. Instead, it focuses on different aspects of the landscape, such as "stump, and stack and stem" and "acres of joints where harvest were", as visualized by Dickinson. **Choice C** is incorrect because it focuses on geographical features like mountains and plains, as well as directions (from East to East again). It does not contain imagery that directly relates to a winter's day or falling snow. **Choice D** is incorrect because while it provides some winter-related imagery, it doesn't directly describe the winter scene with falling snow in the way Choice A does. It is more metaphorical and abstract in its description.

11. **Domain:** INFORMATION AND IDEAS
     Skill/Knowledge: Command of Evidence (Quantitative)

     Key Explanation: Choice A is correct. The table shows that for both studies with passive and active control groups, the SMD is negative for depression and distress, indicating that depression and distress symptoms are reduced after meditation. Further, for well-being, the SMD is positive, indicating that well-being improved after meditation.

     Distractor Explanations: Choice B is incorrect. The SMD for anxiety for studies with active control groups is positive, indicating that anxiety increased after meditation, which is not a beneficial impact. **Choice C** is incorrect. The SMD for anxiety for studies with active control groups is positive, indicating that anxiety increased after meditation, which is not a beneficial impact. **Choice D** is incorrect. The SMD for well-being is positive for both passive and active control groups.

12. **Domain:** INFORMATION AND IDEAS
     Skill/Knowledge: Command of Evidence (Quantitative)

     Key Explanation: Choice C is correct. The graph shows that the projections for 2022 to 2100 are −310k net migrants, which means 310k more migrants left China than entered China. In the early twentieth century, the number of net migrants was generally less than −200k, which is a smaller outflow than −310k.

     Distractor Explanations: Choice A is incorrect. While the graph shows net migrants, the graph does not provide information about absolute numbers of migrants entering or exiting China. **Choice B** is incorrect. While the graph shows net migrants, the graph does not provide information about absolute numbers of migrants entering or exiting China. **Choice D** is incorrect. The graph

shows that the projections for 2022 to 2100 are −310k net migrants, which means 310k more migrants left China than entered China. In the early twentieth century, the number of net migrants was generally less than −200k, which is a smaller outflow than −310k.

13. **Domain:** INFORMATION AND IDEAS
     Skill/Knowledge: Command of Evidence (Textual)

     Key Explanation: Choice A is the best answer. The speaker talks about how it was just like being in chaos without end. The chaos was detached and cool, without offering any possibility of escape. It was like being lost in the middle of the ocean, without seeing the mast of a ship or even hearing about land that might offer some relief or make such terrible anguish easier to understand.

     Distractor Explanations: Choice B is incorrect because here the speaker is only saying that they knew they weren't dead, because they could stand up, and everyone who is dead lies down. **Choice C** is incorrect because the speaker says that it was as though their life had been sanded down so that it could fit into a frame. **Choice D** is incorrect because here the speaker says that they knew that it wasn't night-time because all the church bells were ringing as they did in the middle of the day. None of these choices effectively display the idea of despair and hopelessness as **Choice A**.

14. **Domain:** INFORMATION AND IDEAS
     Skill/Knowledge: Inferences

     Key Explanation: Choice C is the best answer since it reflects the topic brought up in the first sentence about the myths of Japanese culture without requiring the reader to jump to any extreme or inaccurate conclusions. The main idea of the passage focuses on the Japanese saying to avoid being wasteful with examples in their mythology and traditions; this answer reflects that point.

     Distractor Explanations: Choice A might be accurate, but requires the reader to draw conclusions not directly implied in the passage. **Choice B** does not focus on the main idea of the passage, which reiterates ideas of avoiding wastefulness and uses the monsters as examples to reinforce this concept. **Choice D** makes too strong of a conclusion. The passage does not indicate that waste is seen as "sinful", but rather something that would benefit one's life if avoided.

15. **Domain:** INFORMATION AND IDEAS
Skill/Knowledge: Inferences

Key Explanation: Choice C is the best answer as it most accurately draws conclusions about the stories and the theme of "liberated women" by emphasizing their ability to see themselves in these retellings and their power as individual women.

Distractor Explanations: Choice A is wrong because while it is true that the stories show female equality, topics like "darkness" and "murder" do not reflect it. **Choice B** is true for some of the stories, but not all of them. **Choice D** may be true but does not strongly emphasize the liberated women discussed in the first sentence.

16. **Domain:** STANDARD ENGLISH CONVENTIONS
Skill/Knowledge: Boundaries

Key Explanation: The convention being tested is punctuation use with two linked independant clauses. **Choice B** is the best answer because "and" is used to connect two related ideas or facts, which is appropriate in this context to convey that the information about Jupiter's appearance is being added to the previous information.

Distractor Explanations: Choice A is incorrect because "but" suggests a contrast or contradiction, which is not the intended meaning in the context. The sentence is providing additional information about Jupiter's characteristics. **Choice C** is less appropriate because "yet" is typically used to introduce a contrast or contradiction, which doesn't fit the context. The sentence is not presenting a contrast but providing complementary information. **Choice D** is less

appropriate because "for" suggests a reason or purpose, which doesn't align with the context. The sentence is not explaining the reason for Jupiter's characteristics but simply adding information about them.

17. **Domain:** STANDARD ENGLISH CONVENTIONS
Skill/Knowledge: Form, Structure, and Sense

Key Explanation: Choice B is the correct answer. The convention being tested here is subject-verb agreement. The plural subject "adults" agrees with the verb "measure."

Distractor Explanations: Choice A is incorrect because the subject and verb do not agree in number if the sentence reads "adults of this amphibian species typically measures between…" **Choice C** is incorrect because using "is" ("is measuring") will create a subject-verb agreement error since the subject is plural (adults.) "Is" is the singular present tense of the verb "to be." **Choice D** is incorrect because it uses the present perfect tense "have measured," which implies a completed action in the past. It is not suitable for describing a general characteristic of adult wood frogs.

18. **Domain:** STANDARD ENGLISH CONVENTIONS
Skill/Knowledge: Boundaries

Key Explanation: The convention being tested is punctuation use with two linked independent clauses. **Choice B** is the best answer because it uses a comma before "or" to separate items in a list properly. This choice follows the conventions of Standard English.

Distractor Explanations: Choice A is incorrect because it uses an unnecessary comma after "simply." There is no need for a comma in this context, and it disrupts the sentence's flow. **Choice C** is incorrect because it lacks a comma before "or," which is needed to separate the items in the list. Proper punctuation is essential for clarity in the sentence. **Choice D** is incorrect because it places a comma after "or," which is not needed and disrupts the sentence's flow. The comma should be placed before "or" in this context to separate the items correctly.

19. **Domain:** STANDARD ENGLISH CONVENTIONS
    Skill/Knowledge: Form, Structure, and Sense

    Key Explanation: Choice D is the correct answer. The convention being tested here is verb forms. The sentence to be completed requires a past participle verb form to match the past tense context of "trace back." The correct past participle form of the verb is "predating."

    Distractor Explanations: Choice A is incorrect because it uses the present simple verb form of "predate," which creates an error here. The sentence to be completed talks about a collection of lyrics that predates the twelfth century. However, to use "predates" correctly in the same sentence, a determiner like "which" would need to be used. Choice A does not contain a determiner and hence is incorrect. **Choice B** is incorrect because it suggests a future event ("will predate") when the context requires a reference to the past. **Choice C** is incorrect because it implies an ongoing action in the present, which is not appropriate for the context. It also creates a subject-verb agreement error. The plural "are" does not agree with the singular "collection."

20. **Domain:** STANDARD ENGLISH CONVENTIONS
    Skill/Knowledge: Boundaries

    Key Explanation: The convention being tested is punctuation use between a sentence and an essential element. **Choice C** is the best answer because the phrase "as understanding the root causes" functions as a relative clause that modifies the noun phrase "the underlying reasons." The relative pronoun "as" introduces the clause and serves as a conjunction. The comma after "it" is necessary to separate the introductory phrase from the rest of the sentence. This construction is a concise and grammatically correct way to express

the idea that identifying the reasons for turnover is essential for developing effective retention strategies.

Distractor Explanations: Choice A is incorrect because it is missing the necessary punctuation, making it incorrect. **Choice B** is incorrect because it includes a comma after "it" which is not needed and makes the sentence unclear. **Choice D** is incorrect because it lacks necessary punctuation between "it" and "as," making it incorrect.

21. **Domain:** STANDARD ENGLISH CONVENTIONS
    Skill/Knowledge: Form, Structure, and Sense

    Key Explanation: Choice A is the correct answer. The convention being tested here is verb forms. Choice A is the most appropriate option conforming to the conventions of Standard English. It correctly uses the past tense "evolved" to describe Monet's progression over the course of his life.

    Distractor Explanations: Choice B is incorrect because it uses the present perfect tense "has evolved," which implies a connection between the past and the present. However, the passage is discussing events in the past, so the past tense is more suitable. **Choice C** is incorrect because it uses the present continuous tense "is evolving," which suggests an ongoing action in the present. It is not appropriate in this context, as the text focuses on Monet's past progression. **Choice D** is incorrect because it uses the future tense "will evolve," which implies a prediction about Monet's future progression. However, the passage discusses events in the past, making Choice D an incorrect option.

22. **Domain:** STANDARD ENGLISH CONVENTIONS
    Skill/Knowledge: Form, Structure, and Sense

    Key Explanation: Choice C is the correct answer. The convention being tested here is plurals and possessives. Choice C is correct because it uses the proper possessive form "autobiography's" and the correct plural "aims." This choice uses the proper possessive form "autobiography's" to indicate that we are talking about the aims of the autobiography written by Benjamin Franklin.

Distractor Explanations: Choice A is incorrect because while it uses the possessive form correctly with "autobiography's," it does not use the correct plural form of "aim." **Choice B** is incorrect because it is missing the apostrophe in "autobiography's" which is required to show possession. **Choice D** is incorrect because it lacks the necessary possessive form and also uses "aim's" instead of "aims."

23. **Domain:** STANDARD ENGLISH CONVENTIONS
Skill/Knowledge: Boundaries

Key Explanation: The convention being tested is punctuation use between a sentence and an essential element. **Choice B** is the best answer because the sentence requires a restrictive relative clause to provide essential information about the Industrial Revolution and the correct form of the relative pronoun "that" is used to introduce the clause.

Distractor Explanations: Choice A is incorrect because it introduces an unnecessary semicolon and includes an extra "and" before "early nineteenth century". **Choice C** is incorrect because it introduces an unnecessary comma before "and" and after "centuries". **Choice D** is incorrect because it introduces unnecessary parentheses that disrupt the flow of the sentence.

24. **Domain:** EXPRESSION OF IDEAS
Skill/Knowledge: Transitions

Key Explanation: Choice C is the correct answer. The last sentence of the text introduces a contrasting idea (they have reduced stingers, but they have other defensive behaviors) to the previous sentence. In cases where contrasting ideas are shown, words like "however" and "nevertheless" are usually used to show the transition.

Distractor Explanations: Choice A is incorrect. "Furthermore" is used when additional information is being provided to build on a topic already introduced in the previous sentence. This is not the case here, where a contrasting idea is being introduced. **Choice B** is incorrect because a similar idea is not being introduced in the last sentence. Therefore, "similarly" would not be an effective transition. **Choice D** is incorrect because the usage of "though" in this sentence would render it incomplete. "Though" used at the beginning of a sentence such as the one to be completed would introduce a condition (e.g.: though these bees exhibit other … mechanisms, they are easy to kill.)

25. **Domain:** EXPRESSION OF IDEAS
Skill/Knowledge: Transitions

Key Explanation: Choice A, "Therefore," is the best answer. "Therefore" is used to indicate a logical conclusion or result based on the preceding information. In this case, it signifies that the groundbreaking adoption of HFT by algorithmic trading has reshaped the landscape of modern finance as a direct result of the significant contributions made to the development of HFT. By using "therefore," the sentence that follows logically connects to the previous information, suggesting a cause-and-effect relationship between algorithmic trading's adoption of HFT and the transformation of financial markets.

Distractor Explanations: Choice B, "Moreover," is incorrect because it implies that the following sentence will present additional information that supports the previous information. However, the sentence that follows does not provide additional information but rather presents a logical conclusion based on the preceding information. The word "moreover" would be inappropriate in this context as it does not convey the intended logical conclusion. **Choice C,** "In a similar vein," is incorrect because it implies that the following sentence will present information that is similar or comparable to the preceding information. However, the sentence that follows does not provide similar information but rather presents a logical conclusion based on the preceding information. The phrase "in a similar vein" would be inappropriate in this context as it does not convey the intended logical conclusion. **Choice D**, "However," is incorrect because it indicates a contrasting idea or point. However, there is no logical contrast or contradiction between the development of high-frequency trading and its reshaping of the modern finance landscape. The word "however" would introduce an unnecessary contradiction or conflict in this context.

26. **Domain:** EXPRESSION OF IDEAS
    Skill/Knowledge: Rhetorical Synthesis

    Key Explanation: Choice A is correct because it integrates the student's notes to discuss GDP, inflation, and economic recession.

    Distractor Explanations: Choice B is incorrect because though it correctly defines GDP and inflation, it does not discuss recession. **Choice C** is incorrect because though it correctly defines economic recession, it does not talk about GDP. **Choice D** is incorrect because it inaccurately states that a recession is unrelated to inflation rates or the risk of hyperinflation. As per the notes, the economic factors are interconnected.

27. **Domain:** EXPRESSION OF IDEAS
    Skill/Knowledge: Rhetorical Synthesis

    Key Explanation: Choice A is the best answer as it accurately summarizes the main points from the notes. It acknowledges the significant advancements in technology brought about by the Industrial Revolution and their positive impact on the overall standard of living. It also acknowledges the negative consequences of poor working conditions and increased pollution.

    Distractor Explanations: Choice B is incorrect because it suggests that the negative consequences of poor working conditions and increased pollution were merely "despite" the improvements in living standards. It does not acknowledge the significant impact and prevalence of these negative consequences, thus providing an incomplete summary. **Choice C** is incorrect because it implies that the positive impact on living standards was only "marred" by the negative consequences. It fails to fully recognize the substantial and lasting effects of the negative consequences, thereby providing an imbalanced synthesis of the main idea. **Choice D** suggests that the positive effects of the advancements in technology and manufacturing processes outweigh the negative consequences, thus ignoring the significant impact of the negative consequences of the Industrial Revolution.

1. **Domain:** CRAFT AND STRUCTURE
    Skill/Knowledge: Words in Context

    Key Explanation: Choice B is correct. The word "culminating" fits best in the context of the sentence as it suggests that the exploration of themes in *The Great Gatsby* reaches its end point or final stage in tragedy. The word aligns with the information provided in the text, where we have been told that various themes of the novel converge and lead to a tragic outcome.

    Distractor Explanations: Choice A is incorrect because "evolving" implies a continuous process of development or change, whereas the sentence requires a word that indicates a conclusion or final outcome. **Choice C** is incorrect since "resolving" suggests that the themes are neatly tied up or resolved, which is not the case in *The Great Gatsby* where the ending is marked by tragedy. **Choice D** is incorrect because "emerging" implies something coming into view or becoming known for the first time, which does not accurately capture the novel's themes of tragedy.

2. **Domain:** CRAFT AND STRUCTURE
    Skill/Knowledge: Words in Context

    Key Explanation: Choice D is correct because "formidable" is used to describe something that inspires fear or awe. In this case, most of the passage describes how many children have witnessed violence. Thus, the blank part of the last sentence is best filled with the word "formidable," as the sheer number of children witnessing violence inspires fear and awe.

    Distractor Explanations: Choice A is incorrect because "inconsequential" means "not significant". This directly contrasts the information given in the passage which mentions that around 88% of preadolescents had witnessed violence and 10% of children between 1 to 5 years old had witnessed violence related to knives and shootings. As per the passage, there are around 5 million children in the inner cities and the percentage of children who have witnessed violence is high too. Thus, this choice is incorrect. **Choice B** is incorrect because

    the word "sinister" does not relate to the context of the passage since it is usually used to describe something scary that may happen. **Choice C** is incorrect because the passage does not indicate that the numbers are difficult to understand.

3. **Domain:** CRAFT AND STRUCTURE
    Skill/Knowledge: Words in Context

    Key Explanation: Choice C is correct because "discern" means to recognize or distinguish. In the second sentence, adherence was measured to be able to point out the possible inconsistencies.

    Distractor Explanations: Choice A is incorrect because nothing in the passage indicates that the value of adherence was being considered. **Choice B** is incorrect because the word does not suit the context of the sentence. **Choice D** is incorrect because the study was not considering but was trying to prove the possible inconsistencies.

4. **Domain:** CRAFT AND STRUCTURE
    Skill/Knowledge: Words in Context

    Key Explanation: Choice A is correct. The term "piqued" means to arouse or stimulate interest or curiosity. In the context of the sentence, the discovery of the newfound exoplanet, particularly its potential to harbor life within the habitable zone, has sparked significant interest among astronomers. The word "piqued" also fits well in the overall theme of the text because scientists have already been exploring exoplanetary systems to learn more about how the solar system evolved. Therefore, a new exoplanet will arouse interest. Choice A is the most logical and precise word to complete the sentence.

    Distractor Explanations: Choice B is incorrect because "unveiled" suggests that the exoplanet has revealed the interest of astronomers and is a new concept that has just been brought to light. However, this contradicts the initial half of the text where we have been told that scientists have already been exploring exoplanetary systems to learn more about how the solar system evolved.

Choice C is incorrect because "revealed" implies that something previously hidden has been made known, which does not accurately convey the idea that the exoplanet has generated interest. **Choice D** is incorrect as "documented" implies recording or noting something already known, which is not the case here where the exoplanet is a newly discovered object that has generated interest.

5. **Domain:** CRAFT AND STRUCTURE
    Skill/Knowledge: Words in Context

    Key Explanation: Choice D is the correct answer. "Challenging established beliefs" accurately conveys the idea that the discovery is causing a reevaluation or questioning of the established beliefs regarding early human lifestyles. It aligns well with the context of the sentence.

    Distractor Explanations: Choice A is incorrect because "reinvigorating established beliefs" implies a renewed interest or enthusiasm in the established beliefs. It does not convey the idea that the discovery is causing these beliefs to be questioned or challenged, which is the primary focus of the sentence. **Choice B** is incorrect because "excavating established beliefs" doesn't accurately convey the idea of challenging beliefs. It suggests a different digging action related to archaeological work. **Choice C** is incorrect because "underpinning established beliefs" implies support for these beliefs rather than challenging them directly. It doesn't accurately convey that the discovery is causing these beliefs to be questioned or challenged.

6. **Domain:** CRAFT AND STRUCTURE
    Skill/Knowledge: Text Structure and Purpose

    Key Explanation: Choice A is the correct choice as it accurately describes the structure of the text. The poet talks about two roads diverging and how one must always decide between two or more options that situations in life may offer. The poem metaphorically describes how a single choice can change the outcome of one's life.

    Distractor Explanations: Choice B is incorrect because it does not accurately describe the structure of the text. While the poem is set in a forest, the primary focus is on the poet's choice, not on the beauty of nature. **Choice C** is incorrect because it does not accurately describe the essential focus of two choices being available to the poet. While the poet mentions feeling sorry about not being able to travel both paths, the focus is not on offering advice but on reflecting. **Choice D** is incorrect because the poet mentions a journey but does not primarily focus on it or contemplate the passage of time.

7. **Domain:** CRAFT AND STRUCTURE
    Skill/Knowledge: Cross-Text Connections

    Key Explanation: Choice B is correct. Text 1 concludes that bees may be capable of having fun and experiencing this kind of positive emotion. The author of Text 2 acknowledges the validity of this study and prior studies but also cautions that these emotions do not have the level of complexity that human emotions have.

    Distractor Explanations: Choice A is incorrect because the author of Text 2 does not suggest that other insects reach the level of emotional complexity that humans do. **Choice C** is incorrect. The author of Text 2 acknowledges that bees may feel negative emotions, but the author does not propose that bees can only feel negative emotions. **Choice D** is incorrect because the author of Text 2 does not reject the claim that bees can have fun without an incentive in place.

8. **Domain: INFORMATION AND IDEAS**
    Skill/Knowledge: Central Ideas and Details

    Key Explanation: Choice B is correct because the text states that "others suspect mass hysteria or some secret, sinister purpose." This relates to the beliefs surrounding the hum as mentioned in the question.

    Distractor Explanations: Choice A is incorrect as it does not mention a belief surrounding the hum, but mentions a fact ("only about 2% of Taos residents report hearing the sound"). **Choice C** is incorrect because mass hysteria is suspected, as are supernatural origins, but no mention of "hysteria surrounding supernatural events" has been made in the text. **Choice D** is incorrect as the hum has not been consistently described as a whir, hum, or buzz.

9. **Domain:** INFORMATION AND IDEAS
Skill/Knowledge: Central Ideas and Details

Key Explanation: Choice C is correct because according to the text, the author "began that journey through the eyes of an encyclopedic professor" who guided him to China.

Distractor Explanations: Choice A is incorrect because there is no evidence to support the claim that the author had not traveled before. He only mentions he "discovered the other half of the world," meaning he was familiar with one half. **Choice B** is incorrect because the text only mentions a "Philadelphia suburban education." **Choice D** is incorrect because the text offers no evidence that the author had already traveled extensively.

10. **Domain:** INFORMATION AND IDEAS
Skill/Knowledge: Command of Evidence (Textual)

Key Explanation: Choice C is correct because this line from the passage directly refers to physical violence in the form of "blood…gargling from the froth-corrupted lungs."

Distractor Explanations: Choice A is incorrect. This line presents a chaotic scene of people putting on helmets, yelling, and stumbling around, but does not directly mention any form of violence. **Choice B** is incorrect because this line refers to a long, tiring march. However, no physical atrocities are committed or referenced. **Choice D** is incorrect because this line does not reference any physical acts during wartime at all. Rather, this line

mentions patriotic children and what they should not be told.

11. **Domain:** INFORMATION AND IDEAS
Skill/Knowledge: Command of Evidence (Textual)

Key Explanation: Choice C is the best answer. This finding directly supports the claim that annual flu vaccinations are recommended as the best preventive measure to reduce the risk of flu-related complications and transmission. It suggests that higher flu vaccination rates correlate with fewer school closure days, indicating lower transmission rates and fewer flu-related complications.

Distractor Explanations: Choice A is incorrect because it does not specifically address the effectiveness of annual flu vaccinations in reducing flu-related complications and transmission. **Choice B** is incorrect because this statement suggests variability in the effectiveness of flu vaccinations based on virus strains but does not directly support the claim regarding the effectiveness of flu vaccinations as the best preventive measure. **Choice D** is incorrect because it directly contradicts the claim by suggesting that higher flu vaccination rates are associated with higher incidence rates of flu-related complications and transmission, thus weakening the argument for the effectiveness of flu vaccinations.

12. **Domain:** INFORMATION AND IDEAS
Skill/Knowledge: Command of Evidence (Quantitative)

Key Explanation: Choice C is correct. The table shows that it took more days for larvae to reach adult stage in environments with paper leachates than in environments with plastic leachates, which implies that paper cups were more toxic and inhibited the growth of the larvae.

Distractor Explanations: Choice A is incorrect. The table shows that it took more days for larvae to reach adult stage in environments with paper leachates than in environments with plastic leachates, which implies that paper cups were more toxic and inhibited the growth of the larvae. **Choice B** is incorrect. The table does not provide information about the quantity of leachates introduced to each environment. **Choice D** is incorrect. The table does not provide information about the quantity of leachates introduced to each environment.

13. **Domain:** INFORMATION AND IDEAS
Skill/Knowledge: Command of Evidence (Textual)

Key Explanation: Choice D is the best answer. This quotation effectively illustrates the dehumanization and reduction of women to mere objects expected to conform to societal expectations and roles, thereby highlighting the absurdity of such expectations. The woman has been reduced to an "it" or a "living doll" that can perform household chores like sewing and cooking.

Distractor Explanations: Choice A is incorrect because it does not illustrate the underlined claim. While the quote can be interpreted as describing a person who is secreted away in a closet, it does not highlight the absurd expectations society places on a woman. **Choice B** is incorrect because while this quotation illustrates societal expectations, it focuses more on physical attributes rather than the broader theme of conforming to societal ideals placed upon women. **Choice C** is incorrect because it describes the qualities of an object rather than addressing the expectations placed upon women in conforming to societal ideals.

14. **Domain:** CRAFT AND STRUCTURE
Skill/Knowledge: Inferences

Key Explanation: Choice B is the best answer since correctly interprets the idea that individuals will likely be less lonely if they have a "network structure" and "emotional support."

Distractor Explanations: Choice A incorrectly interprets what is stated about the community. It

does not say that lonely individuals do not want to be a part of the community, but implies they struggle to fit into it as is emphasized by the word "cohesion." **Choice C** is wrong because the passage does not indicate what type of health problems loneliness can cause. **Choice D** is wrong because the passage says the study focused on those aged "40-85", not all ages.

15. **Domain:** CRAFT AND STRUCTURE
Skill/Knowledge: Inferences

Key Explanation: Choice D is the best choice since it draws a conclusion recommended by the passage and it states that specific areas of life can be supported. It stands to reason that engaging in music on even a basic level, will improve one's outlook.

Distractor Explanations: Choice A is too narrow by focusing solely on young children, rather than the many groups of people that can be benefited. **Choice B** requires the reader to make an inference not suggested in the passage as it does not suggest that a career can be made out of it. **Choice C** could be arguably true but is slightly off-topic and requires an inference that is not suggested by the passage. Therefore, it is not the best answer.

16. **Domain:** STANDARD ENGLISH CONVENTIONS
Skill/Knowledge: Form, Structure, and Sense

Key Explanation: Choice B is the correct answer. The convention being tested here is subject-verb agreement. Choice B correctly maintains subject-verb agreement, since "have been" agrees with the plural subject "16 children's stories."

Distractor Explanations: Choice A is incorrect because it creates a subject-verb agreement error; "which" refers to "16 children's stories," which is plural. The singular "has been" doesn't agree with the plural subject. **Choice C** is incorrect because "are translated" denotes a present or ongoing situation. However, the translation of Dahl's 16 children's stories has already occurred. **Choice**

D is incorrect because it is in the present tense. The original sentence talks about an action that happened in the past; Roald Dahl had already authored 16 children's stories. The phrase "which _____ into 68 languages and enjoyed by readers worldwide" is describing what happened to those 16 children's stories after they were authored, which is a past action.

17. **Domain:** STANDARD ENGLISH CONVENTIONS
    Skill/Knowledge: Boundaries

    Key Explanation: The convention being tested is punctuation use with two linked independent clauses. **Choice B** is the best answer because in this sentence, the clause after "created" is a contrasting phrase that modifies the previous clause. The phrase "for the purpose of idolatry" is separated from the clause that follows it by a conjunction indicating the contrast that tattoos are not disallowed if they are intended to mark a person's enslaved status.

    Distractor Explanations: Choice A incorrectly uses a dash instead of a space between the contrasting phrases, which is not grammatically correct. **Choice C** uses a comma to separate the contrasting phrase and the clause that follows it, which creates a comma splice error. **Choice D** uses a semicolon instead of a conjunction, which is also grammatically incorrect.

18. **Domain:** STANDARD ENGLISH CONVENTIONS
    Skill/Knowledge: Form, Structure, and Sense

    Key Explanation: Choice A is the best answer. The convention being tested is subject-verb agreement. The singular verb "contributes" agrees in number with the singular subject "wealth."

    Distractor Explanations: Choice B is incorrect because the plural verb "contribute" doesn't agree in number with the singular subject "wealth". **Choice C** is incorrect because the plural verb "have contributed" doesn't agree in number

with the singular subject "wealth". **Choice D** is incorrect because the plural verb "are contributing" doesn't agree in number with the singular subject "wealth".

19. Medium | **Domain:** STANDARD ENGLISH CONVENTIONS
    Skill/Knowledge: Form, Structure, and Sense

    Key Explanation: Choice A is the correct answer. The convention being tested here is pronoun-antecedent agreement. The text mentions "interpreting the material remains of humanity's history". In this case, a plural pronoun must also be used to correctly complete the sentence. Only Choice A uses a plural pronoun.

    Distractor Explanations: Choice B is incorrect because "its" is a singular form that cannot be used with a plural noun ("the material remains of humanity's history.") **Choice C** is incorrect because "they're" is a contraction of "they are" and does not fit the sentence's context. It would create an incomplete and confusing sentence if used here. **Choice D** is incorrect because "it's" is a contraction of "it is" or "it has," and neither of these fits the context of the sentence. Using "it's" would create a sentence fragment.

20. **Domain:** STANDARD ENGLISH CONVENTIONS
    Skill/Knowledge: Boundaries

    Key Explanation: The convention being tested is punctuation use between a sentence and an essential element. **Choice C** is the correct choice because it uses a relative pronoun to introduce a restrictive relative clause that provides additional information about the type of destinations being referred to, without any unnecessary punctuation.

    Distractor Explanations: Choice A is incorrect because it incorrectly uses a comma to introduce a restrictive relative clause that should not be set off by commas. **Choice B** is incorrect because it incorrectly uses a comma to separate the subject "destinations" from the verb "where." **Choice D** is incorrect because it incorrectly uses a comma to separate the adverbial phrase "where South Africans" from the noun "destinations," creating a sentence fragment.

21. **Domain:** STANDARD ENGLISH CONVENTIONS
Skill/Knowledge: Form, Structure, and Sense

Key Explanation: Choice D is the correct answer. The convention being tested here is subject-verb agreement. The singular subject "fresh research" agrees in number with the singular verb "suggests."

Distractor Explanations: Choice A is incorrect because using the plural verb "suggest" creates a subject-verb agreement error. **Choice B** is incorrect because it uses "have" which does not agree with the singular subject "research." **Choice C** is incorrect because it uses the continuous tense that implies an ongoing action, whereas the sentence seems to describe the general findings made by the research.

22. **Domain:** STANDARD ENGLISH CONVENTIONS
Skill/Knowledge: Boundaries

Key Explanation: The convention being tested is punctuation use with two linked independent clauses. **Choice A** is the best answer because it uses a comma before "and" to separate the independent clauses appropriately. A comma is needed to connect these clauses properly in accordance with Standard English conventions.

Distractor Explanations: Choice B is incorrect because it uses an unnecessary comma after "and". The comma is not needed in this context and disrupts the sentence's flow. **Choice C** is incorrect because it lacks the necessary comma before "and." In Standard English, when "and" is used to connect two independent clauses, a comma is typically used before it to separate them. **Choice D** is incorrect because it also lacks the necessary comma before "and." Proper punctuation is needed to separate the clauses to ensure clarity and readability.

23. **Domain:** EXPRESSION OF IDEAS
Skill/Knowledge: Transitions

Key Explanation: Choice C is the correct answer. "The vivacious reds, whites, and yellows on the spiders" are caused by pigments, but the "lustrous blues and purples" are caused by tiny nanostructures. Therefore, we are looking for a word that shows contrast. "Whereas" is the best choice as it is closest in meaning to "but".

Distractor Explanations: Choice A is incorrect because "furthermore" is used when additional information is being given. It is not used to show a contrast. **Choice B** is also incorrect because "similarly" is used when extra information is being given that adds to a point already made. **Choice D** is incorrect because "moreover" may be used when additional information emphasizes or expresses agreement with preceding material in the text. This is not the case here.

24. **Domain:** EXPRESSION OF IDEAS
Skill/Knowledge: Transitions

Key Explanation: Choice C is the best answer. "Indeed" is used to underscore something that is true or has been spoken about or mentioned previously. In this case, "indeed" is the correct answer because the text has so far focused on how the introduction of creative lighting techniques has transformed the field of pet photography. Therefore, using "indeed" emphasizes on the fact that "pet photography's groundbreaking lighting techniques have transformed the way we capture the essence and personality of our furry friends."

Distractor Explanations: Choice A is incorrect because it implies that the following sentence will provide additional information that supports the previous information. However, the sentence that follows doubles down on the preceding information, rather than providing additional supporting information. **Choice B** is incorrect because "in addition," similar to "furthermore," is usually used to add more information to what has been previously mentioned. In this context, however, no more information is being added. Instead, the sentence to be completed underscores what has been previously mentioned. **Choice D** is incorrect because it indicates a contrasting idea or point. However, there is no logical contrast or contradiction between the advancements in creative lighting techniques and their transformative impact on pet photography. The word "nevertheless" would introduce an unnecessary contradiction or conflict in this context.

25. **Domain:** EXPRESSION OF IDEAS
    Skill/Knowledge: Rhetorical Synthesis

    Key Explanation: Choice A is correct because it specifically utilizes the notes to directly highlight the similarity in the way the flu and COVID-19 are spread - through droplets when infected individuals cough, sneeze, or talk. This choice best accomplishes the student's goal of emphasizing the commonality in transmission mechanisms between the two diseases.

    Distractor Explanations: Choice B is incorrect because instead of highlighting the similarities between the spread of the flu and COVID-19, it informs us about the difference in incubation periods. **Choice C** is incorrect because it can mislead us into thinking that the similarity lies in the fact that both diseases can be prevented by vaccines. However, the student's goal was to highlight the similarities in the spread of the diseases, not their prevention. It is a good distractor as it presents a fact but does not directly address the objective of the question. **Choice D** is incorrect because while it is technically accurate in stating both diseases are caused by viruses, does not specifically address the similarity in their mode of transmission, which was the student's objective. This makes it an effective distractor.

26. **Domain:** EXPRESSION OF IDEAS
    Skill/Knowledge: Rhetorical Synthesis

    Key Explanation: Choice D is correct. It accurately captures the transformative impact

of the internet on society, addressing key points mentioned in the notes such as revolutionizing communication, transforming information access, bridging geographical barriers, and shaping various aspects of society. It effectively conveys the student's goal of emphasizing the transformative impact of the internet on society.

Distractor Explanations: Choice A is incorrect as it focuses more on specific aspects of the internet like online shopping and connecting with friends and family, rather than emphasizing its overall transformative impact on society as a whole. It does not address the broader implications mentioned in the notes. **Choice B** is incorrect because while it mentions the internet's impact on creative expression and entertainment, it does not capture the full extent of its transformative impact on society as mentioned in the notes. It does not address the broader implications of communication, information access, and societal navigation. **Choice C** is incorrect because while it mentions a few specific online activities and information access, it does not effectively convey the transformative impact of the internet on society as a whole.

27. **Domain:** EXPRESSION OF IDEAS
    Skill/Knowledge: Rhetorical Synthesis

    Key Explanation: Choice A is the correct choice because it directly contrasts the unique features of the Japanese business world (lifetime employment and consensus decision-making) with Western models (job mobility and hierarchical decision-making). This statement effectively uses the information provided in the notes to underscore the student's aim of emphasizing the unique characteristics of the Japanese business world.

    Distractor Explanations: Choice B is incorrect because it focuses solely on the keiretsu system and doesn't encompass the broader characteristics of Japanese businesses mentioned in the notes, such as lifetime employment and consensus decision-making. **Choice C** is incorrect because though it does highlight unique characteristics of Japanese businesses (lifetime employment and seniority-based pay scales), it falls short of providing a direct contrast with Western models. **Choice D** is incorrect because while this choice does highlight unique characteristics of Japanese businesses (consensus decision-making and the keiretsu system), it doesn't provide a direct contrast with Western business models, failing to fully accomplish the student's goal of emphasizing unique characteristics of the Japanese business world.

1. **Domain:** CRAFT AND STRUCTURE
Skill/Knowledge: Words in Context

   Key Explanation: Choice D is correct. The sentence discusses how A. Mukherjee's book, *AI and Ethics*, adopts a computational lens instead of traditional philosophical or legal approaches. Therefore, "conventional" accurately contrasts with the computational approach, highlighting the departure from traditional methods in addressing ethical considerations related to AI.

   Distractor Explanations: Choice A is incorrect because it suggests a range of approaches, but does not specifically contrast with computational approaches as described in the sentence. The text also specifies that the author has avoided traditional philosophical or legal discussions, thereby indirectly hinting towards "conventional" being the more logical and precise word to use. **Choice B** is incorrect because, similar to Choice A, it does not specifically provide a contrast between other approaches and this specific book's computational lens. It simply implies a wide range of approaches. **Choice C** is incorrect because it does not contrast with computational approaches and does not accurately describe the traditional philosophical or legal discussions that the book seeks to avoid.

2. **Domain:** CRAFT AND STRUCTURE
Skill/Knowledge: Words in Context

   Key Explanation: Choice A is the best answer as a paradox generally means something contradictory. One can also understand this contradiction by reading the text following the underlined word, where the relationship between poetry and solitude is explained.

   Distractor Explanations: Choice B is incorrect because the relationship between poetry and solitude is not similar. **Choice C** is incorrect because while the relationship between poetry and solitude can be complex, the word "paradoxical" specifically refers to a contradiction or inconsistency, rather than overall complexity. **Choice D** is incorrect because "paradoxical"

conveys the idea of a contradiction or seeming inconsistency, which is different from something being unclear or ambiguous.

3. **Domain:** CRAFT AND STRUCTURE
Skill/Knowledge: Words in Context

   Key Explanation: Choice A is the correct answer as "emphatic" means something that has been marked by forceful emphasis. The text also mentions that the brushstrokes are "bold," further implying that Van Gogh's brushstrokes were strong, powerful, and emphasized, adding impact and intensity to his art.

   Distractor Explanations: Choice B is incorrect because it does not accurately capture the meaning of the word "emphatic" as used in the text. While Van Gogh was indeed a successful and creative artist, the word "emphatic" specifically refers to the style of his brushstrokes rather than his overall success. **Choice C** is incorrect because it is the opposite of the intended meaning of "emphatic." Van Gogh's brushstrokes are described as distinct and leaving a strong impression, which is the opposite of hesitant. **Choice D** is incorrect because it is the opposite of the intended meaning of "emphatic." Van Gogh's brushstrokes are described as vivid, leaving a lasting impression, and being a defining characteristic of his art. These traits do not align with the idea of being indecisive.

4. **Domain:** CRAFT AND STRUCTURE
Skill/Knowledge: Words in Context

   Key Explanation: Choice C is correct. It accurately describes the process of deterioration that happened to the skeletons over time due to the acidic soil. "Degraded over time" effectively conveys the intended meaning, which is that the skeletons have been destroyed over time by the acidic soil.

   Distractor Explanations: Choice A is incorrect because "in time" would imply that the erosion has occurred within a specific time period. However, the text focuses on how the acidic soil has caused the destruction of the bodies over many years. Hence "eroded in" changes the intended meaning of the sentence. **Choice B** is incorrect because "perished through" would change the intended meaning of the sentence. Usage of the word "through" would have to be followed by a means through which the skeletons have perished (for example: 8 million people perished through forced labor in the mines.) Since this is not the case here, it makes Choice B an unsuitable choice. **Choice D** is incorrect because the term "dissolved" suggests a transformation into a liquid or another form, which is not the case here. The skeletons are not dissolved but have deteriorated or degraded gradually due to the effects of time and acidic soil, leaving behind only "sand silhouettes" or dark outlines.

5. **Domain:** CRAFT AND STRUCTURE
    Skill/Knowledge: Words in Context

    Key Explanation: Choice D is correct. The passage mentions "Tom's wild exploits." "Exhilarating" is the most suitable choice because it specifically conveys a sense of excitement and thrill, which can be linked to the mention of "Tom's wild exploits" in the passage. The word "exhilarating" is also the most suitable choice as it implies that the escapades in the book are not just ordinary or routine but are filled with moments that are "captivating and delightful".

    Distractor Explanations: Choice A is incorrect because while "energetic" might imply an active and lively character, it doesn't convey the full sense of excitement and thrill associated with the adventures. The text specifically mentions that Tom's adventures are wild and thrilling. Hence, this choice is not as suitable as Choice D. **Choice B** is incorrect because "eccentric" usually suggests an element of peculiarity or oddity. The adventures in Tom Sawyer are exciting and thrilling as pointedly mentioned in the text, but not necessarily unconventional or strange. **Choice C** is incorrect because "elaborate" tends to imply something intricate or carefully planned out. In the context of the passage, "elaborate" does not

convey the sense of thrill and excitement that describes Tom's adventures. Hence, it is not the best choice to complete the text.

6. **Domain:** CRAFT AND STRUCTURE
    Skill/Knowledge: Text Structure and Purpose

    Key Explanation: Choice D is the best answer because it best describes how the underlined sentence functions in the text as a whole. The speaker is confronted with the fact that she will leave Iran and her parents may not join her. While there is a sense of doubt and apprehension, the fact that the speaker starts packing up her things and brings a keepsake from home (Iranian soil) manifests that she has accepted this decision.

    Distractor Explanations: Choice A is incorrect because the text actually suggests that the speaker is apprehensive, illustrating how she doesn't sleep through the night due to nervous thoughts and wonders about life in her new destination. **Choice B** is incorrect because the text does not state how the speaker's parents reacted to the decision because they are the ones presenting the decision to the speaker. **Choice C** is incorrect because the text does not focus on the speaker's inclination to persevering during challenging events.

7. **Domain:** CRAFT AND STRUCTURE
    Skill/Knowledge: Cross-Text Connections

    Key Explanation: Choice B is correct. Text 1 explains that the birds have narrow elevational ranges for each species due to the different temperatures at varying elevations. However, Text 2 explains that the reason for specific elevational ranges is to avoid competition for resources. Therefore, the author of Text 2 is most likely to agree that mountain birds have specific elevations in which they can live, albeit for a different reason.

    Distractor Explanations: Choice A is incorrect because the author of Text 2 does not discuss the genetics of the tropical mountain songbirds. **Choice C** is incorrect because the author of Text 2 does not differentiate between birds living at higher or lower elevations. **Choice D is** incorrect because the author of Text 2 believes that temperature is not the reason for the narrow elevational ranges of each bird species.

8. **Domain:** INFORMATION AND IDEAS
   Skill/Knowledge: Central Ideas and Details

   Key Explanation: Choice B is the best answer. The text mentions that a wise man should follow the path set out by great men so that even if his ability does not match theirs, he will still succeed by virtue of imitating great men. Therefore, this implies that imitation is the easiest way to succeed, irrespective of personal abilities.

   Distractor Explanations: Choice A is incorrect because it directly contradicts what is mentioned in the text ("A wise man ought always… to imitate those who have been supreme"). **Choice C** is incorrect because Machiavelli mentions that clever archers are aware of the strength of their bow and does not mention physical strength. **Choice D** is incorrect because it talks about how men are unable to succeed irrespective of imitating others. In reality, the text argues that imitation is the easiest way to succeed.

9. **Domain:** INFORMATION AND IDEAS
   Skill/Knowledge: Central Ideas and Details

   Key Explanation: Choice A is the best answer because it explains how the researchers determined why cats would be able to walk even if the connection between the spinal cord and the brain is partially fractured. The text states that the researchers show that somatosensory feedback informed the spinal cord about the ongoing movement to keep cats from falling.

   Distractor Explanations: Choice B is incorrect because, as the text explains, it is a cat's somatosensory feedback that keep it balanced even if a partial fracture occurs. **Choice C** is incorrect because the text explains that a cat's spinal cord was informed by the special sensors and not the other way around. **Choice D** is incorrect because the text doesn't indicate that the

researchers specifically studied cats with partial spinal damage or monitored that cat's movement and coordination.

10. **Domain:** INFORMATION AND IDEAS
    Skill/Knowledge: Command of Evidence (Textual)

    Key Explanation: Choice C is correct. This quotation effectively supports the student's claim by emphasizing the presence of complex wit and repartee in Shakespeare's works, aligning with the assertion about intricate wordplay. It also specifically highlights the nuanced character development mentioned by the student, as it mentions that Shakespeare's characters are not only clearly defined but also exhibit dynamic interactions that reveal deeper layers of their distinct personalities.

    Distractor Explanations: Choice A is incorrect because while this option praises Shakespeare's ability to create distinct characters, it focuses more on individual characterization and does not mention anything about intricate wordplay. It does not directly support the claim about wordplay and nuanced character development. **Choice B** is incorrect because it highlights Shakespeare's use of poetic and profound language but does not specifically address intricate wordplay or nuanced character development. It focuses more on the overall quality of Shakespeare's dialogues rather than the specific elements mentioned by the student. **Choice D** is incorrect because while it acknowledges the depth of Shakespeare's characters and their inner thoughts, it does not directly address the claim about intricate wordplay. It focuses more on character depth through soliloquies and asides rather than the broader aspects of wordplay and character interaction.

11. **Domain:** INFORMATION AND IDEAS
    Skill/Knowledge: Command of Evidence (Textual)

Key Explanation: Choice B is the best answer. This finding directly supports the researchers' claim by demonstrating a specific physiological effect of olive oil consumption, a component of the Mediterranean diet ("the diet's emphasis on… healthy fats like olive oil"), on reducing LDL cholesterol, a risk factor for heart disease. This translates to the Mediterranean diet adherence contributing to a reduction of cardiovascular issues.

Distractor Explanations: Choice A is incorrect because it presents information related to overall well-being and depression, which is not directly linked to cardiovascular health and does not support the researchers' claim. **Choice C** is incorrect because while it provides evidence of improved metabolic health among participants following the Mediterranean diet, it does not directly support the researchers' claim regarding the diet's protective effects against heart disease. **Choice D** is incorrect because it introduces a counterargument and suggests that factors other than diet may influence cardiovascular health outcomes, thereby undermining the researchers' claim about the effectiveness of the Mediterranean diet.

12. **Domain:** INFORMATION AND IDEAS
    Skill/Knowledge: Command of Evidence (Quantitative)

    Key Explanation: Choice B is correct. Across all milestones, a lower percentage of 21 year olds have reached life milestones in 2021 than in 1980.

    Distractor Explanations: Choice A is incorrect. Across all milestones, a lower percentage of 21-year-olds have reached life milestones in 2021 than in 1980. **Choice C** is incorrect. This conclusion cannot be reached. While a higher percentage of 21-year-olds reach financial-related milestones compared to child and marriage-related milestones, the percentage of 21-year-olds who reach the house-related milestone is still higher than that of financial-related milestones. **Choice D** is incorrect. This conclusion cannot be

reached. While a higher percentage of 21-year-olds reach financial-related milestones compared to child and marriage-related milestones, the percentage of 21-year-olds who reach the house-related milestone is still higher than that of financial-related milestones.

13. **Domain:** INFORMATION AND IDEAS
    Skill/Knowledge: Command of Evidence (Textual)

    Key Explanation: Choice B is correct. It suggests that artists in collectives engage in collaborations that go beyond a single discipline, thereby pushing the boundaries of creative expression. This aligns with the idea that artist collectives have distinct advantages. It emphasizes the collaborative and horizon-broadening aspects of collectives, which are distinct advantages.

    Distractor Explanations: Choice A is incorrect because it highlights the challenge artists face within collectives when it comes to maintaining their individual artistic identities. It doesn't directly illustrate the advantages of artist collectives. **Choice C** is incorrect because it contrasts the speed of individual artists with the potential challenges of collectives, such as drawn-out debates. It doesn't illustrate the advantages of artist collectives. **Choice D** is incorrect because it only highlights the challenges of creative differences within art collectives, leading to discordant outputs. It does not illustrate the advantages of artist collectives.

14. **Domain:** CRAFT AND STRUCTURE
    Skill/Knowledge: Inferences

    Key Explanation: Choice C is the best answer. The text mentions that most of these voting reform changes are due to the 2022 elections and "reformers are hoping to achieve these transformations before the upcoming 2024 November election." Since the sentence to be completed begins with "however," we can logically expect the sentence to give us some contrasting information to what has been discussed. Choice C states that many of these proposed voting reforms will take decades to fully come into effect, a direct contradiction to what reformers are hoping to achieve. This makes it a logical completion to the text.

Distractor Explanations: Choice A is incorrect because it introduces a new concept, i.e., the role of the upcoming election in the enforcement of these reforms. This does not contradict previous information given in the text and does not align with the use of the word "however," which directly denotes contradictory information will be given in the sentence to be completed. **Choice B** is incorrect because the passage focuses on voting reforms and how they could change the way citizens can vote, not on problems with issues that Democrat Michigan voters could face for several election cycles. **Choice D** is incorrect because although the Democrats in Michigan support early voting, there is no mention of Republicans opposing or supporting this change. Choice D also does not logically complete the text because it does not provide any contrasting information to the previous sentence.

15. **Domain:** CRAFT AND STRUCTURE
    Skill/Knowledge: Inferences

    Key Explanation: Choice A is the best answer since the passage clearly states that those who broke this law believed it to be "tyrannical", and therefore not fair to the people expected to obey it.

    Distractor Explanations: Choice B is not the best option as it requires the reader to make an inference not suggested in the passage. There is no indication that they plan on continuing with these protests. **Choice C** is too general. While the passage discusses many laws that the colonists found unjust, it does not make the claim that they found "all" laws to be unjust. **Choice D** is not the best option as it requires an inference not suggested in the passage. They may be breaking this particular law, but readers cannot infer from this passage that they think it is the "only" way to deal with unjust laws.

16. **Domain:** STANDARD ENGLISH CONVENTIONS
    Skill/Knowledge: Form, Structure, and Sense

    Key Explanation: Choice C is the best answer. The convention being tested is the use of possessive determiners. The plural possessive determiner "their" agrees in number with the plural noun "triangles" and thus indicates that the significance belongs to the triangles.

    Distractor Explanations: Choice A is incorrect because the singular possessive determiner "its" doesn't agree in number with the plural noun "triangles". **Choice B** is incorrect because "it's" is the contraction for "it is" or "it has," not a possessive determiner. **Choice D** is incorrect because "they're" is the contraction for "they are," not a possessive determiner.

17. **Domain:** STANDARD ENGLISH CONVENTIONS
    Skill/Knowledge: Boundaries

    Key Explanation: The convention being tested is punctuation use with two linked independent clauses. **Choice C** is the best answer because "nor" is used to introduce a negative alternative or to continue a negative statement, and it is appropriate in this context to indicate that Jade Snow Wong did not travel solely to her birthplace (the United States) or solely to her ancestral homeland (China). It conveys the idea that her journey encompassed both.

    Distractor Explanations: Choice A is incorrect because "and" does not convey the intended meaning in this context. The sentence contrasts where Jade Snow Wong traveled, so "and" doesn't provide the appropriate contrast. **Choice B** is incorrect because "but" is used to introduce a contrast, which is not the intended meaning in this context. The sentence does not present a contrast between her birthplace and her travel destinations. **Choice D** is less appropriate because "yet" typically introduces a contrast or unexpected result. In this context, "nor" is a more suitable conjunction for indicating that she did not travel solely to one place or the other.

18. **Domain:** STANDARD ENGLISH CONVENTIONS
Skill/Knowledge: Form, Structure, and Sense

Key Explanation: Choice D is the correct answer. The convention being tested here is verb forms. It correctly uses the simple present tense of the verb "endure," which is appropriate for stating general truths or facts. It indicates that Dr. Seuss' influence sustains through numerous adaptations and derivative works, making it the apt choice.

Distractor Explanations: Choice A is incorrect because it uses the future tense form of "endure," indicating a future action. It is incorrect in this context because the sentence is discussing Dr. Seuss' current influence. **Choice B** is incorrect because it does not suit the context of the sentence. "Will have" is typically used to indicate an action or state that will be completed or will still be ongoing at a specific point in the future. It implies a future perfect tense, which suggests that the endurance, in this context, will continue up to a particular future time. Therefore, the use of "will have endured" does not align with the intended meaning of the sentence. **Choice C** is incorrect because it uses the past perfect tense of the verb "endure" suggesting that the enduring influence is in the past. This changes the intended meaning of the sentence.

19. **Domain:** STANDARD ENGLISH CONVENTIONS
Skill/Knowledge: Form, Structure, and Sense

Key Explanation: Choice B is the correct answer. The convention being tested here is subject-verb agreement. The subject "a new generation of virtually noiseless, eco-friendly tractors" is singular, and the correct verb form should also be singular to agree with it. Choice B uses "promises," which is the correct form for singular subjects like this.

Distractor Explanations: Choice A is incorrect because the plural verb "promise" does not agree with the singular subject "a new generation of virtually noiseless, eco-friendly tractors." **Choice C** is incorrect because it uses the future continuous tense. This tense is typically used to describe actions that will be ongoing or in progress at a specific future time. In the sentence, a new generation of tractors that are already developed and exist is being discussed. The sentence is focused on describing their current capabilities, so the simple present tense, as in Choice B ("promises"), is more appropriate to convey this meaning. **Choice D** is incorrect because it uses the present perfect tense which is used to connect the past with the present or to describe actions that occurred at an unspecified time before the present. The use of the present perfect tense would suggest that these tractors made promises at some point in the past, which is not the intended meaning.

20. **Domain:** STANDARD ENGLISH CONVENTIONS
Skill/Knowledge: Boundaries

Key Explanation: The convention being tested is punctuation use between a sentence and an essential element. **Choice B** is the correct choice because it uses a comma appropriately to set off the non-essential clause "that absorb photons from the sun" without disrupting the main sentence structure.

Distractor Explanations: Choice A is incorrect because it includes a comma after "to," which is not needed and disrupts the flow of the sentence. **Choice C** is incorrect because it uses parentheses instead of commas to set off the non-essential clause. While parentheses can be used for this purpose, they are less common in this context, and commas are typically preferred. **Choice D** is incorrect because it includes an extra comma before "to release electrons," which is unnecessary and disrupts the sentence's clarity and flow.

21. **Domain:** STANDARD ENGLISH CONVENTIONS
Skill/Knowledge: Form, Structure, and Sense

Key Explanation: Choice D is the correct answer. The convention being tested here is subject-verb agreement. The singular subject "family" agrees with the singular verb "was," thus completing the text according to the conventions of Standard English.

Distractor Explanations: Choice A is incorrect because "the Aasvik family is on a quest" would indicate that they are currently on a quest, but the text seems to describe a past event ("they stumbled upon.") This choice does not provide the correct verb tense. **Choice B** is incorrect because the singular subject "family" does not agree with the plural verb "were," thus creating a subject-verb agreement error. **Choice C** is incorrect because "the Aasvik family will be on a quest" implies that they will embark on this quest in the future, which is contradictory to the events described in the text.

22. **Domain:** STANDARD ENGLISH CONVENTIONS
Skill/Knowledge: Boundaries

Key Explanation: The convention being tested is punctuation use between a sentence and an essential element. **Choice D** is the best answer because it provides the correct punctuation and structure for the sentence. The commas are appropriately used to set off the nonrestrictive phrase "reminding us," which adds extra information but can be removed without changing the core meaning of the sentence. The placement of "not just a choice but an imperative for humanity" is also correct, conveying that pursuing peace is not merely an option but a necessity for humanity.

Distractor Explanations: Choice A is incorrect because it incorrectly places a comma after "reminding us," creating a comma splice, which is a grammatical error. **Choice B** is incorrect because it uses a comma after "peace," which is not needed. **Choice C** is incorrect because it incorrectly places

commas around "not just a choice," making it seem like an interrupting phrase when it should be part of the main sentence structure.

23. **Domain:** EXPRESSION OF IDEAS
Skill/Knowledge: Transitions

Key Explanation: Choice D is the best answer. "However" logically signals that this sentence, which indicates that there was no difference in depressive symptoms between teens involved in the arts who also did sports and teens involved in the arts who did not also participate in sports, offers a contrast to or refutation of the previous assumption that teens involved exclusively in sports were the least likely to report depressive symptoms.

Distractor Explanations: Choice A is incorrect because "secondly" illogically signals that this sentence merely offers an additional or secondary point concerning the previous assumption that teens involved exclusively in sports were the least likely to report depressive symptoms. Instead, the sentence offers a contrast to or refutation of that assumption. **Choice B** is incorrect because "consequently" illogically signals that this sentence offers a result or consequence of the previous assumption that teens involved exclusively in sports were the least likely to report depressive symptoms. Instead, the sentence offers a contrast to or refutation of that assumption. **Choice C** is incorrect because "moreover" illogically signals that this sentence merely adds to the previous assumption that teens involved exclusively in sports were the least likely to report depressive symptoms. Instead, the sentence offers a contrast to or refutation of that assumption.

24. **Domain:** EXPRESSION OF IDEAS
Skill/Knowledge: Transitions

Key Explanation: Choice B, "Additionally," is the best answer. "Additionally" is used to introduce information that supports and adds to the previous information. In this case, it signifies that the Battle of Marengo bolstered Napoleon's confidence, which is an additional outcome or effect of the battle. By using "additionally," the sentence that follows logically connects to the previous information, indicating that the battle not only secured Napoleon's power and reputation but also had the additional impact of boosting his confidence, leading to further expansion of his empire and shaping European history.

Distractor Explanations: Choice A is incorrect because it indicates a contrasting idea or point. However, there is no logical contrast or contradiction between the impact of the Battle of Marengo on Napoleon's confidence and the outcomes described in the previous sentence. The word "however" would introduce an unnecessary contradiction or conflict in this context. **Choice C** is incorrect because it implies agreement or confirmation of a previous statement. However, the sentence that follows does not provide confirmation but rather introduces new information that supports the previous information. The word "indeed" would be inappropriate in this context as it does not convey the intended addition or support. **Choice D** is incorrect because it indicates a contrasting idea or point. However, there is no logical contrast or contradiction between the impact of the Battle of Marengo on Napoleon's confidence and the outcomes described in the previous sentence. The word "nevertheless" would introduce an unnecessary contradiction or conflict in this context.

25. **Domain:** EXPRESSION OF IDEAS
Skill/Knowledge: Rhetorical Synthesis

Key Explanation: Choice B is the best answer. The notes mention that "there is no evidence that the population is breeding" and that the small population of the African gray hornbill in Florida "may only persist due to continuing releases or escapes."

Distractor Explanations: Choice A is incorrect because it does not explain why the bird will not rapidly multiply in Florida. **Choice C** is incorrect because the notes offer no comparison between

the climate in sub-Saharan Africa and Florida. **Choice D** is incorrect because the notes do not mention that the African gray hornbill is only widespread in open woodland and savannah areas. Instead, it mentions that "it prefers open woodland and savannah."

26. **Domain:** EXPRESSION OF IDEAS
Skill/Knowledge: Rhetorical Synthesis

Key Explanation: Choice B is correct because it highlights a similarity in the patterns of dialogue during the two studies, making it the best choice.

Distractor Explanations: Choice A is incorrect because it does not reveal any similarity in patterns. It tries to distract us by informing that both the neocortex and hippocampus are components of the human brain. This, at first, may seem convincing, but this is not the similarity the question stem asks about. **Choice C** is incorrect because it only outlines the role of the neocortex and does not discuss any similarities in patterns. **Choice D** is incorrect because it mentions only one of the two studies and therefore is not eligible to show the desired similarity in patterns.

27. **Domain:** EXPRESSION OF IDEAS
Skill/Knowledge: Rhetorical Synthesis

Key Explanation: Choice D is the best answer. This sentence emphasizes the proposed mechanism, which is a process by which something takes place, to reduce conservation costs: a market-based trading system of conservation credits that allows nations to offset negative environmental impacts.

Distractor Explanations: Choice A is incorrect. This sentence highlights the need for a conservation mechanism, but it does not mention the mechanism itself. **Choice B** is incorrect. While this sentence mentions the data used in the study, it does not mention the mechanism proposed by the study and its researchers. **Choice C** is incorrect. This sentence mentions the potential impacts of the new mechanism, but it does not emphasize the mechanism itself.

1. **Domain:** PROBLEM SOLVING AND DATA ANALYSIS

    Skill/Knowledge: Percentages | **Testing Point:** Find the percentage of a number

    Key Explanation: Choice B is correct. 12% of 50 can be calculated as $\dfrac{12}{100} \times 50$, which is equal to 6.

    Distractor Explanations: Choice A is incorrect. This is 8% of 50. **Choice C is incorrect.** This is 16% of 50. **Choice D is incorrect.** This is 24% of 50.

2. **Domain:** ALGEBRA

    Skill/Knowledge: Linear equations in one variable | **Testing Point:** Analyzing a graph of a linear equation

    Key Explanation: Choice D is correct. In the graph, the number of houses designed in the year 2000 is 2 which is the y-intercept.

    After 5 years, there were 10 total houses.

    Hence, the architect designed $10 - 2 = 8$ houses in 5 years.

    This means that the slope is $\dfrac{8}{5}$.

    Therefore, the expression is $\dfrac{8}{5}x + 2$.

    Distractor Explanations: Choice A is incorrect and may result from using the reciprocal of the correct slope. **Choice B is incorrect** and may result from not considering the y-intercept. **Choice C is** incorrect and may result from using the reciprocal of the correct slope.

3. **Domain:** ALGEBRA

    Skill/Knowledge: Linear inequalities in one or two variables | **Testing Point:** Solve a linear inequality in one variable

    Key Explanation: The correct answer is 1. To solve the inequality, group like terms together. Adding $2x - 2$ to both sides of the inequality yields $x + 2 + 2x - 2 \le -2x + 5 + 2x - 2$. Combining like terms results in $3x \le 3$. Dividing both sides by 3 results in $x \le 1$. Therefore, the greatest integer

solution of the above inequality would be 1, as x is less than or equal to 1.

4. **Domain:** ADVANCED MATH

    Skill/Knowledge: Nonlinear functions | **Testing Point:** Equation of a parabola

    Key Explanation: Choice B is correct.

    The given function represents a parabola opening upward.

    The function is in vertex form of $f(x) = a(x - h)^2 + k$ where (h, k) is the vertex of the parabola.

    Since the parabola is opening upward, then the minimum value of the function is at the vertex.

    Hence, $y_{min} = k$.

    Since k is equal to -4 in the given function, then $y_{min} = -4$.

    Distractor Explanations: Choice A is incorrect. This is the value of $-h$. **Choice C is incorrect.** This is the value of one of the x-intercepts of the given function. **Choice D is incorrect.** This is the value of one of the x-intercepts of the given function.

5. **Domain:** PROBLEM SOLVING AND DATA ANALYSIS

    Skill/Knowledge: Probability and conditional probability | **Testing Point:** Find the probability of an event

    Key Explanation: The correct answer is $\dfrac{5}{12}$.

    Probability is calculated as $\dfrac{Favourable\ outcome}{Sample\ space}$.

    The favorable outcome would be represented by the parents who voted yes at the meeting which is $36 - 21 = 15$. The sample space would be the total number of parents which is 36. Therefore, the probability would be $\dfrac{15}{36}$ which is simplified to $\dfrac{5}{12}$.

6. **Domain:** PROBLEM-SOLVING AND DATA ANALYSIS

Skill/Knowledge: Ratios, rates, proportional relationships, and units | **Testing Point:** Using ratio to solve a problem

Key Explanation: Choice B is correct. Since the ratio of Grade 7 students to Grade 8 students is $\frac{3}{4}$, then $\frac{no.\ of\ Grade\ 7\ students}{no.\ of\ Grade\ 8\ students} = \frac{3}{4}$.

Since there are 240 Grade 8 students, then

$$\frac{no.\ of\ Grade\ 7\ students}{240} = \frac{3}{4}.$$

Multiplying both sides of the equation by 240 yields no. of Grade 7 students $= \left(\frac{3}{4}\right)(240) = 180$.

Distractor Explanations: Choice A is incorrect. This is the number of Grade 7 students if the ratio of Grade 7 students to Grade 8 students is $\frac{2}{3}$.

Choice C is incorrect. This is the number of Grade 7 students if the ratio of Grade 7 students to Grade 8 students is $\frac{5}{6}$. **Choice D is incorrect.** This is the number of Grade 7 students if the ratio of Grade 7 students to Grade 8 students is $\frac{4}{3}$.

7. **Domain:** ALGEBRA

Skill/Knowledge: Linear functions | **Testing Point:** Creating linear function based on the given data

Key Explanation: Choice C is correct. To create the linear function, use the format $f(x) = mx + b$ where m is the slope and b is the y-intercept.

Since her total savings at Week 0 is $120, then the y-intercept is 120.

The slope is the amount of money she saves per week. Calculating the slope yields $145 - 120 = 25$.

Therefore, the function that best represents her total savings is $f(x) = 25x + 120$.

Distractor Explanations: Choice A is incorrect and may result from not considering the $120 as the y-intercept. **Choice B is incorrect** and may result from using a wrong slope. **Choice D is incorrect** and may result from multiplying x with the y-intercept instead of the slope.

8. **Domain:** ALGEBRA

Skill/Knowledge: Linear equations in two variables | **Testing Point:** Find a linear equation in two variables that represents a line passing through two points

Key Explanation: Choice B is correct. The line has an x-intercept of –2. Substituting 0 for y and –2 for x in the given equation results in $-2m + 0n + 2 = 0$. Subtracting 2 from both sides of this equation yields $-2m = -2$. Dividing both sides of this equation by –2 results in $m = 1$. Thus, the given equation becomes $x + ny + 2 = 0$. It's given that the line also passes through the point (3, 5). Substituting 3 for x and 5 for y in this equation yields $3 + 5n + 2 = 0$. Combining constants on the left side of this equation results in $5n + 5 = 0$. Subtracting 5 from both sides of this equation yields $5n = -5$. Dividing both sides of this equation by 5 results in $n = -1$.

Distractor Explanations: Choice A is incorrect and may result if the line passes through the point (9, 5). **Choice C is incorrect** and may result if the line passes through the point (–7, 5). **Choice D is incorrect** and may result if the line passes through the point (–13, 5).

9. **Domain:** GEOMETRY AND TRIGONOMETRY

Skill/Knowledge: Right triangles and trigonometry | **Testing Point:** Trigonometric functions

Key Explanation: Choice A is correct. Since $\triangle ABC$ and $\triangle ACD$ are right triangles, then the following trigonometric functions can be obtained:

$$\tan(50) = \frac{\overline{AC}}{\overline{DC}}; \ \tan(35) = \frac{\overline{AC}}{\overline{AB}}; \ \sin(50) = = \frac{\overline{AC}}{\overline{AD}};$$

$sin(35) = \dfrac{\overline{AC}}{\overline{BC}}$

The common side of ΔABC and ΔACD is $\overline{AC}$.

Getting the value of $\overline{AC}$ in terms of $\overline{AB}$ yields $\overline{AC} = \overline{AB}\, tan(35)$.

Getting the value of $\overline{AC}$ in terms of $\overline{AD}$ yields $\overline{AC} = \overline{AD}\, sin(50)$.

Equating the two equations yields $\overline{AB}\, tan(35) = \overline{AD}\, sin(50)$.

Dividing both sides of the equation by $\overline{AD}$ and $tan(35)$ yields $\dfrac{\overline{AB}}{\overline{AD}} = \dfrac{sin(50)}{tan(35)}$.

Hence, $\dfrac{\overline{AB}}{\overline{AD}} = 1.09$.

Therefore, the statement $\dfrac{\overline{AB}}{\overline{AD}} < 1.1$ is true.

Distractor Explanations: Choice B is incorrect.
The statement $\dfrac{\overline{BC}}{\overline{AD}} > 1.4$ is false because $\dfrac{\overline{BC}}{\overline{AD}} = 1.34$. **Choice C is incorrect.** The statement $\dfrac{\overline{AB}}{\overline{DC}} > 1.8$ is false because $\dfrac{\overline{AB}}{\overline{DC}} > 1.7$. **Choice D is incorrect.** The statement $\dfrac{\overline{BC}}{\overline{DC}} < 1.9$ is false because $\dfrac{\overline{BC}}{\overline{DC}} = 2.08$.

10. **Domain:** ALGEBRA

    Skill/Knowledge: Systems of linear equations with two variables | **Testing Point:** Creating and using linear equations to solve a problem

    Key Explanation: Choice B is correct. Let a and b represent the prices of items A and B, respectively.

    Since Tom buys 4 pieces of item A and 5 pieces of item B, then this can be represented by $4a + 5b$.

    Since Paul buys 6 pieces of item A and 2 pieces of item B, then this can be represented by $6a + 2b$.

    Since they spend the same amount of money, then

$4a + 5b = 6a + 2b$.

Subtracting $2b$ and $4a$ from both sides of the equation yields $3b = 2a$.

Dividing both sides of the equation by 3 yields $b = \dfrac{2}{3}a$.

Since a piece of item A and a piece of item B costs \$2, then $a + b = 2$.

Calculate the values of a and b using the substitution method.

Substituting $b = \dfrac{2}{3}a$ to $a + b = 2$ yields $a + \dfrac{2}{3}a = 2$.

Combining like terms yields $\dfrac{5}{3}a = 2$.

Multiplying $\dfrac{3}{5}$ to both sides of the equation yields $a = \dfrac{6}{5} = 1.2$.

Hence, item A costs \$1.2.

Substituting the value of a to $b = \dfrac{2}{3}a$ yields $b = \dfrac{2}{3}(1.2) = 0.8$.

Hence, item B costs \$0.8.

Therefore, 3 pieces of item A and 2 pieces of item B cost $3(1.2) + 2(0.8) = \$5.2$.

Distractor Explanations: Choice A is incorrect and may result from calculating the total cost of 2 pieces of item A and 3 pieces of item B. **Choice C is incorrect** and may result from calculating the total cost of 4 pieces of item A and 2 pieces of item B. **Choice D is incorrect** and may result from calculating the amount of money spent by Tom or Paul.

11. **Domain:** PROBLEM-SOLVING AND DATA ANALYTICS

    Skill/Knowledge: Two-variable data: models and scatterplots | **Testing Point:** Line of best fit

    Key Explanation: Choice A is correct. The percentage increase is given by the formula $\dfrac{Increase}{original\ temperature} \times 100\%$. Since there are two recorded temperatures on day 5, the higher temperature would be used to calculate the percentage increase in temperature from the one predicted by the line of best fit. The higher temperature is 5.5°C and the temperature recorded by the line of best fit would be 5°C. Hence, the increase in temperature would be 5.5 – 5 = 0.5. The percentage increase in temperature would be $\frac{0.5}{5} \times 100\% = 10\%$.

Distractor Explanations: Choice B is incorrect. This option is calculated as the percentage of the lower temperature recorded on day 5 compared to the temperature predicted by the line of best fit. **Choice C** is incorrect. This option is calculated by finding the percentage decrease from the line of best fit to the lower recorded temperature on day 5. **Choice D** is incorrect. This option is calculated by finding the percentage increase from the lower recorded to the higher recorded temperature on day 5.

12. **Domain:** ADVANCED MATH

Skill/Knowledge: Nonlinear functions | **Testing Point:** Find the vertex form of a quadratic function given its graph

Key Explanation: Choice C is correct. The vertex form of a quadratic function has the general form $f(x) = a(x – h)^2 + k$, where (h, k) represents the vertex of the quadratic function. From the graph, the vertex is the point $(–2, –4)$, then $h = –2$ and $k = –4$. Thus, the equation of the quadratic function is $f(x) = a(x + 2)^2 – 4$. The graph passes through the point $(0, 4)$. Substituting 4 for $f(x)$ and 0 for x in the equation $f(x) = a(x + 2)^2 – 4$ yields $4 = a(0 + 2)^2 – 4$. Simplifying this equation results in $4 = 4a – 4$. Adding 4 to both sides of this equation yields $8 = 4a$. Dividing both sides of this equation by 4 results in $2 = a$. Therefore, the quadratic function f is defined by $f(x) = 2(x + 2)^2 – 4$, which is choice C.

Distractor Explanations: Choice A is incorrect because $(0, 4)$ does not satisfy the equation $f(x) = 2x^2 + 8x + 8$. **Choice B** is incorrect because $(0, 4)$ does not satisfy the equation $f(x) = 2x^2 + 8x – 4$.

Choice D is incorrect because the equation $f(x) = 2(x –2)^2 – 4$ represents a quadratic function with the vertex $(2, –4)$ and not $(–2, –4)$.

13. **Domain:** ALGEBRA

Skill/Knowledge: Linear equations in one variable | **Testing Point:** Translate a word problem into a linear equation and solve the equation to find an unknown quantity

Key Explanation: Choice B is correct. Let x represent the number of months David follows his plan. Then $3x$ represents the increase in David's hourly rate to solve math questions after x months. Initially, David can solve math questions at a rate of 10 questions per hour. After x months, David will be able to solve $3x + 10$ questions per hour. For his rate to increase to 28 questions per hour, $3x +10$ must be equal to 28. Subtracting 10 from both sides of the equation $3x + 10 = 28$ yields $3x = 18$. Dividing both sides of this equation by 3 results in $x = 6$. Therefore, it will take 6 months for David to be able to solve 28 questions per hour, following the plan.

Distractor Explanations: Choice A is incorrect and may result if David wants to achieve a rate of 19 questions per hour. **Choice C** is incorrect and may result if David wants to achieve a rate of 46 questions per hour. **Choice D** is incorrect and may result if David wants to achieve a rate of 64 questions per hour.

14. **Domain:** ADVANCED MATH

Skill/Knowledge: Nonlinear equations in one variable and systems of equations in two variables | **Testing Point:** System of quadratic and linear equation

Key Explanation: Choice D is correct. Since $y = 5$, then by substituting 5 to y the quadratic equation becomes $5 = –qx^2 + 3x + 7$.

Subtracting 5 from both sides of the equation yields $0 = –qx^2 + 3x + 2$.

Since the system of equations have two distinct roots, then the discriminant is greater than 0.

The discriminant formula is $b^2 - 4ac$ where a and b are the coefficients of x^2 and x, respectively, and c is the constant.

From $0 = -qx^2 + 3x + 2$, $a = -q$, $b = 3$ and $c = 2$.

Substituting the values to the formula yields $(3)2 - 4(-q)(2) > 0$

Simplifying the equation yields $9 + 8q > 0$.

Subtracting 9 from both sides of the equation yields $8q > -9$.

Dividing both sides of the equation by 8 yields $q > -\dfrac{9}{8}$.

Since $\dfrac{9}{8} > -\dfrac{9}{8}$, then option D is the correct answer.

Distractor Explanations: Choice A is incorrect. The discriminant will be less than 0. **Choice B** is incorrect. The discriminant will be less than 0. **Choice C** is incorrect. The discriminant will be equal to 0.

15. **Domain:** ADVANCED MATH

Skill/Knowledge: Nonlinear functions | **Testing Point:** Find the coordinates of the vertex of a quadratic function

Key Explanation: Choice D is correct. The given equation $f(x) = (x - 1)^2 + 20$ is the vertex form of a quadratic function f. The general vertex form is $f(x) = a(x - h)^2 + k$, where (h, k) is the vertex. Since $a = 1 > 0$, then the graph of the quadratic function opens up and it has a minimum, which is the y-coordinate of the vertex. Comparing $(x - 1)^2 + 20$ with $a(x - h)^2 + k$ results in $20 = k$. Thus, the y-coordinate of the vertex is 20. Therefore, the minimum value of the function $f(x)$ is 20.

Distractor Explanations: Choice A is incorrect and may result from conceptual or calculation errors. **Choice B** is incorrect and may result from conceptual or calculation errors. **Choice C** is incorrect and may result from conceptual or calculation errors.

16. **Domain:** ADVANCED MATH

Skill/Knowledge: Equivalent Expressions | **Testing Point:** Find an equivalent expression

Key Explanation: Choice A is correct. It's given that $F = k\dfrac{q_1 \cdot q_2}{r^2}$. Cross-multiplication results in $F \cdot r^2 = kq_1 \cdot q_2$. Dividing both sides of this equation by F results in $r^2 = \dfrac{kq_1 \cdot q_2}{F}$. Since r is a positive quantity (distance), then r is the positive square root of $\dfrac{kq_1 \cdot q_2}{F}$. It's given that $k = \dfrac{1}{4\pi\varepsilon_0}$. Substituting $\dfrac{1}{4\pi\varepsilon_0}$ for k results in $r = \sqrt{\dfrac{q_1 \cdot q_2}{4\pi\varepsilon_0 F}}$ or $r = \sqrt{\dfrac{1}{4} \cdot \dfrac{q_1 \cdot q_2}{\pi\varepsilon_0 F}}$. The square root of $\dfrac{1}{4}$ is $\dfrac{1}{2}$. Therefore, the expression of r in terms of F, q_1, q_2 and ε_0 is $r = \dfrac{1}{2}\sqrt{\dfrac{q_1 \cdot q_2}{\pi\varepsilon_0 F}}$.

Distractor Explanations: Choice B is incorrect and may result if the given formula is $F = \dfrac{q_1 \cdot q_2}{kr^2}$. **Choice C** is incorrect and may result if the given formula is $F = \varepsilon_0 \dfrac{q_1 \cdot q_2}{r^2}$. **Choice D** is incorrect and may result if the given formula is $F = k\dfrac{q_1 \cdot q_2}{r}$.

17. **Domain:** ALGEBRA

Skill/Knowledge: Linear equations in two variables | **Testing Point:** Determine the correct graph of a given linear equation in two variables based on the characteristics of the line

Key Explanation: Choice A is correct. Subtracting $2x$ from the given equation $2x + ay = 3$ yields $ay = -2x + 3$. Dividing both sides of this equation by a results in $y = -\dfrac{2}{a}x + \dfrac{3}{a}$. Since a is a negative number less than -2, then the slope $-\dfrac{2}{a}$ is positive, and the y-intercept $\dfrac{3}{a}$ is negative.

Substituting 0 for y to find the x-intercept in the

equation $2x + ay = 3$ yields $2x = 3$. Dividing both sides of this equation by 2 results in $x = \frac{3}{2}$ or 1.5. Thus, the x-intercept for this line is (1.5, 0). Therefore, the correct graph has a positive slope, a negative y-intercept and an x-intercept of 1.5, and this is true only in the graph below out of the given choices.

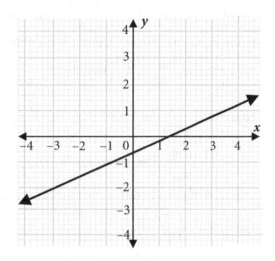

Distractor Explanations: Choice B is incorrect and may result if the x-intercept is $\frac{3}{8}$ and the y-intercept is $-\frac{3}{4}$. **Choice C** is incorrect and may result if the x-intercept is –1.5 and the y-intercept is $-\frac{3}{4}$. **Choice D** is incorrect and may result if the x-intercept is –1.5 and the y-intercept is $\frac{3}{4}$.

18. **Domain:** ALGEBRA

    Skill/Knowledge: Linear equations in two variables | **Testing Point:** Compare the graphs of two linear equations in two variables

    Key Explanation: Choice D is correct. Distributing the left hand side of the first given equation $3(x - 2) = \frac{4y - 8}{2}$ yields $3x - 6 = \frac{4y - 8}{2}$. Multiplying both sides of this equation by 2 results in $6x - 12 = 4y - 8$. Adding 8 to both sides of the equation yields $6x - 4 = 4y$. Dividing both sides of this equation by 4 results in $\frac{1}{6}x - 1 = y$,

or $y = \frac{6}{4}x - 1$. After simplifying the fraction 64 into 32, the first equation can be written as $y = \frac{3}{2}x - 1$. Subtracting 2x from both sides of the second equation $2x - 3y = 3$ yields $-3 = -2x + 3$. Dividing both sides of this equation by –3 results in $y = \frac{2}{3}x - 1$. b is the y-intercept in the slope-intercept form $y = mx + b$. It follows that the y-intercept of the lines $y = \frac{3}{2}x - 1$ and $y = \frac{2}{3}x - 1$ is –1. Therefore, the two lines have the same y-intercept.

Distractor Explanations: Choice A is incorrect and may result if the second equation is $3x - 2y = 3$. **Choice B** is incorrect and may result if the second equation is $2x + 3y = 3$. **Choice C** is incorrect and may result if the second equation is $3x - 2y = 2$.

19. **Domain:** PROBLEM SOLVING AND DATA ANALYSIS

    Skill/Knowledge: Ratios, rates, proportional relationships, and units | **Testing Point:** Calculate the ratio of two quantities

    Key Explanation: Choice C is correct. Let r represent the radius of the smaller circle and R represent the radius of the larger circle. The ratio of the radius of the smaller circle to that of the larger circle is equal to the ratio of the circumference of the smaller circle to that of the larger circle. It follows that $\frac{r}{R} = 0.6$, or $\frac{r}{R} = \frac{3}{5}$. Multiplying both sides of this equation by R yields $r = \frac{3}{5}R$. The area of the larger circle is equal to πR^2, and the area of the shaded region is the difference between the area of the larger circle and that of the smaller circle, which is equal to $\pi R^2 - \pi r^2$, or $\pi(R^2 - r^2)$. Thus, the ratio of the area of the shaded region to that of the larger circle can be written as $\frac{\pi(R^2 - r^2)}{\pi R^2}$. This can be simplified into

$\dfrac{R^2 - r^2}{R^2}$. Substituting $\dfrac{3}{5} R$ for r in the expression

$\dfrac{R^2 - r^2}{R^2}$ yields   This can be simplified into

$\dfrac{R^2 - \dfrac{9}{25} R^2}{R^2}$. Factoring out R^2 in the numerator

yields $\dfrac{R^2 \left(1 - \dfrac{9}{25} \right)}{R^2}$. Canceling out the common

factor R^2 results in $1 - \dfrac{9}{25}$ or $\dfrac{16}{25}$. Therefore, the

ratio of the area of the shaded region to that of the

larger circle is $\dfrac{16}{25}$.

Distractor Explanations: Choice A is incorrect. This is the square of the ratio of the smaller radius to the larger radius. **Choice B** is incorrect. This is the ratio of the smaller radius to the larger radius. **Choice D** is incorrect. This is the ratio of the area of the shaded region to the area of the smaller circle.

20. **Domain:** PROBLEM SOLVING AND DATA ANALYSIS

    Skill/Knowledge: One-variable data: distributions and measures of center and spread | **Testing Point:** Find the mean of a set of numbers

    Key Explanation: Choice C is correct. It's given that the mean of 7 numbers is a, then the sum of the 7 numbers, which is given by the product of the average and the number of values, is $7a$. It's also given that the mean of 4 of these numbers is b. It follows that the sum of these 4 numbers is $4b$. Then the sum of the 3 remaining numbers is the difference between the sum of the 7 numbers and the sum of the 4 numbers, or $7a - 4b$. Thus, the average of the 3 remaining numbers is equal to the sum of the 3 numbers divided by 3, or $\dfrac{7a - 4b}{3}$.

    Distractor Explanations: Choice A is incorrect and may result if the sum of the 7 numbers is a.

Choice B is incorrect and may result if the sum of the 4 numbers is b. **Choice D** is incorrect. This is the sum of the 3 remaining numbers.

21. **Domain:** GEOMETRY AND TRIGONOMETRY

    Skill/Knowledge: Circles | **Testing Point:** Find the radius of a circle given its equation by completing the square

    Key Explanation: 0.99 is the correct answer. The standard form of the equation of a circle with center (h, k) is $(x - h)^2 + (y - k)^2 = r^2$, where r is the radius of the circle. The given equation can be written into the standard form by completing the square. First, divide both sides of the given equation $12x^2 + 12y^2 + 3x - 9y - 10 = 0$ by 12

    yields $x^2 + y^2 + \dfrac{1}{4} x - \dfrac{3}{4} y - \dfrac{5}{6} = 0$, which can be

    grouped into $\left(x^2 + \dfrac{1}{4} x \right) + \left(y^2 - \dfrac{3}{4} y \right) - \dfrac{5}{6} = 0$.

    To complete the square, add $\dfrac{1}{64}$ and $\dfrac{9}{64}$ to

    both sides of this equation, which results in

    $\left(x^2 + \dfrac{1}{4} x + \dfrac{1}{64} \right) + \left(y^2 - \dfrac{3}{4} y + \dfrac{9}{64} \right) - \dfrac{5}{6} = \dfrac{1}{64} + \dfrac{9}{64}$.

    Adding $\dfrac{5}{6}$ to both sides of this equation and

    adding the fractions on the right-hand side yields

    $\left(x^2 + \dfrac{1}{4} x + \dfrac{1}{64} \right) + \left(y^2 - \dfrac{3}{4} y + \dfrac{9}{64} \right) = \dfrac{95}{96}$. Factoring

    results in $\left(x + \dfrac{1}{8} \right)^2 + \left(y - \dfrac{3}{8} \right)^2 = \dfrac{95}{96}$. Thus, the

    radius of the circle is $\sqrt{\dfrac{95}{96}}$ which is equal to

    0.994778. Therefore, to the nearest hundredth, the length of the radius is rounded to 0.99.

22. **Domain:** GEOMETRY AND TRIGONOMETRY

    Skill/Knowledge: Lines, angles and triangles | **Testing Point:** Use similar triangles to find the unknown length of a side of a triangle

    Key Explanation: Choice B is correct. It's given that $ABCD$ is a parallelogram, then $\overline{AB}$ is parallel to $\overline{DC}$. It follows that $m\angle GBF = m\angle FDC$ because they are alternate interior angles. Also, $m\angle BFG = m\angle CFD$ because they are vertical angles. Then the two triangles GBF and FCD are similar because they have two pairs of equal corresponding angles. It follows that their corresponding sides are proportional. $\overline{BG}$ corresponds to $\overline{CD}$, and $\overline{BF}$ corresponds to $\overline{FD}$. Then the proportion can be written as $\dfrac{BG}{CD} = \dfrac{BF}{FD}$. Substituting the given values in the proportion yields $\dfrac{BG}{3.16} = \dfrac{BF}{4.37}$. In the figure, $\overline{AB}$ and $\overline{DC}$ are opposite sides of the parallelogram $ABCD$, then they have equal lengths $AB = DC = 3.16$ cm. It follows that $BG = AB - AG = 3.16 - 1.06 = 2.1$ cm. Substituting 2.1 for BG in the proportion $\dfrac{BG}{3.16} = \dfrac{BF}{4.37}$ yields $\dfrac{2.1}{3.16} = \dfrac{BF}{4.37}$. Cross-multiplication results in $9.177 = 3.16 \times BF$. Dividing both sides of this equation by 3.16 yields $BF = 2.9041\ldots$, which is rounded to 2.9 to the nearest tenth. Therefore, the length of $\overline{BF}$ is approximately 2.9 cm.

Distractor Explanations: Choice A is incorrect and may result if $BG = 1.06$ cm. **Choice C** is incorrect and may result if $AG = 0.92$ cm. **Choice D** is incorrect and may result if $AG = 0.77$ cm.

1. **Domain:** PROBLEM SOLVING AND DATA ANALYSIS

   Skill/Knowledge: Ratios, rates, proportional relationships, and units | **Testing Point:** Directly proportional relationship

   Key Explanation: Choice C is correct. The question presents a direct relationship, which is 1 mile takes 45 minutes to cover. 1 hour is equivalent to 60 mins. Therefore,

   $$\frac{1\ mile \times 60\ minutes}{45\ minutes} = \frac{4}{3}\ miles\,/\,1.33\ miles.$$

   Distractor Explanations: Choice A is incorrect. This is the ratio of Wendy's walk for 1 mile in 45 minutes. **Choice B is incorrect.** This is the result if Wendy walks 1 mile in 50 minutes. **Choice D is incorrect.** This is the result if Wendy walks 1 mile in 100 minutes.

2. **Domain:** ALGEBRA

   Skill/Knowledge: Linear functions | **Testing Point:** Find the value of a linear function

   Key Explanation: Choice B is correct. Substituting 2 for x yields $f(x) = 5(2) - 8$, resulting in $f(x) = 10 - 8 = 2$.

   Distractor Explanations: Choice A is incorrect. This results from adding 2 to 5 and then subtracting 8. **Choice C is incorrect** and may result from squaring 5 and then subtracting 8. **Choice D is incorrect** and may result from adding 8 instead of subtracting 8.

3. **Domain:** ALGEBRA

   Skill/Knowledge: Systems of two linear equations in two variables | **Testing Point:** Solve a system of linear equation based on a word problem

   Key Explanation: The correct answer is 1.20. Let p represent the cost of pens and b represent the cost of books. The first equation would be $4p + 2b = 8.30$. The second equation would be $1p + 4b = 8.20$. Using elimination, multiplying the first equation by 2 yields $8p + 4b = 16.60$. Subtracting

   the two equations results in $7p = 8.40$. Dividing 7 to both sides of the equation yields $p = 1.2$. Therefore the price of the pen is $1.20.

4. **Domain:** ALGEBRA

   Skill/Knowledge: Systems of two linear equations in two variables | **Testing Point:** Solve a system of linear equations with two variables by substitution

   Key Explanation: 5 is the correct answer. It's given that $4x = 8$. Substituting 8 for $4x$ in the second equation $4x + y = 13$ yields $8 + y = 13$. Subtracting 8 from both sides of this equation results in $y = 5$. Therefore, the price of a sandwich is $5.

5. **Domain:** GEOMETRY AND TRIGONOMETRY

   Skill/Knowledge: Right triangles and trigonometry | **Testing Point:** Similar right triangles

   Key Explanation: The correct answer is 18.75. The triangle ABD and ACB are right angled triangles. Using Pythagoras theorem to find the length of AC, $a^2 + b^2 = c^2$ where $a = 20$ and $c = 25$ results in $(20)^2 + b^2 = 25^2$. Therefore the value of b is 15. Subsequently, using linear scale factor, we get $\dfrac{AB}{AD} = \dfrac{CB}{AC}$. This is equivalent to $\dfrac{25}{AD} = \dfrac{20}{15}$ or $20AD = 375$. Therefore $AD = 18.75\ cm$.

6. **Domain:** ALGEBRA

   Skill/Knowledge: Linear equations in one variable | **Testing Point:** Creating and using linear equation

   Key Explanation: Choice A is correct. Let x be John's present age.

   Since Ben is four times as old as John, then Ben's present age is equal to $4x$.

   In four years, John's age will be $x + 4$ while Ben's age will be $4x + 4$.

   Since Ben will be twice as old as John will be in four years, then $4x + 4 = 2(x + 4)$.

   Using distributive property yields $4x + 4 = 2x + 8$.

Subtracting $2x$ and 4 from both sides of the equation yields $2x = 4$.

Dividing both sides of the equation by 2 yields $x = 2$.

Therefore, John is 2 years old now.

Distractor Explanations: Choice B is incorrect and may result from calculating the age of John in four years. **Choice C** is incorrect and may result from calculating the age of Ben now. **Choice D** is incorrect and may result from calculating the age of Ben in four years.

7.   **Domain:** ADVANCED MATH

Skill/Knowledge: Nonlinear functions | **Testing Point:** Interpret the exponential growth formula

Key Explanation: Choice C is correct. Substituting 3 for x in $h(x) = 1,200(1.25)^x$ yields $h(x) = 1,200(1.25)^3$.

Simplifying the equation yields $h(x) = 2343.75$.

Hence, 2344 pencils were used 3 years after the school was opened.

Distractor Explanations: Choice A is incorrect. There were 1,500 pencils used one year after the school was opened. **Choice B** is incorrect. The number of pencils increases by only 25% every year. **Choice D** is incorrect. If the equation is $h(x) = 1,200(1.25)^{\frac{x}{2}}$, then the number of pencils increases by 25% every two years.

8.   **Domain:** ALGEBRA

Skill/Knowledge: Linear Functions | **Testing Point:** Creating linear function

Key Explanation: Choice B is correct. The total number of houses in the residential area can be represented by a linear function with the equation of $f(x) = mx+b$ where m is the slope and b is the y-intercept.

Since the initial number of houses is 5, the y-intercept is 5.

Since x represents the number of years after 1950 and every year 3 new houses are built, then the slope is 3.

Therefore, the function is $f(x) = 3x + 5$.

Distractor Explanations: Choice A is incorrect and may result from multiplying the y-intercept with variable x. **Choice C** is incorrect and may result from multiplying the y-intercept with variable x and not considering the slope. **Choice D** is incorrect and may result from not considering the y-intercept.

9.   **Domain:** ADVANCED MATH

Skill/Knowledge: Nonlinear functions | **Testing Point:** Exponential Decay Function

Key Explanation: Choice A is correct. Since the reserve is decreasing exponentially, then the situation can be represented by the exponential decay function $h(x) = A(1 - r)^x$ where A is the initial value, r is the decay rate, and t is the time interval.

Since the gold reserve of Country A in 1995 is 150 tons, the $A = 150$.

Since the rate is 2%, then $r = 0.02$. Hence, the decay factor is $(1 - 0.02) = 0.98$

Since the reserve is decreasing exponentially at a rate of 2% every 10 years and t represents the number of years after 2015, then $x = \dfrac{t}{10}$.

Therefore, the function is $h(t) = 150(0.98)^{\frac{t}{10}}$.

Distractor Explanations: Choice B is incorrect. This function represents the situation where the reserve is decreasing exponentially at a rate of 2% every $\dfrac{1}{10}$ year. **Choice C** is incorrect. This function represents the situation where the reserve is increasing exponentially at a rate of 2% every 10 years. **Choice D** is incorrect. This function represents the situation where the reserve is increasing exponentially at a rate of 2% every $\dfrac{1}{10}$ year.

10. **Domain:** ADVANCED MATH

    Skill/Knowledge: Nonlinear equations in one variable and systems of equations in two variables | **Testing Point:** Solve a system of equations in two variables where the equations are nonlinear

    Key Explanation: Choice D is correct. Substituting 4 for $x^2 + 3$ into the second equation yields $4^3 = y$, or $y = 64$.

    Distractor Explanations: Choice A is incorrect. This is the value of y if $x^2 + 3 = -1$. **Choice B** is incorrect. This is the value of y if $x^2 + 3 = 1$. **Choice C** is incorrect. This is the value of y if $x^2 + 3 = 3$.

11. **Domain:** ADVANCED MATH

    Skill/Knowledge: Equivalent Expressions | **Testing Point:** Factoring (Difference of Squares)

    Key Explanation: The correct answer is **Choice B**. Find the equivalent expression using the identity $a^2 - b^2 = (a + b)(a - b)$. The expression $16x^2 - 64$ can be represented as $4(2^2x^2 - 4^2)$ and this will therefore be equivalent to $4(2x + 4)(2x - 4)$.

    Distractor Explanations: Choice A is incorrect. Using the identity $(a - b)^2 = a^2 - 2ab + b^2$, this option represents $16x^2 - 64x + 64$. **Choice C** is incorrect. This option represents $16x - 64$. **Choice D** is incorrect. Using the identity $(a - b)^2 = a^2 - 2ab + b^2$, this option represents $4x^2 - 16x + 16$.

12. **Domain:** ADVANCED MATH

    Skill/Knowledge: Nonlinear functions | **Testing Point:** Using exponent rules to solve exponential problems

    Key Explanation: The correct answer choice is **Choice C**. We take the equation $4^4 + 4^4 + 4^4 + 4^4 = 2^t$ and change the bases of 4^4 to 2 which yields $(2^2)^4 = 2^8$. It follows that $4^4 + 4^4 + 4^4 + 4^4 = 2^t$ is equivalent to $2^8 + 2^8 + 2^8 + 2^8 = 2^t$. Combining like terms yields $4 \times 2^8 = 2^t$. Converting the base of 4 to 2 yields $2^2 \times 2^8 = 2^t$. Multiplying the terms with the same base yields $2^{10} = 2^t$.

Therefore, $t = 10$.

Distractor Explanations: Choices A, B, and **D** are incorrect and reflect arithmetic errors in simplifying exponential expressions.

13. **Domain:** GEOMETRY AND TRIGONOMETRY

    Skill/Knowledge: Lines, angles and triangles | **Testing Point:** Alternate interior angles

    Key Explanation: Choice D is correct. Since $\overline{CE}$ is equal to $\overline{ED}$, then point E is the midpoint of $\overline{AB}$. Since figure $ABCD$ is a square, then $\overline{AC} = 2\overline{AE}$. Hence, $\angle AEC = \tan^{-1}\left(\dfrac{\overline{AC}}{\overline{AE}}\right)$. Substituting the value of $\overline{AC}$ in terms of $\overline{AE}$ yields $\angle AEC = \tan^{-1}\left(\dfrac{2\overline{AE}}{\overline{AE}}\right)$. Simplifying the equation yields $\angle AEC = \tan^{-1}(2) = 63.43°$.

    Since $\angle ECD$ and $\angle AEC$ are alternate interior angles, then $\angle ECD = \angle AEC$.

    Therefore, $\angle ECD = 63.43°$.

    Distractor Explanations: Choice A is incorrect. Since $\overline{AC} \neq \overline{AE}$, then $\angle ECD \neq 45°$. **Choice B** is incorrect. This is the value of $\angle CED$. **Choice C** is incorrect. Since, triangle CED is not an equilateral triangle, then $\angle ECD \neq 60°$.

14. **Domain:** PROBLEM SOLVING AND DATA ANALYSIS

    Skill/Knowledge: One-variable data: distributions and measures of center and spread | **Testing Point:** Compare the mean and the median of a one-variable data distribution based on the effect of outliers

    Key Explanation: Choice C is correct. Looking at the shape of the histogram, there appears to be large outliers with respect to the other values of the data set. These outliers are the numbers 20 and 25. Large outliers tend to increase the mean significantly but do not increase the median much.

Therefore, the median of this data set is less than the mean.

Distractor Explanations: Choice A is incorrect because the median is less than the mean. **Choice B** is incorrect because the distribution is not symmetrical. **Choice D** is incorrect because the median and the mean can be compared based on the presence of outliers on the right side of the histogram.

15. **Domain:** ADVANCED MATH

    Skill/Knowledge: Nonlinear functions | **Testing Point:** Analyze and interpret the graph of a nonlinear function

    Key Explanation: Choice D is correct. Since the price of house rent increases exponentially, then the problem can be represented by the exponential growth model $f(t) = a(1 + r)^t$ where a is the initial price, r is the growth rate and t is the time.

    Looking at the graph, the initial price is $200. Hence, $a = 200$.

    Since the dot represents the house price rent in 2004, then the price is $300 in that year. Hence, the price increases by $\frac{300 - 200}{200} \times 100\% = 50\%$ every 4 years. This means that $r = 0.5$. Since x is in years, then $t = \frac{x}{4}$.

    Therefore, the equation is $f(x) = 200(1.5)^{\frac{x}{4}}$.

    Distractor Explanations: Choice A is incorrect. This equation can be used if the house rent price doubles every 4 years. **Choice B** is incorrect. This equation can be used if the house rent price increases by 50% every year. **Choice C** is incorrect. This equation can be used if the house rent price doubles every year.

16. **Domain:** ADVANCED MATH

    Skill/Knowledge: Nonlinear functions | **Testing Point:** Finding the maximum point

    Key Explanation: The correct answer is **3.2**. The maximum value of the function will occur at

$t = \frac{-b}{2a}$. Comparing the given equation with the standard form of a quadratic equation, we get $a = -5$, $b = 2$, and $c = 3$. Substituting these values, $t = \frac{-2}{-10} = 0.2 \ seconds$.

$h(0.2) = -5(0.2)^2 + 2(0.2) + 3 = -0.2 + 0.4 + 3 = 3.2m$.

17. **Domain:** ADVANCED MATH

    Skill/Knowledge: Nonlinear Functions | **Testing Point:** Finding the non-linear function using the given data points

    Key Explanation: The correct answer is **Choice C**. Substitute the coordinate (0, 2.2) into the function $f(x) = 5^{x-1} + 2$, where $f(0) = 5^{0-1} + 2 = \mathbf{2.2}$

    Substitute a second coordinate (1, 3) into the function $f(x) = 5^{x-1} + 2$, $f(1) = 5^{1-1} + 2 = \mathbf{3}$. This is true and therefore it is the function shown in the table.

    Distractor Explanations: Choice A is incorrect. This option represents a function with a y-intercept of 3.2. **Choice B** is incorrect. This option represents a function with a y-intercept of 3. **Choice D** is incorrect. This option represents a function with a y-intercept of 2.4.

18. **Domain:** ADVANCED MATH

    Skill/Knowledge: Nonlinear functions | **Testing Point:** Solving for Nonlinear functions

    Key Explanation: The correct answer is **Choice B**. To solve for the value of $f(4)$, find the function $f(t)$.

    The value of the function $f(t)$ is equal to $g(t - 1)$.

    The value of $g(t - 1)$ is $8(t - 1)^2 - 27$ or $8(t^2 - 2t + 1) - 27$ which results in $8t^2 - 16t - 19$.

    Therefore, the function $f(t) = 8t^2 - 16t - 19$ and the value of $f(4)$ would therefore be $f(4) = 8(4)^2 - 16(4) - 19 = 45$.

    Distractor Explanations: Choice A is incorrect. This option represents the value of $g(0)$. **Choice C** is incorrect. This option represents the value of

$f(5)$. **Choice D** is incorrect. This option represents the value of $g(5)$.

19. **Domain:** ADVANCED MATH

Skill/Knowledge: Equivalent Expressions | **Testing Point:** Solve an equivalent expression using remainder theorem

Key Explanation: The correct answer is –7. To find the value of b and c, first divide both sides of the equation by $(x + 1)$ which yields $\frac{x^3 - 5x^2 + 3x + 2}{x + 1} = (x + b)^2 + \frac{c}{x + 1}$. The value c is considered to be the remainder when $x^3 - 5x^2 + 3x + 2$ is divided by $x + 1$. Using the remainder theorem where $\frac{f(x)}{x - a}$, the remainder is equivalent to $f(a)$. Therefore, since the divisor is $x + 1$, substituting –1 into the dividend yields $(-1)^3 - 5(-1)^2 + 3(-1) + 2 = -7$. Therefore the value of $c = -7$.

20. **Domain:** ALGEBRA

Skill/Knowledge: Linear inequalities in one or two variables | **Testing Point:** Solve a linear inequality in one variable

Key Explanation: $\frac{6}{21}$ is the correct answer. Distribution on the left hand side of the given inequality $2(-3x + 2) - 1 > \frac{9x}{2}$ yields $-6x + 4 - 1 > \frac{9x}{2}$. Combining constants on the left hand side results in $-6x + 3 > \frac{9x}{2}$. Subtracting $\frac{9x}{2}$ from both sides of this inequality yields $-\frac{21}{2}x + 3 > 0$. Subtracting 3 from both sides of this inequality results in $-\frac{21}{2}x > -3$. Dividing both sides of this inequality by $-\frac{21}{2}$ (which flips the inequality sign) yields $x < \frac{-3}{-\frac{21}{2}}$, which is equivalent to

$x < \frac{6}{21}$. Therefore, the value of a is $\frac{6}{21}$.

21. **Domain:** ADVANCED MATH

Skill/Knowledge: Nonlinear equations in one variable and systems of equations in two variables | **Testing Point:** Solving system of quadratic and linear equations

Key Explanation: Choice C is correct. Solve the system of equations by substitution method.

Dividing both sides of the 1st equation by 2 yields $y = \frac{1}{2}x - \frac{1}{2}$.

Substituting this equation to the 2nd equation yields $\frac{1}{2}x - \frac{1}{2} = (2x - 1)^2 - (x - 1)^2$.

Expanding the square of binomials in the right side of the equation yields $\frac{1}{2}x - \frac{1}{2} = 4x^2 - 4x + 1 - x^2 + 2x - 1$.

Combining like terms yields $\frac{1}{2}x - \frac{1}{2} = 3x^2 - 2x$.

Multiplying 2 to both sides of the equation yields $x - 1 = 6x^2 - 4x$.

Adding 1 and subtracting x from both sides of the equation yields $0 = 6x^2 - 5x + 1$.

Using quadratic formula to solve for the values of x yields $x = \frac{-(-5) \pm \sqrt{(-5)^2 - 4(6)(1)}}{2(6)}$.

Simplifying the equation yields $x = \frac{1}{2}$ and $x = \frac{1}{3}$.

Since $\frac{1}{3} < \frac{1}{2}$, then $x_1 = \frac{1}{3}$ and $x_2 = \frac{1}{2}$.

Calculating the values of y_1 and y_2 by substituting the values of x_1 and x_2 to $y = \frac{1}{2}x - \frac{1}{2}$ yields

$y_1 = \frac{1}{2}\left(\frac{1}{3}\right) - \frac{1}{2} = -\frac{1}{3}$ and $y_2 = \frac{1}{2}\left(\frac{1}{2}\right) - \frac{1}{2} = -\frac{1}{4}$.

Therefore, $\frac{y_2}{y_1} = \frac{-\frac{1}{4}}{-\frac{1}{3}} = \frac{3}{4}$.

Distractor Explanations: Choice A is incorrect. This is the value of $\frac{y_1}{x_1}$. **Choice B** is incorrect.

This is the value of $\dfrac{y_2}{x_2}$. **Choice D** is incorrect. This is the value of $\dfrac{x_2}{x_1}$.

22. **Domain:** GEOMETRY AND TRIGONOMETRY
Skill/Knowledge: Area and volume | **Testing Point:** Find the effect of changing a dimension on the surface area of a solid

Key Explanation: Choice B is correct. It's given that the original radius r is decreased by 26%, then the new radius r' is equal to $\left(1 - \dfrac{26}{100}\right)r$ or $0.74r$. Then, the new surface area of the bowl is equivalent to $A_{new\ bowl} = 2\pi r'^2$, which is equal to $2\pi(0.74r)^2$ or $2\pi r^2 \times 0.74^2$. It follows that $A_{new\ bowl} = A_{original\ bowl} \times 0.74^2$ or $A_{new\ bowl} = A_{original\ bowl} \times 0.5476$. The factor 0.5476 is equivalent to 54.76% of the surface area of the original bowl. This is equivalent to a 100% − 54.76% or 45.24% decrease in the surface area of the original bowl. Therefore, if the radius r is decreased by 26%, the surface area of the bowl decreases by 45.24%.

Distractor Explanations: Choice A is incorrect. This is the percent decrease of the radius. **Choice C** is incorrect. This is the percentage of the new bowl relative to the original bowl. **Choice D** is incorrect. This is the percentage of the new radius relative to the original radius.

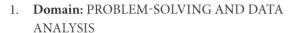

1. **Domain:** PROBLEM-SOLVING AND DATA ANALYSIS

    Skill/Knowledge: Ratios, rates, proportional relationships, and units | **Testing Point:** Similar ratios

    Key Explanation: The correct answer is 27. The ratio 6:4 implies that for every 4 turkeys, there are 6 chickens on the farm. Given that the number of turkeys on the farm is 18, the number of chickens is: $\frac{6*18}{4} = \frac{108}{4} = 27$.

2. **Domain:** ALGEBRA

    Skill/Knowledge: Linear Functions | **Testing Point:** Evaluate a linear function

    Key Explanation: The correct answer is 2033. Since a total of 1,495 cars are sold, then the function becomes $1495 = 22x + 835$. Subtracting 835 from both sides of the equation yields $660 = 22x$. Dividing both sides of the equation by 22 yields $30 = x$.

    Therefore, the company will have a total of 1,495 cars sold in the year $2003 + 30 = 2033$.

3. **Domain:** ALGEBRA

    Skill/Knowledge: Systems of linear equations with two variables | **Testing Point:** Solving for simultaneous equations

    Key Explanation: Choice C is correct. Establish first the variables by assuming that the price of a dress is d and that the price of a shirt is s.

    The total sales amount from dresses she sold in the first week is given by 5 dresses $\times d = 5d$. Hence, the commission received from the sales of dresses would be $30\%(5d) = 1.5d$. The total sales amount from shirts she sold in the first week is given by 20 shirts $\times s = 20s$. Hence, the commission received from the sales of shirts would be $10\%(20s) = 2s$. The equation of the commission she received on the first week would be given by $1.5d + 2s = 65$.

    The total sales amount from dresses she sold in the second week is given by 3 dresses $\times d = 3d$. Hence,

the commission received from the sales of dresses would be $30\%(3d) = 0.9d$. The total sales amount from shirts she sold in the second week is given by 30 shirts $s = 30s$. Hence, the commission received from the sales of shirts would be $10\%(30s) = 3s$. The equation of the commission she received on the second week would be given by $0.9d + 3s = 57$.

The system of equations could be solved by multiplying the first equation by 3 and multiplying the second equation by 2 which yields $4.5d + 6s = 195$ and $1.8d + 6s = 114$.

Subtracting the second equation from the first equation yields $2.7d = 81$.

Dividing both sides of the equation by 2.7 yields $d = 30$.

The price per dress is therefore $30.

Distractor Explanations: Choice A is incorrect. This option is calculated by finding the price per shirt. **Choice B** is incorrect. This option represents the difference between the price per shirt and the price per dress. **Choice D** is incorrect. This option represents the sum of the price per shirt and the price per dress.

4. **Domain:** ALGEBRA

    Skill/Knowledge: Systems of linear equations with two variables | **Testing Point:** Creating and using linear equations to solve a problem

    Key Explanation: The correct answer is **48**.

    Let x be the number of beads used in a bracelet and y be the number of beads used in a necklace.

    Since Hannah used 252 beads to make 4 bracelets and 4 necklaces, then $4x + 4y = 252$.

    Since Jane used 381 beads to make 3 bracelets and 7 necklaces, then $3x + 7y = 381$.

    Calculate the values of x and y using the elimination method.

    Multiplying the 1st equation by -3 yields $-12x -12y = -756$.

    Multiplying the 2nd equation by 4 yields $12x + 28y = 1524$.

Adding the two equations yields $-12x - 12y + 12x + 28y = -756 + 1524$.

Combining like terms yields $16y = 768$.

Dividing both sides of the equation by 16 yields $y = 48$.

Therefore, 48 beads are required to make a single necklace.

5. **Domain:** GEOMETRY AND TRIGONOMETRY

Skill/Knowledge: Right triangles and trigonometry | **Testing Point:** Find the trigonometric functions of a complementary angle in a right triangle

Key Explanation: Choice D is correct. It's given that triangle ABC is right at B, then angles A and C are two acute angles that add up to 90°. The side opposite to angle A in the right triangle ABC is the same as the side adjacent to angle B in the same right triangle. Using the relations $sin(A) = \dfrac{opposite}{hypotenuse}$ and $cos(C) = = \dfrac{adjacent}{hypotenuse}$, it can be found that $sin(A) = cos(C) = \dfrac{BC}{AC}$. Therefore, $cos(C) = sin(A) = \dfrac{4}{5}$.

Distractor Explanations: Choice A is incorrect and may result from conceptual or calculation errors. **Choice B** is incorrect and may result from conceptual or calculation errors. **Choice C** is incorrect. This is the value of $sin(C)$.

6. **Domain:** ALGEBRA

Skill/Knowledge: Linear equations in one variable | **Testing Point:** Creating linear equations to solve a problem

Key Explanation: The correct answer is 7.

Let x be the smallest number, $x + 1$ be the middle number and $x + 2$ be the largest number.

Since the sum of the three consecutive numbers is 12 less than four times the largest number, then $x + x + 1 + x + 2 = 4(x + 2) - 12$.

Using distributive property on the right side of the equation yields $x + x + 1 + x + 2 = 4x + 8 - 12$.

Combining like terms yields $3x + 3 = 4x - 4$.

Adding 4 and subtracting $3x$ from both sides of the equation yields $7 = x$.

Therefore, the smallest number is 7.

7. **Domain:** ADVANCED MATH

Skill/Knowledge: Nonlinear Functions | **Testing Point:** Solving for a nonlinear function

Key Explanation: The correct answer is **4**. The value g represents the initial value of the function or the y-intercept of the graph. The initial coordinate will be $(0, g)$, from observing the graph, this value is $(0, 4)$. Hence, the value of g is equal to 4.

8. **Domain:** ALGEBRA

Skill/Knowledge: Linear functions | **Testing Point:** Using linear function to solve a problem

Key Explanation: Choice D is correct. To create the linear function that represents the total fee in renting and using the boat, use the format $f(x) = mx + b$ where m is the slope and b is the y-intercept.

Since the initial charge of renting the boat is $50, then the y-intercept is 50.

Since the additional fee per kilometer is $20, then the slope is 20.

Hence, the linear function is $f(x) = 20x + 50$ where x is the number of kilometers traveled.

The total distance going back and forth from the island is $62 = 12\ km$.

Therefore, the total amount of money that Vincent must pay is $f(x) = 20(12) + 50 = \$290$.

Distractor Explanations: Choice A is incorrect and may result from only calculating the fee per kilometer going to the island. **Choice B** is incorrect and may result from only calculating the fee per kilometer going to the island plus the initial charge. **Choice C** is incorrect and may result from not considering the initial charge for renting the boat.

9. **Domain:** ADVANCED MATH

    Skill/Knowledge: Nonlinear Functions | **Testing Point:** Finding the function of a nonlinear graph

    Key Explanation: The correct answer is **Choice B**. By observation, the graph exponentially decreases as x increases. The function passes through the point (0, 14) and (1, 7). Substituting the coordinate (1, 7) into the function $f(x) = 14(0.5)^x$ yields $7 = 14(0.5)^1$ which is true.

    Distractor Explanations: Choice A is incorrect. This option represents an increasing exponential function. **Choice C** is incorrect. This option represents an increasing exponential function. **Choice D** is incorrect. This option represents a linearly decreasing function.

10. **Domain:** ADVANCED MATH

    Skill/Knowledge: Nonlinear equations in one variable and systems of equations in two variables | **Testing Point:** System of quadratic and linear equation

    Key Explanation: The correct answer is **71**.

    Since $y = p$, then by substituting p to y the quadratic equation becomes $p = 8x^2 - 2x + 9$.

    Subtracting p from both sides of the equation yields $0 = 8x^2 - 2x + 9 - p$.

    Since the system of equations intersects at exactly one point, then the discriminant is equal to 0.

    The discriminant formula is $b^2 - 4ac$ where a and b are the coefficients of x^2 and x, respectively, and c is the constant.

    From $0 = 8x^2 - 2x + 9 - p$, $a = 8$, $b = -2$ and $c = 9 - p$.

    Substituting the values to the formula yields $(-2)^2 - 4(8)(9 - p) = 0$

    Simplifying the equation yields $-284 + 32p = 0$.

    Adding 284 to both sides of the equation yields $32p = 284$.

    Dividing both sides of the equation by 32 yields $p = \dfrac{71}{8}$.

    Therefore, $8p = 8\left(\dfrac{71}{8}\right) = 71$.

11. **Domain:** ADVANCED MATH

    Skill/Knowledge: Equivalent Expressions | **Testing Point:** Factoring of expressions

    Key Explanation: The correct answer is **Choice C**. Using the identity $(a + b)^2 = a^2 + 2ab + b^2$, the expression $4x^4 + 16x^2 + 16$ is equivalent to $4(x^4 + 4x^2 + 4)$. This is equivalent to $4(x^2 + 2)^2$.

    Distractor Explanations: Choice A is incorrect. This option may be due to conceptual errors. **Choice B** is incorrect. This option may be due to conceptual errors. **Choice D** is incorrect. This option may be due to conceptual errors.

12. **Domain:** ADVANCED MATH

    Skill/Knowledge: Nonlinear Functions | **Testing Point:** Undefined functions

    Key Explanation: The correct answer is **Choice D**. For a function to become undefined, its denominator should be zero. Therefore for the function $f(x)$ to become undefined, $2x^2 - 9x - 5 = 0$. To solve for the value of x using the quadratic formula, $x = \dfrac{-b \pm \sqrt{b^2 - 4ac}}{2a}$, where a is 2, b is -9 and c is -5.

    $x = \dfrac{-(-9) \pm \sqrt{(-9)^2 - 4(2)(-5)}}{2(2)} = \dfrac{9 \pm \sqrt{81 + 40}}{4}$. The value of x would therefore be x is 5 or -0.5.

    Since the question asks for a positive value of x, the correct answer is $x = 5$.

    Distractor Explanations: Choice A is incorrect. This option represents the value of the numerator. **Choice B** is incorrect. This option represents the positive value of the second solution of the equation. **Choice C** is incorrect. This option represents the sum of the solutions to the equation.

13. **Domain:** GEOMETRY AND TRIGONOMETRY

    Skill/Knowledge: Lines, angles and triangles | **Testing Point:** Use similarity of triangles to find a missing length

    Key Explanation: Choice B is correct. It's given that $\overline{DE}$ is parallel to $\overline{CB}$, then $m\angle AED = m\angle ABC$ because they are corresponding angles. The 2 triangles AED and ABC also share a common angle at the vertex A. Then, $\triangle AED$ and $\triangle ABC$ are similar having two pairs of equal corresponding angles. It follows that their corresponding sides are proportional. $\overline{DE}$ corresponds to $\overline{CB}$, and $\overline{AE}$ corresponds to $\overline{AB}$. Then the proportion can be written as $\dfrac{DE}{CB} = \dfrac{AE}{AB}$. Substituting the given values in the proportion yields $\dfrac{3}{5} = \dfrac{3.81}{AB}$. Cross-multiplication results in $3AB = 19.05$. Dividing both sides of this equation by 3 yields $AB = 6.35$. The segment $\overline{AB}$ is the sum of $\overline{AE}$ and $\overline{EB}$. Therefore, the length of $\overline{EB}$ is equal to AB – AE = 6.35 – 3.81, or 2.54 cm.

    Distractor Explanations: Choice A is incorrect. This is the value of AB – BC. **Choice C** is incorrect. This is the value of AB – DE. **Choice D** is incorrect. This is the value of AB.

14. **Domain:** PROBLEM-SOLVING AND DATA ANALYSIS

    Skill/Knowledge: One-variable data: distributions and measures of center and spread | **Testing Point:** Reason about the mean of a set given its median

    Key Explanation: Choice B is correct. To achieve the greatest possible value of the mean, the sum of the 7 integers needs to be the greatest possible. It's given that the median of a set of 7 negative integers is –26. It follows that the fourth integer if the set of values is sorted in ascending order is –26. Then 3 values must be less than or equal to –26, and 3 values must be greater than or equal to –26. To maximize the sum, those values

should be chosen as the greatest possible negative integers. Thus, the set of the 7 negative integers is –26, –26, –26, -26, –1, –1, –1. The mean of this set is the greatest possible mean, and is given by the sum of the values divided by 7, or $\dfrac{-26 - 26 - 26 - 26 - 1 - 1 - 1}{7}$, which is equal to $-\dfrac{107}{7}$.

Distractor Explanations: Choice A is incorrect and may result if the 7 negative integers are distinct. **Choice C** is incorrect. This is the greatest possible mode of the set. **Choice D** is incorrect. This is the range of the set if the greatest possible mean is to be achieved.

15. **Domain:** ADVANCED MATH

    Skill/Knowledge: Nonlinear functions | **Testing Point:** Find a value of the composition of two nonlinear functions

    Key Explanation: $-\dfrac{36}{17}$ is the correct answer. Substituting 2 for x in the expression $g(x) = \dfrac{1}{e^{x-2} + 3}$ yields $g(2) = \dfrac{1}{e^{2-2} + 3}$ or $g(2) = \dfrac{1}{e^0 + 3}$. This can be simplified into $g(2) = \dfrac{1}{1 + 3}$ or $g(2) = \dfrac{1}{4}$. The expression $g(2) - 1$ is equivalent to $\dfrac{1}{4} - 1$ or $-\dfrac{3}{4}$. Thus, the value of $f(g(2) - 1)$ is equal to the value of $f\left(-\dfrac{3}{4}\right)$. Substituting $-\dfrac{3}{4}$ for x in the equation $f(x) = \dfrac{3x}{x^2 - 2x - 1}$ yields $f\left(-\dfrac{3}{4}\right) = \dfrac{3\left(-\dfrac{3}{4}\right)}{\left(-\dfrac{3}{4}\right)^2 - 2\left(-\dfrac{3}{4}\right) - 1}$. This is can be simplified into $f\left(-\dfrac{3}{4}\right) = \dfrac{-\dfrac{9}{4}}{\dfrac{9}{16} + \dfrac{6}{4} - 1}$.

Adding the fractions in the denominator yields $f\left(-\dfrac{3}{4}\right) = \dfrac{-\dfrac{9}{4}}{\dfrac{17}{16}}$. Dividing fractions results in

$f\left(-\dfrac{3}{4}\right) = -\dfrac{9}{4} \times \dfrac{16}{17} = -\dfrac{9 \times 4}{17} = -\dfrac{36}{17}$. Therefore, the value of $f\big(g(2)-1\big)$ is $-\dfrac{36}{17}$.

16. **Domain:** ADVANCED MATH

Skill/Knowledge: Nonlinear Functions | **Testing Point:** Find the expression of a rational function using its graph

Key Explanation: Choice A is correct. The point $(2, 5)$ belongs to the graph of f. Substituting 5 for $f(x)$ and 2 for x in the equation $f(x) = \dfrac{a}{2x+b}$

yields $5 = \dfrac{a}{4+b}$. Multiplying each side of this equation by $4 + b$ yields $20 + 5b = a$. The graph of f also passes through the point $(4, 1)$. Substituting 1 for $f(x)$ and 4 for x in the equation $f(x) = \dfrac{a}{2x+b}$

yields $1 = \dfrac{a}{8+b}$. Multiplying each side of this equation by $8 + b$ yields $8 + b = a$. Substituting $20 + 5b$ for a in this equation results in $8 + b = 20 + 5b$. Subtracting b and 20 from both sides of the equation yields $-12 = 4b$. Dividing both sides of this equation by 4 results in $-3 = b$. Substituting -3 for b in $8 + b = a$ yields $5 = a$.

Thus, the equation defining f can be written as

$f(x) = \dfrac{5}{2x-3}$. It is given that $h(x) = f(x) - 2$,

then $h(x) = \dfrac{5}{2x-3} - 2$. Multiplying the second

term of this expression by $\dfrac{2x-3}{2x-3}$ and adding the

two terms with common denominators yields

$h(x) = \dfrac{5 - 2(2x-3)}{2x-3}$. Distributing the numerator

results in $h(x) = \dfrac{5 - 4x + 6}{2x-3}$. Combining like terms

in the numerator yields $h(x) = \dfrac{-4x+11}{2x-3}$.

Distractor Explanations: Choice B is incorrect. This could define function h if $h(x) = f(x) + 2$. **Choice C is incorrect** because $(4, -1)$, the point 2 units below $(4, 1)$, does not satisfy the equation $h(x) = \dfrac{10}{2x-2}$. **Choice D is incorrect** because $(2, 3)$, the point 2 units below $(2, 5)$, does not satisfy the equation $h(x) = \dfrac{10}{2x+2}$.

17. **Domain:** ADVANCED MATH

Skill/Knowledge: Nonlinear functions | **Testing Point:** Find the expression of an exponential function

Key Explanation: Choice A is correct. The given expression of $f(x)$ can be rewritten as $f(x) = 3(a^x + b) + 2$. It's given that the graph of f passes through the point $(0, 14)$. Substituting 0 for x and 14 for $f(x)$ in the equation $f(x) = 3(a^x + b) + 2$ yields $14 = 3(1 + b) + 2$. Substituting the given $b = a + 1$ yields $14 = 3(1 + a + 1) + 2$. Distribution on the right hand side result in $14 = 3 + 3a + 3 + 2$. Combining like terms yields $14 = 3a + 8$. Subtract 8 from both sides yields $6 = 3a$. Dividing both sides of the equation by 3 results in $2 = a$.

Distractor Explanations: Choice B is incorrect. This is the value of b. **Choice C is incorrect.** This is the result if $b = 10$. **Choice D is incorrect.** This is the value of the y-intercept of function f.

18. **Domain:** ADVANCED MATH

Skill/Knowledge: Nonlinear functions | **Testing Point:** Function translation

Key Explanation: The correct answer is **Choice B.** To solve for the y-intercept, find the function $f(t)$ using the function $f(t + 1)$.

This will be equal to $f\big((t-1)+1\big) = f(t) = 5^{t-1} + 3$.

The y-intercept will be the value of $f(t)$ when t is 0.

$f(t) = 5^{0-1} + 3 = 5^{-1} + 3 = \dfrac{1}{5} + 3 = \textbf{3.2}$

Distractor Explanations: Choice A is incorrect and this would be the value of the intercept if the function $f(t)$ were linear. **Choice C is incorrect.**

This option represents the value of the y-intercept for the function $f(t + 1)$. **Choice D** is incorrect this option represents the value of the y-intercept for the function $f(t + 2)$.

19. **Domain:** ADVANCED MATH

    Skill/Knowledge: Equivalent Expressions | **Testing Point:** Matching the coefficients

    Key Explanation: The correct answer is -7.

    Using distributive property to simplify the numerator of the given expression yields

    $$\frac{2x^2 - 28x}{(3x + 2)(4x - 1)}.$$

    Making the denominators of the other expression the same yields $\dfrac{4ax(4x - 1) + 2bx(3x + 2)}{(3x + 2)(4x - 1)}$.

    Using distributive property to simplify the numerator yields $\dfrac{16ax^2 - 4ax + 6bx^2 + 4bx}{(3x + 2)(4x - 1)}$.

    Combining like terms in the numerator yields $\dfrac{(16a + 6b)x^2 - (4a - 4b)x}{(3x + 2)(4x - 1)}$.

    Hence, $\dfrac{(16a + 6b)x^2 - (4a - 4b)x}{(3x + 2)(4x - 1)} = \dfrac{2x^2 - 28x}{(3x + 2)(4x - 1)}$.

    Matching the coefficients of x^2 yields $16a + 6b = 2$.

    Matching the coefficients of x yields $-(4a - 4b) = -28$ or $-4a + 4b = -28$. Multiplying both sides of the equation by 4 yields $-16a + 16b = -112$.

    Adding the two equations yields $22b = -110$. Dividing both sides of the equation by 22 yields $b = -5$.

    Substituting the value of b to the 1st equation yields $16a + 6(-5) = 2$ or $16a - 30 = 2$. Adding 30 to both sides of the equation yields $16a = 32$. Dividing both sides of the equation by 16 yields $a = 2$.

    Therefore, $b - a = -5 - 2 = -7$.

20. **Domain:** ALGEBRA

    Skill/Knowledge: Linear inequalities in one or two variables | **Testing Point:** Find the value of an unknown quantity for an inequality to have no solution

    Key Explanation: -3 is the correct answer. Distribution on both sides of the given inequality $(k + 2)x - 6x < -12 - 2(3.5x + 5)$ yields $kx + 2x - 6x < -12 - 7x - 10$. Adding $7x$ to both sides of this inequality results in $kx + 2x - 6x + 7x < -12 - 10$. Combining like terms yields $kx + 3x < -22$. Factoring out x results in $(k + 3)x < -22$. This inequality has no solution if and only if $k + 3 = 0$, or $k = -3$. This would result in the false statement $0x < -22$ which has no real solution. Therefore, for $k = -3$, the given inequality has no real solution.

21. **Domain:** ADVANCED MATH

    Skill/Knowledge: Nonlinear equations in one variable and systems of equations in two variables | **Testing Point:** Translate a word problem into a nonlinear equation and solve it

    Key Explanation: Choice B is correct. Let x represent the edge length of the cube before drying, and V represent the original volume of the cube. Then $V = x^3$. It's given that the volume decreases by 26 ml and the length of each edge decreases by 0.15 cm, with 1 ml = 1 cm^3. It follows that $V - 26 = (x - 0.15)^3$. Substituting x^3 for V in this equation yields $x^3 - 26 = (x - 0.15)^3$. Expanding the right-hand side of this equation yields $x^3 - 26 = x^3 - 3x^2(0.15) + 3x(0.15)^2 - (0.15)^3$. Simplifying the right-hand side results in $x^3 - 26 = x^3 - 0.45x^2 + 0.0675x - 0.003375$. Subtracting x^3 from both sides of this equation yields $-26 = -0.45x^2 + 0.0675x - 0.003375$. Adding 26 to both sides of this equation yields $0 = -0.45x^2 + 0.0675x + 25.996625$. Using the quadratic formula

    $$x = \frac{-b \pm \sqrt{b^2 - 4ac}}{2a} =$$

    $$\frac{-0.0675 \pm \sqrt{0.0675^2 - 4(-0.45)(25.996625)}}{2(-0.45)}$$

    yields two roots for x, which are approximately

7.7 and –7.5. Since x is a positive quantity (edge length), then $x = 7.7$. Therefore, the original edge length of the cube before drying is around 7.7 cm.

Distractor Explanations: Choice A is incorrect and may result if the edge length decreases by 0.2 *cm* instead of 0.15 *cm*. **Choice C** is incorrect and may result if the edge length decreases by 0.105 *cm* instead of 0.15 *cm*. **Choice D** is incorrect and may result if the edge length decreases by 0.1 *cm* instead of 0.15 *cm*.

22. **Domain:** GEOMETRY AND TRIGONOMETRY

    Skill/Knowledge: Area and volume | **Testing Point:** Find the volume of a solid formed of other solids

    Key Explanation: 432 is the correct answer. The volume of a pyramid is given by $V = \frac{1}{3} lwh$, where l is the length of the base, w is the width of the base, and h is the height of the pyramid. It's given that the length of the rectangular base is 12 *cm*, and its diagonal is 15 *cm*. Applying Pythagorean theorem to find the width yields $w^2 = 15^2 - 12^2$, which is equal to 81. It follows that the width of the base of each pyramid is equal to $\sqrt{81}$, or 9 *cm*. It's also given that the height of each pyramid is 6 *cm*. Then, the volume of each pyramid is $V = \frac{1}{3} \times 12 \times 9 \times 6$, which is equal to 216 *cubic cm*.

    Therefore, the total volume of the combined solid which is formed of the two identical pyramids is 216×2, or 432 *cubic cm*.

NOTES

Made in United States
Orlando, FL
15 October 2024

52674520R00267